ACROSS THE RIVER

LIFE, DEATH, AND FOOTBALL
IN AN AMERICAN CITY

KENT BABB

HarperOne
An Imprint of HarperCollins*Publishers*

FIRST EDITION

Designed by Terry McGrath

Front cover and interior photography: Emily Kask

Illustrations/football play diagrams: Walter Bethea

Library of Congress Cataloging-in-Publication Data

Names: Babb, Kent, author.
Title: Across the river : life, death, and football in an American city / Kent Babb.
Description: First hardcover edition. | New York : HarperOne, 2021.
Identifiers: LCCN 2020052627 (print) | LCCN 2020052628 (ebook) | ISBN 9780062950598 (hardcover) | ISBN 9780062950604 (paperback) | ISBN 9780062950611 (ebook)
Subjects: LCSH: Edna Karr High School (New Orleans, La.)—Football. | Brown, Brice (Football coach) | African American football players—Louisiana—New Orleans. | African American high school students—Louisiana—New Orleans. | African Americans—Louisiana—New Orleans.—Social conditions—21st century. | Football coaches—Louisiana—New Orleans—Biography. | New Orleans (La.)—Social conditions—21st century.
Classification: LCC GV958.E46 B34 2021 (print) | LCC GV958.E46 (ebook) | DDC 796.332/620976335—dc23
LC record available at https://lccn.loc.gov/2020052627
LC ebook record available at https://lccn.loc.gov/2020052628

---

21 22 23 24 25 LSC 10 9 8 7 6 5 4 3 2 1

AUTHOR'S NOTE

We were on a long bus ride, headed from New Orleans to a road game in Monroe, Louisiana. The man next to me saw a Mississippi cotton field through the window and removed his earbuds.

"I was enjoying the ride until I saw that shit," Marvin Rose said. I could still hear the beat of his Earth, Wind & Fire playlist.

Marv is sixty-three years old, a longtime military man and lifelong civil servant. A few years ago his daughter died in a car accident, and he found refuge as a volunteer on the football coaching staff at Edna Karr High School on the West Bank of New Orleans. Despite his pain, Marv is an incurable prankster and trash talker. I spent parts of a year embedded with the Karr program, and Marv's sense of humor is one reason I usually sat next to him. Another was a mutual curiosity about, and willingness to discuss, our obvious differences: among them that Marv, like every player and coach on the two team buses, is Black. I am white.

When I first saw the cotton, my mind processed it as an unusual sight—just something you don't see every day. But Marv had a deep, visceral reaction. I asked him why, and he explained. His grandmother had been a sharecropper, put to work in fields like that. She'd attended segregated schools and, when she rode a bus, was forced to sit in the back row. Marv himself was one of Karr's first Black students, and hearing racial slurs was just part of his childhood.

So many years later, he shared this perspective—a very different one from mine—from a bus. He always sits in the front row.

I almost didn't ask him about it. Though I'm a reporter with *The Washington Post* and a naturally curious person, discussing race often feels taboo, and part of me wanted to let it go. A different part reminded me that I wasn't just on any team bus. I was on *their* bus, and to not ask and learn would've been a missed opportunity, and a violation of why I was here in the first place.

Throughout the 2019 season, I spent time on Karr's sidelines and in staff meetings, in head coach Brice Brown's pickup truck before games and on the team bus after them, with players and coaches on some of their best and worst days. We spoke often about race and racism, along with similarly complex topics such as identity, mental health, and the criminal justice system. I visited murder scenes, graveyards, jailhouses. I interviewed politicians, grieving relatives, and homicide detectives. I consulted with three local historians and a New Orleans–based crime analyst named Jeff Asher.

Those experiences, and this book, expand on a 2018 article I had written for *The Post* about how Brown and the Karr program were using football to teach life and survival skills to young residents of a city besieged by gun violence. The kids who play football at Karr are teenaged Black males in New Orleans, a city where, in 2016, an eighteen- or nineteen-year-old Black male was fifty-six times more likely to be gunned down than the national average (Asher provided this statistic, as he did many others you'll find in the pages ahead).

Even while working on that original piece, I was struck by how unflinchingly honest Brown is when it comes to his surroundings and in how he speaks to his players, even with a reporter present. I have written about sports, often spotlighting how they intersect with society and culture, for more than two decades. In general, coaches and athletes want to show you the most sanitized versions of themselves, often attempting to conceal their miscalculations, mistakes, and fears. I assume they believe this projects strength, supposedly a core tenet of leadership. But I think it masks not just reality, but humanity as well. No matter our backgrounds, imperfection is something we all have in common, even if we aren't typically comfortable saying it out loud.

To an almost jarring degree, especially given his profession, Brown rejects pretense and inauthenticity. He expects the same of his players and staff. Within minutes of my arrival in August 2018, a senior running back was telling me about the first time he broke into a house. A top assistant coach was sharing an anecdote about how he'd sold marijuana and pills before taking a coaching job at Karr. Brown, whose journey and leadership philosophy I have come to deeply admire, admitted to me that he's driven not by winning games or championships, but by a deep fear that someone else he loves will be cut down by gunfire.

Across the Mississippi River from New Orleans's tourist track is a football program and a school and a world that seemed almost unbelievable before I first crossed the bridge. It's easy to pretend poverty isn't as bad as the news media says, that no matter where you come from, a college education and career success are within easy reach as long as you pull yourself up by your bootstraps and study and work hard. It's especially easy to think that if you look like me, and I must confess here that, regardless of my curiosity and work, I had been content for years to pretend communities like this didn't exist in the United States.

I want to show you this world, and I want you to see it as I did: unfiltered and unpolished. For a time, I considered using pseudonyms when referencing Karr's players, many of whom are younger than eighteen. After all, part of my personal oath when setting off on this exploration of a marginalized community, where some residents have it hard enough, was to do no harm. But Brown and others insisted that I change nothing. They asked that I show their realities, obstacles, and methods precisely as they are. Therefore, no names have been changed and no speech has been modified.

Some of the language is coarse and may be uncomfortable or even offensive to readers. This would include the occasional use of the N-word by players and coaches. I, and my editors at HarperOne, spoke at length about the right way to handle this—influenced by my belief and policy that no white person should ever use this word, spoken or in print. We agreed it is not my place to censor language, but because this is the most divisive and painful word in the English language, we also agreed to use dashes instead of spelling out this word. Do no harm, after all.

This book is a work of nonfiction journalism, and everyone who participated did so with the understanding that their words and actions were on the record. The use of quotation marks signals that the contained remark is written precisely as it was spoken. It's impossible for me to fully appreciate the relationship between Karr's players and coaches, so I avoid judgment in my writing. Other than this author's note and the acknowledgments, I also avoid use of the first person. This isn't my story, after all. It's theirs.

The story unfolded throughout 2019, before the onset of the novel coronavirus pandemic and the murder of George Floyd. But much of this book was written with those events, and their respective aftermaths, as a backdrop and through the privileged filter of a white man's eyes.

I cannot know why Brown and others granted me such exceptional access, though I suspect it was partly *because* of my skin color. Brown does almost nothing without premeditation, and some Karr players had never met—and certainly hadn't held a meaningful conversation with—someone of a different race or completely different set of experiences. One day I was reminded of these differences during a text exchange with another assistant coach. I had expressed sympathy about the plight of Joe Thomas, a Karr player you'll meet. *Don't feel bad for him*, the coach wrote. *Just get his story out.*

I have done so thoroughly and objectively. The overwhelming majority of the reporting is material I personally witnessed. In a small number of examples, scenes and one-off quotations have been re-created with the assistance of court and police documents, credible news reports, and/or accounts by multiple individuals who were directly involved (most instances of this are exhaustively referenced, with additional context, in the Notes and Citations section in the back of the book). With permission, I recorded dozens of hours of audio that included interviews, pre- and postgame speeches, and dialogue. In the handful of times when something is attributed to an unidentified source, these individuals—whose identities I knew—were granted anonymity in print because we agreed the topic was highly sensitive.

At Karr there is a saying that acts as a backbone of the football program: *Give 'em the real.* This essentially means everyone, no matter the circumstance, deserves and receives honesty. The truth may be difficult or painful. But it beats a lie every time.

This book attempts to pay respect to that notion. Marv gave me a real answer on the bus when I asked about the cotton, and though what I heard was uncomfortable, it's sometimes good to sacrifice comfort for understanding. I'm not saying that what you'll read ahead is pretty. I'm just saying this is one season in the life of one football program in one city. As hard as it may be for some of us to believe, this is an American story. And regardless of how any of us may feel about it, it is real.

Kent Babb
Spring 2021

This is for the kids who die,
Black and white,
For kids will die certainly.
The old and rich will live on awhile,
As always,
Eating blood and gold,
Letting kids die.

—*Langston Hughes, 1938*

And also for June, who told me I could.

THE WEST BANK

THE DAY BEFORE Edna Karr High School's first football game, head coach Brice Brown is on patrol. Most nights after practice, he doesn't immediately go home. Instead he drives around New Orleans, calling players to make sure they're still alive.

Sometimes he takes food to hungry teenagers, and other times he mediates some war between parents and kids. Brown often delivers new school shirts, the purple-crested polos that make up part of Karr's school uniform, to their driveways and doors. When a player had no shoes to wear to his grandmother's funeral, it was Brown who drove up in his 2007 Chevrolet Silverado to bring him a new pair. They're all just ways to calm Brown's mind: to hear a kid's voice and know he's okay. In this city, especially on this side of the Mississippi River, that's by no means guaranteed.

Tonight he's giving Joe Thomas a lift home. Joe is an eighteen-year-old linebacker, and Brown worries about him more than anyone. Though he doesn't like driving in Joe's neighborhood, it's better than letting him take the bus or walk.

"Too many night crawlers," the coach says. "Can anything happen over there and pop off instantly? Yep. A lot of times this is where stuff happens."

Brown checks the time on the truck's display. It's a little after nine p.m.

"Still early," he says.

Joe says nothing as he climbs into the back seat and texts his girlfriend, Cassidy. Brown leaves campus and drives through Algiers, a community just outside downtown New Orleans. Joe smiles periodically and looks out the window as he waits for his phone to buzz. Tomorrow is the first game of his senior season, and he and quarterback Leonard Kelly III are two of the team's most important players. They come from vastly different backgrounds and neighborhoods. They've been friends for a decade, Karr admits students from all over the city, and last year Joe and Leonard were juniors on Karr's state championship team, its third Class 4A title in a row. But now they're seniors. This is their team, and its championship hopes and twenty-seven-game winning streak are in their hands. In less than twenty-four hours, they'll take the field against John Curtis Christian School. It, too, is a New Orleans football institution, though when it plays Karr, the cultural contrasts are unmistakable.

Brown has doubts about the game, and about Joe and Leonard. They're good kids, but they've never been asked to lead. Certainly not a team like this.

He drives west toward Joe's apartment, and he's surrounded by tragic reminders of his other mission: keeping players alive. A mile up General De Gaulle Drive is the corner where Brown's father was knifed to death. A mile to the right is where Brown's best friend was gunned down in his car.

It's strange to be surrounded by reminders of the worst days of your life. But Brown is, and they regularly inflame his greatest fears. To the left is another grim milepost: the gas station Brown's former quarterback visited three years ago, a few minutes before he was shot dead.

Brown's phone sits on the tattered center console, silent for now. "You never forget those calls," he says, pressing the accelerator.

THREE YEARS EARLIER, Brown's phone rang on a Friday night in June 2016. It was after ten o'clock, and in this city and at this hour, he knew something terrible had happened.

A familiar sound had indeed cut through the thick summer air. Ten gunshots. Maybe more. Neighbors would say it sounded like a fireworks show. Then, minutes later, the inevitable sounds that follow: ringing phones and anguished voices.

Did you hear about Tonka?

Tollette "Tonka" George had been Karr's starting quarterback in 2010, and he'd led the team to the state championship game. His life was a rap song, his career an urban folk tale. The Cougars' star quarterback, Munchie Legaux, had injured his shoulder a year earlier, and his backup fell ill after a spider bite. Coaches had no choice but to put in Tonka, the team's skin-and-bones wide receiver and punter. He ran for a fifty-yard touchdown on his first play.

He was an unlikely, but almost supernaturally gifted, leader. During his senior year, he led Karr to its first state title game in eleven years. People never forget what you do as a senior, and there are people here who tell Tonka's story as if it's legend. The ambitious kid had done everything he could here but wanted a better life, so he headed off to college and graduated. He made mistakes, though, innocent as they might've seemed. The first had been coming home to see his mama. Tonka was dead seven weeks after his graduation from Alcorn State University.

For more than a half century, New Orleans has reached a dreadful milestone every year: at least a hundred murders. Of the nine US cities that tally triple-digit homicides, New Orleans—population 390,000—is by far the smallest. Outsiders point to Chicago's South Side as the epicenter of American gun violence. That isn't just misguided. It's also viewed as something of an insult to the people of New Orleans. Brown says his classmates at Grambling State University used to argue about, of all things, who'd come from the more fucked-up place. After all, some New Orleanians argue, shootings in Chicago, Baltimore, and St. Louis are largely contained. In New Orleans, shots ring out at any time, in any part of town.

"Murder is almost a part of the fucking culture here," said Rayell Johnson, a veteran homicide detective with the New Orleans Police Department. "The fucked-up part is there's some pride in that."

There are what experts call *murder hot zones*, or places where violent crime happens more regularly. Among those is Algiers, on what is known locally as the city's West Bank. It's part of New Orleans, the vibrantly booze-soaked city cut in two by the Mississippi, and Karr sits in a dimly lit neighborhood on the forgotten side. Parts of Algiers are a mere half mile from the city's bustling French Quarter and are in fact visible from Moon Walk Riverfront Park. But it feels like a different world. There are virtually no tourists, ghost tours, or voodoo shops. You can't get a hurricane or a Sazerac to save your life, and most bars close by midnight.

Algiers is where many of the area's working-class Blacks have lived for decades. There are more here than there used to be, considering New Orleans is one of the nation's most rapidly gentrifying cities. A third of the residents of Old Algiers, the oak-lined historic district, live below the poverty line. Life expectancy is nearly a decade less than the national average, and not just because the sound of gunfire is so familiar. The people who make New Orleans *New Orleans*—those who hose down Bourbon Street and clean ravaged hotel rooms, who painstakingly cook gumbo using time-honored family recipes, who play music and tend bar—can no longer afford to live close to city services such as law enforcement and medical care.

The Irish Channel and the Tremé, both on the East Bank and walking distance from the Quarter, used to be Black neighborhoods. Now they're packed with brunch places, craft beer joints, $600-a-night Airbnbs. White people just swooped in, bought and restored distressed properties, got rich. Rents and property taxes have therefore skyrocketed, driving families—many of whom called a certain neighborhood home for generations—into places where housing is cheap and crime is high.

There's no simple way to explain violence, though one uniquely New Orleans insight is that people from one neighborhood don't often trust anyone from a different neighborhood. People here swear, straight-faced, that someone born in Uptown has a different dialect and even slightly different facial features than someone born two miles away in Mid-City. You carry yourself differently. You play by different rules. Some of this is ultimately part of the city's mythology, not unlike haunted pubs and vampires. But this much is undeniably true: If, like Brice Brown, you were born in the Cut-Off, a poverty-stricken neighborhood in eastern Algiers, it's entirely possible that you and your grandparents grew up alongside neighbors with the same blood. You shopped at the same corner grocery, played in the same parks, walked the same alleys and sidewalks because, well, that's what you and everyone else have always done. Even if there was danger in the vicinity, there was also comfort, and comfort here is the closest thing anyone feels to safety. Even now, Brown lives less than three miles from where he grew up.

Then came Hurricane Katrina in 2005, leveling the city and revealing for a national audience its political and economic weak points. Neighborhoods were destroyed or abandoned, and in some cases razed by shortsighted city officials. Newly homeless residents had to go somewhere, so they poured into unfamiliar communities throughout the city. Broke and traumatized and feeling lost, arguments turned to fights turned to street wars, and hence a phenomenon was born: the neighborhood beef.

An initiated soldier may not identify himself with gang colors or even roll with a regular crew. If only it were that simple. Police would have better luck identifying such actors. Residents could better avoid them. But in some cases, someone who's tangled up in something deadly might not know he's even been indoctrinated. For good reason, people here don't trust the cops, making murders nearly impossible to prevent and similarly difficult to solve. Between 2010 and 2018, only a third of the city's 1,434 homicides resulted in an arrest.

If Tonka George's first mistake had been coming home, his second had been going for a walk on a warm evening and wandering out of his neighborhood. What happened next has confounded relatives, admirers, and even police. Why had he been so careless? What had been so damn important? Had he just been gone too long from New Orleans and forgotten how to move?

Now four years later, Tonka's murder is among the hundreds that remain unsolved. There are no credible witnesses. None willing to talk, anyway.

"For whatever reason, individuals take this position that they're not going to be a snitch," Shaun Ferguson, the NOPD's superintendent and a longtime Algerine, said in an interview. "They want to revert to handling it their own way."

On that Friday night in 2016, Brown answered his phone. He heard the voice of Karr's quarterbacks coach, John Johnson. Brown climbed inside his Silverado, picked up Johnson, and continued toward Old Algiers. Though Brown was certain of the scene that awaited, he was nonetheless afraid of what he'd see. He crept up General De Gaulle, driving so slowly he feared getting a ticket.

He made a right onto Shirley Drive, and a block north he saw the crowd. It was as if a second line had broken out. Brown parked near a neutral ground and saw faces illuminated by police lights. There was yellow police tape stretched between a stop sign and a chain-link fence.

"They killed my Tonka!" he could hear his former quarterback's mother screaming.

Brown just stood there, staring emptily into chaos. Tonka had been a model citizen, had inspired the neighborhood, and, damn, even *he* got killed. It was a stark reminder that, around here, no one is safe. Brown couldn't yet know how much this experience would change him, his coaching philosophy, the Karr football program.

He was only certain of one thing: standing at a crime scene, he never wanted to feel *this* ever again.

THE HOURS AND DAYS following Tonka's murder turned to weeks and months. Brown felt called to do . . . *something*. But as one man, and a football coach at that, what could he do?

Politicians and activists had tried and failed to curb gun violence here. In 2016 alone, there were 486 shootings in New Orleans, and among the dead were the rich and poor, vagrants and dignitaries. That April, former New Orleans Saints defensive end Will Smith had dinner with his wife and a friend at a sushi restaurant in the French Quarter. Smith had played a key role in helping the Saints win the Super Bowl in 2010, providing a sense of rebirth in a city still wrecked by Katrina. On the way home, Smith's Mercedes SUV bumped into the rear of another vehicle just a few blocks from the Quarter. Then he sped away. The other vehicle's driver, Cardell Hayes, followed Smith into the ritzy Lower Garden District, famous for celebrity residents and centuries-old double gallery houses. Smith and Hayes argued, and Hayes produced a .45-caliber Ruger from a holster and unloaded eight rounds into the thirty-four-year-old's back and side. Raquel Smith, his wife, was also shot twice in the legs.

"A tragedy," Mayor Mitch Landrieu told reporters following an incident that horrified the nation. Landrieu had become the city's first white mayor since his father held the office in the 1970s. Mitch had won by promising to curb violent crime in New Orleans. He reminded himself of this by placing a photo of each murder victim into a red binder. By the time he left office in 2018, he'd filled a dozen binders.

Nearly eight months later, shots rang out on Bourbon Street, the nerve center of the city's $9-billion-a-year tourism industry. Bullets tore into the insides of ten bar crawlers, among them a twenty-five-year-old tattoo artist from Baton Rouge. He'd come to New Orleans to celebrate his birthday. Instead he died on the way to a hospital.

"New Orleans is safe," Louisiana governor John Bel Edwards insisted.

Four days after that, former NFL running back Joe McKnight was driving on the West Bank when another car cut him off. McKnight stopped near an intersection in Terrytown, and the other driver shot him three times. He died on the pavement at age twenty-eight.

On and on it went, as young people of color kept dying. And for various reasons, even those with the most power to influence this trend felt overwhelmed.

"How can it not wear you down?" Landrieu would say in an interview years later. "If you're constantly going to funerals and constantly with grieving mothers, you see children—this is just so hard. It never seems like it's gonna end."

Gun deaths became so frequent, so impossible to ignore, that the only sensible way to carry on was to ignore them anyway. Elected officials, stalled by political gridlock, gave up or left office. Police cycled through leadership and tried to pretend its relationship with the city wasn't in tatters. Locals just got used to the sound of gunfire and the knowledge that a neighbor you saw today may be shot dead tonight. When two teenagers were shot outside the Karr gymnasium during a basketball game in January 2017, an administrator pulled Coach Taurus "T." Howard aside at halftime. The shots could be heard inside, but Howard says he was nonetheless told to carry on with the game as if there weren't twin puddles of blood just steps away. Two years later, when two dozen rounds pierced the late afternoon air directly behind the school, Karr's cheerleaders didn't stop jumping rope.

Brown could not abide this. Though he's indeed just a football coach, each day a hundred emotionally vulnerable young men gather inside the four purple walls of the Karr football office. They're here because they just want to play and are willing to do whatever it takes to get onto the field. Brown makes those decisions. And small as his dominion may be, what if he could use his authority—and football's powerful draw—to connect with and reprogram a few dozen kids each year? What long-term impact could it make to have even a hundred kids, who'd grown up surrounded by guns and tragically low expectations, grow into well-adjusted adults? How might they influence others to see their world differently?

Brown's strategy is not complicated. It begins with personal investment and communication. These are children who have irregular access to running water, shelter, and food. Love and mentorship are often scarcer. In communities like this, across the United States, adults tell at-risk kids that without dramatic behavioral changes, they'll wind up dead or in prison before adulthood. They may mean well, but that's not inspiring. It's self-fulfilling. Many of these young people simply accept this warning as fact. Friends and relatives died young, so what do they have to lose? Might as well live hard, use drugs, make money while you can. Where's the logic in planning for a future they won't be around to experience?

Brown takes a different tack. He views each player not as an archetype but as an individual. There is no catchall scared-straight story.

He digs deep into each player's psyche and learns precisely what he needs. Joe Thomas, for instance, grew up surrounded by violence and the drug trade. He therefore responds to entirely different incentives, and stimuli, than Leonard Kelly, whose parents are married and raised him in a middle-class home.

"You have to reach them before you can teach them," Brown says.

Teaching them, though not an explicit solution to gun violence, includes forcing discomfort and cornering them with strenuous discussions. Brown and his assistant coaches speak plainly, often profanely, to players. They simulate challenging, deeply uncomfortable, social scenarios that fluster kids by design. These are meant as psychological stress tests. After all, it's impossible to avoid all conflict, whether in a crime-ridden neighborhood or during a traffic stop. But how do you respond? How *should* you? Just as a quarterback learns to recognize and beat the blitz, young men in New Orleans must learn to identify a possible crisis—and know how to de-escalate it. Around here, that can be a matter of life and death.

The program isn't all about breaking bad habits. It also introduces young people to real, tangible rewards in exchange for sacrifice. They compete for championships and scholarships, and the three dozen former Karr players who, between 2017 and 2019, used football to get a college education are walking billboards for fully committing to the program. Instead of telling players about hotels or fancy meals or the college experience, Karr's coaches show them. They hand out symbols of responsibility along with the real thing: being named to a leadership group called Pride Panel, given an honorary jersey number, or even becoming a team captain. Players can, and often do, call Brown or position coaches at any hour and ask for guidance or support or food. Their mentorship is the rarest thing: predictable.

Brown reminds young people, some of them traumatized and others who've never respected authority or been held accountable, they're capable of amazing things. They can win games, sure, but they can also earn a four-year degree and a six-figure job. They can live anywhere, far beyond where they were born. Though football in much of the United States is facing an existential crisis, considering the spotlight placed on traumatic brain injuries and political polarization, communities such as Algiers rely on the sport as an important incentive and a vehicle to teach life skills and teamwork. Brown, for his part, uses the game to teach players that they can, and should, leave the West Bank forever. But first they must survive.

Players listen to Brown because he's successful. They do as he says because he determines who plays. They trust him because, no matter the day or time, he answers the phone.

In exchange, Brown and his staff ask for only one thing: on Friday nights, players show their gratitude by following the Karr blueprint precisely and, for four quarters, giving everything they've got.

WHEN BROWN IS ANGRY, he's an approaching storm that you hear long before you see or feel anything. He's a mountain of a human as it is, in the neighborhood of four hundred pounds, with a bearded round face flecked with an increasing number of gray strands.

"Pathetic," a voice can be heard calling from down the hall of the football office.

Though he's only thirty-four and finished his own college-football-playing career in 2005, Brown would pass for a decade older. His eyes, often red from exhaustion, bulge from their sockets and sit beneath thick, and usually raised, eyebrows. This gives him a look of permanent skepticism. Brown's voice, though, is his most useful coaching tool. It's a piercing monotone, and he wields it like a sword.

"Fucking pa-*THE*-tic!" he says, louder now, as he walks through a hall and reaches the Karr weight room. This is the team's meeting space before and after practices and games, the program's hub. Joe looks up at Brown from a tattered weight bench, and Leonard sits on the floor. His elbows are on his knees, and he's trying to avoid eye contact. Assistant coaches stare at the black rubber flooring.

Earlier tonight, Karr lost its season-opening game to John Curtis. Fumbles, missed tackles, penalties. Worse, players were lazy and intimidated. The senior class, Joe and Leonard included, revealed its talent deficit, and underclassmen confirmed they're immature. It was the team's first loss in two years.

Brown loves a puzzle, and he has a doozy ahead this season. Almost certainly the most challenging of his career.

"Bullshit. No fucking adjusting. No fucking communication. Bull . . . *shit!*" he says. "Y'all lost the true essence of what Karr really is. And that's fighting."

He slams the rickety door to the coaches' office, disappearing behind it. He lumbers toward his desk and falls into a rolling chair. The head coach's office is a dingy, cluttered time capsule where it's forever 2016, the year Tonka died. The clock doesn't work. The rectangular window is cracked. On the walls there's a poster of that year's state title team, a proclamation from the city council, a framed T-shirt with TONKA printed on it.

Brown, for many reasons, spends most of his life in here. He's often alone, trying to focus on a game that comes easy to him and trying not to worry about what happens if that stops being true. If he starts losing, will kids tune him out? Will they ignore the more important parts of his mission? His credibility off the field, after all, is tied to his success on it. Brown has no children of his own, and he has never married. He has few friends outside football, and lately some of the ones he has here have begun moving away, and on with their lives. Though he talks often about the importance of family, Karr staffers rarely see Brown's mother, stepfather, or the grandparents who helped raise him.

The job, and the parallel nature of this undertaking, is relentless. His motivation comes not from something he'd like to happen but something he hopes will never happen again. He skips meals and rarely sleeps. Though he deeply fears the sound of a ringing phone, he never silences it. He suffers from anxiety, impostor syndrome, and the effects of stress-eating. He hasn't seen a doctor in years.

Brown is a mighty boulder in a river of young lives, but the current is powerful and is wearing him away.

With midnight approaching, Brown finishes his second Coke on the rocks. He sighs. It's time to head back to the weight room, address the players, come up with a plan for the rest of the season. This is a team and a community on its own. Regardless of talking points and good intentions, nobody else is walking through that door to save the West Bank, or this corner of America, from itself.

Brown's knees pop when he stands. A hundred kids are waiting. He's all they've got. The truth is, they're all he's got, too. He slips between his desk and the wall and opens his office door, and in the next room the heads begin turning as their coach rumbles in.

CHAPTER 1

KARR MEN

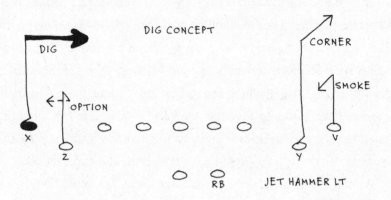

BROWN LOWERS HIMSELF onto damp bleachers, sighing into the Louisiana heat. It's July 2019, and Karr's preseason training camp, held every summer on the campus of Nicholls State University in Thibodaux, Louisiana, is a relentless, sweltering grind.

Brown hates it. Shared dorm rooms, an almost round-the-clock itinerary, and gentlemen of Brown's heft tend to not sleep well on single beds with plastic mattresses. There's almost no air flow in the dorms, or even out here at John L. Guidry Stadium. This swamp-side campus about an hour southwest of New Orleans feels, right now, like the bluest corner of hell.

But Brown knows these are the days that force a cluster of individuals to begin fusing into a team. Coaches use discomfort to their advantage, and it helps them identify strengths and weaknesses for the approaching season. Players begin emerging as leaders, and eventually everyone returns to New Orleans following this period of dramatic transformation.

This is Brown's fourteenth camp. He can sense the weight of each one.

"This might be my last year," he says. He drops his sun hat, a mangled nest of straw that looks to have survived a shark attack, onto the bleacher. "I can feel it."

Brown says the kids aren't listening to him anymore. Neither are his assistant coaches. They're stubborn and entitled, he says. Then again, Brown sounds like a man who's getting older as his surroundings remain static. He is less patient than he used to be, more weary at the constant flow of young people who come to him for wisdom, for guidance, for money. There's usually a few hundred dollars folded in his duffel bag, but it never lasts. Players are always asking for a few bucks, and coaches sometimes ask for help paying their rent, bills, and child support.

As much as Brown wants to, he can't say no any more than he can justify canceling or relocating training camp. It's fulfilling to be so useful, though it's also exhausting. In recent years Brown has tried to outwit not only his players—but also himself, a way to freshen up the routine, keep it spicy. One of his favorite methods is to identify a mantra for the coming season.

One year it was "Owe yourself," which became a conversational catchall. He'd constantly repeat it, partly because players on that team seemed to behave as if they were unworthy of success. Another year it was "God bless you." These sayings have literal, perhaps even inspirational, meanings. But Brown thinks it's hilarious to use them in unexpected ways. As "aloha" can mean both hello and good-bye, "God bless you" can mean anything from "I'm bored with this conversation" to "Happy Thanksgiving" to "Fuck off."

He hasn't yet come up with a mantra for the 2019 season, though it's on a Herculean to-do list for training camp. So for now he's still using the one from last year: "No what the fucks." It's a classic, some of Brown's best work, and in its most accurate sense it means that he longs to go one day or even one hour without something in his orbit making him say, "What the fuck?" He mutters "No what the fucks" when conversations peter out, when he's heading to a team meeting, when he's just sitting alone playing *Toy Blast* on his phone. He thinks it's great.

Yes, Brice Brown is a champion football coach, brilliant play caller, and skilled people manager. He's also a huge nerd.

On the opposite end of the field, training camp's first practice is about to begin. Brown shakes his head because even player warm-ups are a mess. Stretches are supposed to be perfectly synchronized. But assistant coaches aren't paying attention, and players are scattered.

"No what the fucks," Brown says under his breath. Out of the corner of his eye, he sees the team's medical trainer approaching.

Alex Moran works for the Tulane Institute of Sports Medicine in New Orleans, and during training camp, Moran will tape sprained ankles, bandage cuts, diagnose possible concussions. Sometimes she recommends a player sit out one or more practices. Brown thinks she can be overly cautious, but he likes and respects her because she doesn't mince words with the big man, even when delivering bad news. Among Moran's principal frustrations, one she shares with Brown, is teenaged boys' unwillingness to take seriously the dangers of dehydration. Exertional heatstroke kills an average of three football players each year, hospitalizes dozens more, and those numbers are getting worse. Even near sunset, the humidity here makes the air feel like a sticky, thick, ninety-eight-degree sauna. A football helmet can add ten degrees to that, and as soon as Brown sees Moran coming, he knows she's not bringing good news.

Sure enough, Moran tells him Brandon Spincer, a ninth-grade offensive lineman, has taken the hydration mandate a bit too literally. He's pacing near a canopy tent and drinking water. But when his stomach starts to feel full, Brandon jams his finger down his throat and makes himself vomit. Then he drinks more.

Moran reports that she has tried to explain this is counterproductive and, well, a little gross. She doesn't tell him that overhydration can be similarly deadly. But for now, it doesn't seem to matter what Moran tells Brandon. He keeps doing it.

"So you need me to curse," Brown says, and Moran purses her lips.

"Yeah, kinda," she says.

Brown chuckles and stands. He places the straw hat on his head and walks over.

"Brandon, why?" he asks with an exasperated shrug. The young man denies any wrongdoing. Brown drops his shoulders. "I just saw you. I *just* saw you. I looked at you the whole time."

He orders the kid to drop the bottle and rejoin his teammates near the stretching line. Brown shakes his head and mutters to himself.

"No what the fucks," he again says, and Brandon hears him. "B, do you know what that mean? It's like: You stick your finger down your throat, I say: 'What the fuck?'"

The confused young lineman jogs away. Brown wanders onto the practice field to check in on various position groups.

"Drink the water!" he thunders. "If you don't, I'm gonna fuck you up."

Quarterback Leonard Kelly is practicing the option, but his pitch to the running back is rushed and sloppy. Jamie Vance, a senior cornerback, just lost his temper and berated a younger teammate before ignoring his position coach's attempt to calm him down. The defensive line is disorganized, and the wide receivers are a wreck. This is a problem. Brown's catch-and-run spread offense is a symphony in pigskin. He is the conductor, and Leonard is the principal soloist. But the receivers are the violins: the group that, ideally, comes together to create something big and beautiful. Brown's offense relies on receivers making relatively simple catches before using their athleticism to outrun defenders. Before that can happen, there must be timing and precision.

During this first rehearsal, Dany'e Brooks commits a false start, and Aaron Anderson whiffs on an important block. Destyn Hill, whose tall and slender frame seems in conflict with "Fat," his nickname since he was a chubby offensive lineman in park ball, keeps making the same mistake when he runs a basic dig route. After sprinting fifteen yards, Fat is supposed to make a sharp ninety-degree turn toward the center of the field. Instead, his pivots are "rounded," which costs him speed and could mean that he and Leonard's pass won't get to the same place at the same time.

"Look at yourself!" receivers coach Omari Robertson shouts at Fat. "Fuckin' terrible."

Brown watches and periodically shakes his head. Eventually he blares an air horn to end practice. Players remove their helmets and squeeze water into their mouths. Then they form a semicircle around Brown and take a knee for the coach's postpractice assessment.

"A lot of y'all was being cussed the fuck out today," Brown says. "Just take that shit."

Film review and a leadership group the team calls Pride Panel, both opportunities to meticulously—and mercilessly—dissect players' mistakes, will come later tonight. For now, Brown strikes an inspiring tone: pointing out that Ryan Robinson, a ninth-grade defensive back, has a chance to start at safety. Even Brandon Spincer, who a little earlier was puking under a tent, has a chance to someday anchor the Cougars' offensive line. He just has to fully commit himself and master his position's most minuscule details.

"Because if you want to win," Brown says, "it comes down to what?"

"Little shit," the voices say back to him in unison. They've heard this many times.

"So how can you get more?" the coach says. "How can you *give* more, even when you make a mistake?"

He pauses. After fourteen summers of this, Brown's public speaking technique is well honed.

"You go to Karr. So your reality and your imagination *have* to be big," he says. "Because if you have limited mind-sets, then you're going to have limited goals. Then you're going to have limited dreams. And you're going to have a limited reality."

Players are nodding, and so are a few of Brown's assistant coaches. A few of them played for Karr and once heard versions of these same remarks.

"Everybody understand that?" Brown says.

"Yes, Coach," the voices say, and after a final prayer, the cluster disbands. Players begin collecting their equipment.

Brown starts toward the stadium's exit. But before he leaves the field a senior linebacker jogs up to his coach. His number 7 jersey is cinched up, revealing his trim abdomen. Of everyone out here, perhaps no one grew up with a more limited imagination or more modest dreams than Joe Thomas. When he addresses Brown, he does so with deference. He asks if they can speak privately back at the dorm.

Brown agrees, and Joe sprints up the stadium's concrete stairs. He runs past his dawdling teammates. When he's out of sight, Brown takes a deep breath. He's all too aware of how Joe grew up, and the environment he's trying to escape. Considering the things Joe has endured, it's nearly impossible to guess what he'll tell Brown.

"Whatever it is," the coach says, "it ain't good."

He considers the possibilities. It's going to be a long night.

"What the fuck," Brown says.

PLAYERS CARRY THEIR equipment back to Ellender Hall, and Brown climbs into his banged-up Chevy Silverado. Condell "Tiga" Benjamin, Karr's volunteer equipment manager and the coach's reliable body man, takes his place in the passenger seat.

The pickup does more than transport water coolers and football equipment. It is Brown's mobile command center, the vehicle he uses to roam New Orleans when he worries about his players' well-being or safety. Like most everything that belongs to Brown, it's in pretty rough shape. The center armrest is torn, allowing yellow foam to spill out, and he recently backed into an empty school bus. He was so relieved the bus was undamaged that he didn't bother getting the dent in his truck fixed. The back seat is a cross between a junkyard and a football museum: cups and discarded snack wrappers sharing space with clothes and boxes containing heavy trophies.

"Coach of the year shit," Brown says, apologizing for the mess as he starts the engine and gases it back toward the dorm.

He drives without speaking, and he and Tiga mouth the words to the old R&B jam whispering from the radio. Brown parks near the dorm's entrance, and he walks in to find assistant coaches stacking sixty boxes of pizza onto tables.

"Your change, sir," Marvin Rose, a squat ex-Navy man, says. Earlier Brown fished $400 from his duffel bag. Marv hands him all that's left.

"Eight dollars?" Brown says. "Ah, fuck."

He stuffs the bills into his pocket as players file in, and they grab a plate and attack the boxes. As grueling as training camp can be, there are upsides. Everyone is together and accounted for, and kids don't have to worry what, or if, they'll eat. If anything, they're overfed and in awe of the bounty that's available to them. Breakfast and lunch are daily buffets with build-your-own omelet and grain bowl stations and all-you-can-drink smoothie and juice bars. The student lounge in Ellender Hall is stocked with snacks almost around the clock, and team leaders have the freedom to walk across the parking lot to Chick-fil-A. This, like most everything in training camp and in fact in Brown's program, is by design. Any time Karr leaves New Orleans, be it a road trip during the season or preseason camp, Brown wants to impress players with the world beyond their home city. He highlights the differences, unfairly on occasion, and speaks of New Orleans as desperate and crumbling. Other places are overflowing with beauty, peace, and abundance.

Brown sits in an armchair and watches as the hundred teenaged jackals tear into the pizza. Though he could've swiped a slice or two before the players arrived, he resisted. It's almost nine o'clock, and the coach hasn't eaten all day.

"I'll get something later," Brown insists. Even he knows this is untrue, and he catches himself immediately. "I'll drink a Coke. I need to hydrate anyway."

Joe polishes off three slices and stuffs his plate into an overflowing trash can. Then he heads toward Brown. The coach takes a breath and sits up in his chair.

"So what's the deal?" he asks, and the young man sits on a side table.

Joe is square-jawed and handsome, with close-cropped hair and tattooed arms packed with new muscle. His eyes are the color of a pecan shell, and if he doesn't understand something or if he distrusts you—most everyone, at least at first—they latch on to you. He speaks softly everywhere but the football field, and because of a tendency to misspeak and a thick lisp made worse by braces, Joe often keeps his secrets to himself. And he has many.

Brown knows them, and almost all involve Joe's mother. Joe leans toward his coach and whispers, and it's immediately clear this story is no different.

A few months ago, Keyoke Thomas was arrested and charged for possessing crack with the intent to distribute. She pleaded guilty and was sentenced to at least a year in prison. Keyoke has been "on the block," which is how she describes selling drugs, since she was a teenager. Joe is her only child, and over the years he has gotten used to his mother occasionally going away. He tries to carry on and pretend nothing happened, and this includes staying in the apartment they used to share. Joe can't just tell the landlord he's living there alone, another secret, and usually he cobbles together the monthly $200 rent. Sometimes Ms. Diane, the woman Joe believes to be his paternal grandmother, slips him some cash.

This month was different. Before Joe came to school to catch the bus for his ride to Thibodaux, he saw a notice on the apartment door.

Brown listens to Joe's retelling and squirms in the armchair. Then he calls for Nick Foster, a deeply loyal assistant coach who acts as Brown's consigliere, to join them.

"Tell coach everything," Brown says, and Nick leans in.

"I got a conviction notice," Joe says.

"Conviction?" Nick asks. He looks confused before untangling the words. "*Eviction.*"

"Ihh-viction?" Joe asks.

"E-, yeah. *Evict.*"

With that settled, Joe repeats the story. He says he offered the landlord rent money, but that wasn't enough. The landlord demanded an additional $80 as a late fee. Joe doesn't have that, and now he fears not just moving out but explaining to Keyoke that he has lost their home. That, in his mother's absence, he'd failed.

Brown says that, if it comes down to keeping Joe from being homeless, he's got $80 in his duffel bag. But Brown points out that he doesn't like Joe's neighborhood, or that he spends so many nights there alone. Cypress Park sits on a quiet but sketchy corner of Algiers. There's often a drug dealer posted on a corner a few steps from Joe's front door, undeterred by the bright halogen light on a pole. Neighbors sit outside and smoke weed in a common area, and Joe greets them on his frequent walks to McDonald's. It's the only food he can afford, and he eats there so often that employees greet him by name.

Brown suggests an alternative: instead of staying in the apartment, Joe could spend a few nights with Nick. He lives in a house in suburban

Terrytown, has a young family, is a damn fine cook. It's not unusual for Karr's coaches to take in kids for a few nights, especially if there's trouble at home or danger in the vicinity. It's just part of the job here, and players are encouraged to ask for shelter, or transportation, or a few dollars for food or clothing, rather than seek these things out in other ways. Even if coaches don't outright hand over cash, they often know of options to get these basic necessities. Indeed Joe has thought about it, and he truly hates being alone. But it's not that simple. Keyoke has done so much for him, he says. He can't live with the thought of letting her down.

"I just have a bad feeling about it," Brown says.

Joe's eyes flood, and when a few teammates approach, he turns his head so they will not see. Brown continues, pointing out that Joe's stubbornness is both his greatest strength and biggest weakness. He reminds Joe that he has come a remarkable distance, one that even a year ago seemed unthinkable. But if he wants to finish it, to achieve his dream of playing college football, he has more to do. Brown tells Joe he is taking on too many responsibilities and cutting himself no psychological slack. As much as anything, this could threaten his future.

"You're trying to prove, like, you can do all this shit," Brown says.

Joe nods and wipes his eyes. Brown and Nick agree to continue the discussion later. Tonight's previously scheduled team meeting is about to begin, and Brown asks Joe to address the team. Over the next three days and nights, Joe will be among fourteen players who'll actively campaign to be one of five team captains. Players cast their votes on the final night of camp, and between now and then, Joe needs to earn their respect. Brown reminds him that honesty is a pathway to trust.

Nick pats the kid's shoulder, and Joe joins his teammates and sits cross-legged on the floor. Brown knows Joe, considering his scar tissue and some of his leftover instincts, could be either his greatest triumph or his most devastating failure. The next few months will determine Joe's future, and ultimately the strength of the Karr program.

The meeting begins, and Brown keeps his seat as Nick calls it to order before inviting Joe to the front. The young man smiles and pops to his feet. Nick leans on a pool table as Joe begins.

"A young man like myself," he says, "has got to grow up."

He talks about hopes for the coming season, and for a fourth consecutive state championship. Then he pivots to other matters resting heavily on his heart. He shares that his mother is in jail, that all the McDonald's has fattened him up, that earlier today he walked outside and saw a paper tacked to his front door.

"I got a conviction notice," Joe says.

Nick, zoning out before this, snaps his head up.

"Got a *what*?" he says. "What you got?"

The other boys laugh, and soon there's a chorus of voices correcting Joe.

"Eeeeeviction!"

Joe drops his head, and he bursts into laughter, too. Humor is just one of the ways he has learned to survive. He turns to look sheepishly at Brown, who is shaking his head.

"This motherfucker," the coach says.

AFTER AN HOUR of speeches, instructions, and warnings, most players are dismissed to their dorm rooms. But fourteen young men remain in the lounge and begin sliding armchairs toward a wall to form a U.

These are the members of Pride Panel, a sort of tribal council composed of team leaders selected by coaches because of their on-field ability and maturity. It's also the psychological centerpiece of training camp, and perhaps the Karr program at large. Most of the players are upperclassmen, though a few are sophomores. Each player will be asked not just to speak, but to analyze the day's events on and off the field. He'll be expected to point out what—or who—was successful, or not. Each opinion will be directly, and harshly, challenged by coaches, and there are several purposes for this: to put kids on the spot and make them as uncomfortable as possible. Most important, it's to have them make choices under duress—and to experience the consequences.

"Ain't no right answer," says Nick, who Brown uses in this and other situations as his bad-cop enforcer. "We just try to put their ass in a pickle."

It's almost 12:30 a.m. when the meeting begins, and what unfolds over the coming hours can seem disorganized and madcap. But nothing about Pride Panel happens by accident, including the late start. Brown, like government intelligence officers and interrogation specialists, knows humans are less willing to lie when they're deprived of sleep. That's ultimately the point of this: tell the truth, take your licks, and we can all get to bed.

There's also the seating arrangement. To continue the orchestra analogy, players are ranked by not just their importance to the team but also their reliability. Joe sits in the first chair, and Leonard is in seat number 14. He is Karr's starting quarterback, and eight months ago he led the Cougars to the state championship. But a while back he lied to teammates about a girl he was dating. Nothing is worse than lying to Pride Panel. This earned him more than just a demotion from second to last chair. It got him "silenced." He's forbidden from speaking until his teammates decide Leonard has served his punishment. This has been going on for months.

Players sit directly across from their counterpart on the team, and in Joe's case, he faces Fat in the second chair. They are different in almost every way, yin and yang. Joe is the blue-collar, humble, inglorious linebacker. Fat is a dynamic, supremely gifted, swaggering wide receiver. Tall and lean, Fat smiles even when he shouldn't and wears his hair in bleached yellow twists. His soft facial features conceal a ferocious desire not just to succeed—but to perform. He calls himself "Fatastic" and dreams of playing in the NFL and becoming a superstar on the level of his hero, Odell Beckham Jr.

When Brown assigned jersey numbers a few months ago, he considered these personality contrasts. Three numbers—2, 5, and 7—are sacred in the Karr program, and being assigned one of the legacy numbers is both a high honor and a mighty burden. Overachieving leaders and defensive backs Shakiel Smith and Elcee Refuge once wore the 7, seen as the emotional rock of the program. Tonka wore the 5, which is now awarded to a player who displays selflessness and sacrifice. As for the 2, charismatic former receiver Racey McMath and running back Ronnie Jackson achieved legendary status wearing the number, and today it recognizes the star of the show. The 5 is announced in an annual ceremony before Karr's first home game, but during Pride Panel a few months ago, Brown presented Joe with the 7 and Fat with the 2. A considerable achievement, to be sure, though Brown reminded both players of a caveat: he, and only he, can take this away at any time.

Pride Panel begins, and Fat's responsibilities include reciting minutes from the group's previous meeting.

"We talked about our assignments in camp, the schedule, and how everything is gonna go," he says, speeding through the exercise.

"What do you mean?" Nick asks, an attempt at slowing Fat down. "You're bad at detail."

"And we talked about bringing Leonard back," Fat says.

Brown, sitting in a chair and silent until now, issues a loud and exaggerated sigh.

"It's amazing how y'all start off with bullshit," he says. "You fucking forgot what the fuck the meeting was about?"

Fat shifts in his chair and looks Brown in the eye. Tonight is Fat's sixteenth birthday, and despite his youth, he has already learned one Pride Panel maxim: no matter what, you never change your answer. Doing so is an admission that you didn't feel strongly about your first one—and, worse, is an act of submission.

"He was telling us the itinerary," Fat tells Brown, "and what we want from it."

"Why couldn't you say that?" Nick says.

"I did say that."

Coaches move on, Fat exhales, and now it's Joe's turn. His job is to analyze the day's practice and take a stand: Was today more good than bad, or more bad than good? And why?

Joe speaks clearly, if softly, and points out the day was good. But the roster lacks experience and maturity—something coaches are all too aware of.

"There's not too many vets out there. It's beaucoup young dudes," Joe says, using a frequently used example of New Orleans slang, passed through the generations and a reminder of the region's French and Creole influence. "I feel like we need to motivate them more. Like, that shit was intense today. But it's gonna pick up tomorrow."

"So you need to give them directions and shit?" Nick asks.

"Yeah, 'cause they was fucked-up," Joe says. "They was tired. They running to the water. They need that bitch."

But Joe made a mistake of his own during practice. Nick points out that he directed players to line up for stretches on the wrong side of the field. So what good are his directions to others if Joe doesn't fully understand his own responsibilities?

"That's me," Joe says, tapping his chest.

Nick shakes his head. Not good enough.

"It can't be no, 'That's me, my fault; I fucked up,'" he says. "I understand that's your accountability. But right now, at this point in the season, ain't no fuckups. Ain't no wrong mistake. That's a simple, direct order, and you couldn't even get that right. Sit down, man, go to the next person."

Nick looks disappointed in Joe, and the young linebacker locks his eyes on a coach he deeply respects. Now Fat is up again, and while they're on the topic of personal responsibility, he kept running that rounded, imperfect dig route today. This is a problem, not just for Fat but for Omari, his twenty-eight-year-old receivers coach.

"How many times he keep telling you to stop rolling them digs?" Brown asks, pointing toward Omari.

"He didn't tell me that," Fat says. "He said post it."

Some teammates laugh at Fat's audacity. But Joe doesn't. He doesn't have Fat's natural talent. This is his shot. It's serious for him, and he doesn't appreciate screwing around.

"Y'all not really being accountable," Joe tells Fat, though he's referring just as much to the entire offense. Earlier today during what was supposed to be a conditioning period, Joe caught offensive players goofing off instead of lifting. "Y'all doing the same shit y'all was doing in the weight room today. Now it's coming on the field. What the fuck, son?"

"I never roll my digs," Fat says. "I don't."

Brown is pleased when Joe weighs in, though it's Omari he ultimately wants to hear from. So Brown turns the conversational screws, amplifying the tension. He thinks Omari is too laid-back, and Brown wants him to take charge. Brown spins toward the young coach, who a decade ago played wide receiver at Karr, and challenges him. Is he *purposely* teaching his receivers poor technique? Omari sits up in his chair.

"I told you to do what with your digs?" he asks Fat.

"Post up and square down at the top," Fat replies. This is an admission he's not running the route exactly as drawn.

"So *now* do you roll your digs?" Nick says. But Fat knows he can't back down.

"No," he says. "I don't roll my digs."

This sends Nick into a frenzy, and now he's screaming at Fat, who stares blankly ahead. Nick points toward Omari.

"So he's wrong?" he asks. "He don't know what he's talking about?"

"He know what he's talking about," Fat says. He's trying not to show emotion or send this confrontation into overdrive.

Is Fat just being obstinate? Nick asks. Does he not understand the dig-post concept? Brown asks. Omari says nothing. Ratcheting the tension once more, Brown suggests either Fat or Omari has brought more dishonesty to Pride Panel.

"This same shit y'all punish Leonard for, for lying," Brown says. "My book, no sin is greater."

Brown again looks toward Omari.

"Y'all don't have no control in that room," he tells him. Omari and Mike Thompson share responsibilities coaching wide receivers. Omari handles the bigger outside wideouts, and Mike oversees the speedier slot receivers. "None. Prisoners running the prison."

Nick suggests Omari had better do or say *something*. In his second season on the Karr coaching staff, Nick points out he is in danger of losing not just the respect of his players, but of his colleagues, too.

"You know what I think?" Omari finally says. "I don't have a problem expressing it to the Pride Panel. Um, I told him last night I think he's not in it right now for Karr."

Now it's personal. Omari is saying what others have been thinking: that Fat, who before his junior season is attracting recruiting interest from some of the nation's most prestigious college football programs, cares more about his own future than that of the team. That he's not a "Karr man," an honorary title that means a player is willing to sacrifice himself for the sake of the team. Omari continues, suggesting Fat may have the talent to help the Cougars, but his lack of character is dishonoring the team and the number 2 jersey.

"I disagree," Fat says calmly, and Omari explodes.

"I don't give a *fuck* what you're saying!" he says.

This reaction is highly unusual for Omari, who is soft-spoken almost to a fault and usually presents himself as a peer to players. It's part of what he learned playing college football at Southern University, though it now makes him an outlier on Karr's coaching staff. Brown prefers an in-your-face style, and recently he has been pushing Omari to be more assertive. Especially with Fat, whom coaches are worried is getting too much, too soon—so much adulation from outsiders, before he's mature enough to handle it.

Now pushed to the edge, and facing an audience, Omari is unloading.

"All this shit is coming prematurely for you," he says. "You not ready for the shit that's been happening. Is it a blessing? Yeah, it's a blessing. But you didn't earn it."

Omari knows training camp isn't just an evaluation period for players. Coaches are being analyzed, too. Attempting to impress Brown, Omari makes his move.

"Until I see otherwise," he tells Fat, "you are no longer a starter. Motherfucker, don't put that fucking jersey on tomorrow. You go out there with fucking Under Armour on."

Fat doesn't say anything. Neither does Brown.

"Do *not* wear that fucking jersey," Omari repeats. "Do you understand me?"

"I understand," Fat says flatly.

But has Omari pushed hard enough? Has he satisfied the boss? After a moment, Omari leans back in his chair and finishes it.

"Out the room," he tells Fat, barely above a whisper. "Now."

Brown raises his eyebrows, as eager as anyone to see what happens next. But he says nothing. Fat stands and walks toward a door leading to a stairwell. When he reaches his room, it's almost 2:30 a.m.

He makes a decision. He slides the number 2 jersey over his head and onto his torso, carefully tucking it into his pants. Then he steps into the hallway and heads downstairs, stopping at the heavy door that leads to the student lounge. Just before opening it, Fat looks through the square window, takes a deep breath, and makes the sign of the cross.

During Fat's absence, Pride Panel moves on. Players are called on, more confrontations ensue, answers are offered. A wide receiver promises his position group will be more focused tomorrow.

"How y'all gonna do that?" Joe asks.

A defensive back mumbles through a coach's question about body language.

"Speak up," Joe instructs.

Several players fumble through responses about their top priority for training camp.

"Fuck," Joe interjects, "I just need everybody to be together."

Then behind them, a door opens. A few players see Fat marching in wearing the 2, and when they laugh, Joe tells them to shut up.

"You really doing this shit?" Nick asks. Fat keeps walking back to his seat.

On his way, he parades in front of Omari, who reaches out and grabs a fistful of jersey.

"Take it off," he tells Fat. The young man refuses.

"You didn't give me the jersey, O," he says.

Fat tries to step forward, but Omari blocks him. He grabs the jersey with his other hand.

"Take the jersey off, Fat," Omari says. "Take it off, bro."

There's only one person who can order the jersey's removal, and that's the same person who assigned it months ago. Fat just stands there, and Omari, still strong from his college days, adjusts his grip on the neck of the jersey. Nick stands up, ready for what seems inevitable. The other coaches push their chairs back, making space.

"Why you doing all that?" Fat says. "I'm not about to fight you, Coach."

"Take the jersey off," Omari repeats. His voice is louder. "Take the fucking . . . jersey . . . OFF! Take the fucking jersey off!"

Omari jerks hard on the neck, slinging Fat forward. The armchairs squeak as they're pushed across the tile. Omari keeps tugging on the jersey, trying to pry it off the kid, and both lose their footing. Omari falls back into his chair and Fat tumbles into his lap and blurts out something unexpected. With tears in his eyes, it's all he can muster.

"I love you, Coach!" he says.

"That's enough, O," Brown says finally. "Take the jersey off; give it here."

Fat does, tossing it at Omari's feet. He retreats to his chair and tries to avoid crying. Omari slides deep into his seat with embarrassment. Even Brown knows he let this go too far. Nobody speaks for a long time, and it's clear in this moment that this isn't yet a team. It's a cluster of strangers trying to find their footing and their voices.

Brown asks if anyone is willing to share what they're feeling. A coach says he can feel his anger issues flaring up. Another points to the book of Proverbs and its teaching that loving a child means acts of tough, even harsh, discipline. Another asks if it's okay to step outside to get some fresh air.

"Anybody else?" Brown asks, but there are no takers. "Listen, I done been here a long-ass time. I done seen some crazy shit, but that was some crazy . . . *shit.*"

He takes a breath before continuing.

"Y'all stuck," he says. "Stuck physically, stuck emotionally. Everybody pushing and pulling. Everybody got their own story. Everybody got their own struggle and shit like that. But for y'all, y'all got to embrace the struggle. Like, sometimes you've got to fight yourself in order to overcome yourself."

Some faces stare intensely toward the coach; others are glazed over. It's past three in the morning, and players are scheduled to be on the field in five hours.

"You've got to recognize your weaknesses and your shortcomings," Brown says. "And you've got to fight, and you've got to battle that shit every day. If a motherfucker call you an 'I guy,' you better accept that shit and fight that shit every day so you can become a 'we guy.'" He scans the room, locking on any eyes looking back at him.

"Fight yourself so you can overcome it," Brown says. "If you choose to walk away, you choose to give up. And y'all like to spill shit over to the next day, 'cause you don't want that confrontation. Your perception and reality is two different things. You don't want that struggle. You just want the success. You just want the glamour. You don't want the struggle. You don't want the pain. You don't want the blood. You ain't want none of that shit."

Fat is looking at the floor with his bottom lip quivering. Omari's hand is on his chin, as if in his mind he's replaying the choices made over the last hour. Nick sits on the arm of a chair, staring at nothing. Joe, though, is looking at Brown as if the coach is speaking directly to him.

"Some of y'all want a handout. But I got news for you: ain't nothing in this world free," Brown says. "Ain't no handouts."

THE FINAL DAY of training camp is the longest, hardest, most important. Coaches and upperclassmen work with young players on the finer points of football, and making it on this team. They spend a half hour repeating the fight song, at varying tones, tempos, and volumes. They work on the right way for offensive skill players to turn toward the sideline in unison. They practice, again and again, how to properly line up and salute the flag during "The Star-Spangled Banner."

Though these processes take hours, perfection will take weeks. The team ends the day with speeches and skits, the most memorable of which is Brandon Spincer's spot-on impression of Brown. The final act is the most important, and most grueling: the selection of captains.

Members of Pride Panel file into a small room a little after midnight, taking their usual seats at desks shaped into a U. There's a lectern in a corner near a mounted television with loose wires, and coaches sit behind players for what promises to be harsh cross-examination. Following a vote, five captains traditionally emerge.

Before pitches begin, Fat asks if he can address Pride Panel. Nick obliges. Fat looks toward Omari.

"I just want to apologize to you, Coach, for doing some bullshit," he says. "I just hope that we can move forward, and our relationship can continue for life."

Omari nods but doesn't speak, and Nick asks if Omari wishes to add anything. The receivers coach, whose easygoing nature and light skin tone have earned Omari a reputation as an outsider, says he and Fat spoke and made peace. He says he'll leave it at that.

"Ain't no secrets in Pride Panel," Brown calls out.

Omari sighs, visibly incredulous, and offers a cursory elaboration: he and the kid met, Fat apologized, they moved on. That was that.

Brown shakes his head in frustration, but he insists they carry on. Joe goes first, and his pitch is straightforward: Coaches know his story, the things he has seen and experienced, what football means to him. He wants to identify and teach the next Joe Thomas, he says, and go on to represent Karr and the values that changed, and might've saved, his life.

Joe retakes his seat, and Fat makes his way to the lectern.

"My goal," he says, "is to get other people better."

It's a thin argument that lacks thought and personality.

"How?" Nick asks.

"To get other people better," Fat says.

"*How?*" Nick says again.

"You gonna show 'em how to round your digs?" Brown asks. Fat shakes his head and sighs.

He starts again, and in this moment there's more than just inexperience and youth on display. There's deep insecurity and a thirst for affection, both of which Fat normally conceals under layers of bravado. When he continues, it's as if *Destyn* is speaking, not *Fatastic*. He explains that every receiver, every individual, is different. That means the way he runs a dig route might be different, too. He mentions past Karr captains and the ways they inspired him; how he dreamed of someday wearing the purple and gold and leading the Cougars' chill-inducing pregame entrance.

Coaches listen, and some nod. Others aren't buying it. Norm Randall, a longtime Karr assistant and a man who takes pride in challenging players, is among the skeptics. He wonders if Fat, considering his dueling personas, even knows the difference between himself and the character he seems determined to play.

"You are very fucking talented. The sky is the fucking limit," Norm says. "Don't take what I'm telling you as personal. I'm telling you the truth about how I feel, right? It's your job to change that. You've got to *want* to change that. Everybody ain't Karr men.

"Everybody don't come back to help the program. Everybody don't care about raising kids in the community. And that's fine. But don't sit up here and give me no bullshit. If you want to change it, change it. Prove us wrong. But come here and say that; say: 'I want to be a captain, I'm still working on my fucking self. If you guys allow me to work on myself and be around you guys and learn from you guys, I think I can change and become a Karr man.' I'll take that any fucking day; I'll ride or die with you in the back alley. But you've got to tell the fucking truth about who you are."

Fat retreats, and though coaches won't tell him this, they're encouraged. Next comes Leonte Richardson, a tall and skinny running back, followed by cornerback Jamie Vance. They make their pitches and take their licks. Earlier this week, it was Jamie who exploded at a teammate during practice, and during Pride Panel he wore University of Arkansas apparel. Jamie has committed to play college football for the Razorbacks, but coaches expect players—even star players with bright futures—to focus on the moment, and their remaining work at Karr. Wearing college logos is a signal that Jamie is using high school as a stepping-stone, which around here is a show of disrespect.

"I know who you are," Norm tells Jamie. "I've been watching you. You're a good kid with a good heart. But your whole goal is that fucking shield that says NFL on that bitch. If you want to be a part of that family, you have to make sacrifices and open yourself up. And if you do that, you'll become a Karr man because you'll do it the right way. If not . . ."

Norm pounds the table.

". . . you'll just be Jamie."

The minutes turn to hours, and a receiver is ripped apart for being too rehearsed, a running back is attacked because he's perhaps too injury-prone to be taken seriously as a captain, a sophomore linebacker clumsily admits he can sometimes be a "bitch."

Coaches start to react, but Joe beats them to it.

"That should've never came out of your mouth," he says, ordering the young linebacker back to his seat.

After thirteen proposals, there's one last candidate. Leonard makes his way to the corner. He has, for the first time in months, been unsilenced and allowed to address Pride Panel. Before he can, coaches pile onto him about the girlfriend who Leonard put before his teammates. Is she really that good in bed? one asks. She got diamonds in her private parts? demands another. Why can't you give her up? one more asks.

Leonard laughs, offers answers, and adamantly denies he's still seeing the girl. His responses seem defensive, and he's unable to just ignore coaches who are deliberately trying to rattle his cage.

"That's why you're so guilty," Brown says, staring deep into his quarterback's eyes. "Your guilt just pours out of you."

Leonard looks away.

"We all drop the ball sometimes. It's how we learn from our mistakes," Brown continues. He wonders aloud if Leonard's teammates will vote for him anyway.

If they don't, Leonard would be Karr's first starting quarterback in Brown's nearly two-decade tenure to not begin the season as a captain. And the thing that bothers the coach most, he tells Leonard, is how uninspired Brown is to stump for him.

If this were Aldon Clark or Munchie Legaux or Speedy Noil, Brown says, he'd be pounding on the table arguing for him. If it was Tonka, he'd come across it and fight anyone suggesting doubt.

Leonard looks at Brown and, in a hushed voice, speaks to his coach.

"I have a question," he says. "Why wouldn't you do that for me?"

Brown looks up, exploring his mind for the right words.

"This is different," he says. "And don't take what I'm saying wrong: you're just cut from a different cloth."

Leonard is staring at Brown, who continues.

"A lot of the qualities that made them so special as captains, you don't have," he says. "I couldn't imagine a Pride Panel telling Munchie Legaux that he's silenced."

A true Karr man would've fought for himself. Wouldn't have just defended himself but risen above it, been bigger than a single mistake. In fact, Brown tells him, he would've reminded his teammates he was a state championship fucking quarterback, the big man on campus, and nobody silences *him*.

"But you accepted it," Brown says. "I can't imagine that. You let somebody take something away from you that God gave you: a voice."

After absorbing the words, Leonard nods and walks silently back to his chair. There's nothing he could say now anyway. He'll be remembered not by what happened, but by how he responds.

An assistant coach stands and distributes pencils and half sheets of paper. Players can write up to three names, and Pride Panel will learn who has qualified for the captain's line tonight, before Brown announces them to the rest of the team tomorrow morning. The ballots are handed to Brown, and another coach begins tallying the votes.

Players filter out of the room and wait in the student lounge. When the last one leaves, Nick stands and slams the door.

"So much talent, so little direction," Norm says.

Joe, Jamie, Leonte, and Fat have at least five votes, enough during a typical year to qualify. Leonard, with only two, does not. After the fight with Omari, someone asks, what message does it send to elevate Fat to captain? One more example of too much, too soon?

The coaches debate this, and other possibilities. What about Tygee Hill, a wiser-than-his-years sophomore defensive tackle who might be the most talented player Brown has ever coached? Which is more important, when it comes to Leonard, tradition or making him understand the long-term consequences of a lie?

"Leonard's my dude," Brown says, "and maybe I need to get over the shit. But I ain't over it yet."

"You always tell me to let that shit go," Norm tells him.

"Yeah, but this one I can't get over."

Brown sighs, looking at the names.

"This is a fucked-up little team," he says.

He says he has an unusual idea. What if, for the first time, coaches hold off on naming captains until closer to the season opener? Just call it an extended audition period, Brown says, and see who shows the most growth over the coming weeks. It's unusual, but the assistant coaches like it. Maybe fucked-up teams need to be managed in fucked-up ways.

Nick opens the door and calls down the hallway. Players retake their seats, and Brown explains the staff's decision. He says nothing about the votes. Besides, Brown continues, what difference does it truly make to be named captain?

It's just a title, after all. An honor, an ambition, a goal. But nothing more than an artificial reminder of your value as a player and individual, Brown points out, and what does it say about you if the absence of that affects your performance? Who would even confess to such a thing? Now that he thinks of it, Brown wants to know. He asks for players to raise their hand if it would actually matter to them, if not running onto the field as a captain tomorrow morning would diminish their play and feelings of self-worth.

He waits, scanning to see if anyone dares raise a hand. No one does. Brown begins reciting the following day's practice schedule and travel itinerary for when the team returns to New Orleans. As he reads aloud, Brown can see, out of the corner of his eye, one hand start to slowly go up.

THE STAIRWAY DOOR OPENS the next morning a little before nine, and players stream in and sit on the floor. Joe is among the last to arrive, and he does so without a shirt. He barely slept after Pride Panel, though that's not unusual for him.

For years now, Joe has had a recurring nightmare. He's sleeping, and someone kicks open the front door. They're here to kill Keyoke, his mother. Sometimes they turn the gun on Joe, too. But the dreams always end the same way: His instincts tell him to protect his mother, to stop the gunman, and he never can. She always dies. Even after Joe snaps awake, he is left with persistent feelings of guilt and shame, for he has failed not only the person he loves most—but the one who, throughout his childhood, trained him for moments like this.

These dreams have continued since his mother went to jail, so his way of coping is to just avoid falling asleep. If someone comes, he'll be awake and ready. And if not, at least he won't be afraid.

After Pride Panel's dismissal a little before five a.m., Joe went dorm room to dorm room to see who was still awake. When Dylan Smith, a senior defensive lineman, faded around 6:45, Joe gave in and went to bed. He slept maybe two hours. Now he's wrestling a T-shirt over his head, rubbing sleep from his eyes.

"So you're tired as a motherfucker," assistant coach Mike Thompson tells him. Joe smiles, revealing the silver braces covering his teeth. But not his thoughts.

When another coach blows a whistle, players begin streaming through the doors and into the morning heat. Training camp's final session is a walk-through run entirely by players, traditionally the team's new captains. Coaches sit in the bleachers and observe.

Only one player will lead today's stretches and drills, and because there are no secrets in Pride Panel, Joe had to come clean last night. Yes, "captain" is merely a title. But to him it is an honor that once seemed impossible. If he could walk into a room or onto a field and be this team's *captain*, what else might he be capable of?

Brown suspected the traumatized young linebacker felt that way. His challenge to see if Joe, or anyone, would be honest enough to admit a perceived weakness had been one last test. Joe raised his hand, and in the hall a few minutes later, Brown took the young man aside. Congratulations, he told Joe, and get ready for the weight of leading a team like this. It is one that needs many things, Brown knew, but most of all it needs a protector.

"I hope y'all figure this shit out," Brown told him. He followed this with a saying that would eventually succeed "No what the fucks" as the coming season's mantra. "Good luck," he told Joe.

On the way to Guidry Stadium, Joe blinks away the sting in his eyes as he jogs down the sidewalk. He threads past Leonard and Fat, who are still under the impression Karr has no captains. Joe runs past the other members of Pride Panel before stopping near a stadium tunnel. While players wait for a gate to be unlocked, Joe pulls on his jersey and smooths the 7 on his chest.

The gate opens, and teammates file through an opening and down concrete stairs. And when they reach the field and take their usual places for stretches, the players turn to see Joe facing them, standing alone on the captain's line.

CHAPTER 2

THE BOY WHO PLAYED WITH TRUCKS

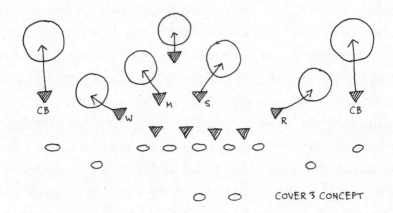

COVER 3 CONCEPT

RHONDA GEORGE LEANS AGAINST her only son's tombstone and runs her fingers through purple silk flowers. It reminds her of rubbing Tonka's hair. So many times he'd crawl into bed with his mama, snuggling up, and even as an adult he'd ask so pitifully if she could play with his hair. And she'd groan and roll her eyes, though she could never say no.

Now she can barely recall its texture, how spongy and soft his little Afro was. She wishes she could.

It's early September 2019, a little more than three years since Tonka died alone, scared, bleeding just three blocks from home. His murder remains unsolved, and his killer is still at large. Deep down Rhonda knows she'll probably never learn who killed Tonka, or why. Her shock and despair have turned to restlessness and outrage, and visiting

McDonoghville Cemetery to talk to Tonka is among the only things
that provide actual comfort.

"I really don't understand," she is saying on a particularly humid
Thursday afternoon on the West Bank. "I'm trying to . . ."

Rhonda takes a deep breath.

"I'm not gonna say I'm trying to *cope* with it," she says. "Because
you didn't deserve this."

She lifts her glasses and wipes away tears. Cars hum in the distance
as they cross the Crescent City Connection, the twin cantilever bridges
that cross the Mississippi River and link the two New Orleanses. Like
most days, Rhonda has the cemetery to herself. She smooths the dec-
orative gravel atop the grave and dusts off a tombstone engraved with
the shape of a football and a message: "LONG LIVE #5."

In a few hours, it will be "Long Live 5 Night" at Behrman Stadium,
when Karr kicks off its regular season against John Curtis. Brown des-
ignates one game each year to memorializing his former quarterback.
This season he has chosen perhaps the most anticipated high school
game in Louisiana: two defending state champions squaring off on
Karr's home field.

"You know what Coach Brice is doing for you?" Rhonda asks Tonka
as she tidies his grave. "He worships the ground . . ."

More tears. She forces a smile.

"Joooohhnn *Curtis,*" Rhonda says, imagining the evening's crowd
and its energy. "Boy, that would've been your game."

A silent moment passes; when she has finished cleaning, Rhonda's
fingertips again find the purple flowers.

"I know you're smiling," she says.

DURING LEONTE RICHARDSON's pitch to be a captain, he did remarkably little talking. Instead, Karr's assistant coaches told stories. Many

of them involved the best and worst thing about the young running back: his fearlessness.

Mike Thompson referenced a scalding practice in late spring, and Leonte just wouldn't stop. It was something to behold. Leonte, tall and muscular but thin, refused water and rest—even when coaches told him it was okay. Eventually, he collapsed and had to be rushed to the hospital. As Thompson recounted the episode, which had genuinely frightened coaches, it was as if Thompson couldn't decide if it had been inspiring or a cautionary tale.

"A Karr man will die for this shit," he told Leonte and the rest of Pride Panel. "N——s telling you: 'Stop working, take a break, man.' And you're like: 'I gotta do it; I can't let 'em down.' You were really willing to die for that shit, like, literally."

Norm Randall, who coaches special teams and defense, went next. During a team-building outing at a paintball course, Randall's nine-year-old son, Baylon, wanted to roll with the big boys. Leonte invited Baylon to join his team, though that's not what left an impression on Norm. It was that, after Baylon became separated from the group, leaving him vulnerable and afraid, Leonte ran over and wrapped his arms around the boy. Their opponents closed in and opened fire as Leonte shielded Baylon. Even days later, Leonte's back was still bruised and flecked with light blue paint.

"That's my brudda," Leonte said that night. His thick New Orleans mumble is distinctive even among his teammates.

Brown, sitting in a corner, had been silent. Because Leonte grew up only a few blocks from Karr's campus and started hanging around the program as a child, Brown has known him for years. The coach sat up in his chair and spoke.

"You remind me a lot of Tonka," he said, a comparison he issues neither lightly nor frequently.

But by then Brown had made a decision. He had one last honorary jersey number to assign, and if 7 is the team's backbone and 2 is its sizzle, whoever wears the 5 is the program's soul. That had been Tonka's number, and each year Brown gives it to the player who most exemplifies selflessness, the way Tonka had. The other two numbers mean more to the team, perhaps, but none is more precious to Brown than the 5. He decided Leonte was deserving, not just because of what he'd already done but because of what coaches were about to ask of him. Though Leonte would receive enough of his teammates' votes to qualify as a captain during normal years, Brown knew he needed to single out Joe and elevate him alone. Brown knew Leonte would understand.

And he did, though as training camp ended and the team returned to New Orleans, Brown could find himself both fascinated and alarmed by Leonte. As Coach Mike had pointed out, the kid was something of a paradox. He often ignored instructions to pace himself, and he'd occasionally berate a teammate in the weight room for something as meaningless as improper squat form. He screamed at other players for drinking water or catching their breath, dismissing them as a "bitch" in comically dramatic fashion. Leonte kept pushing, pushing, pushing beyond even his own body's alarms. Eventually players and coaches just got used to Leonte passing out or disappearing to get intravenous fluid. Brown began referring to the kid as a "walking hazard."

This was confusing to Leonte, because didn't coaches want maximum effort? He had inherited unremarkable genes, and at five feet ten inches and about 160 pounds, he is strong but fragile. He is quick but not fast, too skinny to be an every-down running back, too short to be a dynamic wide receiver. Leonte is just big, fast, and strong enough to get your attention—but neither big, nor fast, nor strong enough to keep it.

College recruiters had ignored Leonte, and this gnawed at him. No scholarship offers, no interest, no nothing.

"All my life I been an underdog," Leonte says. Though he can be defensive about the attention he doesn't get, another part of his paradoxical nature is that he relishes being seen as a blue-collar player who must fight for every opportunity and superlative.

Leonte, like so many young people here, grew up surrounded by bullets and blood. Eventually he became almost desensitized to death. He saw his first dead body when he was thirteen, and now five years later, he estimates four close friends have been cut down by gunfire. It's just something you learn to live with here, and Leonte needn't leave his home for reminders of its permanence. A decade ago, his uncle Chris moved in with Leonte's family after a bullet pierced his spinal cord and left him paralyzed.

Leonte's boyhood chore wasn't feeding the dog or cleaning his room. It was making sure Uncle Chris was taking his pills and not refusing to eat. As much as Leonte wanted to, he never asked how or why Chris had been shot, not just because reliving the trauma might be painful. But also because the answer didn't matter. It happened, and all anyone could control was what followed.

The other thing Leonte noticed was how fast people here just . . . move on. His four friends? Uncle Chris? Most people forgot about them. Their lives and accomplishments were just erased.

Which perhaps explains why Leonte does not dwell on the past, the limits of his body, or college recruiters who ignore him. He cannot control those things. But he can pack muscle onto his frame, outwork most everyone on the practice field, pay closer attention to football's finer points—the "little shit"—than teammates do. Indeed he speaks, walks, even shakes hands with remarkable purpose. If someone offers a weak handshake or, God forbid, a casual left hand, Leonte doesn't just refuse to take it. He'll stand there, staring at you from behind slit-shaped cat's eyes, and provide a step-by-step explanation of the *right* way to shake someone's hand. He has done this to no less than Brown himself.

These are the actions of a young man who craves attention, in a sport whose infrastructure is fueled by it. Leonte is, for better or worse, a performer. If a defender bulldozes into his thigh with a helmet, Leonte will parade around the sideline, moaning in pain. His voice is a high-pitched whir, and coaches designate him to begin the daily reciting of the Lord's Prayer. "Ayy, whose father?" Leonte asks his teammates, who then respond in unison. "*Our* father, who art in heaven . . ."

If Leonte breaks a long run or catches a tough pass, he sometimes retreats to the sideline and makes sure a reporter saw and noted it. Every day is the Leonte Show, and it is reliably amusing—to almost everyone.

Though heart and passion are precisely what Brown wants in an overachieving player, Leonte's theatrical reaction to every . . . single . . . mistake (or triumph!) is a source of great annoyance for the coach.

Leonte simply refuses to lower the volume, regardless of the circumstances, and weather, offensive assignment, and coaches' advice to modulate himself can all go to hell. Brown can't decide if Leonte is the best possible example for his teammates or the worst.

"You almost died!" Brown yelled at Leonte once, a reminder of the day his stubbornness (or determination!) led to Coach Mike performing chest compressions as an ambulance drove onto the practice field.

But Leonte just stared back at his coach, eyes narrowed, because even after knowing him for so long, Brown still doesn't get it. It isn't death that Leonte fears.

It is the possibility of being forgotten.

A DOZEN OR SO YEARS EARLIER, nobody associated Karr football with dreams of immortality. The team usually made the playoffs, but in the dicey aftermath of Hurricane Katrina, the school itself was a social melting pot with a football program struggling to find itself.

The storm had decimated New Orleans in August 2005, forcing residents to either evacuate or take refuge in the Superdome, the hulking downtown stadium where the Saints play home games. The seventy-three-thousand-seat building became an emergency shelter, which gradually became a hellscape. Rapes, murders, and suicides were common, and shared restrooms overflowed with people and their various fluids. And, in the most perverse way, that was better than what was happening outside. Rescue teams traveled from house to house, spray-painting an *X* on the walls as a code to other recovery workers of what they'd find inside. On the top right was the number of current hazards. On the bottom right was the number of dead bodies the house contained.

This, astonishingly, was an American city, and the world watched as bodies floated down flooded streets and a once-vibrant metropolis tore itself apart. Katrina unmasked corrupt politicians and a compromised police force, and it revealed deep cracks within the city's government and education system. The Orleans Parish Public School Board lacked adequate insurance on its resources and in fact had no record of how many schools it actually controlled. After estimating that 126 facilities fell under its jurisdiction, a consulting firm later discovered that more than 200 schools actually reported to the board.

Most were damaged and closed for months. Sixty thousand children, many of them at ages seen as particularly important for emotional development and behavior regulation, were on indefinite recess. Some wandered, fell into trouble, had nothing to do but seek thrills and cash and drugs. But three dozen schools had sustained zero or minor damage. Four months after Katrina made landfall, the city announced that Edna Karr Magnet School was among those that'd be recommissioned as a charter high school whose student body would come from the entire city. Suddenly kids who'd grown up rarely leaving their neighborhoods, and in fact avoiding people from outside their immediate vicinities, found themselves studying, existing, and playing together.

"I don't care where you were before Katrina," Karr's principal told the student body in December 2005. "Now you're all Cougars."

Rhonda George was among the quarter million residents who'd evacuated. She and her two children took refuge with extended family near Atlanta, and she prayed for her home city to survive and heal. She pleaded with God, just as she'd done a dozen years earlier, when Rhonda asked the Lord to bring her a son. She had a daughter, Tiffany, but Rhonda had always wanted a boy. She wanted to love and shape him, to teach and learn from him.

God was always listening, so into the world came baby Tollette. He was a porky thing from birth, with rolls of fat collecting around his elbows and knees. That's the real reason an uncle called him Tonka: he was built like a truck. But it sounded better when the same uncle bought him a yellow toy truck for his first Christmas. He loved it. The only toy he liked better was a football. Rhonda tossed it to him and taught him to press his hands together to catch, and as the years passed, the two became inseparable.

She went to his park ball games in New Orleans, screaming for her little superstar from the bleachers. They grew closer because Tonka could be moody, sarcastic, withdrawn—and so could Rhonda. He had his mother's eyes and impatient smirk, and by the time he was a teenager and the family fled to Atlanta, Tiffany had learned to roll her eyes at how her brother and mom laughed at the same things and finished each other's sentences. They seemed like soul mates, this mother and son.

Eventually New Orleans reopened, the Superdome emptied and got a good cleaning, and Rhonda returned home to begin rebuilding. Tiffany and Tonka remained with their relatives in Georgia, and when Rhonda finally gave the all-clear for her kids to rejoin her, Tonka walked in with tears in his eyes.

"Don't do that to me again!" he demanded of his mom. They agreed to stay together from now on, no matter what.

Tonka got into Karr in 2008, and the first thing he noticed was the diversity in its halls. The faces were mostly Black, but there were stuck-up kids from New Orleans East coexisting with country-asses from the Cut-Off and junior gangsters from Uptown. If Tonka listened closely, he could untangle some of his teammates' accents. And they noticed a thing or two about Tonka, too: the most obvious being that, at a rip-roaring 155 pounds, he was more Prius than dump truck.

Jabbar Juluke was Karr's head coach then, and he made Tonka a wide receiver and punter. Juluke and his twenty-five-year-old offensive specialist, Brice Brown, had begun retooling Karr's offense. The school had been running a slow-paced veer option for decades. The attack, as methodical as it is antiquated, relies on deception and ball control. Though it peaked in the 1970s at the University of Houston, it was simple for teenaged players to understand, and it limited the mistakes commonly associated with high school football.

Brown wanted to modernize Karr's offense using a variation of the spread he'd learned as a college player at Grambling State. And with a vast landscape of talent now available, Juluke and Brown could install skilled athletes at every position and go all in on an attack that is perhaps the polar opposite of the veer. The spread relies on quick strikes, sound quarterback and receiver play, and high risk. Turnovers are often as possible as eye-popping scores, and sometimes the difference between those results is timing, precision, and most of all, an intelligent and thoughtful quarterback with lightning-fast instincts.

In 2007 and 2008, Karr made it to the second round of the Louisiana state playoffs. Then in 2009, Brown inserted Munchie Legaux at quarterback. Munchie wasn't just a six-foot-five, two-hundred-pound prototype. He was the first player to combine physical talent with mental acuity, fulfilling Brown's vision. Most mornings they met at 6:15 to watch film and establish the weekly game plan. But Munchie had a lazy side, and if he overslept or planned to skip school, he'd awaken to see a familiar presence standing in his bedroom.

"Get your ass up!" Munchie would recall Brown booming. The quarterback's mother trusted Brown so much, and knew her son so well, that she gave the coach a spare house key. Once Munchie was up and his heart rate had normalized, off they'd go to the school.

But in 2010, Munchie was playing for the University of Cincinnati. Juluke and Brown had almost no one with experience running the spread. No one but the shrimpy mama's boy wearing number 5.

Before Tonka's first game as a starter, he was terrified. He didn't even want to play quarterback. He preferred playing receiver, believing that position gave him a better chance of being recruited to play college football. But he'd agreed to play out of position because the team needed him. Rhonda whispered a message in his ear before that first game, and it became their private tradition.

"Stay focused; play the game," she told him. "Let God do the rest."

Karr lost its opener to St. Paul's, a predominantly white Catholic school in New Orleans's northernmost suburbs. But after that, something unexpected happened. Tonka settled into the rhythm of Karr's new offense and led victories against Destrehan and Jesuit, larger schools that reached the previous year's Class 5A playoffs.

Tonka wasn't especially big, fast, or strong—not enough to keep your attention, anyway. But Karr kept winning, largely on Tonka's heart and attitude, which was big and bad enough to overpower seemingly any opponent. He could inspire his teammates one day and blast them the next, and he seemed almost supernaturally tuned in to what the group needed to hear. The Cougars sliced through rival New Orleans programs McDonogh 35 and Warren Easton, and they racked up confidence and wins.

Sometime that season, a Karr assistant coach named Ajenavi "Ace" Eziemefe suggested a new pregame entrance to match the team's swagger. Tonka wanted to run onto the field to Jay-Z's "I Just Wanna Love U," because he was a hustler, baby, and another teammate suggested the Archie Eversole anthem "We Ready." But Christopher Herrero, the school's young band director, had a different idea. One day he directed his low brass section to play a long concert F followed by a D. Then he motioned for the drums to fill rapidly into the background, and players listened and felt themselves swaying back and forth.

Herrero had played this piece, based on David Banner's "On Everything," as a student in the Jackson State University marching band. The song isn't especially famous, but it samples something even more obscure: the dramatic musical introduction of King Jaffe Joffer's motorcade in *Coming to America*, the 1988 Eddie Murphy romantic comedy. In the film, it's more than a song. It's an announcement—the arrival of Zamunda's king, and with him something menacing and powerful is approaching.

Tonka and his teammates loved it. Before games they'd gather in an end zone as Herrero directed the band to play what would be called "The Rock." Some players would crawl on all fours, mimicking an actual cougar on the loose, and the group reassembles to begin rocking in unison to their left and right to higher-pitched horns. Then, with the music building to a crescendo, players burst onto the field.

After the 2010 regular season ended, Karr beat Wossman and Northside in the playoffs. The team leaned as much on Tonka's intelligence and instincts as his comfort running the spread. Then the Cougars stomped Teurlings Catholic in the state semifinal, and for the first time since Katrina, Karr would play in the state championship game, held in the Superdome, a building that five years earlier hosted ruin and rot.

Rhonda sat in the bleachers, looking for her baby. She watched as

Tonka led "The Rock" in the end zone, before the team ran onto the field to face Franklinton High, a school in the easternmost part of Louisiana. By then Karr had won thirteen consecutive games. Perhaps more impressive, the Cougars and their quarterback hadn't just found each other and established harmony. Katrina, for all it had destroyed, wound up creating something, too. Upstarts and misfits had fused to reach the state's grandest stage, and they were one win from immortality.

Tonka's mama stood when number 5 zipped down the field and threaded through defenders. Rhonda screamed so loud as Karr's quarterback reviewed his options, found openings, and sprinted forward again and again.

"Come on, Tonka!" she kept calling from her seat. "Run!"

MIDAFTERNOON NOW on this Thursday in September 2019, and the door opens to Karr's weight room. Joe enters first, followed by four teammates.

With the regular season approaching, Brown invited each of the young men into his office. Jamie Vance, the lean but short-tempered cornerback, walked in and closed the door. He took a seat on the pleather love seat facing Brown's cluttered desk. Joe was already a captain, Brown explained, but he couldn't lead the team alone. Jamie's path to this point had been different from Joe's, but it had nonetheless led him to the captain's line.

"Your process is your own," Brown told him.

Next came Dylan Smith, a stocky and occasionally immature linebacker. Brown then sent word for Fat to come into his office. After the training camp scuffle with Omari Robertson, Brown had accepted Fat's apology to his coaches and the Pride Panel. He'd returned the number 2 jersey. Now Brown was elevating Fat to captain, the group's only junior.

The last player was, besides Joe, the most obvious. Leonte took his seat, which because it sits slightly lower than Brown's desk makes its occupants literally look up to the coach. Brown informed Leonte he was now a captain.

"It's your voice that moves the people," the coach said. "Just don't get so emotional."

As notable as were the four new captains, so was the most glaring omission: Leonard, the team's starting quarterback. Brown had decided he needed to work out his personal entanglements, on top of the fact that Brown was skeptical teammates would listen to Leonard's instructions.

Along with increased responsibilities, Karr's captains receive certain privileges. Each has direct, round-the-clock access to Brown, who in the nonfootball universe is easygoing and almost mayoral. But here he sits on an exclusive and intimidating throne. If Brown is the profane and ramshackle pope, the captains are his cardinals and assistant coaches the Swiss Guard.

While most players dress for games and practices in the locker room, captains are granted entry to the weight room. Each is assigned one of six barbell racks as his own station. Joe, the team's heartbeat, has the rack in the room's center; at his left is Fat, and to Joe's right is Jamie. Dylan's station is in the rear left corner, and in the opposite corner one rack has been left vacant in case Brown decides to expand the captain's line. Like Pride Panel, nothing about the weight room is without intention. Leonte's rack, therefore, is directly in front of a wall featuring framed eight-by-ten photographs of Karr luminaries: Devon Francois wearing his Alcorn State uniform, Elcee Refuge lined up at Kent State, Noel Ellis Jr. crouching in his Texas A&M gear.

Leonte has been placed closest to reminders of the young men and former captains who built the Karr program. Those who'll never be forgotten. But there's no picture of the former quarterback whose ghost seems to haunt these halls. Tonka's presence nonetheless looms over the program at all times, around all corners. Now his old jersey number is draped onto Leonte's weight rack.

There are reminders of Tonka, subtle and obvious, almost everywhere. This is the same weight room he used. Past the locker room and down the hall are the classrooms where he and Brown once studied opposing defenses and planned their attacks of them. Then there's the dank gymnasium and the school's auditorium, where the school held Tonka's funeral. Hundreds packed into the bleachers and saw his open casket, a thin sheet covering half his face. This is the cost of being remembered in a place like this, where years later people talk not only about the things you accomplished, but the memories and moments that were stolen away.

On this afternoon, Karr's five captains file in and take their places. Leonte's eyes are drawn to the jersey and a number and memory he's now partly responsible for. He says he wants this, sure, and seems to crave its attention and pressure. But is he up to it? Can anyone truly take on Tonka's uniform and legacy?

For now, Leonte sits on his bench and prepares for kickoff. In three hours, two Louisiana football heavyweights will collide, and a clash of approaches and cultures will be on display. J.T. Curtis, the legendary coach of the school his father founded in 1962, strictly forbids profanity and deploys the veer option offense. If Brown's spread is a lightning strike, Curtis's veer is a patient boa constrictor. You know it's there. You know it plans to encircle you. It is an attack you see coming but nonetheless cannot stop.

Curtis is a seventy-year-old white man who coaches mostly white suburban kids. Because of the school's twenty-seven state championships, tonight is a showdown pitting tradition against modern, efficiency against speed . . .

"The n——s," assistant coach Nick Foster says, "against the white boys."

As this Thursday afternoon advances, Karr's players begin their various pregame rituals. Tiga, the team's equipment man, stalks around the weight room in a red bow tie and Guy Fawkes mask. Norm lights a stick of incense and places it on a shelf. Fat checks his social media mentions, and Joe is continually interrupted to deal with some crisis of the moment. Just now in the gymnasium, a fight has broken out between a Karr student and Trent Washington, a junior wide receiver who has become a source of increasing alarm among coaches. After being suspended from the team during the summer, Trent was recently reinstated—but is again bringing trouble into the program.

Leonte tries to ignore the ordeal. He picks up the purple 5 jersey and admires it before draping it again on the rack. He begins dressing, and because Leonte is Leonte, he has assigned deep importance to every step of this process. Dressing for the game will take him ninety minutes. He snaps a clear visor into his helmet, pulls on a white sleeveless undershirt, slides on one pair of socks before a second. He wrestles with a purple compression sleeve on his left arm until it—and the GOD FIRST printed on it—is just right.

Then he pushes in a pair of earbuds and hits play on his iPhone, disappearing inside his playlist. He bobs his head as he unties his cleats with his teeth, wipes down his helmet, bites down on a new mouthpiece.

A new song starts, and Leonte likes this one. "RN4L," by Lil Durk, is an anthem to the streets and a hymn of survival and caution, about living as much and as hard as you can before you're inevitably cut down.

Been around with my brothers, you give me endurance,
I ride with two Glocks
And I'm thinking 'bout getting insurance
Tryna do me like 2Pac

Leonte closes his eyes, but he doesn't sing along until the chorus hits. When it begins, he dramatically lifts his arms and sings: "They told me don't die young because I'm talented!"

ON THAT FATEFUL EVENING in June 2016, Tonka was lonely and wanted to smoke. He texted a friend and asked if he'd left a "gar"—a blunt—in his car.

Like rolled up one? the friend replied.

No the pack, Tonka said.

But the friend didn't find anything, eliminating the need for him to drive to Tonka's. This was the first domino in a sequence that would end a young life. The next was Tonka calculating that a Shell station, which sold cigars, was five blocks away. He normally hated walking, so he called Tiffany to ask for a ride. She was asleep and didn't answer. Other friends were busy on this Friday night, Tonka's car needed transmission work, and his mother was at a bar called Richard's, sipping from a glass of Crown Apple.

So Tonka, tipping over another domino, stepped into his slippers and opened his front door. The air was warm but not unpleasant, and a breeze drifted across the river and cooled the air. He set off, down the walkway before making a right onto Lauradale Drive. Then he pushed in his earbuds and FaceTimed La'Keilla Veal, a young woman Tonka knew from college. They talked once or twice a day, sometimes about life or nothing at all. He usually didn't say much about Tyriell, his longtime girlfriend.

Tonka had spent the previous seven weeks trying to bridge a gap in his life. This is not uncommon among recent graduates, especially those who are the first in their families and social circles to attend college. You have the people and experiences that made you, and they're not always compatible with the moments they made possible.

In Tonka's case, he had his world in New Orleans and a very different and expanded one at Alcorn State.

Six years earlier, Karr had lost the 2010 state championship on the cruelest of fourth-quarter scenarios: Tonka fumbled to effectively end the game. He was inconsolable, but college scouts who had come to the Superdome noticed the undersized quarterback's gritty performance. Tonka would later sign a scholarship agreement to play wide receiver at Alcorn, in Mississippi about three hours from New Orleans.

Rhonda cried the day she drove him to college, cried the whole way back, cried when she sat alone at home. They had vowed after Katrina that they'd never leave each other's side. Now they were breaking their promise. Rhonda knew it was the right thing to do, reminding herself that her chubby little boy was now a lean and muscular man whose education would be free. She would attend Alcorn games, home and away, and when she couldn't get out of work, she'd sneak into the break room and cheer. She overnighted him red beans and turkey necks and sent him a bicycle so he wouldn't have to walk to class. Tonka's friends made fun of him for being a mama's boy, and they learned they could joke about a lot of things, but never about Ms. Rhonda.

Regarding Tonka and his mama, "He doesn't play," said Brandon Vessell, another wide receiver and Tonka's former roommate.

As much as he shared with his mother, there were things he kept to himself. She didn't know he sold the Tootsie Roll Frooties she sent him, or that he'd developed a taste for CÎROC vodka. Tonka told almost nobody when he heard troubling whispers from back home: old friends who increasingly spent their weekends fighting neighborhood rivals. The incidents kept occurring, the beef kept escalating, and eventually one of Tonka's friends got shot. Retaliation is just the law of the streets in New Orleans, and Tonka tried to play peacemaker. But he preferred to stay out of it, keeping his thoughts to himself and his secrets locked in his iPhone. Because he also spent time with multiple ladies, both at school and back home, he changed his passcode often.

When Tonka graduated, he thought about moving to Texas, as an uncle suggested, and starting a new life near relatives who'd been there since Katrina. But Tonka wouldn't leave his mama.

He dreamed of trying out for the Saints, but more realistic was a career in graphic design. He'd get a job and moonlight as a football coach at Karr, teaching what he'd learned and sharing his road map out of New Orleans. Tonka had followed the blueprint precisely: play in the Superdome, earn a scholarship, use football to get an education.

On that warm Friday in June, Tonka talked to La'Keilla as he crossed General De Gaulle Drive, a busy thoroughfare in Algiers. He walked into the Shell station's well-lighted parking lot and passed by the gas pumps, where—another domino—a red Honda Accord had parked. Tonka opened the door, ringing the bell inside, and bought a cigar and lighter before leaving. He went back the way he came. La'Keilla, at home in Mississippi with her family during Alcorn's summer break, kept talking to him on her laptop. She was doing other things, though, and the chatter was mostly mindless.

Tonka walked out of the light and again crossed De Gaulle. He dodged the cars as he made his way toward Shirley Drive. The red, two-door coupe eased out of the parking lot and followed him. It drove slowly as it approached Tonka from behind and then sped up after passing him. The Honda made a U-turn a block down, and the driver parked and turned off the headlights. The passenger door opened as Tonka made a left on Vespasian Boulevard.

In Tonka's pocket, alongside his purchases from the Shell station, was the fully loaded pistol he ostensibly carried for protection. It had never been fired. And it never left his pocket—not when the Honda's passenger walked toward him, not when the stranger lifted his gun toward Tonka, not when the dark street briefly lit up amid several loud pops.

The man turned and ran back toward the car, which sped away moments later. La'Keilla heard the gunshots and clicked on the FaceTime window. Because Tonka's iPhone had fallen to the pavement, all she saw was darkness. All she heard was gasping.

"Tonka!" she shouted. "TONKA!"

An elderly woman who lived on Vespasian heard the commotion and made her way outside. She saw the young man lying near a sewer drain and bleeding from his head and torso.

"Hold on, baby," she told him as she hurried inside to dial 911, the first of many calls that night regarding the status of Tonka George.

La'Keilla ran into her parents' bedroom with her laptop still open. She tried, hysterically, to explain what happened, and La'Keilla's father tried to calm her. He took her computer and closed it, which disconnected the FaceTime call.

And as the moments passed and silence resettled over a peaceful boulevard 140 miles away, Tonka's phone glowed as it lay faceup, fading a few seconds and then going dark.

AN HOUR BEFORE KICKOFF, Leonte and Rhonda are standing on opposite sides of a chain-link fence. They have very little in common, are separated in age by more than three decades, possess vast differences in life experience. Yet here they are, less than ten feet apart at Behrman Stadium, tragedy and tribute bending their paths. Now, those paths have merged.

The woman in her midfifties, wearing a T-shirt printed with a photo collage of her son, looks silently toward the field through rimmed glasses and flooded eyes. The eighteen-year-old man, in a helmet and pads, nods exaggeratedly as players leave the locker room and cluster near a gate.

"Number 5! Number 5!" five-year-old Carlie Williams calls toward her new favorite player.

"His name is Leonte," Tiffany George, Carlie's mother and Tonka's sister, tells her.

"Leonte!"

He looks toward Carlie and issues a quick wave. His focus returns to the scoreboard and its countdown to kickoff. When the gate opens, Leonte will take his place on a forty-yard line and lead stretches alongside four cocaptains, who are gathered closest to the gate and will take the field first.

"Let me out!" Jamie yells.

"I gotta go!" Fat calls.

"Stop holding me back!" Leonte shouts.

Two assistant coaches, Thompson and Ellis, scream for players to stay back. The young men appear ravenous and uncontrollable, and coaches shove them and yank on their jerseys in a futile attempt at restoring order. Players push back and keep screaming, desperate to be released. It's all part of the show, an elaborate intimidation ritual aimed at John Curtis.

"I gotta get out!" Leonte says again, and at last coaches swing open the gate and players pour through the opening. Herrero stands on a bleacher and conducts the marching band's performance of the Karr fight song.

When players reach their previously assigned warm-up stations, captains turn and face them. Most everything about this massive stage production is meticulously choreographed long in advance of opening night. The team's animated senior running back, standing to Joe's left near the center of the field, steps forward to call the assembly to order in a most Leonte way.

"Turn this bitch out!" he screams, punctuating each word. "The moment here! Ain't no more waiting!"

The clock ticks down, the sun is on the horizon, and back near the gate Rhonda is surrounded by relatives. She's holding an oversized frame that contains more photos of Tonka, and in them he is forever alive and smiling.

She watches as players run routes and catch passes, and four minutes before kickoff, they gather in the north end zone. Most hop with excitement, though Joe is among those who stand solemnly. Herrero signals his tubas, trombones, and baritones to start "The Rock." Band members issue a concert F and then a D, and several players drop to all fours—action-starved cougars at last unchained—and crawl toward midfield. Nick Foster and assistant coach Shak Smith grab them by the collar and direct them back toward the group. The drums enter, filling the background, and the horns go silent. The drums continue, faster now, and football players use this as a cue to form a tight cluster and lock arms. Trumpets sound three rapid-fire notes, announcing the arrival of the West Bank's kings, and players sway slowly, menacingly, to their right. Then their left. Fireworks take flight behind the field goalposts, and players charge forward before reaching the Karr sideline.

The music stops, and Rhonda walks slowly toward midfield. She can smell the sulfur of spent fireworks, hear the hush that has fallen over the crowd, feel the weight of the frame and the moment. Sometimes she addresses the crowd on "Long Live 5 Night," though more often she's too emotional and allows the public address announcer to relay her previously written thoughts.

On this evening, she walks onto the field and is surrounded by family. Karr players lift their hands and extend all five fingers. Then this year's 5 walks forward to join Rhonda, who presents Leonte with the frame before speaking into his ear.

"Stay focused; play the game," she tells him. It's the same motherly advice she gave Tonka nearly a decade earlier. "Let God do the rest."

Leonte's eyes give way to tears, which stream past his helmet visor. He drapes one arm onto the shoulders of Tonka's mother, the other onto his own mom's shoulders. The group then releases purple and yellow balloons.

Rhonda and Leonte stand together and look up. They watch the balloons as long as they can, because like a memory the balloons are floating away, growing faint and small as they drift into a darkening summer sky.

IN THE AFTERMATH of Tonka's death, Rhonda felt unmoored. Despair turned to acceptance turned to a desperate hope that justice would prevail. She cried. She prayed. For the first time, God wasn't listening. Perhaps the only thing that buoyed her was that the New Orleans Police Department assigned Detective Rayell Johnson to investigate Tonka's murder.

Johnson was young and Black, energetic and reassuring. After appearing on several episodes of the true crime television show *The First 48*, he was also mildly famous.

"I *know* he's gonna solve this," Rhonda's sister-in-law announced when Johnson arrived a few hours after Tonka's murder. "Mr. First 48!"

But Johnson would let her down, too. Weeks passed. Then months. The air turned warm and thick, and one evening in September she drove to a place she hadn't visited in a long time. Rhonda parked near Behrman Memorial Park, walked toward a small booth, and bought a ticket to a Karr football game. She sat in the bleachers and watched as the young men in purple and gold sprinted and blocked, making their tackles and catches. The quarters passed, and eventually Rhonda realized she felt something she hadn't in months: relief. Maybe even joy.

She kept returning, week after week, home and away. Football was her therapy, the only thing that gave her peace. Especially after Brown began handing out number 5 as a legacy jersey, Rhonda could watch the young man wearing it and pretend it was 2010 again.

On this evening in 2019, the pregame ceremony concludes and Rhonda makes her way back toward the gate. She passes New Orleans Saints players Alvin Kamara and Teddy Bridgewater on the sideline, here for the biggest football game in the state, before recognizing an old friend from Algiers. Rhonda and Shaun Ferguson know each other from the Krewe of NOMTOC, a social club on the West Bank that spends most of the year preparing for Mardi Gras. Ferguson is also New Orleans's superintendent of police, meaning he's the NOPD's top cop and Johnson's boss's boss. Rhonda asks where Tonka's case stands. It's been three years, she reminds him. Ferguson forces a smile, gives her a hug, and asks Rhonda to call him tomorrow.

She harrumphs and heads toward her seat. It's blisteringly hot here, and without a breeze the Spanish moss on the park's ancient oak trees is still. It feels like 103 degrees, and the warm air carries the scent of hot dogs and fried catfish, and locals press cold drinks and smuggled-in beer cans to their necks. Herrero's marching band avoids the traditional standbys; instead, it plays brassy versions of "The Thong Song" and "I Got 5 On It."

Rhonda walks through a gate, climbs a small staircase, and takes her place inside a small cluster of family. They watch as John Curtis returns the opening kickoff eighty-three yards to Karr's eight-yard line. Rhonda grimaces when the Patriots' quarterback, Collin Guggenheim, runs straight into the defense and past Joe for the game's first touchdown—a disastrous start for Karr, whose coaches are livid.

The Cougars' offense, Brown's specialty, takes the field. The first series of the season can sometimes act as a good barometer for a team's fortune for the coming season. Leonard approaches the line of scrimmage and analyzes the defense's alignment. He sees one safety in the deep center of the field and the two outside cornerbacks lined up ten yards from receivers. John Curtis is showing Cover 3, and Brown has taught Leonard, as he once did Tonka, that this coverage has many vulnerabilities. One is that, because of the space between the corners, it is susceptible to quick, short passes.

Leonard changes the play from a run to a pass, and after the snap he drops back and zips a short throw toward wide receiver Darrell Hills. His assignment is a curl route, a short pass that exploits the free space between the receiver and corner. Darrell catches the ball, breaks two tackles . . . then fumbles. John Curtis, clearly not intimidated by Karr or its pregame theatrics, recovers.

"I'm gonna have to go down there!" Rhonda shouts in frustration.

Eventually Karr takes over again on offense, and Leonard hands off to Leonte, who plays like he lives: full tilt. He barrels into defenders, and if he takes a hard hit, he gets up writhing in agony before shaking it off.

"He's fired up," Rhonda says when he collides with an opponent. "He's fired up now!"

She keeps watching, temporarily forgetting the pain of these last three years. Rhonda claps almost constantly, stands if there's even the appearance of a big play, shouts until she's nearly hoarse. Then number 5 zips down the field, threading his way through defenders once again.

"Come on, run, Leonte!" she shouts, jumping on the bleachers. "Run!"

CHAPTER 3

INTERSECTION

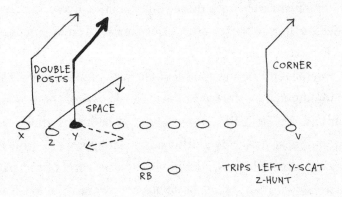

BROWN WALKS QUICKLY off the field at Pan American Stadium following the Cougars' third game. It was an imperfect but encouraging 38–12 victory against Warren Easton High. After losing to John Curtis two weeks earlier, Karr has now won two games in a row. Leonard conducts an interview with a local newspaper reporter, and Brown eavesdrops.

"We knew it wasn't over after one quarter," the quarterback is saying of Karr's ability to overcome an early 12–0 deficit. "Because we play all four quarters."

Brown rolls his eyes and continues walking toward the gate where his truck is parked.

"Podium talk," he'll say. He doesn't care for the hyper-rehearsed, inauthentic way Leonard sometimes speaks. And not just to the media. He occasionally talks like this to coaches, and Brown worries it's a sign

Leonard cares less about the product he delivers than the *appearance* of the product. Nothing shortens Brown's fuse more than a lack of genuineness—especially from his most important player.

Leonard and Brown are exceptionally close, having spent hours together most every day since Leonard became Karr's starting quarterback in 2018. Weekday mornings are for studying opposing defenses and recognizing tendencies, patterns, and soft spots. Afternoons are for installing plays that attack those vulnerabilities. Every Sunday during the season, they're at each other's side almost all day—brainstorming, drawing plays, dreaming.

Leonard is athletic and good-looking, with caramel skin and a square face highlighted by thick eyebrows. He also knows how to weaponize his charm. He looks into your eyes as he listens, those eyebrows clustering near the bridge of his nose, and appears to achingly care about the same things you do. It's just another form of *podium talk*, of course. Leonard can say, do, be whatever you need him to be, and that malleability is what drives Brown berserk.

But Leonard is also perhaps the smartest quarterback Brown has ever coached. He retains information and adjusts to the game's split-second developments in a way that confounds and devastates defenses. Teammates and Karr fans compare Leonard to Russell Wilson, the Seattle Seahawks' undersized but brilliant quarterback. He idolizes Wilson and studies his game, and he brags about meeting Ciara, the R&B singer and Wilson's wife, when she visited Karr to speak to students as part of a workshop. She even posed for photographs wearing a Karr football "3-peat" shirt in front of the school's massive trophy case.

"Take risks and be bold," she told the kids. Leonard was almost giddy.

Boldness and risk-taking have never been a problem for him. In fact Brown sometimes worries about how often Leonard's poor judgment undermines his charisma and smarts. Usually it's restricted to off-the-field clownery, though not always. It's enough of a concern that Brown believes it could jeopardize more than just the team's immediate future.

Considering who Leonard usually hangs out with, it could actually put his safety at risk.

Brown passes through the gate and reaches his truck before climbing into the passenger seat. He doesn't drive himself to or from games, leaving that to a trusted aide. He uses the rides to defragment the tightly packed hard drive of his mind, and having a chauffeur also makes him feel a little like Nick Saban, the legendary coach at the University of Alabama. Brown sits shotgun, and Pat Johnson, Karr's school resource officer, takes the wheel. Marvin Rose, a volunteer assistant who's more taskmaster and comic relief than coach, sits in the back seat and provides running commentary on whatever passes through his mind. Tonight it's the fact that a tray of leftover pulled pork, which Officer Pat intends on taking home, looks like dog food. Though nobody asked him, Marv loudly announces he wouldn't eat that crap if he were starving.

Brown, trying to tune out Marv, closes his eyes and massages the bridge of his nose. After another long week, he just wants to turn his brain off. But his phone keeps ringing with some crisis of varying severity on the other end. He can't just ignore it.

An assistant coach calls to tell Brown that a player's mother is waiting at the school, because she believes a different assistant punched her son in the stomach. Another call alerts him that not only is starting center Joe Hayes being loaded into an ambulance with a severe ankle injury, Karr's new medical trainer has been unable to locate the lineman's mother. Another call from Leonte, who rushed for two touchdowns tonight, admitting he's severely dehydrated after again refusing to drink enough water. Muscles are cramping throughout his body, and the trainer briefly takes the phone to warn that without an IV, Leonte could go into cardiac arrest.

"They're trying to send me to the hospital," Leonte says.

"Well, go!" Brown tells him.

The coach ends the call and sighs.

"Maybe if he hadn't done all that *performing*," he says of Leonte's behavior, "this shit wouldn't be happening."

Officer Pat makes a left into the school's rear entrance, eases the truck over the curb, and crosses the practice field. Marv is still imploring Pat to throw away the rotgut leftovers. Brown's phone rings again, and when he sees the name on his display, he chuckles. It's Leonard's father, calling like he always does, wanting to relive and analyze his son's heroics.

Brown takes a breath and answers, and Leonard Kelly II jumps right in: Man, that thirteen-yard scoring run in the third quarter. And how about that twenty-seven-yard throw, right on the money to Fat, for another touchdown?

The coach mostly listens, though there is something Brown needs to discuss with Leonard's daddy. Four months ago, Leonard II bought his son a car. Though it's a traditional rite of passage between a father and son, Leonard II and Brown agreed to wait until the time was right to actually give it to him. Then Leonard lied to Pride Panel, got himself demoted and silenced, was passed over as a captain. Since April, with the novelty worn off, Brown has been holding on to the key to a 2006 Acura TL. Tonight it's in his hip pocket. He and Leonard's daddy decided that if Karr beat McDonogh 35 and Warren Easton, a sign he'd bounced back and was finally growing up, Brown would present Leonard with the key in front of his teammates.

Brown, though, has a bad feeling. Leonard and Joe Thomas have known each other since middle school, and despite stark differences in how and where they grew up, they're best friends. Leonard's family lives in a quiet suburb in New Orleans East, on the other side of the Mississippi River and a world away from most of his Karr teammates. His parents are married, and the family takes regular vacations and, because Leonard II leads something of a double life, occasionally travels to professional sporting events. Leonard's dad doesn't just push and protect his elder son; he insulates him from any and all discomfort.

Joe is deeply fascinated by Leonard's home life, and Leonard by Joe's. They spend weekends together, text constantly, cruise the city for reasons Leonard's daddy doesn't know about and may not understand. After all, nobody receives more *podium talk* than the quarterback's earnest but naïve father.

Brown knows a few of these secrets. He wants to tell Leonard II that some of Karr's players are flying high after tonight's win. Some, including his quarterback, might be feeling a little too good about themselves. So, well, how should he put this? Brown wants to protect Leonard and Joe but not violate their trust.

"You gonna pick him up?" Brown asks Leonard II, but he and his wife are heading to a party.

The coach pauses. His quarterback's father isn't getting it. So he chooses his next words carefully: Joe has been spending time in the Fischer Development Neighborhood, a community with treacherous pockets a dozen years after its notorious housing projects were torn down. Sometimes he crosses the river and socializes in the Seventh Ward, where he used to live. Assuming he and Leonard will be together, adding a new car for Leonard to hormones and feelings of invincibility could form a deadly equation.

"So I . . . you know," Brown continues, "you've just gotta watch it."

Leonard II finally untangles what Brown is trying to tell him.

"No, no," he says. "He's gonna come home tonight. Tell him to come home tonight. Fuck that."

They keep talking, and though the quarterback has waited months to get his car, they decide he'll have to wait a little longer.

"If them two together," Brown says, "you've got two fucking bottle rockets with no fucking stick on it."

"B, let that n—— know go home, you heard me?" Leonard II says, alarm now in his voice. "Tell him go to his fucking house."

Brown ends the call and climbs out of his truck, lumbering up a ramp and into the Karr football office. Players begin filing in, draping their jerseys on a laundry bin and arranging their shoulder pads on a rack. Brown stands near a back extension platform and watches as Joe and Jamie walk into the weight room businesslike, Fat not so much. He's wearing only a jock strap, dancing toward the locker room.

"You have *got* to start wearing pants," Brown tells him. The young receiver smiles and disappears through a doorway. "You got a ass like a ho, too."

A moment later Leonard walks in, drops his number 3 jersey—a nod to his full name, Leonard Kelly III, and to Russell Wilson—into a bin, and Brown steps in his path.

"Your daddy said don't go by Joe's. He wants you to get dressed and go straight home," he says, and the eighteen-year-old quarterback's shoulders drop.

Brown says nothing more. He walks away before Leonard can respond, starting toward his office. He changes out of his sweat-drenched khaki pants and plops into a rolling chair. Then he opens the top drawer of his desk, reaches into his pocket, and drops in the Acura key before pushing the drawer closed.

A DECADE AGO ON THE Fourth of July, Stank woke up and saw his mama holding a gun. She asked if he'd ever shot one of these. The boy said he hadn't. She shook her head, saying, *Get up, boy, you're nine years old. It's time.*

They walked to the front door of their apartment, and she stood behind Stank. She handed him the pistol and wrapped her arms gently around his. Her body a support beam, she leaned into him and guided his arms upward, to a roughly forty-five-degree angle above the horizon. She told him to squeeze the trigger, and he did, popping off five rounds into the early-morning sky. Stank was a natural, and his mama was proud.

Keyoke Thomas rarely called her son Joe back then, and carefully teaching him to fire a gun was her way of showing affection. This, to her, was an important milestone for her growing son. She loved her only child more than anything, and like all parents of young children, she wanted him to be protected and strong. So to condition him, she'd sometimes drive him to an unfamiliar neighborhood, Slidell or the East, and demand he get out. She'd instruct him to find his way home. Then she'd drive away.

Other times they'd be driving around, and Keyoke would ask Stank about some landmark they'd passed. If he confessed to not paying attention, she'd punch him and issue a reminder: if you recognize where you are, you can never be lost.

One day Stank came home from a playground with a bloody nose. He was eight or nine. Keyoke asked what happened, and he said another boy beat him up. She asked if he'd fought back, catching a beatdown but giving the other boy everything he had. He shook his head, and Keyoke exploded.

"This is what them n——s gonna do!" she told him, proceeding to whoop her little son's ass until he started defending himself.

It took a long time, and many beatings, before this made sense to him.

"At the time she was doing it, I was like, 'My mom really don't like me. She gonna kill me,'" Joe would say much later. "I understand now."

This might be an unusual parenting style, but New Orleans—in particular the corners Joe grew up knowing—can be heartless and dark. It feels no compassion and usually offers no warning. Keyoke promised herself that her boy would grow up neither unprepared, nor unaware, nor soft. If he couldn't negotiate a city that shows its teeth, she decided, she'd have failed him.

Back then, mother and son behaved as if they existed in a two-person society. Keyoke had been selling drugs since her teens, and betrayals, reprisals, and even murders had just become part of her routine. Partners, friends, relatives—everyone could, and usually did, let you down. In middle school, Keyoke had goals, though she had no idea how to achieve them. Teachers grew impatient and frustrated, and in time they all threw their hands up. Keyoke's mother disowned her when she was sixteen; foster parents tried to love and reassure and tame her, but eventually they gave up, too. So in a universe of liars and cheats, Keyoke and Joe could be honest with each other. In a world of predators, they could trust each other. In a city this brutal, she alone could teach him to survive—teaching adaptation and awareness by conditioning him to feel comfortable amid brutality. Nothing else, and nobody else, mattered.

Joe was eight when he was playing basketball with an older cousin. Some other boys approached, one of them put a gun to the cousin's head, and squeezed the trigger. Joe watched a pool of blood spill from his dead cousin's skull and spread across the blacktop. When he later sought consolation from Keyoke, he instead received a cold explanation. The cousin had played dice for money, and after winning a dollar, he'd pocketed the dollar and walked away. This, according to the streets' gospel, is poor gambling etiquette. The cousin had fucked up, Keyoke explained, and this is what happens in New Orleans when you fuck up.

Keyoke taught him how to dribble a basketball, the sport she'd played before getting kicked out of Booker T. Washington High, and how to make five dollars last three days. She trained him on how to "finesse," which is what she called sweet-talking the cops and girls, and when Joe told her he didn't plan to kiss a girl until college, Keyoke told him this was no place for a passive little bitch.

"Booooy, once you start feeling that pussy . . ." she told him, and though Keyoke identifies as gay, on occasion she'd find herself in bed with a man.

Two of those times were in late 2001. A few weeks after both encounters, Keyoke learned she was pregnant. She would never be certain who Joe's father is, and the two most likely candidates were gone. A man named Joe, for whom Keyoke would name her son, would be shot dead while he talked on the phone with Keyoke. The other, Darrel Jones, is still serving time after being convicted of manslaughter not long after Joe was born. Like most everyone else, Keyoke would tell Joe, these men had failed them and couldn't be counted on.

There was only one thing, in fact, that had never failed Keyoke: money. A full pocket made her feel special, powerful, independent. She'd felt almost addicted to money's comfort and the rush of pursuing it. She came of age working various blocks on the East Bank, though in 2005 Katrina forced Keyoke and Joe to Houston. She joined a gang there, the 52 Hoover Crips, and she'd teach Joe to never trust anyone wearing orange, the traditional color of a Hoover Crips rival. They returned to New Orleans when Joe was about ten, and they sometimes spent the night in abandoned houses. Keyoke found this unacceptable and often found herself slinging pills and weed on the Gert Town corner of Olive and Fern Streets.

She parlayed her earnings not just into a steady home, big televisions, and game systems. Keyoke and Joe went shopping every Thursday, and she'd spend $500 on herself and $500 on her son. He walked the neighborhood, and occasionally went to school, wearing jewelry and expensive sneakers. Once she dressed him like a little pimp and sneaked him into a nightclub.

Their apartment wasn't far from Olive and Fern, and though it was small, Keyoke was proud of it. She bought a leather sofa and an entertainment system, and she and Joe spent each Saturday sweeping the floors and emptying the trash. Sundays were for washing clothes. Sometimes they'd come home and find the door slightly ajar, discovering the apartment had been emptied. Joe will say every home he has ever lived in was robbed.

So she'd return to the block and get to work on replacing their things. She beefed up, making herself more intimidating at more than two hundred pounds, and by the time Joe was a teenager, he saw himself as Keyoke's protector. As her lookout, he'd stand watch a few dozen yards away while she worked, looking for cops and rivals, usually palming a little Glock. He'll say much later that he never shot anyone, though if he'd witnessed someone getting crosswise with his mama, he would've.

Often around three in the morning, he'd sheepishly approach Keyoke and beg her to come home. Sometimes she said no, a money addict out here chasing a fix, and on occasion the police would show up and put her in handcuffs. Keyoke would go away for a while. In 2004 it was for marijuana charges; in 2007 for possession and trespassing; in 2009 after getting caught with ecstasy and painkillers; and 2013 on more drug charges.

But she always came home, though Keyoke was clear-eyed about the realities of her profession, and its inevitabilities. Someday, she told him, she'd be gone and he'd be on his own. Joe needed to be a man now; that's why she had taught him all this.

Keyoke would sometimes smile at Joe and ask if he wanted to smoke weed with his mama. He was old enough now, she'd point out, so why not? If Joe said yes, Keyoke—short but broad-shouldered—would deliver another beating.

Sometimes, in fact, she slipped neighborhood boys a few dollars to pick fights with her son. Keyoke would watch from afar to see if he held his own. She signed him up for park football, an attempt at further toughening him up, and at home she'd fire a football at Joe's head or challenge him to tackle her.

She eventually taught him to avoid walking anywhere. If that was impossible, he should never go back the same route he came. He was to zigzag back home, in case robbers or killers were tracking him. If you're inside, she instructed, never let anyone—no matter who it is— call you outside. She trained him how to react when you hear gunfire: don't start running, because in a panic you might accidentally run *toward* the shooter. Instead, lie on the ground, assess your surroundings, and crawl toward a secure hiding place.

"Beaucoup tests," Joe would say later. If he failed one of them, his mother's response was at least consistent. "I caught whoopings a lot."

In 2016, not long before Keyoke was arrested and convicted of theft and domestic abuse, she signed Joe up for a citywide admissions lottery to attend one of the schools run by InspireNOLA. Applicants rank their preferred schools, and Keyoke ranked Karr—an aging but prestigious school across the river from where they lived—as her top choice. Roughly 10 percent of the twenty-five hundred applicants to Karr are admitted, according to the school's principal. One day someone reached out to say Joe had been accepted. He celebrated by partying on Canal Street and getting hit by a car, and on the day of orientation, Keyoke drove him to the West Bank. She didn't know or trust anyone there, so she cursed out anyone who asked why Joe's face was all busted up. "He's blessed, ma'am," one teacher would say Keyoke dismissively snapped whenever anyone asked her son if he was okay.

Karr's faculty was introduced to this peculiar family at Joe's baptism, when Keyoke screamed profanities at him for not sitting up straight. Football coaches received their initiations during an evening meet-and-greet for parents and staff, during which Keyoke loudly expressed her dissatisfaction with the event's timing. Usually she was on the block and earning money by this time of day.

"Y'all got me meeting about shit I fucking *know!*" Brown would recall Keyoke shouting, drawing stares and raised eyebrows before she stormed out.

Joe was something of a wild stallion himself. He struggled to make eye contact with teachers and coaches and often slept through classes. He ran through the halls screaming, a mop of long twists spraying from his head. He posed for pictures in which he flashed gang signs or held wads of cash. If someone asked him to pay attention or tried to discipline him, he might casually stand and leave the room. He beat up kids who made fun of his lisp or called him stupid or said his mother was a gangster. He skipped school or showed up late, and when he was there he was antisocial and short-tempered.

"Get the fuck out of my face," one former teacher recalled him saying when he asked Joe to hand over his cell phone.

He seemed to enjoy football practice, especially the part that involved knocking the piss out of the player across from you. Joe was a young man with obvious trust issues that made him suspicious, defiant, and even violent. For the first while, coaches allowed him to be as savage as he wanted to be. He at least showed up, though usually not on anyone else's schedule. Over time coaches began noticing marginal changes. He stopped shouting and cursing when anyone tried to correct him or provide advice. He attended school, at least most of the time, because that's a prerequisite to playing football. If coaches threatened to kick Joe off the team, he'd behave . . . better.

He was often exhausted, and coaches learned why: he had frequently been awake, trying to coax his mother back inside, until three or four in the morning. One day Norm Randall pulled a bleary-eyed Joe aside and asked a question: How long can you keep this up? Norm challenged him, as he has done other players, to choose a side: football or the streets. It's unsustainable, and dangerous, to try both.

Joe made his choice, and one afternoon in April 2019, he finished a spring practice and tried calling Keyoke. She didn't answer. He assumed she was on the block and would call him back. He tried her again hours later, before he went to sleep. Nothing.

The next morning he woke and saw a missed call from an 866 area code. By then he'd learned this came from the Orleans Parish Sheriff's Office, and Joe set off for school wondering what criminal charges had befallen his mother this time. They were, in fact, considerable: possession with the intent to distribute cocaine and crack, and a separate charge for obstruction of justice. She had violated her probation and also faced a bench warrant from the 2016 arrests. There were two additional "municipal attachments," or what New Orleans calls leftover court appearances or granular responsibilities from past cases. These keep many residents, the overwhelming majority of whom are Black, entangled within the justice system for years. Keyoke would be sentenced to three years of "hard labor" in a Louisiana state prison.

Eventually Joe's phone rang, and he saw the 866 area code. He answered and heard his mama's voice.

"Stank," Keyoke said. "They finally got me."

EVEN ON SUNDAY MORNINGS in autumn, the French Quarter has a soundtrack. It's subtler than when the sun is down, but there's a certain symphonic cadence. Power washers blast the remains of Saturday night from sidewalks, and card sharks and poets make their pitches in Jackson Square. Sketch artists speak over the faint sound of a distant trumpet.

But things aren't always as they appear, and that's part of the allure. The horses that pull carriages down Decatur Street are actually mules, and fast-talking riverfront shoe shiners are constantly looking to game unsuspecting tourists. On this Sunday, a man approaches a visitor on a staircase and bets him a $20 shine that he can guess where he got his shoes. Sure, the out-of-towner agrees, and the local points to the visitor's feet.

"I said where you *got* 'em, not where you *bought* 'em," the silver-tongued huckster says, pulling a cloth from his back pocket.

To survive here means to establish, and perfect, your own hustle. This is true for the chefs and mixologists, the stripper who swipes your cigarettes while you're at the cash machine, and the kid with the French horn and the sob story. The only way to avoid getting taken is to speak the language, learn the angles, know how to move. Speaking of which, up the way is a proud hustler working his corner, Poydras and Lasalle Streets, same as he does most Sundays this time of year.

"Welcome to my world," Leonard Kelly II says outside the Super-dome, and out here he's neither a charter school administrator nor the father of four children. He is, simply, the "Ticket Man."

Today the New Orleans Saints will host the Carolina Panthers, and Leonard II has tickets for the best seats. He's constantly on the move.

"Tickets, tickets," he says, walking from one corner to the next, fanning his inventory and raising it into the air.

Three decades ago, the soundtrack of Leonard II's Sunday morning may very well have included gunshots. He grew up in the Magnolia Projects in Central City, and he was eleven the first time he watched a man die. Everyone here, it seems, remembers witnessing their first murder, yet another rite of passage that's as gruesome as it is inevitable. He remembers the blood, of course, but Leonard II also recalls how everyone else just went about their day.

He vowed to pursue a different kind of life, deciding his future children would never walk these streets and feel that mix of fear, disgust, and powerlessness as someone close to you bleeds out. He had no idea how to achieve such a thing, and neither did his parents. But Leonard II decided to just be the best he could at whatever he did.

He studied, earned good grades, got accepted into Grambling State University—the first member of his family to attend college. But then he got his girlfriend, Demetrice, pregnant. They were both seventeen. It was over.

Except it wasn't, because Leonard II was determined not just to leave the Magnolia Projects behind but to be the daddy he'd never had. Leonard II barely knew his own father growing up, though later in life they'd reconnect. He spent weekdays at Grambling before driving the three hundred miles southeast to New Orleans every weekend to see Demetrice and their baby daughter. He graduated, Leonard II and Demetrice married, and a few years later their first son, Leonard III, was born. Another daughter and son would follow.

Their lives felt new, but to Leonard II, they remained incomplete. He worked in administration at a school on the East Bank, and it paid okay. But life is too short for just okay, so one Sunday morning he walked down Claiborne Avenue to the Superdome. Leonard II bought some cheap tickets, sold them for a profit, and felt a rush he wanted to repeat. He kept returning, earlier and earlier each Sunday, tinkering with his sales pitch and negotiating skills. He studied the fundamentals of economics, supply and demand, and used social media to learn the nuances of internet ticket brokerage. He produced a commercial and started a spreadsheet on his laptop of big-money games: Louisiana State vs. Alabama, for instance. Cashing in meant investing his earnings in lower-tier events to eventually buy dozens of tickets to those major games.

Eventually he'd save enough to buy Demetrice an Infiniti sedan and the family a house near the banks of Lake Pontchartrain. Though it contained big televisions and fine furniture, nobody broke in. Leonard III never witnessed a murder, and he played baseball on a mostly white team and football at a private middle school. The Kellys spent some weekends at the Superdome, where Leonard II always kept the best seats for his family. Occasionally he'd surprise his children with not just tickets to a game but airfare and hotel accommodations when the Saints played in California. If they stayed home, the pop of gunfire never interrupted the evenings, which is when Leonard III is off doing whatever eighteen-year-old boys traditionally do. His mother and father, meanwhile, sit at their square table and sip chardonnay.

"I earned it," Leonard II says one evening, motioning toward his kingdom. "*We* earned it. Together."

"We tried to shield them," Demetrice says of their kids.

"From the struggle," Leonard II says.

Occasionally Leonard III joined his father on Sunday mornings at the Superdome, though the young man never liked it much. The mornings were too early, and though Leonard II let his son keep whatever he earned selling tickets, to young Leonard it felt like too much work. It's indeed lucrative but exhausting, and ticket brokers are constantly on the move, haggling with strangers and evading the cops. Leonard II motions toward a worn-down old man in a neutral ground in the middle of Poydras. He's been out on these streets, running this same hustle, for decades.

Leonard II, who at thirty-nine is bearded and squat, figures that he'll someday be that old man waving tickets and standing in the cold. He's okay with that, as long as his children never have to do this. He wants them to be better, to sleep in on Sundays, to never have to work this hard to make a few bucks. He wants his son to *play* in stadiums like this, not sell tickets outside them.

"It ain't their business to know this," Leonard II says.

It is around this time that he notices a fan in a Drew Brees jersey negotiating with two ticket brokers. He jogs over, physically getting between the fan and the sellers, and hijacks the deal. The fan continues toward the Superdome, but Leonard II follows him. He keeps talking, refusing to let the fan walk away. Eventually the exasperated man stops. Worn down, he agrees to Leonard II's price: $400 for two tickets, which he bought a few minutes earlier for $50 each.

The fan removes his billfold and hands the cash to the Ticket Man, who smiles and tells the fan to enjoy the experience. Then he takes a breath, feeling the rush once more, before again noticing the old man in the neutral ground. He's arguing with a rookie police officer about something, and Leonard II's smile fades. He figures he should walk over and see what's going on.

The old man, after all, is his father. His name is Leonard I.

In the days and weeks after Keyoke disappeared into her prison sentence, Joe drifted between his old life and his new one. Though he was seventeen and a rising high school senior, with an expanded support system and worldview, his mama had always been his rock.

Now she was gone.

At first he drew closer to the world they'd known together. He picked fights, befriended gang members, skipped school. He tried to stay awake most nights, though when he inevitably fell asleep on the sofa in their apartment now at Cypress Park, he did so with a gun in his hand. Keyoke was seventy miles away in a women's prison south of Baton Rouge, but Joe kept looking for ways to feel close. He got a tattoo with KEYOKE in swirling letters down the length of his upper arm, and on Saturdays he cleaned the bathroom and scrubbed dog piss from the tile floors. There was comfort in their weekend routine.

He tried cooking, his mother's favorite hobby and most impressive skill, but he was no good at it. He boiled cabbage until it was a sad gray slop, and another day he stirred frozen corn niblets into white rice.

Hungry and defeated, Joe decided deliverance was a mere five blocks away. So each night he opened his front door and started toward McDonald's. He threaded through the men clustered in the complex's U-shaped parking lot, past the drug dealer on the corner, beginning a nightly walk by crossing Vespasian Boulevard. That's the same street that, three years earlier, Tonka was gunned down on while making a similar trek.

But Joe had to eat, and after securing his meal, he obeyed lessons that Tonka never had—results of a childhood spent in Keyoke's security awareness training. Joe zigzagged home, never retracing his steps, and never stopped minding his surroundings. He'd pass through shadowy backyards or take the long way home, and if he suspected someone was watching or following him, he'd adjust his movements accordingly. Sometimes he hid in an empty house or jolted down an alley, waiting in the darkness, pistol palmed, until the perceived threat was gone.

Eventually he'd make it home. He bolted the steel door behind him, and at last he opened the brown bag and dined.

As elaborate as this routine may seem, Joe will insist Cypress Park is the nicest, quietest, most peaceful place he's ever lived. Gunfire is uncommon, and break-ins are rare. If Joe Thomas were capable of relaxation, he could do so here. But his mama trained him to never let his guard down, and to ignore Keyoke's teachings would be to dishonor her.

A few months after Keyoke reported to prison, Brown invited the young man to talk, if he wanted to. At first he declined, preferring to keep his thoughts to himself. Gradually he opened up. He liked to talk about football and self-improvement and the coming season, and Brown encouraged those discussions. Weeks passed, and Joe occasionally talked about his mama, his persistent fears, the uncertainty of a future he could barely imagine. Sometimes he insisted he was used to, and in fact comfortable in, isolation and danger. Other times he cried.

Brown usually listened, a tactician surveying the field, before deciding on a plan of attack. Many of the kids who stream into the Karr football office come from trying, complicated backgrounds. Their lives, in many cases, are emblematic of Joe's walks home from McDonald's: zigzagging, unpredictable, pocked with dangers real and imagined. But, at least in Brown's analysis, the young men themselves are uncomplicated. They need, and often crave, nothing more than structure, affection, and a sense of purpose. The only question is how to deploy those concepts to each individual. Brown's listen-first approach is twofold: it builds trust and lets the kid vent, and it allows Brown to begin decoding the specific things the young man needs.

Tonka, for instance, was a little man who needed to feel big. Ronnie Jackson, a dynamic running back with a big personality and anger issues, had to be challenged during frequent shouting matches with Brown and frequently thrown off the team. It was a mental reboot that forced him to confront life without football, but also a reminder to the young alpha that Brown might be aging and slow, but he's still the biggest, baddest dog in the yard.

According to Brown, Joe, whose square shoulders, piercing eyes, and gravelly voice project toughness and invulnerability, is actually just a tenderhearted young man who needs more affection—and to feel valuable. In late spring 2019, five months before the season began, Brown told Joe that he had an idea. The coach sold it to the kid as a risk that could make or break the coming season, and maybe he was crazy for even considering it. But he was going to add Joe to Pride Panel's first chair, effectively putting him in the team's most important leadership position. Was he up for it?

Joe said he was, and Brown immediately told him to stop talking. This mantle depends not on words but actions. Joe nodded, left his coach's office, and got to work. A year earlier, when an assistant coach called roll each day before practice, it was questionable whether Joe would be there. But now, every day, he was on the rubber flooring, sitting cross-legged and announcing his presence. He didn't just lift weights; he trained with ferocity and determination that teammates noticed. Joe pulled young players aside, and becoming an extension of Brown, sometimes draped an arm across a troubled teammate's shoulder and other times cussed him the fuck out. It just depended on what the kid needed to hear.

The weeks passed, and Joe felt pulled in opposite directions. Down one path was the life he knew, and down the other was a future Joe *wanted* to know. One was familiar but dangerous; the other was mysterious but promising. Joe went to the barbershop and told the man with the clippers he was tired of looking like a drug dealer, so off came the fountain of twists in favor of a close fade. He packed on muscle, studied his defensive playbook, stopped carrying his Glock.

When Keyoke had a court appearance, Joe would take the bus to the courthouse and sit in the gallery. His mama would steal a glance at her boy, now looking more like a man. Joe looked taller now and wore a modest goatee. When he visited her at the prison, Keyoke would marvel at the changes, and on occasion two people who wanted the world to see them as emotionless and fierce would cry together, even as glass separated them and they stared at each other from opposite sides.

"Just keep ya fuckin' head up," Keyoke told him.

"Mama," Joe said, "I'm all right."

Then he'd take the long ride back to New Orleans, and the next morning he didn't sleep in. He reported for school, sneaked to the football office between classes, stayed late to quiz his position coaches, Brennan Harris and Nick Watkins, on defensive concepts. He hated going home now, avoiding Cypress Park at all costs, and some evenings he'd be among the last to leave school. Increasingly often he'd ask a teammate to let him crash, and usually that teammate was Leonard. The boys had been friends since park ball before they reunited at Karr.

The friends played video games, talked football, watched NBA games on the family's big TV. Joe slept over so often that he called Leonard II "Pops."

A short time before the season started, Joe was with his teammates and felt called to share something. He knew he'd cry, but it was something he had to do.

"I really love playing with y'all, but I'm going through some shit," he said, and sure enough here came the tears. "I know I be hard on y'all, but I really appreciate you. Y'all make me come back every day, and like last week I was just sitting at the house, just sitting around thinking: I *need* to be here with y'all."

Joe paused, attempting to swallow the lump in his throat. The young men on the floor looked up at him.

"Y'all are my motivation and why I keep coming, and the coaches, too," he said. "And I really appreciate every one of y'all, and I just want to thank y'all for everything. Y'all my real family."

BECAUSE LEONARD COULD LIFT the curtain on a world Joe had never seen, the young linebacker thought he should return the favor.

One night they drove to the Lower Ninth Ward, to a neighborhood known locally as the CTC, which is short for "Cross the Canal." By day it's a trendy arts enclave that neighbors the Industrial Canal. After sunset, its visitors would suggest CTC stands for something else: "Cut-Throat City." Closed businesses and abandoned buildings are common, and so on occasion are shots fired.

Joe thought Leonard would find the CTC educational, so they agreed to attend a summer party there. Leonard was on edge even before they arrived. Then he saw men carrying guns before a car sped by—often the preamble to a drive-by shooting. Leonard started to run, but Joe stopped his friend and assured him that as long as Joe was with him, he was safe.

"I'm with my partners," Joe told him. "You're good."

Much later, he'd still find Leonard's reaction to this scene, which Joe found wholly innocuous, highly entertaining.

"You running, and you don't even know where you going," he'd say. "I thought that was so funny."

Though Joe enjoyed basking in the comforts of Leonard's home in New Orleans East, he also came to believe Leonard's parents ultimately did him a disservice. He speaks about Leonard's upbringing with a tinge of pity, in part because of the adventure and fun the quarterback surely missed out on. But Joe also believes Leonard's lack of exposure to New Orleans's grittier pockets, and inability to navigate them, could cause him problems. Leonard is, in Joe's analysis, "green"—naïve to an almost dangerous degree. Brown believes Joe is good for Leonard, at least under the right circumstances.

Joe is visibly scarred by his youth, and even now, he perceives many situations and strangers as possible threats. He believes that makes him well-equipped; that his upbringing, merciless as it was, is just what it takes. He insists that, no matter his education or success, he'll someday raise his own children as Keyoke raised him. Leonard, on the other hand, has never existed in a universe without shelter, air conditioning, and consistent (if occasionally overbearing) support.

And adversity, Joe believes, is inevitable. He wonders how Leonard will react if he's off at college and finds himself in a jam. Will he be able to wriggle out of it himself, or will he need to call Daddy? Is he prepared to defuse a tense situation, or will he say or do something that escalates it?

"Say you pull out a gun on me and you trying to rob me. Do not panic," Joe says in an admittedly extreme hypothetical, adding that the immediate response to this stress can mark the difference between living and dying. "I'm gonna wind up forcing you to kill me because I'm doing stupid stuff."

In his demonstration, Joe says nothing and extends his arm to offer an invisible wallet.

"Here. Do what he said," he says. "What would Leonard do? Man, probably shit on his self."

Joe laughs again, though this conceals a true anxiety about his friend's preparedness for the wider world. He also worries for Jamie Vance, another teammate from a two-parent household who Joe claims is "green." Which is why, when the three friends hang out on weekends, Joe feels a responsibility to provide a crash course in the Keyoke Method.

One time Joe took Leonard and Jamie to a dice game in the Fischer. Jamie was uncomfortable from the outset, though he realized this was part of the point.

"They looking at you like, 'Who is this? What you bringing him back here for?'" Jamie would recall.

The game began, and Joe would evaluate his friends' play and their reactions to wins and losses. If they celebrated to a disrespectful degree or talked too much shit (or not enough), Joe would correct them. He watched Leonard roll a 7 or 11, which in the safety of a casino is a stand-alone win. But in street craps that's only the first round, and your opponent expects a chance to win his money back. At one point Leonard won, collected his perceived winnings, and Joe started "talking to him reckless," as he put it.

"Man, what, you trying to dick me out or something?" he said, aggressively getting in Leonard's face.

After gauging Leonard's reaction, Joe broke character and let his friend off the hook. Then he explained that, when Joe was eight, it had been a dice game just like this when Joe's cousin won his round, snapped up his cash, and walked away. He wouldn't live long enough to right his wrong.

If Joe, Jamie, and Leonard were cruising Canal Street, Jamie sometimes drove his mother's car. If he went too slow or sunk too deep in the driver's seat or had his hoodie pulled low, Joe would correct him.

"Bro, what the fuck you doing?" Jamie would recall him saying late one night. Joe went on to lecture his friend about the little things that attract unwanted attention, from either the cops or locals looking for trouble.

One time Jamie got mad at Joe about something neither of them would remember. But both recalled Jamie approaching Joe from behind and slapping him in the head. Joe breathed through his fury before putting Jamie in a choke hold, calmly turning the sneak attack into a teaching moment.

"You never do that," he told his friend. Joe explained that if you're going to confront someone, the proper way to do so is face-to-face— never from behind. "That's how you get killed."

Joe could be equally puzzling and captivating to Jamie and Leonard, who indeed learned from their friend but never fully understood him. It confused Jamie when he called Joe to offer him a ride to school, and Joe flatly declined before hanging up.

It wouldn't occur to Jamie, nor would it to most people, that Joe's mother had drilled into him an unrelenting belief system that had hardened into a survival code. If you're inside, Keyoke had taught her son, never let anyone call you outside. *Anyone.* This included one of Joe's closest friends, and though Jamie's offer had been innocent, Joe had no way to be certain of that. Nor could he know where Jamie had been before this and who might've put him up to making this call. It'd have been different if Joe had *asked* for a ride. But unsolicited? That's a red flag.

Jamie shrugged it off as Joe being Joe, unpredictable and a little weird. But the code is the code, and as much as Joe tried, he couldn't make his friends—certainly those he saw as privileged—understand it. Not completely, anyway, and regardless of whether his choices strain his friendships or paint Joe as bizarre or force a layer of distance between him and the rest of society, precisely following the Keyoke Method has kept Joe alive this long.

SUNDAY MORNING AFTER the Warren Easton game, and Leonard is the first player to arrive at the Karr football office. Today is a marathon day of injury treatment and initial game prep for Catholic High, a formidable program in Baton Rouge. Coach Brown, using an English classroom as meeting space, greets Leonard with questions.

"Whose party was your daddy at Friday?"

"A cousin's."

"What did you do last night?"

"Went to bed early."

"Who were you with?"

"Nobody."

"Mm-hmm," Brown says, lifting his eyebrows and cutting his gaze away, a favorite expression of Brown's that conveys both suspicion and dismissiveness.

"You gotta trust me," Leonard tells him. "*Got* to."

Brown mostly does, though he won't tell him that. Like his father, Leonard sometimes misses the coach's hints, which aren't exactly subtle. Two nights ago, Brown addressed the team after the Easton win. He made an announcement: the captain's line would be expanding by two. Senior defensive lineman Josh Randall was joining, and so was Leonard, who sat on the mat and smiled as he received pats on the back from his teammates. He had reached this carrot at last, and Brown was eager to see how he'd react. For the moment, Brown wanted to use Leonard's journey as an example for the younger players, many of whom prefer instant gratification.

"If, for one second, he had believed that he wasn't a team leader or he wasn't a captain," Brown told the group, "if he would've had that limited mind-set, then he would've had a limited outcome. You can't let other people's limited imaginations affect what the fuck you do."

With that piece of business complete, that left only that damn Acura key. In its life it has traveled from a Honda factory in central Ohio to a dealership in Louisiana to its first owner's home in New Orleans to the top left desk drawer of one Brice Michael Brown. As Nick Foster and Omari Robertson begin commiserating with Leonard over the fledgling game plan for Catholic, Brown dispatches Tiga to retrieve a small black bag from his desk drawer. In a moment the key will be traveling again, beyond the head coach's office and through the weight room, past the purple lockers and into Karr's rear hallway. Now it reaches an English teacher's hobbled desk, propped up by a copy of *The Elements of Style*.

Maybe it's because Brown is surrounded by quotes from Shakespeare and Chaucer, but the coach is up to his throat in symbolism: the black leather bag contains so much more than the key to a used car. Brown is on the verge of handing over a token of his trust, the fortunes of a vulnerable football program, the hopes and dreams of a hundred young men outside on a concrete landing, waiting to dunk themselves in an ice bath to reduce lingering swelling after Friday night's game. Joe is out there treating a sore shoulder, and Jamie is in the tub scrolling Twitter. Just this morning, he informed the University of Arkansas he was decommitting in order to reopen his recruiting. He had received a scholarship offer from the University of Louisville, in his mind a bit more prestigious than Arkansas, and Jamie wanted to make himself available in case a college football superpower came calling. Trying to be whatever recruiters wanted him to be, Jamie underwent a full rebranding and was willing to change no less than his name. At least on social media, he was no longer Jamie. He became "Greedy" Vance, borrowing from Greedy Williams, at the time a rookie cornerback with the NFL's Cleveland Browns.

Brown sits at the desk and sighs, an attempt at beating back a strengthening feeling of regret. He overpowers this emotion the same way he does all of them: by immersing himself in the finer points of football. Brown stands and begins drawing play diagrams on the classroom's whiteboard, emptying ideas from his mind, erasing a route or a blocking assignment, and drawing something new. When he likes something, he asks Nick what they should call it. After all, calling a play is deliberately complex; it's as much about confusing your opponent as relaying Brown's choice to the quarterback.

Karr, like most teams, has dozens of plays. Maybe hundreds, considering each one has multiple variations, shifts, motions. And Brown is always adding. Occasionally he stumbles upon something new: an alignment or pre-snap motion. In football offense, anything new can be confusing to a defense, and confusion is a major advantage.

Brown stops drawing, admires his latest creation, and he and Nick debate its name. Each play call uses a cluster of code words that should be confusing enough that a clever, or devious, opponent can't intercept the call—but simple enough for high school players to grasp it.

"Call it 'Florida,'" Brown says. "Or you want a one-syllable?"

"It's your play," Nick says.

"You'd rather 'Flag'? Or 'Fox'?"

In this case, both words signal the same play: a route combination that features a "fitch" concept, one receiver on a fade route and another running a hitch. The coaches agree on "Fox," but this isn't the end of the process. After Brown calls his play verbally, Nick then translates it into a series of hand and body gestures to relay the play to the quarterback.

Nick stands to demonstrate possible ways to signal "Fox" from the sideline. He twists his rear end toward Leonard and waves a hand above his waist, mimicking a fox's tail. Even if you understand and appreciate football, there's something strange about watching a thirty-four-year-old man pretending to be a fox. But here it's just part of the Sunday routine. Though the purpose is to surprise the defense, opponents aren't the only ones who get mixed up.

"That look like 'Brown'!" Brown says, meaning it's too similar to a different signal and could lead to miscommunication.

"I'm going through it," Nick says, smiling through the absurdity of this exercise. "It ain't a full signal, god*damn*!"

To make matters more puzzling, Nick wants a separate word—"Blue Fox" or "Brown Fox"—to signal the direction. Usually "Blue" means the play should go to the left and "Brown" to the right. This time, Nick wants the words to mean the *opposite*. It's . . . a lot, and even coaches' eyes are glazing over.

"This shit confusing the fuck outta me," Brown says. Then he snaps into a more hopeful tone. "I'm gonna have it by tomorrow."

He starts drawing a new play. Football games are often won and lost before kickoff, and coaches such as Brown are chess masters who can predict—and exploit—an opposing team's mistakes. If they line up *here* on defense, then Karr must adjust by doing *this*, which will then lead them to do *that*, so then Karr will have to . . .

On and on it goes. That's the game, even at the high school level. It grows only more complex in the college and professional ranks, where defenses disguise coverages and offenses spend dozens of hours studying game footage just to identify something minuscule to reveal the defense's intentions. What makes Brown's approach unusual, and successful, is that he prepares like a college coach. He watches film on his iPad, looking for defensive leverages and mismatches, and Brown installs pre-snap motions that often confirm what he has recognized.

At this point, the game becomes less chess than poker. If Leonard can do something that forces a defender—almost always a defensive back—to tip his hand early, he'll almost always know where the ball should go even before he snaps it.

Brown, still standing at the whiteboard, has a new idea. Leonard takes notes as his coach narrates.

"If they're playing us Quarters," Brown says—he has noticed that Catholic frequently uses the Cover 4, a concept that uses four deep defensive backs and three underneath linebackers—"the safety is *here* and the nickel is *here*."

He's scribbling a play he has used before—but never with pre-snap motion from the inside, or 'Y,' receiver. In this iteration, Leonard will have three receivers to his left, and Fat is the 'Y' and will line up closest to him. Fat's assignment is a deep post route toward the center of the field. There's a fourth receiver to Leonard's right, but everyone except Fat is a decoy, designed to draw defenders away. A moment before the snap, Fat will take a few steps to his right, then turn and retake his original position.

"So when he motions *here*," Brown continues, "what that corner gonna do? He's gonna outside leverage. So watch this."

He keeps drawing. The defense, which studies film of its own, may suspect this play is coming. But the motion could throw coaches and players off with only a second or two before the snap. Who should the cornerback cover now? What should the safety do? Everyone will have to make a choice, and just as their mental gears are turning, Leonard snaps the ball.

Brown just sees all these moving pieces in his imagination. He's a football version of John Nash, the lead character in *A Beautiful Mind*, and he gets annoyed when staffers reveal that they don't possess this same extraordinary spatial intelligence or process information with similar speed. Which, truthfully, is everyone.

"This should work," Brown says, pleased with himself. He names the play "Trips left Y-scat Z-hunt," or just "Z-hunt" for short. "Look at it, O."

"I need a piece of paper," Omari says.

"No, bitch," Brown says. "Come look at it right here."

They examine it together, and Brown's mind is still computing. A single play, as simple as it is brilliant, now has him thinking about possibilities that seemed impossible even earlier today.

"I don't know if we should show this shit for now or state-championship-type shit," Brown says. His assistants laugh, but the big man isn't joking. Maybe for the first time this season, he's thinking about another trip to the Superdome.

The staff settles on the beginnings of a game plan for Catholic, and Brown takes a long breath. It's time for one last thing, and it's even more complicated than attacking Catholic's defense. Brown unzips the black bag in front of him and removes the Acura key. Nick slides a desk toward Leonard's and leans toward him.

"You're not a little boy no more," Nick says, his voice low and imploring. "You know how you and Joe was the clowns and all that type of shit? Y'all the leaders, and you've gotta act like it."

In other words: Joe grew up. It's time for Leonard to do the same. Now Brown is holding a symbol of coaches' faith in him to do just that, and he's pointing its metal end at Leonard like a knife.

"This is something that can be taken away," the coach says. Brown sees the car, and Leonard's response, as a chance to see how the young man handles a new level of freedom, not unlike when Joe was promoted to first chair. "All those pats on the back that you're getting, that's six inches away from a kick in the ass. Period. And I'm closer than six inches. I'm one inch off your ass. I'm one mistake off your ass."

Leonard looks his coach in the eye.

"I'm gonna show you," he says.

"You're saying that," Brown says. "But what you say and what you do is two different things."

Brown lists the possible mistakes Leonard can make—being late, having too many teammates rely on him for pickups, running out of gas—and stabs the key on a notebook as he recites them. He says he doesn't worry about Leonard's judgment when he's on campus or in the football office. But when he disappears out of coaches' view? That's different, and even after all this time, Brown doesn't quite know if *podium talk* is a manner of speaking for his quarterback, or if it's becoming a way of life. What is real, and what is bullshit? Does Leonard even know?

"Are you gonna tell your daddy you're gonna go by Joe house and you're gonna go by a little girl house? Yeah, you're gonna do that," he says. "But I'm telling you, if you do me that, I'm gonna slap the shit out you. Ain't gonna be no conversation."

"I got it," Leonard says, barely above a whisper.

Though Brown has no kids of his own, and speaks to young people in his own way, he at least seems to understand a central tenet of parenting: that attempting to control every action and insulate young people from the world's dangers is, ultimately, futile. You just teach them all you can in the time you have, and then you hope it was enough.

Brown extends his arm, offering Leonard the key. The quarterback stands, smiling, and takes it.

"Good luck," Brown says, and though this is his motto for everything, it feels particularly appropriate now. Leonard leaves the classroom and heads toward the school's rear exit.

The key is traveling once more, and Leonard walks into the parking lot and uses it to unlock his new car. Climbing behind the wheel, he's still smiling. The dashboard is cracked, and the power lock doesn't work on the driver's side. Otherwise, the car is in good shape and has clearly been cared for; it has never been crashed or abandoned or flooded.

He inserts the key into the ignition and turns it, gently shifting the car into gear before creeping toward the street. Leonard makes a left and takes it easy over a speed bump before braking at a stop sign where two roads, Huntlee and Berkley Drives, intersect. Though they go perpendicular and come from different places, same as Joe and Leonard, their paths are inextricably connected.

Leonard stops, checking his left and right. With no cars approaching, he at first moves the vehicle slowly. Then the Acura disappears behind a row of trees, Leonard once again out of coaches' sight, and in the distance the engine can be heard accelerating as vehicle and driver charge intrepidly up the road.

CHAPTER 4

SUNKEN CITY

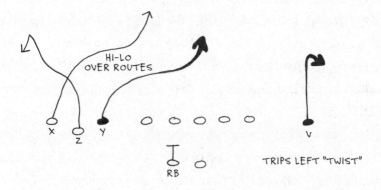

HI-LO
OVER ROUTES

X
Z
Y

RB

V

TRIPS LEFT "TWIST"

AFTER THE SEASON-OPENING LOSS to John Curtis, assistant coach Norm Randall asked Brown if he could address the team.

The result itself wasn't what bothered Norm. After all, John Curtis is a Louisiana football juggernaut that has played in thirty-seven state championship games. Coach J.T. Curtis has led the team for more than a half century, and after so many years, the program's message and machinery are time tested and well honed. No, Norm was concerned by *how* Karr had lost: eight penalties, three fumbles, seven dropped passes. Defensive players looked tentative, and they missed tackles and blew assignments. Offensive players were repeatedly out of sync.

The continual mental errors were alarming to Norm, though not exactly surprising. After a dozen years on Karr's coaching staff, he has developed a theory. In general, players here are aggressive, confident, and fearless—until they play an opponent from a predominantly white school. In those games, they lose their tempers. They abandon their training and make mistakes. Norm believes they play as if they don't deserve to win.

New Orleans is a city that's still coming to terms not just with its troubling racial history, but how it acknowledges the fact that an estimated 135,000 enslaved Africans were bought and sold in and around the French Quarter. In modern showings of the 1726 watercolor *Veue et Perspective de la Nouvelle-Orléans*, the foreground—showing naked slaves hauling timber on the West Bank and rowing themselves across the river—is often cropped out. The city didn't commission historical markers to note its involvement in the slave trade until its tricentennial in 2018.

Gentrification has applied ongoing strain. In many historically Black neighborhoods, rents and property taxes have increased to levels many families simply cannot afford, forcing longtime residents to abandon or hastily sell homes they've occupied for generations. They've been pushed, therefore, into parts of the city that feel almost foreign, farther and farther from hospitals, public transportation, and police stations. Though this has improved somewhat, in 2015 it took police an average of an hour to dispatch an officer following a 911 call. In some primarily Black neighborhoods, such as New Orleans East and Gentilly, the wait doubled. It's even worse for nonviolent crimes.

Displaced residents aren't just physically uprooted from their homes, neighborhood, and comfort zones. They often carry harsh emotional burdens that, in particular for children, can lead to higher risk of anxiety and depression. Parents are given no handbook for how to soothe their kids or even explain to them the complex reasons they're moving yet again. Residents don't say much about why they distrust or fear the police, and how justice here is a mirage. What's the point in a conversation about how the median income in Black households in New Orleans is $25,806, and in white households it's three times that?

These things just *are*. And, in a city and country where Black and brown people have been ignored, pushed aside, and beaten down for generations, many New Orleanians just accept that this isn't a place where white people lose.

Not in net worth or home ownership, not in admissions at top colleges or approvals on loan applications, not in incarceration rates or even life expectancy. Not even, Norm believes, on the football field.

"They look at it like: if we're Black," he says, "we *can't* beat them."

The crux of his theory is that players believe teams such as John Curtis or Catholic or Neville are smarter, better coached on fundamentals, play with more discipline. It's an old stereotype. And it's no more true, and no less lazy, than suggesting Black teams win only because they have bigger, faster, stronger athletes. But if a notion is passed on long enough, merely adopted without pushback, it seems to *become* true. Norm, though, refuses to accept this.

That's why he is standing here near midnight, arms outstretched on the weight racks assigned to Jamie and Joe. A hundred pairs of eyes look toward him.

"Now listen," he begins. "They can be as humble as they want in the paper and tell you everything they want. Say: 'They're a good team; they can run, they can catch.' Man, fuck that. They ain't telling their fucking team that. They're telling their team you a bunch of n——s who are undisciplined, who got penalties, who shot they self in the foot."

Norm is a rectangular man, broad-shouldered more than fifteen years after his last football game but softened by a successful career in information technology. His face is intense and curious, his demeanor playful, his worldview shaped by being the son of a Black father and South Korean mother. Most everyone in the football office thinks about race, though nobody confronts it as frequently or relentlessly as Norm.

"I don't give a fuck if it's just two mistakes, fellas," he continues. "It *can't . . . fucking . . . happen!*"

He pauses, having worked up a sweat.

"We fucking blew it together," he says, looking into the eyes of Karr's captains, Joe and Jamie and Leonte and Fat. "But you know what the problem is? Motherfuckers getting tired. I'm talking about leaders. I'm talking about n——s that matter on the team. Gotta tell a n—— to fucking keep their eyes open. Gotta tell n——s to stand up."

Brown, standing behind Norm, is nodding.

"You wanted to win tonight in front of a fucking packed house," Norm says. "And you didn't because we didn't stay true to our principles and our keys. That's the little details of the game."

He takes a breath.

"That's the difference between us and every other Black school," he says. "We *want* to do the little details. We *want* to be disciplined. And when you don't do it, and when you shoot yourselves in the foot early, you done lost, dog. You done lost."

LIKE SO MANY SUBJECTS that might seem taboo elsewhere, Brown's program runs toward the incendiary issue of race, not away from it. At the center of Karr's philosophy is an at-all-costs avoidance of bullshit. Coaches are brutally honest about a young athlete's play on the field, his survival skills off it, the world—and the prisms through which it views people of color—he hopes to navigate after crossing the Mississippi River for good.

This involves harsh confrontations, and the occasional social experiment. Years ago, St. Paul's Episcopal School in New Orleans kept beating Karr during the regular season. It made no sense. Karr played in the state championship game four times between 2010 and 2015, and during that time St. Paul's never advanced beyond the third round of the playoffs. The Wolves went 4–1 against the Cougars during that span.

"We couldn't put our finger on it," Brown says with a dash of sarcasm in his voice. According to longtime St. Paul's coach Kenny Sears, the Wolves football team is about 90 percent white.

Brown says that, during some of those games, Karr players would report hearing St. Paul's players using the N-word between snaps (Sears was asked directly about this in an interview, and he denied knowledge of his players using such language. He insisted he would strongly discipline any team member who used a slur). Brown says players responded more with inquisitiveness than fury. They often asked coaches why the other kids would call them such a thing.

Brown encouraged players to shrug it off, saying later that players were simply told to "turn the other cheek." But the emotional effect seems undeniable. In those games Karr players consistently abandoned their fundamentals, made uncharacteristic mistakes, in general looked overwhelmed and at times intimidated by an inferior opponent.

But rather than simply dropping St. Paul's from the yearly schedule, Brown kept penciling in the Wolves, usually at the beginning of each season. Conditioning comes not from avoiding discomfort but from meeting it head on—and, eventually, overcoming it. In 2016, Karr finally beat St. Paul's before doing so again in 2017 and 2018. Through psychological reconstruction, painful and slow as it was, Karr stopped viewing St. Paul's as a team it should lose to—and instead saw the Wolves as a team the Cougars were supposed to beat. In 2019, Brown finally stopped scheduling games against St. Paul's. He was tired of counseling players about what they sometimes heard on the field, but more than that, this particular majority white program was no longer useful to him.

John Curtis and Catholic could be, though. So he agreed to games against those programs for early in the 2019 season. Brown's assistants suspected this was a questionable act of self-sabotage, and considering how Brown treats himself, that theory tracks. But the coach's actual motivation was simpler: with a senior class that had lost one game in three years, the mad social scientist with a coaching whistle just wanted to see how the kids responded.

And, in that first game, they had done so poorly. Brown expected as much, and it gave him a chance to dust off a few old tricks. During Karr's first practice after the John Curtis game, Brown made players warm up and lift weights in silence. They hadn't communicated when it counted. So now they could forego verbal communication when it didn't. Instead of clapping to signal a new stretch or exercise, captains had to pantomime smacking their hands together. In Brown's analysis, this was one more privilege that, if taken for granted, can be taken away.

Then again, players hadn't been the only ones who'd fallen victim to Norm's theory. A few assistant coaches had done the same.

It's important to point out that Brown isn't just tearing a hundred young people down to their emotional studs before initiating a rebuild. He's doing the same with many of his staff members, in effect reprogramming the reprogrammers. When a young defensive backs coach was chirping with players late in the John Curtis game about putting injured wide receiver Aaron Anderson back into the game, the assistant had no idea Brown could hear him. Or that Brown would call out the staffer in front of the team during his postgame address.

"You've got motherfuckers, D.B. coaches and shit, talking about: 'Where's 4 at? Where's 4 at?'" Brown said, referring to Aaron's jersey number. "Man, shut the fuck up and do your fucking job. Next motherfucker do that shit, you gonna be dismissed on-site."

The assistant coach's momentary lapse in judgment hadn't just been a show of insolence that could undermine Brown's message or even divide the team. It was a self-defeating act that, Norm says, is a tired instinctive response that plays into Black male stereotypes and is frustratingly typical, he says, of so many boys and men Norm grew up with, played football alongside, and now works with.

"I feel like we give up so easily," Norm says. He goes on to describe a troubling chicken-and-egg scenario in which young men grow up believing their futures are limited—and then do things that turn that belief into reality.

When Norm attended Southeastern Louisiana University about an hour northwest of New Orleans, he noticed how inclusive the community felt. The white and Black students all went out drinking together, but then the next morning the white kids tended to power through their hangovers. The Black athletes, Norm says, cut class and slept in. During football practices, Norm himself frequently had no idea what coaches meant when they told him to line up in the "three-technique," a common pass-rushing alignment in which two interior linemen attempt to control the center of the line of scrimmage. At Karr, coaches never taught players such advanced methods. Defensive linemen were simply told to be the toughest motherfuckers on the field, and to go get the ball carrier.

Now, because of something he was never taught, Norm was being yelled at, called names, and judged in an arena in which nearly half of all college football players in the United States are Black while only about one in ten head coaches is an American of color. It would've been easy, he says, to give up.

"You're cursing me out because I don't know," Norm says. "Now I'm mad at him, but I should really be mad at the people that didn't prepare me to come here. People want to say: 'White folks has done us wrong,' or blah this, blah that. But we don't look at our own self."

In a country where skin color too often determines advantages, and college football is built on a foundation of unpaid labor, largely by a minority workforce, both things can be true.

"My whole thing with the kids is: Don't believe that you're not disciplined," Norm continues. "Don't believe that we can't wake up on time and be places on time and do things the right way and be just as tough and gritty as them. Right? We might not have the same upbringing. We might not have the same financial background. But that's not a fucking excuse."

By the time Norm joined Karr's coaching staff, where he'd bring a detail-oriented and in-your-face coaching style, he was working as a technology consultant for New Orleans's bustling trade show industry. During high school, he had no idea what an IT professional even does, let alone how someone pursues such a career. But one day his father brought home an America Online disc, Norm downloaded the software, and away he went—a life changed but only by chance.

But no one at Karr, which was a prestigious magnet school, exposed him to that possibility. At first this made Norm feel anger. Then he channeled this into trying to alter the mentalities and ambitions of a new generation, though this proved far more difficult than he'd initially thought. What he found, year after year, is that in a nation where kids can do and be anything, so often in poor neighborhoods, young people are told to simply ignore their circumstances and succeed anyway. But many of those same kids are offered neither consistent guidance nor an easy-to-understand road map out of their current environment. They come to believe their hopes of making it rely solely on industries they know: professional sports, say, or becoming a rapper. When those dreams inevitably fall flat, frustration can turn to resentment and anger. In places like New Orleans, that can metastasize into something worse.

"You don't *have* to go pick up a gun," Norm says. "You don't *have* to go sell weed and get the easy, quick money. Why we can't just do it right? Why we can't just struggle and do it the right way?"

Sitting on a padded table in Karr's training room, Norm shakes his head.

"All this time we were told dreams that really wasn't realistic," he says, "and we believed it."

WITHOUT REALIZING IT, in early 2014 Brown was about to set into motion his boldest and most important social experiment. Brown had been Karr's primary offensive play caller for years. But now under head coach Nathaniel Jones, he was being promoted to offensive coordinator and would therefore be vacating his duties as offensive line coach.

Karr posted the job, and one day Jones invited Brown to meet a particularly unusual candidate. Chris DeGiovanni wasn't a Karr man, wasn't even from New Orleans. He hadn't played college football and, at age twenty-eight, had only coached the high school game for a few years. But he was confident, brash, knowledgeable.

Brown walked in carrying a Sno-Ball shaved ice treat and saw DeGiovanni for the first time. Something unexpected drew Brown's attention: DeGiovanni, a puff of close-cropped sandy hair sitting above skeptical eyes, is white.

It was obvious to Brown that Jones saw DeGiovanni as something of a courtesy interview. That and being a source of entertainment. Jones had put DeGiovanni through a battery of strange tests, first asking him to whoop and holler as if he were trying to get kids hyped before a game, then shift into the character of an introspective and earnest sage. Jones asked DeGiovanni to repeat to Brown what DeGiovanni had said earlier. *How* had he said he'd handle the Black kids who'd challenge him, curse at him, or get in his face?

"I'm gonna *get* them out of my face," DeGiovanni said. Jones could barely hide his laughter.

Brown just looked blankly at the stranger and took another bite of his Sno-Ball. Eventually Jones asked the big man if he had any questions, and Brown blurted out the first thing that came to mind.

"What's your favorite play?" he asked.

DeGiovanni stood and approached the whiteboard, and he began emptying the contents of his imagination. He scrawled what appeared to be a basic strong-side zone-read, a play that requires the quarterback to note a defensive end's movement immediately after the snap and quickly decide whether to hand off to the running back or run it himself. But DeGiovanni's play, which he called "Prime," was an inverted version of the traditional play: a run to the side with weaker blocking protection; to make matters more precarious, there was no tight end to provide extra blocking help. His play was built on misdirection and relied on a wide receiver, in general smaller than a tight end, to block—not just putting more pressure on the quarterback to make the correct read, but to do so in an instant.

Other coaches had insisted the play would never work. Very few high school quarterbacks can read defenses and process information that quickly. Or, more precisely, they're rarely trusted to do so. Most high school offenses, after all, are designed to eliminate risk and limit the quarterback's responsibility. Even in some college offenses during the rise of the spread offense over the last decade, a play with four receivers and a running back might appear to have numerous receiving routes and possibilities. But the truth is, most plays have a predetermined end point. Coaches, not the quarterback, read the defense before the snap and decide which receiver *should* be open. This divestment of critical thinking doesn't build players. It forms automatons who run an assigned play and have little idea how to adjust. And it's one reason why so many star college quarterbacks struggle in their transitions to the NFL game, where coaches call plays but rely on the quarterback to make pre- and post-snap adjustments, based on the defense's alignment. It's also why DK Metcalf, the Seattle Seahawks star, was the ninth wide receiver selected in the 2019 NFL draft. After reviewing film of Metcalf's three seasons running basic routes at the University of Mississippi, largely because that's what Coach Hugh Freeze's offense asked of him, scouts feared that he'd struggle in his transition to the professional game.

But even on the high school level, Brown allows players the freedom to make changes and be creative. Though he has veto power, Brown expects his quarterbacks—from Tonka to Leonard and everyone in between—to know the opposing defense. They must be able to recognize its coverage and identify possible leverages, or the angle of attack defenders take immediately after the snap, that reveal possible vulnerabilities. Brown actually hands out a written test every week with hand-drawn coverage diagrams and hypothetical scenarios. If his starting quarterback does well, that's usually a good sign Karr is going to win.

So when DeGiovanni was talking as he drew up his play, Brown was intrigued. And not just because he wanted to someday steal DeGiovanni's play and deploy it against Warren Easton or Neville.

Another side effect of living on the West Bank and existing within a tightly wound neighborhood culture is that, even in high school, many kids arrive at Karr having never met a white person. It's a demographic group that simply lives elsewhere, and for better or worse, most students here have never experienced in-your-face racism firsthand. Brown recognized they eventually would, be it in a restaurant or against a predominantly white opposing team or if they are pulled over by police. By then, with stress high, the reaction might be severe—leading to uncomfortable, or perhaps deadly, consequences. Brown believes emotion, especially unchecked emotion, can be a weakness. That's why he relentlessly conditions players to experience and respond to all manner of assholery.

But how can a football coach condition players to racism? With an entirely Black staff, how could he begin to simulate these inevitable, visceral reactions while having them occur in a controlled setting?

A few days after DeGiovanni's interview, Brown strongly encouraged Jones to hire the little white candidate. Jones reluctantly agreed, and even during DeGiovanni's first days, when he would be introduced and referred to only as Chris D, the players responded precisely as Brown hoped they would.

"Who the fuck is this white man?" Chris D says he kept hearing, and at first Karr's offensive linemen ignored their new coach. They took their questions and concerns to Brown, who suggested they kindly fuck off.

At first Chris D tried to handle this politely, having shaped his coaching and chemistry teaching personas from the *Stand and Deliver* and *Dangerous Minds* handbooks. These are children, after all, and when he learned some of the boys' stories, he couldn't help but feel sympathy. But Brown warned him that, hard as it may be to believe, communicating with Karr kids with respect and as peers—at least in the beginning—is a mistake.

Chris D kept resisting, figuring that can't possibly be true. And when students asked him for ten dollars, he'd sometimes oblige. He'd calmly ask unruly children to please chill out. Then one day a young man stood up from his desk, casually removed his penis, and filled a cup with his own urine. Then he flung it at a female classmate, and when pandemonium erupted, Chris D had no idea what to do. Fights broke out regularly, kids danced on their chairs during lessons, and one student called his chemistry teacher neither Mr. DeGiovanni nor Chris D. Instead the student referred to him only as a "bitch-ass n——."

One day mayhem broke out once more, and with the kids ignoring Chris D's pleas for calm, he walked toward a desk. Without further announcement, he threw the desk against a wall. The kids' eyes widened, and their asses returned to their seats.

Chris D stopped feeling sorry for the kids and started being honest with them. He came to learn that, despite a powerful impulse of white guilt, sympathy isn't just pointless. It's a show of submission.

"Kindness gets taken advantage of," Chris D would say, "and they'll see you as weak and, 'I can get five dollars out of this motherfucker; next time I'll get twenty.'"

In the football office, he tried to stay cool when running back Ronnie Jackson purposely bumped into him in the locker room. Ronnie came from a broken home, fell in with a crowd that robbed houses, was using football to lift himself toward a better future. But a soft touch wasn't exactly what Brown had hoped for when he'd lobbied for Chris D. So he encouraged the novice coach to curse at Ronnie, get in his face, kick his ass if it came down to it. Brown *wanted* Chris D to mix it up with players and bring those unspoken feelings and questions to the surface. Because only then could they be confronted and recalibrated.

So one day Ronnie passed Chris D again and drove his shoulder into the coach's chest.

"You a bitch," Ronnie announced. Teenager or not, Chris D went after him.

Ronnie found himself in a headlock, Chris D got himself pinned to the floor, and eventually teammates broke it up. Though the two competing rams were shamed and out of breath, the message had been received. Ronnie never called Chris D a "bitch" ever again.

The months and years passed, and Chris D settled in not only as Karr's offensive line coach but as Brown's lily-white bouncer. On a muggy afternoon in May 2019, the team's spring program was just beginning. Coaches were handing out T-shirts in the coaches' office. Players were invited into the cramped room two at a time, and Brown ticked their names from a spreadsheet.

Chris D stood in the doorway and granted—or refused—entry. A wiry tenth-grade running back wasn't in the mood to wait. Chris D knew the kid's story well: incarcerated mother, a childhood spent bouncing among foster homes, experiences and expectations that had pushed him to the brink not just of success or failure, but of life and death.

"If you don't go to the edge with him," Chris D would later say of this particular player, "he's gonna fall off."

On this day the running back kept returning to the doorway. He wanted to do things on his own schedule and tried to push his way in.

Brown, like a Mafia boss, nodded toward Chris D as a signal to put a stop to it. So the white man engaged the kid, and in an instant, they were scuffling in the hallway, arms entangled as they drifted past a dumbbell rack. Nobody here seemed to believe this was particularly cruel or unusual, and barely anyone noticed when Chris D ended the confrontation by slinging the impatient and troubled young man into a potted plant.

THE YEARS AND SEASONS PASSED, and Chris D found himself mixing it up with players and coaches alike. He and Ronald Davis, a former Karr player who'd become the assistant offensive line coach, got into a fistfight before a game because of a disagreement that boiled over. Chris D and Nick Foster got into shouting matches so often, usually about football philosophy, that Brown called them into his office once and threatened to fire them both if they couldn't work out their differences.

Chris D became so comfortable as Brown's bulldog that he sometimes forgot he was in someone else's house. Coaches blanched at his presence for any number of reasons, skin color included, and the truth is Brown saw that as a benefit.

To be complacent in football is to fall behind, and Brown dislikes the idea of anyone around here being too comfortable. Though he complains about the bedraggled Karr football office, with cracked windows and ancient equipment, he uses its modesty as a metaphor for players' backgrounds. Brown's fight against contentment is ultimately why he'd schedule John Curtis and Catholic within the first four games of the 2019 season, because he believed coaches and players had grown accustomed to winning and, well, needed a kick in the teeth.

Chris D understood and supported his boss's rationale, and even this grated on his colleagues. Though Nick and Ronald and Norm and Omari had played college football and had known Brown for decades, and were more importantly OG Karr men, some saw Chris D as a yes-man. Brown and Chris D could lose themselves for hours talking about new techniques, advanced formations, never-before-seen plays. They'd disappear for long lunches or elaborate dinners, talking football all the while, going on walks around City Park to talk about what they'd uncovered on their iPads as they ventured deeper down the rabbit hole. He and Brown were usually together, and in lockstep, despite being opposites in most every way.

Brown had played college football and learned the game the traditional way. He'd been his college coach's understudy before taking his education back to Karr and eventually building his own program. Chris D was self-taught and spent his college years not on a sideline but as a seafood cook. He became an investment banker who hated his job, then a would-be attorney who kept failing the LSAT. Football, of all things, was his Plan C. He learned the game by watching blocking drills and making notes on offensive line trivia: proper stances, hand placement, hip rotation. He drew diagrams of defensive coverages and blitzes he'd seen in games, studying them as if a math problem. He learned to identify weaknesses and memorize an offensive play that could—no, *would*—exploit it.

When he was satisfied with a play's chances, Chris D would log into *Madden NFL*, the wildly popular and highly sophisticated video game, and bring it to life. At one point he was among the nation's top-twenty Madden online players, he says, and it was because he "became obsessed." He tinkered with motions and shifts, pre- and post-snap reads, unbalanced receiver sets and funky alignments—anything that could reveal a defense's weak points.

He and Brown, despite their football educations, had arrived at a philosophically similar place. Unlike others, they could each see on-field sequences in their minds. They also agreed that the best attacks bend, if not outright break, traditional rules. Most offenses are believed to have limitations. For instance, the spread almost always relies on a tight end as an extra blocker and hefty receiving option. But Brown prefers speed over power, and that's ultimately what had intrigued him about Chris D and "Prime." It defied tradition and challenged custom, and plays they both liked seemed to have only one rule.

"Just score," Chris D would say later. "Nothing else matters."

And that's football, no matter the level, at a glance: the defense has no choice but to guess what the offense might do. With enough study and memorization, offensive coaches (and some quarterbacks) can look across the line of scrimmage and *know* not just where the defense has put its emphasis—but, more important, where it has not. It's why Peyton Manning became notorious for his "Omaha" pre-snap call after making adjustments based on what he saw at the line. Manning and his teammates usually broke the huddle with multiple plays; "Omaha" was just a quick, easy-to-understand indicator word that announced they were going to Plan B. Tony Romo, the retired quarterback and CBS football analyst, can similarly evaluate a defense from the press box and "predict" which offensive play is coming. The ability has earned him a $17 million annual salary and the nickname "Romostradamus." The truth is, he just knows how to spot a defense's intentions. This same—if simplified—pursuit is why Brown and Leonard meet for two hours before each school day to watch defensive game film.

In the end, Chris D and Brown became close not just in spite of their differences. It's because, deep down, they both believe football can be hacked. All a coach needs is enough time and patience—along with, perhaps, a photographic memory like Brown's, and a willingness to devote his entire life to mastering the game. What could be easier?

"Our offense is designed to find a weak point in every defense," Chris D says. "The answer is in our playbook. We just have to find the right answer. Once we find the answer, it's over."

On Fridays, it was Chris D who found himself on the sofa in Brown's office, contemplating final preparations as Nick and Norm and the rest sat in swivel chairs in the assistants' office. Then the head coach and his top assistant would head toward the stadium, Brown in the passenger seat of his truck and Chris D behind the wheel. They'd spend a few more minutes talking football before showtime. They'd wonder aloud if they'd missed something, if the defense has implemented a new wrinkle just for Karr. No matter the opponent or game plan, the soundtrack of these drives was always the same: "I'm Not Tired Yet," a rollicking gospel anthem by the Mississippi Mass Choir.

> *Been running by day and praying by night*
> *I'm not tired yet!*
> *I've gotta get going it's a mighty hard fight*
> *I'm not tired yet!*

Chris D always backed the truck in at the stadium before giving Brown a few minutes of solitary quiet time. Eventually the big man would lumber out and make his way to the Karr sideline. After kick-off, Brown would stand on one end of the coaches' box and Chris D would venture to the opposite end. Unlike many offensive play callers, Brown doesn't use a "script"—a predetermined sequence, regardless of the defense, of the first fifteen or twenty plays. He doesn't even hold a list of possible plays. Instead, he coaches and makes calls based on feel and what the defense shows him. Though Brown says his playbook contains hundreds of possibilities, there are games in which he'll call slight variations of the same ten plays. "Casino," a short route to the flat, is perfect for a lanky running back such as Leonte, especially on second and long. "Z-hunt," the killshot play with two deep posts, is tailor-made for a big and fast receiver such as Fat. "Twist," a high-low read that requires the quarterback to assess a defensive back's movement immediately after the snap, is ideal for a smart and instinctive player such as Leonard.

Before Brown calls a play, he surveys the defensive front and talks into his headset to Chris D. Standing thirty yards away and evaluating the secondary, Chris D relays what he's seeing. Then Brown makes his choice—"Jet Daytona right stick draw," for instance, is the simplest play in the book: a handoff to the tailback and a run up the middle. Nick then translates the words into signals, which the quarterback interprets and shares with his ten teammates.

He'll then take his place in the shotgun formation to evaluate the defense for himself. He can determine whether or not to make an adjustment or send a receiver in motion to confirm or challenge what he sees. He then lifts his hands waist-high, as if to prepare for the snap, before Karr's quarterback, running back, and receivers all twist their bodies in unison toward the sideline. This is Brown's final opportunity to overrule the quarterback's read. He can either issue a last-second change or stick with the original play.

This happens fifty times a game, each time unfolding in no more than thirty-nine seconds. When the ball is finally snapped, the offense and Karr's sideline usually know precisely where it's headed and roughly how many yards are at stake. But not always, especially against the state's best defenses. But Brown and Chris D have a hack for that, too. Brown often calls a play during Karr's first possession, a trial balloon just to see if their preparation, planning, and eyes were worth a damn.

"We didn't give a fuck if it worked," Chris D says. "We didn't give a shit if we threw an interception."

This is chess, not checkers, and football is a game that requires foresight, sequencing, and a willingness to sacrifice. What coaches get in exchange is more valuable than a single possession, turnover, even a touchdown. It's verification, even in the first quarter, that Karr is winning tonight. More than likely in a blowout.

"We'd be like: 'This is it. This is the answer,'" Chris D says. "The next time we're going to score on one play. And by the time they figure out what we're doing and adjust, we've got thirty-five points on the board."

THREE WEEKS BEFORE the 2019 season began, Chris D was on Karr's practice field when his phone rang. The voice on the other end asked him a question. Chris D said yes.

For the previous four seasons, Karr had achieved what few football programs ever do: consistent, formidable success. There weren't just ambitious, highly talented players walking these halls. There wasn't just a genius, no-nonsense coach with an exacting style and intricate scheme. And there wasn't just a staff of assistant coaches, some offering love and others fear, each providing a different perspective on matters of background, worldview, even race.

It has become cliché to call successful teams a result of "chemistry." But that's what this was: a cluster of individual elements that, when combined with heat and shock, can be either explosive—or fuse into something else entirely.

Recommending Chris D in 2014 had indeed been Brown's riskiest gambit. But he had been the final, occasionally unstable addition to the Karr compound. He ingratiated himself into the local culture to such a degree that his New Jersey accent disappeared, replaced with a Louisiana drawl, and he went to a Black-owned barbershop every two weeks for a high-top fade. Nick Foster granted him "honorary Black status" during training camp in July 2019, and Chris D was so at ease here that some players actually believed he *was* Black, albeit with extremely fair skin.

Joe, who'd never met a white person before Chris D, remained skeptical about the coach's race even after Brown corrected him.

"They got white people in Africa," Joe insisted.

"You really just don't know what you're talking about," Brown said.

"I'm saying, like, how he talk."

In Brown's first four seasons as head coach, the program would compile a 53–6 record while outscoring opponents by an average of twenty-four points. It reached the state championship game all four years. After the 2018 title, Chris D held the championship trophy and cried, wondering aloud if he had somehow stumbled into the most important and fulfilling work of his life.

But there was another reason he wept, for deep down he knew there were no worlds left to conquer. Not in high school, anyway. He and Brown joked sometimes about graduating and taking their system to college. Both men secretly wanted to test it. Brown had been approached by college programs after the 2017 and 2018 seasons, but he kept returning to Karr, its dingy halls and cluttered football office, its comfort.

Chris D, though, applied to college jobs he was convinced he'd never get. But on the practice field that day it was the head coach calling from the University of Virginia's College at Wise. The tiny outpost, whose campus is in Virginia's foothills near the Tennessee border, needed an assistant offensive line coach. And though the timing stunk, at least for Karr, Chris D couldn't say no.

He spent a restless night wondering how he'd tell the players. A few had spent nights at his house after fights with relatives, and because he never did get good at saying no to a hungry kid, Chris D spent evenings driving for Uber so he could slip one of his linemen a couple bucks without going broke. But more than that, he worried about what he'd say to Brown. The season opener against John Curtis was less than a month away, the offense needed further tweaks, and overall the roster was a mess.

When he walked into Brown's office the next day, explaining his decision from the fake leather sofa, the burly man asked why he was acting like this. This was an amazing opportunity, Brown told him, precisely what they'd dreamed about.

"*Go*, motherfucker," the boss said. They finished the conversation by imagining working together again someday. Maybe this time Brown would call plays on head coach Chris D's staff.

Chris D loaded his truck and started toward rural Virginia, leaving Brown without his right-hand man, disciplinarian, and social X-factor. But there was no time to mope, so Brown kept sadness at a distance by retreating into his football lab.

He promoted Ronald Davis to replace Chris D as offensive line coach, though Brown worried the inexperienced and laid-back Ronald wouldn't get into players' faces as much as Chris D had. He deputized Nick as the team's enforcer and top assistant, though Nick was increasingly distracted by job and health crises. Nick had lost his teaching position before the season, and his father, Ethridge Foster Sr., was diagnosed with dementia. Nick himself has diabetes, and his brother was recently admitted to the hospital with pneumonia.

Brown tried empowering his two wide receivers coaches, Mike Thompson and Omari Robertson, by giving them more authority. But each kept disappointing Brown, who called them out for tiny infractions. Their deadly sin, in truth, was that neither was Chris D.

Brown's best friend was gone, off pursuing a dream they'd once shared. He kept refusing to confront this reality, the very thing he forces his players to do on a daily basis, and Brown indeed kept struggling. He could seem reactive and withdrawn, and as always therapy came in locating and attempting to erase the weaknesses of others. During the Warren Easton game, Brown wandered toward the receivers during half-time. Mike was providing an animated talk, and Brown tried to interject.

"We good," Mike told him dismissively. Seeing this as a show of disrespect in front of players, Brown blew up. Though everyone could agree that telling the boss to effectively go away is a bad idea, it was more slip of the tongue than purposeful act of insubordination.

Brown kept stewing, and late that night he called Mike into his office and said he was thinking of firing him. While he made up his mind, Mike would be suspended from the next day's staff meeting. Brown ultimately kept Mike on staff, but not without additional con-sequences. Though Mike and Omari are supposed to be equals, they interpret most everything as a symbol of their dominance. Mike, for instance, stands on the sidelines during games and Omari watches from the press box. Knowing Mike views this as a symbol of his authority, Brown switched the coaches' roles, sending Mike to the press box and the game-day hinterlands, effectively a demotion.

Brown made a big deal about Omari using this as a moment to take charge, and in fact become the next Chris D, albeit with some recalibration of his own. Omari had shown a glimpse of passion and urgency during the training camp scuffle with Fat. Though nobody was exactly proud of how that'd gone down, Brown wanted to see more of that from Omari—more sparks, if not explosions.

But Omari was perpetually, and frustratingly, laid-back. His eyes are sleepy, and his voice is monotone. Brown kept trying to inspire him. He invited Omari to chart plays and look for patterns, one of Chris D's old jobs. Brown sometimes complained that Omari's play designs were uncreative and that he sometimes didn't process information quickly enough. He rolled his eyes when Omari tried to impress his boss with confidence.

"Their secondary is terrible. It should be Bombs Over Baghdad," he said during the staff meeting before the Catholic game. "We should put up fifty."

Brown raised his eyebrows skeptically and laughed. He then chided his assistant for creating false expectations. It was just the latest example of everyone continuing to disappoint the boss.

THREE DAYS BEFORE CATHOLIC, the team is out of sync. Monday practices are for installing Brown's newest plays and familiarizing players and coaches with terminology and hand signals. Tuesday is for repetition, the first steps of the slow march toward perfection.

But that seems a mighty distance from here, as wide receiver Darrell Hills keeps running the wrong route and dropping passes.

"What the *fuck* are we doing?" Omari shouts. "God-fucking-DAMN!"

Brown ambles by, watching Leonard and the receivers during a seven-on-seven drill. There's no pass rush, so this is supposed to be easy. But Leonard's timing is off, in part because the offensive line has been decimated by injuries and Leonard is overcompensating and rushing his throws. Joe Hayes, the team's center and timekeeper, has been out with a high-ankle sprain since the season's third week. Left tackle Kenny Bannister, the line's most naturally gifted blocker, hasn't been healthy all season. Even at the skill positions, Fat's hip hasn't felt right since he dislocated it in spring practice, wide receiver Aaron Anderson hurt his knee against John Curtis, and running back Kevin Marigny's shoulder and ankle have been bothering him. Leonte usually complains of *something* debilitating, though Brown and Karr's trainer have discovered that if they just let Leonte moan for a while, his injuries tend to improve.

But Leonard is in hero mode, trying to improvise with thread-the-needle passes. This isn't what Brown's offense is designed for; it's a symphony, after all, not a jazz ensemble. In Leonard's study session with Brown this morning, the quarterback struggled to recognize coverages and spot weaknesses against Catholic, which uses multiple defensive fronts and frequent shifts.

Karr just doesn't seem like itself this week, and it has made for a noticeably tense environment. Leonard sails another pass over Fat's head, Dany'e Brooks drops another easy catch, Darrell is still confused. Leonard walks toward him to explain his assigned route.

"Don't . . . tell him . . . *SHIT*!" Omari screams. Even Brown is surprised by the reaction.

Wednesday and Thursday practices come and go, and on Friday morning players board buses and coaches carpool to Baton Rouge. Officer Pat, who replaced Chris D as Brown's game-day chauffeur, navigates the Silverado toward Louisiana's capital city as Brown chews his nails. Leonard wasn't exactly stellar on his written test yesterday, and Brown knows Catholic's defense will have some surprises waiting.

Officer Pat pulls the truck through a stadium gate, and Brown climbs out to learn that Tiga, the team's loyal but occasionally forgetful equipment man, left Karr's Gatorade back in New Orleans. It has just been one of those weeks.

"No what the fucks," Brown mumbles. It's an oldie but a goodie. Tiga and several freshmen tear-ass across the field to ask Gabe Fertitta, Catholic's head coach, to borrow a water hose.

The coach invites them to help themselves, and he overhears Tiga and Marv instructing players to be careful with the fucking hose, to fill the fucking coolers, to put the fucking hose back on the fucking cart just the fucking way it was. Fertitta grew up in New Orleans and makes his living as a football coach, so he doesn't exactly have virgin ears. But he nonetheless chuckles at the differences in the two programs' approaches. Catholic High, an all-boys private school with $12,000-a-year tuition, fields a football team that's about 70 percent white. Fertitta's players are, in many cases, children of privilege and means—kids who may not be fluent in the language of Karr men.

"That kid learned a life lesson," Fertitta would say. "We just borrowed something that doesn't belong to us, and we're gonna make sure we return the thing exactly the way we borrowed it. If it had ten F-bombs in it, so what?"

Fertitta, as it happens, is fascinated by these cultural contrasts, and of the stereotypes that often follow white and Black schools into games. A day earlier, he'd posted on Twitter that fans would see that Catholic has big, strong, fast athletes and that Karr is "extremely [disciplined] and well coached." The inverses of each notion was just as true.

About an hour before kickoff, players head up a hill and into the visitors' locker room. Norm is waiting for them with a message he has been crafting all week. He wants players to imagine what their parents, grandparents, and ancestors had felt—and to try to channel that energy into their play. Tonight, he tells them, can be an equalizer. Tonight, Karr can prove its players take a back seat to no one.

"They think we dumb. Think we're undisciplined. Think we were late for practice," Norm tells players. "We've got a lack of respect, and they get *all* the respect. So again: just like any other young Black kid, we've gotta—what?"

"Prove ourselves," the kids say.

"Just fucking prove ourselves again," Norm says. "And again and again and again and *again* until that bitch over, and *you* make a n—— bow down."

The door opens, and players pull on their helmets and spill onto the field. The sun dips behind the bleachers of Memorial Stadium, a horseshoe-shaped structure that's nearly seventy years old. Players line up for "The Rock," and Nick screams at the cluster for being disorganized and sloppy even now.

That much doesn't change once the ball goes up. Karr commits a personal foul on its first possession. Brown reminds Leonard on the sideline to stop rushing his passes, assuring him he can take an extra second or two to read Catholic's defense. It keeps changing its defensive front and adding a safety on certain plays, and it's clear the Bears' attempts to confuse him and restrict the center of the field are working. With Aaron injured and Fat a target of double teams, Leonard's most athletic receiving options are unavailable.

Karr's defense isn't helping. It keeps missing tackles, making the Bears' quarterback, Jackson Thomas, look like Lamar Jackson. Karr allows two touchdowns in forty-seven seconds.

Shortly before halftime, Leonard finally looks comfortable and leads the offense toward the end zone. Brown calls a time-out to talk about "Twist," the high-low read play that's a Leonard specialty. When Catholic shows Cover 3 match, a variation of the three-deep defense in which inside cornerbacks "match" the routes of the slot receivers, Brown will call the play for what should be a touchdown. All Leonard has to do is read the nickel corner after the snap. He'll either be covering the receiver running a seam route, or the one who'll run a comeback. He can't be in two places at once, so one of the receivers will be wide open.

Leonard returns to the field, and Catholic falls into Brown's trap. But after the snap, Leonard panics. The nickel is assigned to the seam, but Leonard ignores Reynaud Shields, who's open on the comeback. He sees Fat running deep downfield, and he throws toward him. Leonard watches as the ball floats, as if in slow motion, directly to safety Michael Cerniauskas, who steps out of his zone assignment and intercepts the pass. He returns it ninety-eight yards for a touchdown.

Brown removes his headset and slams it on the turf. Leonard slinks back to the sideline and tries to hide. Brown finds him, demanding to know what the hell he saw. Leonard offers that Fat ran the wrong route, which isn't true and isn't just a way to compound his mistake. It's a glimpse at Leonard's worst instinct, trying to save himself with a lie.

"Sit your ass down," Brown yells. Leonard heads to the bench as reserve quarterback Khamani Simmons pulls on his helmet, jogs onto the field, and immediately throws an interception of his own.

In this moment, Brown makes several decisions. The first is that Leonard will be experiencing the rest of this game from the sideline. The next is that Karr's problems, its psychological roadblocks, might be bigger than even Brown had been willing to admit.

"Learn from this shit," Brown screams toward Leonard during half-time. The quarterback stares forward and says nothing, having been silenced once more.

Leonard II sits with his family in the bleachers, wondering aloud about Brown's strategy. Why isn't his son going back onto the field? Why do coaches seem willing to concede defeat? After two quarters, Brown has decided Karr cannot keep up with Catholic. Trying to do so could lead only to more injuries. The 47–12 loss will be the most lopsided defeat in Brown's head coaching career and the worst since St. Paul's won by twenty-seven points four years earlier.

When the scoreboard completes its cruelly slow tick-down, Norm heads up the hill. He and other assistant coaches wait for Brown.

"I'm not ready for this tongue-lashing," Norm says. But when Brown reaches the crest, he's surprisingly calm. He made his peace earlier, not just with this whooping but perhaps with the fate of the season, too.

"When you're coaching football," he tells his staff, "it teaches you humility. My concern is the want-to of the senior leadership—the drive and purpose. They think they can just show up and win."

Nobody says anything. Maybe that's part of the problem. Everybody, players and coaches, keep waiting on someone else to save them. Brown continues.

"This game was won on Tuesday," he says.

Brown finishes, the coaches say a quick prayer, and Officer Pat heads off to retrieve Brown's Silverado.

"Let's get the hell out of Baton Rouge," Norm says.

"Hell," Brown says, "they're gonna *kick* us out."

FOR THIRTEEN AGONIZING DAYS, Brown tried twisting his coaching Rubik's Cube. Karr had an open date after the Catholic game, and this provided time to experiment—and, of course, to sulk.

This team bad, Brown texted Chris D during a particularly dark moment.

Though Brown's ultimate message is only loosely tied to football, he knows his power to shape young lives off the field is tied to his success on it. Suiting up for Karr and competing on Louisiana's grandest stage is an ambition. But if the program fails to win a state championship, endures a rebuilding season, or starts losing, will Brown's influence dissolve? He already worries the kids have started tuning him out. Though he tries to project the air of a man above such worry, he deeply fears that the downside to gaining the power to change lives is that he'll inevitably lose it.

So rather than accept that this team is "fucked-up" or just bad, Brown kept trying to hack his own program. The answer, as he and Chris D always told each other, was in there somewhere.

He decided everyone here was just a little too pampered. He took away Leonard's car and considered stripping Joe and others of their captaincies. He threatened cruel and unusual punishment: players rolling, shoulder over shoulder, the length of the field. He tried exhausting them, attempting to make them so physically miserable that they'd change.

"A late player is a lazy player," Brown barked at them one afternoon, during an endless series of core exercises. "A lazy player is a loser."

He blew his whistle to initiate fifty more Russian twists. Then fifty more in-and-out crunches. Then fifty more seconds of sled holds. Leonard and Leonte moaned between sets, and a few of the meatier offensive linemen could barely lift their heads. But after forty-nine seconds, Brown blew the whistle again and accused one player—*you know who you are*—of relaxing one second early.

"You guys think you're all the way there, and you'll be one play short," he said. The truth was no player had quit early. He just wanted to make a point. "You can't be satisfied with that. It's got to make you uncomfortable to have somebody take the easy way out. You gotta believe in shit like that. Again!"

He kept tinkering with his coaching staff. He needed to find the right balance of fresh eyes and energy, experience and wisdom. Coaches had grown complacent, too.

But what else could he do?

One day he called Chris D with an idea. Karr already had two wide receivers coaches, Mike and Omari. But for different reasons, they tested Brown's patience. Mike had his head in the clouds too often and seemed too interested in being players' friend. Omari could be emotionally distant and too reserved.

Brown told Chris D that he'd be adding a third wide receivers coach. At least on the field, it seemed entirely unnecessary—tinkering for tinkering's sake. But the kids needed a jolt, so one day he called a specialist named Alan Boyd and coaxed him out of retirement.

Boyd is middle-aged and detail oriented, built strong as if he shares genes with a wheelbarrow. He's loud and profane, even for Karr, and he wears a purple "KC"—Karr Cougars—hat backward. He's tireless when it comes to throwing passes to receivers, and he doesn't mind being Brown's bad guy.

There's another reason Brown thinks Boyd can shake up the team. Though he's just another pawn on a psychological chessboard, there's something that makes him different here. Perhaps his very presence will make everyone a bit less comfortable. Alan Boyd, loud, confrontational, and kind of mean, also happens to be white.

CHAPTER 5

ONE FOOT IN

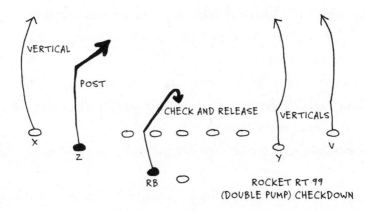

ONE NIGHT AFTER PRACTICE, Joe asks Brown for a lift back to his apartment. The coach agrees, on one condition: they stop on the way to get dinner together. Joe doesn't say no.

Along with Tiga, who almost always catches a ride from Brown, they walk into Karr's dimly lit front parking lot and climb into the Silverado. He navigates the truck south, to the suburb of Harvey and one of the big man's favorite haunts: New Orleans Seafood & Spirits. It's a high-end spot with a vast assortment of menu options, many of them just as Brown likes them: fried.

Joe's dining choices usually consist of either the Hot 'n Spicy Mc-Chicken sandwich or two cheeseburgers and fries. The truth is he's a little intimidated. Brown is just hungry, though, and he sees this as a chance to broaden Joe's horizons.

A host leads Brown, Joe, and Tiga to a square table near the back of the restaurant. Joe eyes the plates on other tables packed with massive portions. They take their places, a server approaches with tall glasses, and Joe watches as the man fills each glass with ice water. Brown immediately gets down to business, studying the menu.

"Now look," Brown says. "These voodoo rolls 'bout to fuck your head up."

Joe has no idea what a voodoo roll is, or what to expect from this experience. With his mother locked up and his money running out, he has recently taken to going to bed hungry. He stares at the menu as if it's written in a different language—which, frankly, it kind of is.

"The Catfish Lafayetta, you might like that," Brown says, having ordered it many times. "You like fried fish?"

"Anything fried," Joe says. Brown purses his lips as if to say: *Now we're talking.*

The server returns, removing a notepad for what will be a king's feast: cups of crawfish chowder and a dozen buttery chargrilled oysters with extra bread. Brown orders two servings of voodoo rolls, which are crawfish tails and a cheesy stuffing packed inside a spring roll wrapper and fried. They haven't yet decided on main courses.

"I'm gonna do an Arnold Palmer sweet," Brown tells the server, who turns to Joe.

"Arnold Palmer sweet," he says.

The stranger disappears, and Joe relaxes his shoulders. He thought Brown was taking him to Golden Corral, the all-you-can-eat cafeteria that's a crowd favorite during Karr road trips. Before tonight, that's the nicest restaurant Joe has ever been to. That or maybe IHOP.

The soup arrives first, and Joe watches as Brown looks the server in the eye and thanks him. Joe does the same. Brown begins explaining one of his many food-based theories: that soup is highly polarizing. After all, some people crumble saltines into the bowl, and others dip a full cracker into the broth. It's obvious he has passionate thoughts on these matters, and that either choice is a peek into someone's soul. Brown, presenting his single cracker, is a dipper. Into the soup it goes.

Joe opens his packet, removes a cracker, and dips it. Brown grumbles about the missing Arnold Palmers. He points out the restaurant is busy and the server should be trusted to get it right.

"You don't even know that man to trust him," Joe says. He looks suspiciously at Brown.

A moment later the drinks, half sweet iced tea and half lemonade, arrive alongside two heaping plates of voodoo rolls. Joe watches Brown carefully unfold his cloth napkin and place it in his lap. Joe again follows. Then he slides a voodoo roll onto his plate and takes a crunchy bite of the rich, cheesy, fatty goodness. This isn't just food. For someone used to boiled cabbage and McDonald's, it's a fucking revelation. Joe raises his eyebrows to note the dance occurring between his taste buds and brain.

Brown is still studying the menu, trying to think of a meal that's new to Joe but isn't so exotic it'll scare him off. The Catfish Lafayetta is still calling to him.

"So check this out," Brown says. "They're gonna have fried catfish, and they're gonna top it with crawfish stew."

"All right: gumbo," Joe says. At least he has heard of that.

"*Noooo*, motherfucker," Brown says. "Look. Catfish *topped* with crawfish stew, over rice."

This isn't just a dish the coach wants to introduce to Joe. It's a world he has never visited, but one Brown wants him to know, appreciate, and strive for. Joe laughs at how strongly his coach feels about all this.

"You've got to learn to appreciate some of this stuff," Brown says. "I used to think McDonald's was the best, too."

ALMOST TWO DECADES EARLIER, a kid a lot like Joe was struggling to find his place at Karr and beyond. Like Joe, he didn't like to go home or be alone. He was also thoughtful and curious but often retreated into his own mind, even in the company of others.

Doc's friends would tease him mercilessly. They were interested in dating and drinking, and Doc was perfectly happy going to a parade with his grandmother. He liked sprawling Sunday dinners and singing in the choir. He preferred talking about things like Greek mythology and astronomy, matters of depth and mystery that are impossible to fully explore.

Karr's varsity basketball coach was a short white man named Roch Weilbacher. Weilbacher saw that Doc's mind worked differently, as if he were someone bound for the high sciences or medicine.

Though Doc didn't play basketball at Karr—he was a dedicated football player—Coach Roch liked having him around the team. He had a solution for his aversion to solitude: Doc would be the team's water boy. He tagged along on road trips, and Roch invited him to sit with coaches during pregame meals. Roch had learned that hungry kids don't just eat alongside the person who feeds them. They open up. They talk. Eventually they trust.

These days, Roch is the only person who calls Brown anything but "Coach" or "Brice" or "B." Indeed, to Roch Weilbacher, Brice Brown will always be "Doc." And with Brown's uncanny recall, he can reconstruct certain moments that have been seared into his memory. What he was doing when Katrina hit. Tonka's death. His first state championship as a head coach. Another of those images is the time Roch took the basketball team to Semolina, a kitschy Italian place in suburban Metairie. Brown, used to his football coaches providing pizza or burgers with strawberry soda after games, can remember the gloss of the laminated menu at Semolina and the ecstasy he felt at considering so many possibilities.

He ordered a dish called Shrimp Roban. Though he had no idea what it was, Roch assured him that getting something new was part of the fun. Brown dug in, momentarily ignoring that the dish comes with scallions and that he hates vegetables. (Many years later, among the spoils of being a successful head coach is that most everyone in your kingdom goes along with everything you say. This includes Brown's dubious insistence that he's allergic to "green"—not *greens* but green, the color. He claims he can eat nothing of the sort without a severe reaction.) The rich, buttery Shrimp Roban was like opening the door to an alternate world.

"This is how you eat when you make it," Brown would recall thinking. He took bite after intoxicating bite.

With the young man distracted, Roch asked Doc what he really wanted to know: *How's Scoota doing?*

Scoota was Roch's shooting guard, a handsome and charismatic young man named Guy Henderson. (Yes, Roch had a nickname for everyone.) Guy and Brown had grown up together in the Cut-Off, and Guy was everything Brown wasn't: gregarious, comical, social. Still, they were best friends. Guy was the Karr football team's quarterback, and Brown was his 260-pound left tackle. He was the player literally responsible for protecting Guy's rear end. He did so on and off the field, though Guy sometimes moved so fast that Brown couldn't keep up.

Guy liked to skip class and chase girls. Brown says now that Guy had one foot in the Karr program and one foot out. This, he'd teach his own players much later, is untenable. You have to be fully committed or, well, gone. Back then it was usually Brown who tried talking sense into Guy. He reminded him practice was important, and that even small mistakes could affect his future. Another reason Brown's friends made fun of him was because he was the kid who did everything right. Guy, not so much. But they did have one powerful, if grim, thing in common: both their fathers had been murdered. Around here that's as good a thing to bond over as any.

In 1999, Guy Henderson Sr. had been gunned down in the Cut-

Off following a dispute about money. The trauma seemed to scar Guy Jr., or at least convince him life is short and better lived hard. Brown, on the other hand, was a toddler when his dad, Burnell, was stabbed near an intersection close to the Fischer Projects. Brown, for his impressive memory, only remembers his grandmother telling him that his father was dead. It's possible Brown never followed up, or never got curious, or just doesn't like talking about it. Regardless, all Brown has to say about this subject is that his daddy died right there on the sidewalk.

Because of this link and others, Scoota trusted Doc. But he didn't always listen to him. He'd sometimes sneak out the school's back door, prowl the streets of Algiers, show back up for football practice with red eyes. Occasionally "Brother Nick," or what Roch called running back and defensive lineman Nick Foster, would be with Scoota as they roamed the backstreets. Doc was no good with girls and lacked the stomach for anything illicit. Usually he was content playing spades with family.

"Old man shit," Nick would say later. He says Brown was a forty-year-old man trapped in the body of a fifteen-year-old. Guy was the silly one, Brown the straight man, Nick the social chameleon who could get along with anyone. Nick could be untamed one day and disciplined the next.

But Brown kept the other boys grounded and had a coach's temperament long before he actually was one. In truth that's the perfect makeup of a successful football team: rebels and rogues at the skill positions and scoring points, an austere protector or two making the machine work.

By the time Brother Nick, Doc, and Scoota were seniors and team captains in 2003, Karr wasn't among the best teams in Louisiana. But it was good. The offense thrived under new head coach Jabbar Juluke, who'd begun implementing the spread offense. Its concepts were demanding, fast, versatile—an offense with vast depth, and that could never be fully explored. Brown was in love.

Karr won six games in 2003 and entered the playoffs as the state's number ten seed. Its first opponent was South Terrebonne, a predominantly white school in the southeast Louisiana bayou town of Bourg. The Gators ranked twenty-third of the thirty-two playoff teams. They would travel to Algiers to face Karr on its home field.

But Karr, a heavy favorite, was tentative and disorganized: penalties, turnovers, dropped passes. When the final horn sounded, the scoreboard read South Terrebonne 24, Edna Karr 14. The Cougars' season was over, and so were the high school careers of three friends who'd formed the team's soul. They were devastated. Everyone was.

Juluke, in fact, seemed to take it harder than anyone. When the team made it back to campus and gathered in the gym, Juluke was crying. He couldn't bring himself to address players. They sat in the bleachers and looked at one another, and assistant coaches didn't budge. Wasn't someone going to say *something*?

Finally someone stood, walked down the stairs, and faced the players. It was Brown, who outside his group of friends rarely said anything. Weeks earlier, Brown's cousin had been shot dead on the streets of Algiers. His great-grandmother had recently died of natural causes. With so much pain and death coursing through his life and those of his teammates, it seemed absurd to consider a lost football game the end of anything.

"We feel like we failed. But the mistakes we made are small," the captain told his team. "The end gotta come."

THE THREE FRIENDS splintered after high school, though they promised to reunite. Nick enrolled at the University of Alabama at Birmingham and, without a football scholarship, walked onto the football team as a defensive end. Brown and Guy went to Grambling State, the iconic historically Black university in northwest Louisiana. They too were walk-on players for the football team.

Brown played college football not because he loved it but because he was good. It was a hobby as much as anything, something the cool kids do. He never thought there was a viable path to the NFL. At least not as a player. Instead, Brown wanted to be a civil engineer and take antiquated structures and make them more efficient and modern.

Guy, for his part, didn't think far into the future. Today had the potential to be too much fun to be worrying about tomorrow. Instead of remaining on campus to study his playbook, he'd return to New Orleans on weekends to work the concession stands at Behrman Stadium or the Superdome. He'd make a wad of cash, have a good time, then head back to school.

"A wild card" is how former Grambling coach Melvin Spears describes Guy.

Spears had trouble connecting with Guy, who didn't return to Grambling after his freshman year. But he had no such trouble with Brown. Their minds worked in strangely similar ways. Spears had spent a few years coaching high school and college football in the 1990s, but he walked away to take a job as a mathematician and software programmer with Honeywell and Motorola. He worked on a 1997 project called Iridium, which launched sixty-six connected satellites into orbit to form a "constellation" that'd span the globe with Motorola communication services.

When he wasn't thinking about a $5 billion enterprise that relied on rockets launching from Russia, China, and the United States, Spears's mind sometimes drifted back to football. The way he saw it, defensive players could cover only a finite amount of terrain. So Spears mentally separated the field into vertical quadrants. Factoring in a safety's responsibility of covering the back portion of, say, a depth of thirty yards, eleven defenders must cover forty-eight hundred square feet of territory. It's impossible, which is why the most efficient defense is the "zone," which assigns players to patrol a small area of the field.

But rather than predicting where those defenders *might* be, what if Spears could use pre-snap motions and other identifiers to know where those players *would* be? Basketball players use open space to their advantage, and they take the ball up the court knowing the play could change at any moment. Teams use movement as a weapon and attack, and adjust, based on how the defense is trying to stop them. Football teams, at least traditionally, run their offenses precisely as drawn and just dare the defense to stop them. Spears wanted to invert that convention and borrow from basketball. So he took principles from the "Stretch" concept, which assigns number values to what the quarterback and the offensive linemen are seeing from the defense and allows for change right up to the snap. He merged this with the "West Coast" offense, which spaces the defense out across the field— expanding the terrain it must cover with four or five receivers. Legendary San Francisco 49ers coach Bill Walsh used the "West Coast" offense to win three Super Bowls.

When Spears went to Grambling as an assistant coach for Doug Williams in 1998, he brought these ideas with him. Players were understandably confused by an offense Spears called the "Tiger Stretch." But in actuality, it couldn't have been simpler. In those days, the spread was still a novel concept in college, and defenses barely bothered to conceal their intentions. Spears and his offense helped Grambling win three consecutive Black college national championships. When Williams took a job with the NFL's Tampa Bay Buccaneers in 2004, Spears replaced him as head coach.

Brown and Guy were members of his first team, and became subjects in his football experiments. They watched loads of film, including basketball footage, and were sent to ROTC military science classes to learn discipline. They went to Toastmasters International meetings to learn communication. Spears's quarterbacks didn't just have to be perceptive and athletic. They had to be, as the coach puts it, "presidential."

"The guy that leads the whole army," Spears says. Grambling's commander in chief was someone interested in a role in student government and who dressed and looked and spoke like a leader.

If Spears's quarterback was the team's face, Grambling's offensive linemen were its brain. Blockers were expected to recognize and understand not only their assignments, but opposing defenses' movements and tendencies, too. If the defense adjusted during the game, the offensive line could sense it was coming.

Though some freshmen struggled to grasp the coach's abstract methods, Brown took to them almost immediately. Each week Spears gave each offensive player a written test, one of several techniques Brown would bring to Karr. Brown almost always aced his exam and tutored other players on complex plays, such as "Rocket Rt 99," which has four deep receiving routes and which Spears says players nicknamed "bin Laden" because Grambling used it to bomb opposing defenses. On plays such as that, Brown didn't even have to study. He could just visualize the moving parts in his mind.

"He sees it all," Spears would recall of his star pupil. Still, at six feet tall, Brown didn't actually play much.

He completed most of his academic requirements in three years, but Brown still needed internship credit to graduate from Grambling. It so happened that Karr offered just such an internship in its physical education department. Brown could coach football and learn at Juluke's feet, then return to Grambling for whatever lay ahead. By then the young man had fallen in love with the game and its nuance, in particular the way both can be manipulated. He dreamed of coaching for the New Orleans Saints, or maybe Louisiana State or Alabama.

Following Brown's internship, he told Spears he was forgoing his final year of eligibility as a player. He wanted a head start in coaching, and Karr had an entry-level job available on its football staff. He never went back to Grambling. The months turned into years, Brown kept discovering new hacks, and Juluke kept promoting him. He was calling plays at age twenty-five and was a head coach by thirty. He gave up on his dream of coaching the Saints, and if stepping-stones toward his dreams presented themselves, Brown either ignored or missed them. He says now that he has become a "prisoner" of his own success, and he now warns players and assistant coaches to avoid falling into a trap.

Periodically Brown checked in on Nick and Guy, both still kind-hearted and lovable, both still drawn to the fast lane. Nick had given up on some of his own dreams, including becoming a dentist. He sold pills on occasion, he says now, or a few ounces of weed. On occasion he took on bigger risks, and those come with a fatter payday. Nick says he transported drugs from Birmingham to Atlanta. A successful trip could score him about $10,000.

Then one day the blue lights hit, and Nick found himself in the Jefferson Parish Correctional Center. He says he was stripped, searched, shackled. To make matters worse, Nick's mother had recently been diagnosed with cancer. He dreaded confessing his mistake to her. Nick says he spent two weeks in jail before ultimately being sentenced to probation. In that time, he promised himself that he'd never embarrass himself, or his family, ever again.

But how would he make a living? One day he called an old friend and asked for advice. Brown invited Nick to stop by Karr one afternoon so they could talk. By then Brown was offensive coordinator, and Juluke listened to him on personnel decisions. After his conversation with Nick, Brown talked Juluke into hiring him to work with Karr's running backs. He would learn Brown's modified version of the "Tiger Stretch," which by 2013 Karr had adopted and would use to reach the Louisiana state championship game four years in a row. The attack is a scaled-down version of the offense used by Andy Reid, the Super Bowl champion NFL coach, and relies on run-pass option plays and a quarterback who must make split-second decisions.

Nick showed an aptitude for conceiving new plays and shifts. But he was most valuable to the Karr staff because he had something Brown lacked: experience in society's underbelly. He could speak the language of the streets with a proficiency Brown never could. Nick is built like a Pontiac GTO: low to the ground and sturdy. He doesn't so much look at your face as he studies it, searching for clues into your soul or at least your intentions. Nick has no problem admitting he doesn't trust strangers, or (at least initially) white people. His face is round, though he has lost most of the chub from his days as a defensive lineman, and on game days he is recognizable because of his backward visor and a slight pigeon toe. His intellect, immaculately groomed beard, and thin-rimmed glasses paint him not as a traditional football coach as much as the cool, understanding headmaster at a private school.

Nick's voice is his defining feature. It's gravelly and low, that GTO with a rusted-out muffler. He liberally decorates his sentences with calm, piercing profanity.

Brown told him, years ago, that when he addresses the kids, do so with honesty. Brutal honesty, if necessary. "Give 'em the real," everyone here says, and that often means communicating on players' level: curse words, thick accents, slang. Brown had been surprised by how Karr kids responded to his own stories. He'd earned trust by sharing that, like so many of them, he had been raised by strong, independent women. He, too, had experienced tragedy. He'd come of age wanting more than what he'd been born into, and he worked hard and achieved it.

Nick took this to a different level. He's capable of deep discussions about the future or the past, but his value here comes not from just a football mastery but his willingness to curse a kid out. He's comfortable being the bad guy. If Ronnie Jackson skipped practice again, it wasn't Brown who went looking for him. It was Nick going from drug house to drug house until he found him. Then he dragged Ronnie out and smacked him around on the sidewalk.

"A lot of them don't like confrontation," Nick says. "But it's the only way to get results."

Brown and Nick were realizing that football, at least here, has the power to offer direction and purpose to wandering souls. Brown called Guy sometimes, still looking for his footing nearly a decade after he left Grambling, and they'd talk about the old days. Usually Guy asked his old protector for a few dollars, just till he got back on his feet. Brown was terrible at saying no. But he hated himself for loaning Guy money again and again, so he usually sent Nick to make the handoff.

Brown nonetheless kept calling, not just trying to reconnect with Guy but to save him. Football had lifted Nick out of certain circumstances, and Brown suspected it could do the same for Guy. Brown refused to give up, still determined to protect his old friend's backside. If Guy didn't answer the first time Brown called, the coach would immediately call back. Guy always answered the second call.

Shortly after Karr's 2014 season ended, Brown called Guy once, then twice. He answered, and they talked about an idea Brown had: Guy could join the coaching staff. Perhaps working with kids could be a reset. Guy loved it. They agreed to meet for lunch on the final Monday of December.

That morning, Guy never called to confirm, and Brown shrugged it off. Just Guy being Guy. Brown instead invited Dennis Lore, a former longtime assistant coach at Karr, to ride with him to Lafayette to check in on a former player who was then in college. They'd stop at a seafood restaurant along the way and enjoy the big lunch Brown and Guy were supposed to have.

They were on Interstate 10 when Brown's phone chirped: **You hear about Guy?** He called Nick, who'd received a similar message—albeit with a few more details. Nick was already running across his front lawn, climbing into his car, speeding toward an intersection in Algiers not far from Behrman Stadium. Brown hung up with Nick and called Guy. He didn't pick up. Brown called a second time. Nothing.

"He always answers," Brown muttered. Lore pulled his truck onto the shoulder and lowered the radio.

A moment later, Brown's phone rang. When he answered, he heard Nick's gravelly voice. He was standing next to police tape, looking toward a ditch maybe two miles from where Guy's father had been shot dead years earlier.

From here he could see Guy's blue Kia, pocked on the driver's side with bullet holes. Nick's tone softened. He was looking at Guy now, dead in the driver's seat. Nick said he could see their old friend's arm dangling across the steering wheel.

THERE'S A REMARKABLE consistency in Brown's life, not just with the relentless tragedies and the way they've hardened into chronic anxiety and survivor's guilt. But also in how he deals with it all.

This is a man who, no matter what he accomplishes, deprives himself of joy. If emotion is a weakness, as he likes to say, satisfaction and happiness are not exempt. When Karr won its third consecutive state championship in December 2018, players and assistant coaches partied in the weight room and danced as Sheck Wes's "Mo Bamba" rattled the windows. Nick and Chris D cried and took pictures, wondering aloud if they'd reached their professional mountaintops. Brown, though, sat alone in his office and sipped from two kid-sized bottles of Powerade. He stared at a team photo taken a few days earlier and lamented how it could've turned out better.

Rather than take even a moment to reflect, Brown ruminated on a formidable to-do list and the coming stresses of the new year. He worried that, without the structure of football season, players he loved wouldn't just drift. They could die. The program, Brown has convinced himself, can change the lives of those who exist within it: Ronnie, Joe, even Nick. But once the season ends and everyone leaves that protective bubble, they become vulnerable. Brown doesn't drive around the city at night because he truly thinks he can save a kid's life. He does it to ease his restless mind, and to remind players that Big Brother Brice is out there. It's a way for him to tell himself he's doing *something*.

Brown also tells himself he's too busy to be happy. That there are higher priorities. Brown lives, though, as if he doesn't *deserve* happiness. His clothes are ratty, his truck is a wreck, self-care and even personal hygiene are a distant priority. Before the 2019 season, Brown said his coaching salary is $77,000 per year. He estimated that at least a third of that goes to clothing, feeding, and supporting people within his orbit. He hands out cash for staffers' travel, including parties and reunions he doesn't attend. He paid for one coach to attend a wedding in California. If someone's family cannot afford medical care, Brown reaches into his wallet.

Before Karr's prom in 2019, Brown drove Ronnie and Joe to a formalwear shop where they shopped for tuxes. Brown, meanwhile, usually plods about in weathered sneakers and a Karr hoodie he's had since 2010. Back then it was purple, but it's so faded now that it's more of a dark pink. The cuffs are frayed, and there are gaping holes in the elbows. Brown jokes that he should trash it. But 2010 was the year Tonka was Karr's starting quarterback, and he led the team to the state title game. Throwing away the hoodie would be to throw away a piece of Tonka, and that's something Brown just can't do.

There is one thing Brown allows himself, of course. It is perhaps the only thing that brings him visible joy: food. Since that fateful basketball team dinner at Semolina years ago, Brown has associated restaurants not just with pleasure and satisfaction but with success. He eats out several nights a week, ordering a bounty not just because he and his dining companions are hungry, but because he can. Brown has "made it," and he feels a responsibility to share.

In July 2019, Brown forgot his own birthday. He had driven a few Karr players to a summer football camp at the University of Houston. When Joe called to offer his greetings, Brown decided he'd celebrate by going to Pappadeaux, a popular seafood chain. He brought staff members and friends, and when the $400 bill came, the birthday boy slapped down his credit card.

This is common, even when his dining companion can afford to pay. Brown still has regular lunches with Coach Roch, who still refers to Brown as "Doc." One day Roch gently pointed out that Brown's weight seemed to be spiking. Never a slim man, Brown passed three hundred pounds while at Grambling. Friends suspect he surpassed three hundred fifty shortly after Guy's murder, when Brown was elevated to head coach twenty-six days after the funeral, and he seemed to stress-eat like never before. Nick urged him to seek actual therapy, and Brown did research it. But then he got busy again, supposedly, and never scheduled a session.

Among Brown's encyclopedia of slogans, one centers on self-sacrifice and is at once inspiring and alarming: "You have to give a life to save a life." This means that lifting up Karr's players and staffers comes at a steep cost, perhaps even the ultimate one.

Brown says he weighs three hundred eighty-seven pounds, though he admits in the next breath that it's been a long time since he actually stepped on a scale. Some colleagues suspect four hundred came and went long ago. Brown has gone years without seeing a doctor, partly because doctors hector you about bad habits. Though his and Chris D's friendship is ultimately rooted in advanced football, Brown also liked that Chris D never hounded him about ordering that extra side of pancakes or opening another Coke.

For reasons Brown himself admits are flawed, he has created a world in which he makes the rules. His community believes him (or at least doesn't challenge him) when he insists on a diet that may be harming him. There is no Coach Brown that Brice can ask for help, no one to offer him the kind of tough love he administers daily.

Behind the jokes and top-of-the-football-hierarchy machismo, the truth is that Brown occupies a demographic group that is more likely to suffer from depression and anxiety while being less likely to actually seek out professional help. Around here, asking for treatment in dealing with stress or trauma is seen as a show of weakness, even as men such as Brown are aware they inhabit a world in which Black men just die young. Deep down he believes he's no exception, and he pays little mind to the fact that his own choices could fulfill this prophecy. What was it he told his Karr teammates after losing to South Terrebonne in the 2003 playoffs? *The end gotta come.*

"A motherfucker like Brice," Nick says of his friend and boss, "he's gonna die the way he wanna die."

Surrounded by almost constant death, Brown simultaneously keeps surviving and punishing himself for doing so. Whatever he receives, and in fact earns, he either devalues or gives away—a burly, tattered Robin Hood of the gridiron. This seems to almost be the only way Brown can live with himself.

In July 2019, he sat in his dented truck while wearing his faded hoodie, watching his team during a special teams drill. Alex Moran, at the time the team's medical consultant and de facto trainer, walked up and offered a concern about players getting dehydrated. She volunteered to visit a nearby Walmart for gallon jugs of pickles, whose salty and vinegary brine is an old-school (and cheap) way to flood players' bodies with electrolytes.

"How many jars?" Moran asked, and Brown thought about it. Four or five, he finally estimated.

"Need some cash?" he said, reaching for his billfold.

ON THIS EVENING at New Orleans Seafood & Spirits, Brown leans back in his chair and exhales. Joe, who ordered a platter of fried catfish and shrimp with another side of shrimp, is still eating.

The server brings to-go boxes for Joe and Tiga, and the check. Brown explains to Joe the concept of tipping, which seems especially perplexing to the young man, just giving away money you don't have to. Brown tells him he's got a lot to learn.

"Put your napkin on the table," Brown instructs.

Bellies full, the three of them retreat to the Silverado. Tiga is in the passenger seat and Joe sits in the back. The truck isn't fancy, but it's safe—a four-wheeled extension of the Karr bubble. Brown puts it in gear and accelerates toward Algiers, a community with so many memories, good and bad. Brown doesn't say this to Joe, but he's struck by how the ripples of the past spread inevitably toward the present. Brown, so straitlaced and driven, once counted two of his Karr teammates as best friends. One, like Leonard Kelly, was carefree and likable, just a kid so preoccupied with having fun that he didn't always notice the traps in his path. The other, like Jamie Vance, could get along with anyone—someone who just came and went with the breeze.

It's one reason Brown is so drawn to Joe, because Brown *is* Joe, or at least he was. And he wants to show him the way forward, just without so much heartache. Maybe Joe can be the protector Brown wasn't, considering the coach still beats himself up for failing to save Guy.

With Joe's face illuminated by the glow of his iPhone, he tells Brown he'll be meeting his girlfriend, Cassidy. But she's afraid of

Joe's neighborhood, so she has asked to meet him at the McDonald's down the road.

Brown pulls into the well-lit parking lot, and Joe scans the vehicles.

"Right here, this silver car," he says. Browns pulls the truck next to a parked sedan.

Joe opens the door, the protective barrier pierced, and warm air rushes in. Joe steps out and pulls on the passenger-door handle of the silver car. But it's locked. It's the wrong vehicle. Brown is rattled, so many baked-in fears converging. Around here, a simple misunderstanding paired with bad timing can end a young life. Brown's voice is tense when he asks if Joe should call his girlfriend again. But, no, Joe remembers Cassidy's car is black, not silver, and he notices it parked along the road.

Brown takes a deep breath, an attempt at lowering his heart rate.

"All right, Coach," Joe says. "Love y'all."

"Good luck," Brown says. He watches Joe get into the car before backing out of the parking space.

He and Tiga are silent as Brown pulls onto General De Gaulle Drive. Every day, sometimes morning and night, Brown gives his equipment man and sidekick a ride. He appreciates Tiga's loyalty and, because Brown doesn't like to be alone, enjoys the company.

After a right onto Hancock Street in Old Algiers, Brown accelerates toward a cluster of small apartments and houses. On the right, maybe a hundred yards from Tiga's place, is McDonoghville Cemetery, and out among the tombs are the final resting places for Guy, Tonka, and Brown's father. All of them, right here.

Brown hasn't stepped into the graveyard since Tonka's funeral in 2016. He has never visited Guy's grave and in fact has gone years since seeing Guy's mother. Brown knows it'd dredge up emotions he has conditioned himself to ignore, and seeing Guy's old bedroom—untouched since his death—would bring back memories. He's just not ready to go there, neither into Guy's house nor into this shadowy corner of his mind.

He passes the cemetery and makes a left into a short driveway. Tiga climbs out carrying his to-go box. Brown says he'll see him in the morning before backing up and going back the way he came. He passes the graveyard on his left and says nothing, just a man with regrets who has found a steady way to punish himself day after day.

CHAPTER 6

TULANE AND BROAD

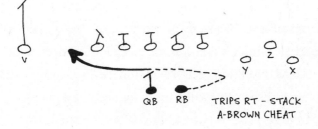

RHONDA GEORGE COULD SEE the detective from a distance, dancing and smiling, having a big time. Rayell Johnson was at a parade on the West Bank, dressed in his sky-blue New Orleans Police Department uniform.

Nearly three years had come and gone since Tonka died. Three years of Rhonda's solitary visits to McDonoghville Cemetery. Three years of Karr games, breakdowns, shouting matches against God. Johnson, the NOPD's most recognizable homicide detective, hadn't called Rhonda in months. No updates. No suspects. No nothing.

"Well, hello there," Rhonda told Johnson. The floats passed and the brass bands played. Her eyes narrowed.

The detective recognized her, and his shoulders dropped. His smile vanished. Young and well-built, he is identifiable not just because of his mocha skin and youthful freckles but because of his recurring appearances on the A&E police docudrama *The First 48*, a show that examines the critical first hours of a murder investigation. When shock is still raw, Johnson's celebrity and determination are often enough to bring hope to a shattered family. It's also no small thing that in a profession notorious for being disproportionately more white than the communities being policed, Johnson is Black. He's ambitious and successful, but he's not immune to frustration. He's overworked, and occasionally the NOPD temporarily reassigns him and other detectives to crowd control. After all, the city's image and revenue stream are tied to special events and tourism. Like so many other things, pausing investigations is just part of Johnson's job. It is for every NOPD detective.

But instead of sulking, Johnson sees these diversions as a chance to enjoy himself. Especially when the assignment is a parade.

"Ms. George, I . . ." he started to say, but Rhonda cut him off.

"You're out here walking the street," she'd recall saying. "But you can't call me back?"

He tried to explain. But Rhonda didn't care what he said. Didn't Johnson get it? Tonka wasn't just some name on a case file. This was her *son*.

Attempting to soothe a still-grieving mother, Johnson said he understood. He promised to call her Monday. Before turning to walk away, Rhonda told him not to bother.

ON THE EVENING of June 24, 2016, Johnson was at home when his phone rang. An email sent earlier that day listed his name in red type, meaning he was "up"—first in line to be assigned a murder. It's a strange thing for your phone to ring and know someone is dead, to consider the devastating reverberations already coursing throughout a family and a neighborhood and a city.

But that's the job. Just as Johnson got used to the sound of ribs being cracked open by a medical examiner and pools of blood at a crime scene, he learned to accept the realities of his work. Most of them, anyway.

"We've got a thirty," Johnson's supervisor told him. That's Louisiana police code for murder. A young man lay dead two miles from Johnson's home.

He changed clothes, sliding a dress shirt over bulging arms decorated with tattoos. Those are reminders of his other life. He snapped his own Glock 27, which he prefers over his department-issued pistol, into a leather shoulder holster and clipped NOPD badge number 1127 to his belt.

By the time he made it to Shirley Drive, a crowd had gathered. "Ah, who the hell is this?" Johnson would recall thinking. He wondered if the victim had been a celebrity.

He parked his Crown Vic on the shoulder and walked slowly toward the onlookers. Johnson listened, trying to overhear their chatter. Among the tentacles of New Orleans culture is a general avoidance of talking to the cops, apparently even as you lay dying. When the two young men were shot in Karr's front parking lot in February 2017, one of the victims refused to identify the gunmen as he clung to life in an ambulance. The eighteen-year-old literally took what he'd seen to his grave, not just because of legitimate fears of reprisal in a city that largely polices itself, but also because it's part of an unspoken, generations-old code.

But humans, here and in general, like to tell others when they know something juicy. Sometimes gossip is laced with truth: a physical description, a number of shooters, a vehicle. So Johnson walks slowly, listening for valuable pieces of information, taking mental notes. They're not talking to the cops directly, but they're also not keeping quiet about what they've seen or heard.

Johnson gets it, and he grew up distrusting the cops as much as anyone. He was born in 1981, a year after a white NOPD officer named Gregory Neupert drove his cruiser into the Fischer Projects. He went missing and was later found with his pistol still in its holster and his throat torn out by a bullet. Seven revenge-minded cops marched into the Fischer, rounded up Black residents, interrogated and tortured a few they believed to be witnesses. Some were beaten with phone books, others had plastic bags placed over their heads until they talked, and many were marched through the neighborhood at gunpoint. Those officers, who'd become known as the "Algiers 7," took what they'd learned and raided the homes of two individuals who may or may not have been involved in Neupert's death. Three people, including a resident's girlfriend, weren't arrested, charged, and brought to trial. They were shot dead in their own homes.

The FBI got involved, and a conspiracy indictment would be handed down. But a New Orleans judge threw out criminal charges against the seven cops. It became a bitter, if foreboding, chapter of US history four decades before persistent police violence against Black Americans led to viral social media videos, mass protests, and calls for comprehensive police reform.

Johnson grew up, therefore, in a New Orleans reeling in the immediate aftermath of this ugly period. Later, he says, he'd experience discriminatory policing for himself. When he was a teenager, a white NOPD officer stopped him, searched him, hauled Johnson off to jail for driving a vehicle that didn't belong to him. There was also a white woman's driver's license and Sam's Club card inside. The cop ignored the fact that Johnson worked for his father's rental car business and was returning the vehicle to the lot.

"Just, fuck y'all," he'd remember thinking about the police.

Because this is just what you do, Johnson refused to talk to investigators when a beloved cousin was gunned down. He got good at outrunning cops after sneaking into nightclubs, picking fights, occasionally selling drugs. Johnson failed out of Southern University in Baton Rouge and dreamed of being a rapper. He wrote rhymes about the juxtaposition of being blessed with intelligence but cursed by having been born in a place where ambitious Black boys sometimes bump their heads on low ceilings.

He alternated between the right and wrong sides of the law so often that Johnson sometimes imagined himself as a character with a split personality. "Ray-L" was a fledgling gangster who carried a gun and sold weed. "Rayell" was a straitlaced and fun-loving young man who, after Katrina wiped out his dad's business, took a job in the Sears tool department. "Rayell" was carefree and responsible, and he moved on to driving an armored truck. "Ray-L," meanwhile, fantasized about robbing that truck.

One day a colleague confessed that he'd be applying to the police academy. Johnson jokingly called his partner a turncoat, then he decided to submit an application of his own.

"How the fuck you gonna be a police?" Johnson says some friends said. Maybe they were joking about him selling out his own culture. Maybe not.

He nonetheless promised that'd never happen, instead suggesting his background and skin color would help him change a broken department from within. Johnson cut off his braids, tucked in his shirts, eventually clipped on a badge. Indeed he could relate to, and communicate with, people from various backgrounds and on both sides of the law. This ability to bridge divides helped him advance quickly from street cop to robbery detective to homicide. If a suspect in an interrogation room ignored him, Johnson might recite lyrics by Curren$y and talk about how the local rapper used to sell Johnson discounted PlayStations when he worked at Toys "R" Us. Other times he'd roll up his sleeves and show the tattoos on his left arm, or share a few pictures of himself with gangsters, or reveal that a relaxing evening means cleaning his Glock and sipping his Martell straight.

He got so many reluctant witnesses to cooperate, got so many breaks, that he solved his first half-dozen murders. Over three years, he cleared 38 percent of his cases. That's high for a police department that makes an arrest in only one in three murders, and on the office whiteboard where the NOPD's nineteen homicide detectives tracked their closures, Johnson ranked fifth over a thirty-six-month stretch.

When producers from *The First 48* came looking for a compelling lead character to follow through the streets of New Orleans, they quickly discovered the young, handsome detective who could solve the impossible. Johnson was a husband and new father, and his easygoing nature and confident idealism made him a no-brainer. It didn't hurt that he could act. In fact it was something Johnson, who long ago learned to present himself in different ways to different audiences, did every day.

"What the *hell*?" he says in his first onscreen appearance. He cocks an eyebrow in an episode titled "Dead Wrong," just before a dramatic cut to commercial. Johnson uses video surveillance, a tireless work ethic, and that uncanny ability to get witnesses to talk to make an arrest and bring closure to a grieving family.

"That's how I roll," Johnson tells his colleagues at police headquarters in the episode's celebratory final scene. Then he delivers the perfect sign-off. "There's plenty more to do."

And he wasn't wrong. In 2013, New Orleans had the second-highest murder rate in the US: 41 homicides per 100,000 residents. By 2015, the murder rate among Black male New Orleanians was more than twenty-five times the national average. In other words, Johnson's phone never stayed silent for long. When it rang, he'd suit up and head toward another grisly scene. Johnson enjoyed the puzzle of an investigation, and it satisfied Johnson's craving for purpose—and, sometimes, attention. Occasionally bystanders at a crime scene recognized him from television. Once someone asked him to pose for a selfie, which Johnson says he refused.

That didn't happen the night Tonka died, and Johnson mostly blended in as he filtered through the crowd. He tried to collect leads, and eventually he reached yellow tape at the edge of the road. He flashed his badge and ducked under the barrier. A blue pop-up curtain shielded the victim's body from view, and Johnson noted the bullet casings on the pavement and in the grass. Near a storm drain was an iPhone, lying faceup.

When Johnson peeked over the curtain, he saw a twenty-three-year-old man wearing slippers and shorts. The detective's eyes were drawn toward the victim's muscular calves. Johnson immediately wondered if the dead man had been a football player.

ONLY THIS TIME, nobody talked. It didn't seem to matter what Johnson did. There was no credible chatter at the crime scene. Grainy surveillance video from a camera posted a hundred yards away yielded only the make, model, and color of the shooter's vehicle, the red Honda Accord. Johnson's attempts to get information from witnesses or leads from confidential informants, including a few old friends, failed.

The detective retraced Tonka's steps and found nothing particularly noteworthy. He'd kissed his mama good-bye before she left for work and later played pickup basketball in the Cut-Off. Then he went home, walked to the gas station, bought his cigar at the same time the red Honda was getting gas. But who'd been in the vehicle? Someone Tonka knew or even trusted? Or, perhaps more likely, someone beefing with some of Tonka's friends—one of whom had been shot while he'd been at Alcorn State?

The way it works in New Orleans is that, if you're feuding with someone or a group of someones, you try to bring physical or emotional pain to your rival. You attack or kill one of their members, they come back and hit one of yours, and on and on it goes. These wars, often one neighborhood faction clashing with another over a botched drug deal or just the perception of disrespect, can span years and end dozens of lives. These groups and conflicts aren't exactly sophisticated, nothing like a Mafia family or even a traditional street gang. But the objective is similar: get one of your enemy's leaders. And if you can't kill him, then you kill someone he cares about.

Johnson suspected, but couldn't prove, that one or more of Tonka's friends had become involved in one of these wars. Was Tonka even aware of it? Had he been warned?

The detective couldn't know, and the most frustrating thing was that potential answers lay in the NOPD's evidence room. Johnson believed Tonka's iPhone contained information that could break the case open. But nobody knew Tonka's passcode, and not only did the NOPD lack technology to bypass it, this murder occurred when Apple and law enforcement agencies were battling over privacy rights.

Johnson had generated persons of interest in Tonka's killing. But without a direct tie to this or another crime, he had no leverage to compel anyone to talk. Months passed, and a group Johnson suspected kept having its people killed, then retaliating. He wondered if Tonka had been a pawn or was even gunned down in a case of mistaken identity.

"Even after he was murdered, them dudes were looking for somebody to kill," Johnson would say in one of several interviews much later. He refused to disclose certain details of his investigation because Tonka's case remained open. "They didn't know who to kill. But somebody had to die."

He kept knocking on doors, asking questions, trying to crack the code of the locked iPhone: first using Tonka's birthday, then parts of his Social Security number. No luck. Then six weeks after Tonka's death, Johnson's phone rang again. A murder in broad daylight in

New Orleans East. Two months after that, another call: a thirty-six-year-old father of ten shot dead in Algiers and his tire shop burned. Two months later, another murder following a triple shooting near Behrman Stadium.

On and on it went, and by the end of 2016, Johnson was juggling roughly a dozen unsolved murders—more than twice the workload the Bureau of Governmental Research recommends. Homicide detectives gave up tracking their scant closures on the whiteboard, and a few of Johnson's colleagues decided their job was impossible and just quit.

Since 2013, when a consent decree between New Orleans and the United States Department of Justice went into effect, the NOPD had been in rebuilding mode. An investigation into the years following Katrina found a department-wide culture of toxicity: corruption, police brutality, cover-ups. The most infamous example was the death of Henry Glover, a Black man and thirty-one-year-old father. In those first waterlogged days after the storm Glover went to an Algiers strip mall to thumb through looted baby clothes. A white NOPD officer named David Warren noticed Glover inspecting the goods before shooting Glover dead. Another officer drove Glover's car and body to a levee along the Mississippi River before torching the vehicle and Glover's remains. Following a series of fabricated police reports and a wide-ranging conspiracy, dramatically inflaming racial tensions that had existed since the "Algiers 7" disaster, Warren wouldn't be arrested for five years. After being initially sentenced to more than twenty-five years in prison, Warren was acquitted during a retrial and wound up serving about three years.

Around that same time, Mayor Mitch Landrieu, who'd campaigned on a promise of curbing violent crime, agreed to the federal investigation into the NOPD and the consent decree. Landrieu argues now that the agreement would rebuild the department on a foundation of ethical policing and was as necessary as it was expensive: a $55 million bill to taxpayers. Leon Cannizzaro, the city's district attorney and a supporter of the hypercontroversial stop-and-frisk policing, criticized Landrieu and the federal intervention. He'd claim it neutered the NOPD and prevented cops from doing their jobs.

"We've got to get out from under this consent decree," Cannizzaro said in an interview in early 2020. "We have got to do that, because the police have got to be allowed to go out and be police. They cannot be proactive. They can't go out and look for criminal activity, which is what good law enforcement officers do. They're simply reactive."

Johnson, for his part, tried to press forward. He remained hopeful, even while working for a police department that overspent its overtime budget and paused new hiring. The NOPD had no crime lab and farmed out forensic evidence to state police. Five superintendents occupied the department's top job over fourteen years as cops faced almost constant whiplash on changing priorities, approaches, and procedures.

Homicide detectives attended autopsies in a fire-damaged former funeral parlor that lacked proper ventilation. "Oh, God, I couldn't get that smell out of my nose," Johnson says as he forces a laugh.

Morale, and productivity, cratered. An average of ten cops a month left the force and weren't replaced. The year Tonka died, Johnson was one of sixteen detectives in a city of 390,000 residents and 175 homicides. He took on murder after murder, and because of slashed personnel, Johnson and other detectives often set aside cases while they worked crowd control during the Final Four, College Football Playoff games, or Mardi Gras.

Cops worked longer hours with stagnant pay, and Johnson made ends meet for his growing family by earning overtime as he patrolled the French Quarter overnight in a squad car. Sleep-deprived and overworked, a bleary-eyed Johnson still reported each morning to the corner of Tulane and South Broad Avenues and attempted to reacquaint himself with the growing stack of case files on his desk. Each one had its own nuances, and Johnson's mind became a frequently clogged pipeline of thoughts and ideas.

His segments on *The First 48*, once just a fun side project, now offered fulfillment and perhaps even therapy. Trying to preserve his flickering optimism, he chased the high of those appearances by volunteering to appear in department-produced videos, such as those wishing New Orleanians happy holidays.

During his downtime, Johnson nerded out to cop shows and imagined himself on a TV or movie set. He prepared for his inevitable star turn by lifting weights and marching into homicide wearing pressed shirts, a carefully cinched necktie, a caramel-colored shoulder holster. He saw himself in the tireless but cocky Frank Pembleton on *Homicide: Life on the Street*. He was a proud and dogged lawman like Andy Sipowicz from *NYPD Blue*. On Johnson's many social media accounts, he is "Robocop."

His swagger and sunny demeanor drew admirers. But it also generated eye rolls, in particular from his more beaten-down colleagues. "Here comes the movie star," Johnson says one detective consistently greeted him.

He ignored the jeers, or tried to. He vowed to never become so jaded and tried to convince himself that older detectives were relics of an antiquated and racist system. Johnson, he told himself, could represent the future of the NOPD, and of policing.

But as time passed, Johnson's coworkers grew increasingly weary. And not just of his theatrics and public persona, but his proximity to and comfort in New Orleans's underbelly. One detective confronted Johnson and alerted their supervisor after discovering social media photos of Johnson hanging with a few notorious friends. When Johnson used his department-issued vehicle for a personal project, another detective found out, reported him, and got Johnson suspended.

He tried like hell to shrug it all off. Was this just the personal cost of systemic advancement? Of being ambitious? He still dreamed of being a rapper, and a man who once divided himself into contrasting characters wrote lyrics about being defined by more than one thing. Some of his verses were simpler, and Johnson liked to mentally disappear into a fantasy world that didn't involve petty colleagues, grieving relatives, a constantly ringing phone.

His first full song, "9ine to 5ive," was about nothing more than having a day off from work. One day, just for kicks, Johnson rented out a bar in the Tremé and recorded a music video. It begins *First 48*–style, Johnson in his shirt and tie pulling up at a fictionalized murder scene. Then the beat starts, and the video cuts to a very different Johnson. He's wearing gold chains and a black muscle shirt that exposes his tattoos. Surrounded by friends—some cops, others criminals—Johnson allowed "Ray-L" to come out and play.

> *Every day, out here on the case*
> *Yeah, I'm off today, got time today*
> *Now what them haters said?*
> *Let me be great.*

When it was finished, a few of Johnson's colleagues watched on YouTube. Some told him they were impressed by the production and the music. Others ridiculed him for the song's unimaginative lyrics and how this proved he didn't take police work seriously. One detective complained to superiors and again got Johnson disciplined.

Feeling micromanaged and misunderstood, Johnson sometimes found himself indulging a new hobby: drinking, increasingly when he was alone. He thought more about a career in Hollywood, an escape from all this. Other times he'd rebound, summoning the fading wisps of vanishing idealism, and read a text from someone who counted on him.

He'd slip back into a character that was harder to portray convincingly: Detective Rayell Johnson, inexhaustible crime fighter and hopeful beacon in a broken land.

I'm going to continue to do everything in my power, he texted one day to Rhonda, **to get you closure.**

MORE AND MORE OFTEN, though, Rhonda heard nothing. She had only one murder to think about, and in her grief, she did so constantly. She realized Johnson was overworked, that witnesses are scared of cops, that the NOPD and city government are a mess.

She just didn't care.

Johnson didn't arrest anyone in the first forty-eight hours after Tonka's death, and neither would he during the first forty-eight months. Days and weeks passed without an update or even a response, and Rhonda tried to keep the case at the front of Johnson's mind the only way she knew how.

This ms .George, she texted one day.

This Ms.Rhonda George, she texted the next.

This Ms. Rhonda George, she texted the day after that.

If God had failed her by allowing Tonka's death, she could at least trust the handsome Black detective to bring her peace. She saw Johnson as her hero, her light, and she was desperate for him to power through the limitations surrounding him.

"I'm just trying to figure out *why*," she'd say a long time after burying her son.

Rhonda moved into a new house, and trying to empty her routine of hellacious memories, she turned her new living room into a shrine of comforting ones. A curio cabinet filled with photographs and newspaper clippings, a life-sized cardboard cutout of Tonka, toys and chalk drawings given to her by strangers. There were photos of him during and after games, when he'd helped to further expand Brown's offense with highly advanced plays such as "Trips rt-stack A-brown cheat," a zone-read that requires decisiveness and athleticism. Rhonda sought refuge at Karr games, not just getting to know the kids like Leonte, who wore her son's old number, but loving them. She saw players as parts of her extended family. Yearning for someone to mother, she called them and prayed for them and offered them advice. She sat in the stands and cheered for them as if it were her son on the field.

When Carlie, her granddaughter, asked why her uncle had to go to heaven, Rhonda tried to hold back tears. Usually she failed, and after a while she stopped apologizing for another breakdown. If friends told her to be strong, to move on and stop crying, Rhonda stopped counting them as friends.

Other than despair, patience was hardest. Even under ideal conditions, justice can be sluggish. Rhonda, though, demanded urgency and singular focus. She felt no remorse about the unfairness of these expectations. These are humans, uncles and brothers and sons, not just cases in a stack.

Johnson, as delicately as he could, tried to explain that each of his investigations is equally important. Rhonda, as politely as she could muster, explained she could not accept that.

These were individuals from the same places, from the same side of the river, whose paths had crossed because of a tragedy they now shared. But as days and weeks turned into months and years, it was becoming clear they struggled to understand each other or even communicate. Johnson wanted to send updates when they were meaningful. Rhonda just wanted reminders that Tonka still mattered to someone besides his mother.

I haven't heard from you, she texted him one afternoon.

Nothing new as of now, he replied.

Rhonda texted or called or emailed day after day, and many times Johnson just didn't respond. So, in her desperation, she did what so many residents do in New Orleans: she sidestepped the cops and took matters into her own hands.

One day she noticed a red two-door Honda and followed it. When it parked and the driver walked away, she crept close enough to the license plate to snap a picture. She combed her old neighborhood and knocked on doors, asking residents what they'd seen or heard that night in June 2016. Did they have a security camera? Could she review the footage?

Rhonda called La'Keilla Veal, Tonka's friend in Mississippi and the young woman who'd been the last person to hear his voice. An interrogation of sorts, Rhonda asked what they had talked about and the tone of Tonka's voice. Had he described something he saw— anything—as unusual? Rhonda talked to so many people that she established a list of six possible suspects that included real names and aliases. Some were the same names Johnson had highlighted, though he couldn't tell her that.

She reviewed their social media profiles, printing out posts with even a loose connection to Tonka. Friends and relatives told Rhonda she was going too far. Some suggested she was putting her own life in danger. Her pastor sprinkled holy water on her and prayed for her to know peace. Rhonda's daughter, Tiffany, begged her mother to remember not only that she had a granddaughter to live for, but another child, too.

Yet it's just something Rhonda couldn't do. After a while she stopped expecting anyone else to understand.

"Me and you against the world," she'd say at Tonka's grave some days. "Come to me. *Tell* me who done this to you."

If Rhonda happened upon something she found interesting, she'd text or email it to Johnson. When he didn't reply, she'd take her findings to a private investigator for a law firm in Algiers. But the investigator sounded just like Johnson, insisting hard evidence or witness accounts were the only paths forward. Indeed a year after agreeing to look into Tonka's case, the investigator had filled exactly one page of a legal pad. He hadn't even pulled the incident report from the night of the murder.

Rhonda kept digging. She had no idea how she'd feel if she actually achieved closure, whether it'd ease her pain or make it worse. But stopping, when to her everyone else had caved to passivity, was not an option. One day while searching her list of suspects, she happened upon a photograph of a young man wearing a Karr hoodie and a high-top fade. She'd become convinced he had been in the Accord that night. No evidence, just hope and whispers. But wasn't that enough to go talk to him? What if he slipped up and said something revelatory or implicating? Rhonda identified the young man's parents and found where they worked. She implored the private investigator to confront them; see what they say, how they react. The investigator refused.

So facing another dead end, Rhonda once again sent the photo to a familiar phone number, but one she'd been avoiding.

Can you talk to him pls, she texted Johnson. **Please Please Please Bring him in he is going to crack. . . . I have FAITH IN YOU.**

Three weeks passed before he responded. But the consent decree had hamstrung cops, especially those lacking evidence. With police under a harsh microscope, he couldn't just go snatch up a private citizen and rattle his cage. The skull-cracking days of yesteryear were long gone.

Rhonda was unmoved, and she decided Johnson wasn't constrained by ethics or legalities but by fear. She suspected he'd been compromised somehow, or just didn't want to get mixed up in a culture of endless bloodshed (Johnson adamantly denies this). But Rhonda nonetheless went over Johnson's head, emailing Shaun Ferguson, the NOPD superintendent and Algerine whom Rhonda has known for years.

Couldn't Ferguson *make* Johnson round up these individuals? Or assign a detective who would?

"I trust that my people are doing everything that they can to bring peace," Ferguson would, in an interview later, recall telling Rhonda.

Continually let down by men with supposed power, Rhonda imagined working her way up the chain and barging into the offices of Leon Cannizzaro or Mayor LaToya Cantrell, who succeeded Landrieu and unveiled her own fifty-year crime plan. Rhonda disappeared into the satisfying, if fictional, realities of crime shows and compared the detectives she watched with the one she actually knew. A favorite was *Law & Order: Special Victims Unit*, whose gruff and no-bullshit Fin Tutuola, played by Ice-T, would be proactive where Johnson seemed so reactive.

"I wish I could just talk to Ice-T," Rhonda would say one afternoon. She'd sheepishly admit she watches too much TV.

Flipping channels one evening, she stopped after recognizing New Orleans's distinctive architecture. Indeed the show was exploring a murder that had transpired here. Rhonda, a fan of *Criminal Minds* and *Chicago P.D.*, had never seen an episode of *The First 48*. She gave it a try, watching until the camera cut to an interview with the case's lead investigator. But the sight of Johnson on her television was so disgusting that she immediately reached for the remote.

Rhonda's faith, she realized, wouldn't be rewarded. Not here. The system is too broken, the city too set in its ways even amid attempts to modernize. She kept telling herself justice would come, that closure was attainable if she kept fighting. That if she kept shouting, eventually the right person would hear her.

But in her most honest moments, she'd acknowledge that hope was being beaten out of her. She felt alone in her quest, and Rhonda would accept a cruel truth about living in New Orleans: no human, with so many flaws inherent to the species, is capable of overpowering a decades-old structure. Certainly not one that deincentivizes results and shames the ambitious. Elected officials and cops talk big, but they're neither motivated nor strong enough to save this city from itself. The job is too big, too dirty. There are no heroes here, she'd come to believe, at least not where they're supposed to be.

I know I haven't talked to you, Johnson texted Rhonda one morning, ending a month of silence. **I didn't forget about you.**

Yes you did, she replied.

MOST DAYS AFTER WORK, Johnson goes to a cigar bar in the French Quarter to have his first drink. Usually his second, too. Smoke on the Water is a venerable cop hangout, and Johnson likes to unwind with a good smoke while listening to two retired homicide detectives share war stories.

The older retiree stayed on the force as long as he could, juggling murders and chasing bad guys for thirty years. He says he'd give anything for just one more case. The younger one is different. He did his twenty-five years, got his pension fully vested, then got the hell out. He doesn't miss it. Eventually he just realized, as so many idealists do, that he was too small to effect systemic change. You either leave the decay entirely or you conform to it. That second ex-cop realized as much, and after he retired, he never looks at his phone. He sleeps better now than he ever did.

Johnson, still a long way from retirement, wonders which of these guys he'll someday be. He knows which one he wants to be: the retiree who turned in his badge, turned off his brain, and never looked back. But he also knows himself, and though his colleagues (and maybe Rhonda) think he doesn't care enough about his work, the truth is that he can't stop thinking about it. In the shower, while he's trying to sleep, during vacations and days off.

"Rayell," the carefree and optimistic side of himself, is no more than just another role he plays. Just another fictional character, the first one he ever created.

"I know I act like I don't give a fuck," Johnson will say. "But I give a fuck more than anybody. I want to solve *every* fucking case. I want to be perfect."

The hobbies aren't side hustles, he says. The dreams of Hollywood neither interfere with nor obstruct his work. They're just silly little fantasies, a method of escape from a reality of constant blood, heartbreak, and personal disappointment. Then again, New Orleans ended its contract with *The First 48* in 2016, so this diversion isn't so reliable anymore.

That's one reason he goes to the bar. Johnson's mind drifts more often toward frustrations with an environment seemingly incapable of change. The murder case that fell apart in court, the witnesses he can't get to talk, the realities of policing in a violent city. As much as anything, Johnson says he thinks about the iPhone the NOPD's digital forensics team can't seem to penetrate.

Who, he wonders, had Tonka talked to that day? Was there chatter about some altercation? Something involving one or more of Tonka's friends?

"There's *something* in that phone. I just know it," Johnson says. "That's gonna be the thing that opens this thing back up. There's gonna be conversation in there: 'Man, fuck that dude.'"

But he can't know. At least not yet.

"My Hail Mary, last resort," he says, sighing now. He has thought about this case, and so many others, for years. "I just want to see what's in this phone."

Time keeps passing, leads keep vanishing, hope keeps dissolving. Johnson suffocates his thoughts inside a cloud of cigar smoke and cognac-fueled talk of bygone days. Eventually he heads home, greets his wife, and checks in on his two kids. Then he walks into his backyard to pour another drink. Then another.

"I would like to say I'm not an alcoholic . . ." he'll say. He never completes this thought.

Though Johnson and Rhonda view the world and its atrocities through different lenses, there are many things they share. Both are on an insufferable search for peace. Both frequently feel isolated and overpowered. Both struggle to silence the suggestions of their own minds.

Rhonda finds catharsis, such as it is, by continuing her impromptu investigation. Johnson does so by relentlessly trying to shed his own skin. But with no producers calling, and his name climbing the up-list to catch the next murder, there's only one thing left to do. He reaches for the Martell and hopes his phone gives him just a few more moments of silence.

CHAPTER 7

HITCH

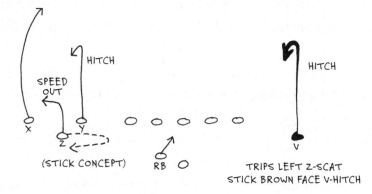

LOOKING BACK, they would describe the young woman as a blur. Skinny. Light skin and short twists. Maybe sixteen.

She had run onto the field at Behrman Stadium after Karr's 44–0 win against Eleanor McMain High and approached wide receiver Trent Washington. Her left hand never left her jacket. Was there a gun inside? She said there was. She kept shouting, inches from Trent's face, about how she was here to put fifteen bullets in his chest. What a shame, she said, to splatter blood all over his pretty yellow jersey.

Then she ran away. Scooped up a backpack near a chain-link fence and disappeared through a gate, past a ticket booth, into the trees. Leonte, who seemed to know the young woman, rejoined his shell-shocked Karr teammates. Coaches, who prepare for so many scenarios, had never practiced this. Receivers coach Mike Thompson sprinted toward an idling police cruiser. Norm Randall directed his two sons, Baylon and Liam, to follow an athletic department colleague and move away from the crowd.

"Helmets on, helmets on!" Norm shouted. Players slid on their equipment, designed for protection against big hits, not bullets. But it was all they had if the young woman, wherever she was, started shooting.

Coaches pushed players inward, forming a tight cluster of young bodies. Then they circled the kids for an extra layer between her and them. Their eyes scanned the faces of a hundred strangers on the field. Everyone on the field was a possible threat. The hive began inching off the field and toward Karr's buses.

"We're sitting ducks," Norm would recall thinking as he braced himself for the inevitable crack of gunfire.

EVERY SPRING the doors open at Karr's football office, and around three dozen wide-eyed freshmen stream in. They are unknowns, and almost immediately coaches begin assigning kids to certain classifications. Wide receivers and blockers and pass rushers, of course. But also the initial diagnoses of what each kid needs, and how he should be coached.

Some freshmen, loud and confident, must be tamed and reminded that football is a collective game of sacrifice and teamwork. Others have sustained obvious psychological trauma, signaled by a hesitancy to speak or make eye contact. They must receive frequent reminders that they are valuable and loved.

Each year there are a half-dozen Joes, several Leonards, one or two Fats. One way or another, their words and actions will announce who they are, where they're from, what they'll require. Many are from broken homes. A few have already sold drugs or are used to carrying a gun. Some have never been held accountable. Once coaches identify who is who, they can begin addressing the freshmen not as interchangeable parts but as individuals. Brown and his assistants hold one-on-one meetings and share their own stories of personal success and failure, which lowers social barriers. In many cases, they provide counsel, transportation, and food. This builds trust. Once or twice a year, a player will get into a conflict at home and need a place to stay while things cool down. Every Karr coach has opened his home at some point. One time a kid ran away from home and was missing for two days. It was his position coach he finally called, not his parents. After another player insisted that the welt on his arm was a result of getting "popped with chicken grease," as his mother had instructed him to say, it was a coach who took him to a doctor to receive treatment for a staph infection. This establishes respect.

"You have to reach them before you can teach them," Brown likes to say. With enough effort and time, a flock of wildly divergent personalities and souls can be formed into a team.

And though it may seem obvious for coaches to treat each individual as a unique being, this tends to be something lazy coaches and failed business managers ignore. In fairness, Brown's way is time-consuming, grueling, exhausting. His method is also not foolproof, and every few years, a player slips through the cracks.

When the freshman class entered before the 2017 season, Trent Washington seemed like a Leonard. His parents had been married since 2003, and because Trent's brother is fourteen years older, they doted on and supported Trent as if he were an only child. His mother, Gwen, is a special education teacher at Karr. His dad, Trent Sr., is a bus driver and sports fanatic who played high school basketball. He could frequently be seen (and heard) in the crowd at Karr games. The parents moved Trent from De La Salle, a private school in Uptown, to Karr because Brown won championships. Succeeding here would give their son the best possible chance to earn a college scholarship.

Trent was quiet during those first weeks at Karr, but he made friends fast. He and Fat, along with Dany'e Brooks and Destin Refuge, hit it off. Coaches identified the four friends as talented boundary pushers who were highly impressionable and perhaps insecure. But they were considered ultimately harmless. Other freshmen would require more immediate, and thorough, intervention.

Time passed, and Trent became a starting wide receiver before Fat and Dany'e. He was nimble and strong. But sometimes he missed practice or skipped school. Coaches heard whispers about tension at home, in part because Trent preferred football over basketball, his father's preferred sport. Gwen and Trent Sr. argued about this and other things, she would say in an interview, and she'd leave him before coming home. This circle continued for a while.

One evening Trent walked in during another argument, and he punched the family's television. The screen cracked, and blood streamed down his hand.

"I can't control my anger!" Gwen recalled her son shouting.

She enrolled him in therapy, where he met with a counselor each Saturday. Gwen filed for divorce, hoped things would improve, tried to follow the counselor's advice by surrounding Trent with positivity. Instead, Trent blew his midnight curfew by staying out till two, and sometimes Gwen's coworkers reported that Trent acted out in class.

"If anybody told him anything he didn't like, he'd react in a negative manner," Gwen said. She adds that she let many of Trent's infractions slide, an attempt at avoiding his triggers.

Coaches, though, believed he was crying out for discipline. That, in fact, he needed confrontation, not a soft touch. They noticed dark stains on his lips and a loss of muscle definition. Sometimes he looked as though he hadn't bathed in days.

Brown kicked Trent off the team, one of the coach's go-to moves. It's ultimately a bluff, though the kid doesn't know that. He is nonetheless barred from the football office for a few days, and Brown will say kids rarely think about how much the game and team mean to them until both are taken away. It also reestablishes coaches as no-nonsense authority figures, and almost always the kid slinks back and apologizes. It's rare that Brown actually bans a player for good.

Trent, though, kept making mistakes. Brown did not allow him to join the team for training camp in July 2019. Instead he invited Trent to "find himself" during an extended time away from football. But sometimes he didn't answer coaches' calls, and they heard troubling rumors.

"He don't give a fuck about *nothing*," Fat told Coach Mike, who oversees slot receivers and is Trent's position coach.

Players were hearing that Trent had gotten himself mixed up in something dangerous and had no idea how to get out of it. But if they knew more than that, it never reached the coaching staff. Then a few hours before kickoff against John Curtis, players ran to the gym to break up a fight between Trent and another student at Karr. The other boy, players kept hearing, had been a snitch.

One day Brown summoned his two receivers coaches, Mike and Omari Robertson, into his office. What should the team do? Omari had grown frustrated with Trent, in particular that he'd been born with advantages other teammates lacked. Omari recognized privilege from his own life, and resented that Trent had taken it for granted.

"Trent has a father. Has a mother. They have money. It's not like they're struggling for anything," Omari would say. "He wants to be a gangster, wants to be a thug. He *wants* that lifestyle."

But Mike didn't want to give up on him. Jovial and with high cheekbones, Mike's most identifiable features are dreads that reach his waist and an incurable weakness for second chances. He's an innovative route designer, though not quite so creative as the team's unofficial DJ. Each day Mike kicks off football practice by plugging his phone into an outdoor speaker and blaring Phil Collins's "In the Air Tonight" during stretches. Used in various movies and TV shows, and made popular again by Mike Tyson's cameo in *The Hangover*, the song has become a symbolic anthem of menace.

Mike Thompson's own youth had been creased by unresolved trauma, in his case having fled New Orleans after Katrina for the Dallas suburbs. His comfort and plans felt shattered, and he dealt with this by alternating between ambition and rage. Football had been a constant, and despite periods of tumult the game eventually led him to Louisiana College. He played tight end and earned a degree in kinesiology, then later he played arena-league football. He vowed to return to his hometown and devote his future to mentoring young Mike Thompsons who perhaps felt as lost as he had.

Sitting in Brown's office, Mike said he wanted to give Trent another shot.

"If I don't save him," the young coach said, "nobody will."

So that day after practice, Mike called Trent but got no answer. He drove to the family's home in nearby Gretna, a community on the West Bank. When he arrived the windows were dark. Mike knocked on the door, but nobody answered.

Gwen had given Mike the front door's key code, and though he was nervous about what he might see, he punched in the numbers anyway. The television was on in Trent's bedroom, and a plate of food was warm but untouched. But no Trent, so Mike kept looking.

He finally saw the young man through a kitchen window, sitting alone outside. He quietly opened the back door.

"How you been?" Mike said, announcing himself. Trent looked at him with alarm before appearing relieved that it was Mike and not someone else.

Mike sat next to him, and they began by talking football. Karr was 2–2, Mike told him, and Aaron Anderson's knee was still bothering him. The offense could use a quick and athletic slot receiver to ease pressure on Fat and provide an extra option for Leonard. Trent said he wanted to come back, but he'd become entangled in something untenable. Besides, Trent said, he was uncertain Joe and the other captains would allow him back.

"*They* want you to come back," Mike would recall saying.

So did Mike, though not without changes. For one, he'd have to behave like a freshman again—no frills, no seniority, just another unproven kid trying to earn his place. Rather than having one foot in the program and one foot out, Mike told him, it was time for Trent to pick his side.

"I want to play," he told Mike.

"Show me," the coach said.

THIRTEEN DAYS BEFORE Karr's first game, two young men walked toward a parked car a little before midnight. Similar to the sequence Tonka initiated three years earlier during his fateful walk, this was the first domino. It would soon tip over and bump into the second one.

On this dimly lit corner near a Family Dollar, a struggle ensued between the vehicle's twenty-three-year-old driver and the two young men. One of them reached for a gun, and several pops could be heard in the shopping complex across the street. Bullets entered the driver's torso and arm. The two young men ran away, disappearing into the night.

The driver suffered life-threatening injuries but would survive the attack. For the moment, the second domino teetered but remained upright.

Eventually police cruisers came and went, the sun rose, and the West Bank carried on as if more blood hadn't been spilled onto its pavement. Bystanders whispered about what had happened the night before, though eventually they quieted.

On the following Monday, Karr held its first football practice of the week. Trent had been invited to rejoin the team, but he didn't show up. He came to school occasionally, attended practice sporadically. Brown allowed him to lift weights but neither to play in games nor practice. He wasn't even allowed the honor of wearing a Karr jersey. He worked out and stood on the sidelines in a T-shirt and, at least on that Thursday, got into a fight with the supposed snitch. Leonard talked to Trent, and so did Joe.

"Let this be your future," Joe told him, reminding Trent that not long ago it had been Joe at this crossroads. Now look at him.

The receiver appeared to do everything right during the season's first four weeks. But in early October during the football team's bye week and essentially a recovery period, something caused a deep vibration that made that second domino wobble for the first time in six weeks. The Jefferson Parish district attorney charged Trent with attempted second-degree murder in connection with the shooting outside the Family Dollar. If it advanced, the sixteen-year-old would be tried as an adult.

Karr's players and coaches were unaware when this second domino fell, though it did so with a vengeance. It crashed into the third, which was Brown reissuing Trent's old number 84 jersey and inviting him to rejoin practice. Later that week, Brown designed a play with his befouled receiver in mind.

"Trips left Z-scat stick brown face V-hitch" is a complicated call for a simple route combination. It calls for three wide receivers to line up on Leonard's left side. The single receiver to his right is the "V," or "Viper," receiver. The play's first read is an attack on the Cover 3 zone defense in general and on a cornerback's soft coverage specifically. The "Viper," in this case Trent, is to run a "hitch" route: a sprint forward to give the impression of a deep fly route, which Cover 3 is designed to prevent. But after ten yards, Trent will abruptly stop to face Leonard, who by then should have the ball on the way toward Trent's left shoulder.

The route is easy, a good reintroduction to game action for Trent. Against Eleanor McMain, less famous for its football program than the fact that the rapper Lil Wayne went there, would be a midseason tune-up for Karr. The risk in involving a rusty, potentially out-of-shape receiver was minimal. Coaches decided Trent should be rewarded for his hard work, and as far as they knew, an apparent recommitment to football and avoiding trouble.

Mike, who like all other coaches claimed no knowledge of the charges Trent faced, remained at Trent's side during his first weeks back. Together they worked on the receiver's footwork, the right way to explode forward immediately after the snap, the proper way to pivot after catching the ball and turning upfield. Trent hadn't caught a pass from Leonard in months, and besides, Leonard wasn't the same quarterback he used to be.

After the interception and benching at Catholic, he'd become more determined and focused than before. He arrived early for meetings with Brown. He could identify opposing defenses more reliably, diagnose hacks for them more quickly. Now practicing with a wide receiver who had drifted, and who needed a confidence boost, Leonard's passes were crisp and timed perfectly. They nailed the play every time.

When Friday arrived, fifteen days after Trent's arrest and subsequent release on bail, more dominoes had begun falling. Perhaps Brown should've sensed it, considering how everything seemed out of sorts throughout the day. Responding to a forecast that included evening thunderstorms, Karr and McMain agreed to a 3 p.m. kickoff, four hours earlier than normal. Karr's school buses arrived late to the school, and when they transported players to Behrman Stadium, they accidentally parked in the wrong lot. Players had to lug their equipment across the field and into the home locker room.

Brown sat in his truck and tried to stay calm. He muttered to assistants before the game that he was tempted to take his frustration out on McMain. Maybe he'd make the poor Mustangs his stress ball and hang eighty points on them. But Omari suggested such an onslaught could bring on bad karma, and Brown rolled his eyes but agreed.

He instead used the game as an opportunity to experiment. He deployed receivers who almost never played meaningful snaps, and Leonard threw touchdown passes to a sophomore and junior who rarely participated. When the time came, Brown noticed McMain showing Cover 3 and spoke his play call into the microphone on his headset: "Trips left Z-scat stick brown face V-hitch." Nick Foster signaled it to players.

Leonard snapped the ball, and Trent exploded forward—sprinting, stopping, turning. But when the ball arrived, on time and in the right spot, it bounced off Trent's hands. He dropped it. The public address announcer nonetheless announced that Leonard Kelly's incomplete pass had been intended for Trent Washington.

That announcement wound up being the final domino, because a young woman in the bleachers heard it. Her eyes followed Trent Washington, number 84, as he retreated to the sideline. She watched him as Karr won, improving to 4–2 on the season. It was cause for celebration, and after the teams shook hands at midfield, Karr players had unexpected time to congratulate one another. Brown, who usually hurries players toward the parking lot, lingered with everyone else. After all, they had to wait on the buses to come from the opposite side of the stadium.

While they waited, the skinny young woman descended the bleachers, passed through a gate, dropped her backpack near a fence. She walked onto the field and approached Trent and announced herself as the sister of the twenty-three-year-old who'd been shot in the torso and arm. She'd known exactly where Trent would be on this afternoon, and the jersey number that would identify him. She said she was here for revenge. Trent, according to Karr coaches' recollections later, challenged her to get on with it. Some would recall an unnerving look of acceptance on Trent's face.

Leonte, usually so high-strung and dramatic, calmly approached her and spoke calmly. He placed his hand on her wrist and tried to lower the temperature. Coaches believed Leonte held her arm in order to keep her hand, and whatever she might've held in it, inside her pocket. A few went so far as to suggest Leonte's soothing presence might've saved lives. Asked directly about this later, Leonte narrowed his eyes and smiled but would not share details of the encounter or any knowledge of the young woman. Another player ran toward Mike, who was directing players toward the approaching buses.

"Coach Mike!" one of them called. "Come see."

Then, for reasons nobody fully understood, the girl just turned and ran off. She swiped up her backpack and disappeared into the darkness between Behrman Park's massive oaks.

"Helmets on!" Norm kept calling, and after clustering together and herding toward the exit, rattled players and coaches reached the buses at last.

Police directed Trent to a secure vehicle, where he sat in his pads alone. Someone spotted his mother's car and, after flagging her down, explained what had just happened. She raced toward the vehicle and found her son. He rode with his mother back to Karr.

"It's all made-up stories," Gwen would recall Trent insisting in the incident's hazy aftermath.

The buses started back toward campus, and Officer Pat diverted from his usual meandering route back to the school. He drove Brown's truck, with its shell-shocked owner sitting silently in the passenger seat, down the well-lit and heavily traveled General Meyer Avenue.

At one point, someone else crossed General Meyer on a bicycle. The young woman made her way home, about a mile from the stadium and near an intersection in Algiers. When she arrived a little after 6 p.m., there was a silver car waiting.

Gunshots indeed rang out on this early evening, as storm clouds gathered and cast a shadow over the West Bank. One of the bullets pierced the young woman's right thigh, just before the four-door sedan sped away. Soon an ambulance arrived to take her to a hospital, and some time later an emergency worker asked if she had any idea who might be responsible for this; if she suspected anyone of setting this line of bloodstained events in motion.

She said she did.

LATER THAT NIGHT, after hours of discussions with police and officials from the school and InspireNOLA, Brown couldn't sleep. Trent's mother had assured them this was a case of mistaken identity, and Trent told the NOPD he hadn't been involved in the Family Dollar incident. But Brown struggled to parse fact from speculation. As his mind kept playing the earlier scenes on a loop, he kept thinking about what *could* have happened.

Had the young woman actually brought a weapon to Behrman Stadium, either in her jacket or in the backpack? What if she'd brandished a gun or even shot Trent or another player? Or fired into the crowd? Or hit one of the coaches' children, playing catch on the field?

For the first time, Brown told himself, it was his football program—designed to save kids from gun violence—that had put them in danger. If the young woman had been looking for Trent, she knew where he'd be, when he'd be there, how to find him.

Brown finally dozed off around 3 a.m., though he kept waking up and alternating between guilt and fear. The next day he groggily reported to the football office and found his staff similarly shaken.

Some had been afraid, others filled with regret for not knowing about Trent's arrest, and at least a few responded with anger.

Nick, the program's resolute fixer, beat himself up over leaving the stadium early. He had no idea anything had gone on until he arrived at the school and chattering coaches began filing in. Nick wished he'd been there. He said he would've ended it.

But deep down he knew his presence would've solved nothing, and in the short term it might've escalated an already hyperintense situation. In the longer term, well, this is New Orleans. A man had been shot. By the law of the streets, revenge in some capacity seemed inevitable. Nothing here just fades away, and Nick was acutely aware of that even after the young woman ran off.

"Ain't no making peace with that shit. It's kill or be killed," he said, suspecting the drive for revenge would continue. "And there ain't no warning."

The echoes of Tonka's death were unmistakable. Brown and Nick talked about the right way to proceed. Brown addressed the staff, challenging coaches, already spread thin because of a particularly vexing team and the kids' ever-growing list of needs, to work harder. To dig deeper and learn if there were other players dancing on the razor's edge.

"We're not trying to just win a state championship," Brown told them. He reminded them of the program's true mission.

Nick spoke next. He told colleagues that regardless of the affection they might have for Trent, one player cannot be allowed to endanger the others. Dozens of people had been put in harm's way because of one kid, whether or not he'd been at Family Dollar. Coaches had tried not just to teach Trent but to reach him, but the program by its very nature is imperfect. Now it was time to move on.

What did Mike think? He'd vouched for Trent, talked to him, loved him.

He sighed and thought about what had happened.

"To follow him to the game . . ." he said, trailing off. But what had truly bothered Mike had been Trent's response to the confrontation. He hadn't looked bewildered or even scared. He was bold, as if he'd been waiting for something like this. "I just want him to be all right. He's really a good kid. He really is."

In forty-eight hours, though, Trent's teammates would again stream through those doors. If these four purple walls no longer stand for safety, they stand for nothing.

"No matter how much I love him," Mike said, "you gotta leave some of what you love behind."

And so it was decided: Trent would be indefinitely suspended. The coaches closed their meeting by agreeing to recalibrate on Monday and attempt to move on. Karr's next game was against cross-town rival Landry-Walker. With two losses and the playoffs approaching, every game mattered. The postseason felt simultaneously important and not important at all.

Brown dismissed his assistants, and the men scattered to deal with the preceding events in their own ways. Nick kept thinking about Trent's way forward, believing his only means of survival was to leave Louisiana forever. Mike had to talk himself out of driving back to Trent's house and asking him what was true. The reason he didn't was because Mike was scared of what he'd learn.

"Some shit," he said, "you just don't need to know."

Brown, for his part, went home and started a movie. He turned up the television as loud as it would go, trying to control the air traffic of his mind with distraction and noise. He tried to nap, an attempt at soothing himself with silence. But neither worked. Only one thing could provide solace on a matter this serious. So that evening he climbed into his truck, drove south to Harvey, and parked at Ditali's, a cozy Italian café.

He ordered wings and a full portion of shrimp fettuccine, topped with chicken. Usually it's large enough for two. But there was only one man sitting here, and when the dishes arrived and his table was full, Brown took his fork and went digging for peace, surely waiting near the bottom of his pasta bowl.

WHEN MONDAY AFTERNOON arrived, players walked in before practice and took their places in the weight room. Mike called roll but didn't say Trent's name.

Fat and Dany'e had been freshmen wide receivers with Trent. They had entered together, faced many of the same challenges, fought some of the same battles. Now one of them was gone. Fat sat on his captain's bench and stared into space. Though Dany'e isn't a captain, he nonetheless has an important job. Before coaches address players at team meetings, Dany'e hops off the floor and calls the meeting to order in an extremely Karr way.

"Where my n——s at?!" he yells, punching the air.

"Uh-*UHHHH*!" his teammates shout back.

Nick stood and faced them. As always, he believed not in altering or even sugarcoating the truth. Karr men deserve, and receive, honesty. Nick began by pointing out the obvious: Trent isn't here. For the foreseeable future, he told players, he is dismissed from the team, probably from school entirely. There are many things people here don't know, Nick told players, but Trent made mistakes and violated the Karr code.

"You chose to go right," he told the young men looking up at him. "Sometimes you gotta let the people going left alone."

He closed by reminding players they're safe here. If only here. He asked them to assure their parents that coaches are doing everything in their power to protect their kids. Practices, usually open to the public and accessible through the campus's back gate, will be closed from now on. The doors leading to the football office, often casually left ajar, will be locked day and night. And on game day, school buses and coaches' private vehicles will be chaperoned by a police escort.

Another NOPD cruiser will be stationed in front of the school, and bright floodlights will be installed on the school's facade.

"You're protected," Nick said again.

A few miles away in Gretna, a mother is at home with her son. She's trying to make sense of the previous days and weeks, what's real and what's not. For now, Gwen insists Trent was misidentified. She'll say he was just as shocked as anyone by what the young woman had accused him of doing. At home on the night of the confrontation, she says, Trent adamantly denied involvement in anything nefarious. She chose to believe him.

Gwen was nonetheless whipsawed by the situation. She was frightened for her son's safety and angry at some of her own coworkers at Karr.

As time passed, Trent would continue facing felony charges. Throughout this process, school and charter administrators superseded football coaches' decision and dismissed Trent from the school. While he awaited trial, he wasn't allowed on Karr's campus.

Gwen says she's confident Brown and the other coaches did right by her son. They tried to use football to help him overcome the very real issues at home and in his life. She says she's not angry at them. But she does feel betrayed by Karr's administration. Gwen says she tried to speak with her bosses and beg them to reconsider. But on the advice of attorneys, she says, they refused to discuss changing Trent's status. She says she wrote letters to the school board, maintaining her son's innocence and pleading for him to be readmitted. She says the letters were ignored.

"These people who I call my colleagues are failing my child," Gwen says. "This is a minor child that you're throwing to the wolves. You threw him to the wolves."

She continues.

"He's been walking around the street while me and his dad are at work, doing nothing. Because we can't babysit him," Gwen says. "So this is what you did to him. He could've possibly got shot or whatever; you pushed him out into the street because you said he was a risk. You punished him already. He's *been* punished. I don't know what else you want from him but blood."

ON THIS FIRST DAY BACK at Karr football practice, most everyone feels naked and vulnerable. The doors are bolted and the gates padlocked, but revenge finds a way. Nick wonders aloud if there's some way to send word into the streets that Trent isn't here anymore, that any would-be assailant would be coming to the wrong place if they come to the field looking for Trent.

Coaches try to curb their anxiety with football, assuring kids and themselves that the situation has been dealt with and that everyone is moving on. Players pull on their jerseys and helmets and jog onto the practice field. Then they take their places for warm-ups, and Mike jogs toward the speaker and plugs in his phone. He plays the same song he always does, though its lyrics, about feeling deceived and empty, are especially evocative today.

Well, the hurt doesn't show, but the pain still grows
It's no stranger to you and me

When Collins's iconic drum solo kicks in, players jump and scream before breaking off into small groups based on their positions. In that way, today is no different from any other. Drills begin, and Leonard fine-tunes his footwork and zips sharp passes to Fat and Dany'e and others. Leonte tucks the ball between his arms and dramatically crashes into whomever he can. Joe crouches into a ready position and prepares to shut down any ball carrier who dares run his way.

A few minutes into this, a white Dodge Charger with black trim approaches the rear gate. It slows and then stops. This is an unusual time for a car to be here. Eyes dart toward the vehicle, maybe eighty yards away, and after a moment the Charger slowly backs off.

Practice continues, and Tiga's phone rings. He answers it and immediately sprints toward the school. It's Brennan Harris, Karr's linebackers coach, calling. He's running late for practice, slowed by traffic on the Crescent City Connection. That was his Charger out back. He'd forgotten that the gate would be locked.

Tiga agrees to let Brennan in through a locked side door, and Tiga hurries through the hallway and releases the bolt. Parked now in the front lot, Brennan rushes inside. Tiga closes and relocks the door, and they jog through the hallway and onto the field, heading out with everyone else into the lonely open.

CHAPTER 8

HOMECOMING

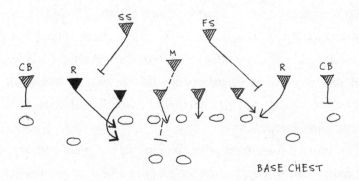

BASE CHEST

JOE'S AUNT OFFERED to pick him up from school one day. His mama had taught him to never accept unsolicited rides. Cautious as usual, Joe at first said no. His aunt insisted. She had a surprise for him.

Joe agreed, family being family, and he climbed in. Off they went.

At first the aunt suggested they were heading to Academy Sports, a sporting goods store not far from Karr, to buy Joe some new pants. But she continued past the shopping center and carried on west. They had to pick up Joe's niece first, his aunt said.

Now he was nervous. Where were they really going? He'd made a mistake.

In the months since Keyoke went to jail, Joe had established a routine and gotten used to his mother being away. Brown and Nick Foster took care of him sometimes, Joe had a steady girlfriend, and on occasion he spent the night in Gentilly.

Diane Eagleton had introduced herself to Joe a few years earlier, suggesting she was the young man's paternal grandmother. Neither could know for sure, considering Keyoke had never been certain which of her male companions had impregnated her, either the dead one or the one in prison. But Joe looked so much like Ms. Diane's son, Darrel, now serving his manslaughter sentence at a facility in Baton Rouge, that she was convinced.

Joe, yearning for traditional displays of affection and love, went along with it. Keyoke never cared much for Ms. Diane, but she was gone and Joe hated being alone. So when Ms. Diane invited him over, he usually said yes. They talked and looked at old photos and worked on jigsaw puzzles. At Christmas she bought him an Xbox. All this was well and good, though sometimes he wondered if these comforts were making him soft.

This crossed Joe's mind as he rode through Algiers with his aunt. His old instincts would've never permitted him to get in this car. Increasingly nervous, he demanded to know where they were going.

Fine, his aunt said. They were heading to Joe's apartment at Cypress Park. But the destination wasn't the surprise; it was who was waiting there.

Keyoke had been granted early parole, a December hearing expedited because of her good behavior (and a Louisiana prison system trying to decompress its notoriously overcrowded facilities). She'd been released that morning.

At first Joe believed his aunt was pranking him, and he yelled at her for being so cruel. But when the car stopped in the complex's parking lot, he saw the front door open. Then he saw Keyoke.

"That's my mama!" Joe said. He opened the vehicle's door and ran toward her.

They fell into each other's arms as their eyes flooded, just the two of them, the way things used to be.

KEYOKE AND JOE went to Academy Sports as planned, and she helped her son pick out a few things for school. Though only a few months had passed since her arrest, she marveled at how much her son had grown. She quietly lamented the things she'd missed.

She wanted to come watch him practice. She said she'd be at every game. She vowed to never miss another moment.

After a few days, Keyoke met with Brown and Nick. She thanked them for looking after her son and teaching him. At the end, she requested a Karr shirt to wear to games. Then she asked for a few dollars. Her electric bill was due, and she was already behind on the rent. Her bank accounts were empty.

"I did fucking time," she said. "Now they zeroing me out."

Brown and some other members of the community collected $400 to help Keyoke get back on her feet. But she didn't pay bills. Instead, Keyoke went to the grocery store. Among the many things prison takes away from you is the opportunity to do what you love, and for months now, Keyoke had been dying to cook. She planned an enormous feast to welcome herself home, and to make up for lost time with Joe. She invited her sister and niece to join them, and though the party was small, Keyoke made jambalaya, baked chicken, macaroni, corn, fried chicken, and dirty rice. She stayed in the kitchen for hours, and the leftovers would last for days.

In those first days, Joe slept peacefully for the first time in months. He didn't worry as often about his mother's safety. With Keyoke no longer incarcerated, he was confident he'd perform better on the field and bridge his old and new lives. He was eager for his mother to meet Cassidy, a Karr cheerleader who'd introduced him to sushi (and tricked him into thinking wasabi was ice cream). Joe imagined Sunday dinners and Christmases with Keyoke and Ms. Diane. He wanted to share his accomplishments and elaborate dreams with his mother, because she is who'd made them possible.

Joe told her that he wanted to be an entrepreneur and someday op-
erate multiple businesses, maybe a tattoo shop and a car wash. Maybe
he'd come full circle and run his own McDonald's franchise.

But all this sounded complicated to Keyoke. Her idea of making
money had always been simple, and on her schedule. She walked outside when she felt like it, slung a little product, filled her pockets with
cash. Joe was talking about a long-term plan that involved maneuvering
she'd never considered. Besides, it was hard enough for Keyoke to
remain focused on the challenges of today.

She'd vowed after this last conviction to never go back to prison,
and that of course meant never returning to the block. As the days
passed, Keyoke learned how hard it is to break old habits. Like so
many of the six hundred thousand Americans released from prisons
each year, Keyoke lacked education or a meaningful work history.
Now she was among the 27 percent of formerly incarcerated people
who are unemployed—a rate higher even than the general population's
unemployment rate during the Great Depression. Among Black women,
that percentage doubles.

At age thirty-five, Keyoke worked on her first résumé, though she
had no idea what to put on it. She'd once spent a month working
for a temp agency, and while incarcerated she completed her general
education development requirements and took a few college courses.
There wasn't much else to add.

She filled out job applications and researched how to get a commercial driver's license. Most of the time, prospective employers didn't call
back. There's no guidebook for returning to society or finding your
footing in the legal economy or even how to deal with the stress of
it. Before, during, and after incarceration, women face greater risk of
mental health disorders than men and, during the first months after
release, are at an elevated risk of major depressive episodes and suicidal thoughts. There's nothing easy about reentry, made all the more

difficult by social stigma, insomnia, and persistent sadness and anger. At least in the beginning, Keyoke tried to remain hopeful, and to keep the promises she'd made to Joe and herself.

"Trying to be a truck driver, do something different—Uber driver, something. Taxi driver, something," she said not long after coming home. "Long as I don't sell no more rocks."

The old itch was persistent, though, and Keyoke always claimed she was addicted to money. She indeed missed the feeling of a full pocket, the sense of independence and power it granted. It was all right outside the apartment door. While she'd been away, the City of New Orleans had installed bright floodlights to discourage dealers from posting up at Cypress Acres Drive and Vespasian. But the city would need something stronger to depress its mighty drug trade, or the pangs flaring up inside one of its newly freed residents.

"I be trying to stay inside," Keyoke said. "I ain't strong yet. I won't lie to you. I ain't strong. I see it's getting close to my baby graduation, and I *need* a graduation. I need to send him all the way out."

Though Keyoke's parenting philosophy may seem unorthodox, it's hard to argue against its effectiveness. Like Brown says about coaching Karr kids, strategies that may seem gratuitous to outsiders may be necessary to prepare young people for the harshness of life here. Among Karr's players, Joe stands alone as what Brown wants a young man to be: mature, aware, circumspect. He scrutinizes strangers, and Keyoke's way of teaching him developed this and actually helped him find the right people to trust. In other words, she taught him to survive his first eighteen years, then brought him to Brown, who could then teach him to live and thrive in the decades to come.

Joe's escape had always been Keyoke's motivation. As brutish as she acts with an audience, as tough as she looks at 230 pounds and tattooed, deep down she's still a single mother who wants better for her son. She treasures the memories she has of him, quietly sending old pictures and hoping you feel what she does. There's Joe toddling around in baggy jeans and an Allen Iverson jersey. Here he is with his arm around his mother, both of them making hand signs.

"They sum good pic," she writes. Getting Joe to graduation, to her, would validate what she'd done. It'd be her finish line. She needed to see it.

But for everything she had taught Joe, there was one thing she'd never prepared herself for: sharing him. He had school and football and social responsibilities, and he was gone much of each day. Since Keyoke had been gone, Joe had learned to compartmentalize his life and stay on schedule. When he was home, Joe and his mother talked and dreamed and laughed about the past. When he was at school, or with Cassidy, or at Ms. Diane's, Keyoke's mind drifted. She used to have a bigger television and nicer furniture. She used to be able to get their two poodles professionally groomed. Now it was up to her to bathe and clip them, and afterward she'd look upon her work and frown.

Keyoke isn't a proud crier like Rhonda George, doesn't dwell powerlessly on the past like Gwen Washington. She channels her feelings of insecurity into aggression, usually, or busy work. She distracted herself by cleaning the house and vacuuming the staircase carpet. She picked up stuffing from dog toys and a puffy chair they'd chewed on. She scrubbed dried piss off the tile.

"You know how long it took for me to get that dog smell out of here?" Keyoke snapped at Joe one evening.

"So—oh my *God*!" he shot back. He pointed out that he'd spent weekends not with friends but borrowing supplies from the football office and maintaining the apartment. He did not mention having to navigate a possible eviction.

"You cleaned your room," Keyoke said.

"When I was here by myself," Joe said, "I was worrying about cleaning everything else *but* my room."

They argued, made peace, promised to do better. Then, invariably, Joe left again. Keyoke clicked her teeth but claimed to accept that her little boy wasn't so little anymore. Soon she was alone again, the television blaring and the poodles yapping, and at one point she got so bored that she walked across the living room. She put her hand between the vertical blinds, leaned close to the window, and looked outside.

THE NOVELTY of KEYOKE's homecoming wore thin, and so did her patience with Joe. They argued increasingly often, and sometimes Keyoke made threats. She could always return to the block, she told him. How would he like that?

The truth was, he didn't just hate it. It was Joe's deepest fear. She knew that, and it served as her time-and-again nuclear option. Usually after the fact, she felt bad about it.

Joe tried to shake off his mother's warnings, but they stressed and distracted him. When he was away from home, he daydreamed about where his mother was and what she was doing. He missed tackles, zoned out during assignments on the field, found himself getting fooled by a ball carrier's basic trickery. A sophomore and junior linebacker makes these mistakes. Joe was supposed to be beyond them.

One night after practice, Nick drove to Cypress Park in an attempt to play peacemaker. He parked his sedan on the street, passed through the cloud of marijuana smoke outside the apartments, looked through the steel door. Keyoke was cleaning again. She hadn't yet gotten to the mangled dog toys or an empty box in the entryway.

"Chill out, chill out!" Joe shouted at the poodles as they announced Nick's arrival. After walking into the living room, Nick settled into an armchair in the corner.

Keyoke turned off the vacuum and sat in a folding chair next to

Joe. Short and thick, she looks older than she is, and her ashen skin and raised eyebrows make her look cynical and tired. Her dreads are tied back, revealing a "Predator"-style undercut. Distressed jean capris show a few of the tattoos on Keyoke's calves. She has a gold Grillz covering her teeth, and when she's uncomfortable or impatient, she sucks on the purple and yellow snakebite piercings in her bottom lip.

"Y'all doing me wrong," she tells Nick, jumping right in. She still doesn't have the Karr apparel she'd been promised. "I ain't even have a shirt since I been home."

Nick assures her that's easy. He'll send something home with Joe tomorrow. Now, what's this really about?

Keyoke takes a breath. She frequently initiates confrontations, and it's clear her default setting is to project strength and even aggression, a well-practiced survival instinct from a life on the block. But her body language undermines this persona. Her eyes drift to the floor, and she shifts in the folding chair.

"He ain't really spent time with me since I been home," she says of Joe. "But you gotta make time with them girls."

"Here you go," her son says. He forces an uncomfortable smile.

"Being real."

Nick responds calmly. He's a parent, too, but he's also a son. His mother died of cancer years ago, and now he only has his father, Ethridge. Months after his dementia diagnosis, Ethridge's health is deteriorating. Nick visits him most days in a memory care facility, and he wonders how much time his dad has left. Nick tells Joe that there's nothing like the pain of regret, something he learned the hard way. He doesn't wish it on Joe.

"Make time for your little woman," Nick says. "But you gotta make time for Mom, you know?"

Joe nods, and Keyoke looks at him and asks if he'll be running for homecoming king. Joe explains that Brown prefers that Karr's captains

focus on the team during the season. Keyoke sighs at the thought of
one more memory she'll miss. She was gone last spring when Joe went
to prom. Where are the photos Joe promised her?

He grimaces and says they're still at Ms. Diane's house. He pledges
to bring them home soon. Keyoke shakes her head and explodes.

"I don't need no handout," she says. "For real, people starting to make
me think I need 'em. I ain't used to that. Might as well get this money."

There she goes again. Nick speaks up.

"Soon as you get that feeling," he says, "I just need you to think
about Joe."

"I know," she says. "I went the other day; I was about to get in them
streets, and my baby hit my head. I said: 'Lord, I can't do him this.'"

There's a quiet moment, and Keyoke is ruminating. Every parent, if
they've done their job well, sees their usefulness fade. But her mistakes
have denied her precious memories with her only child, and now Joe
is dividing his vanishing youth with other people. Usually it's Ms.
Diane who's the beneficiary, and who Keyoke increasingly sees as a
competitor.

"I understand she trying to be a grandma," she continues. "But
she do it overextreme sometimes. You could never compete with me,
because I've been here from day one. When I didn't have nowhere
to go—sleep, nothing, no Pampers or nothing—I had to do this on
my own."

Nick and Joe are silent, allowing Keyoke to vent. Her voice is getting
louder, and she's pointing in the air with her index finger. Joe stares
at the white tiling, scratched up by the poodles' nails.

"Bitch, I did this on my *own*," Keyoke says. She has talked herself
into a fury. "My son grown now. You know what I'm saying? I never
called y'all and asked y'all for a motherfucking thing. Never."

She pauses.

"I ain't beefing with her," she continues. "It's just that—respect my mind, what I did. Your son ain't do a fucking thing. He been in jail all his life. Respect what I did do. Y'all at a game watching my baby and seeing his future and what *I* done did."

She doesn't like that Ms. Diane buys things for Joe. Keyoke believes this is an attempt at buying her son's affection, and siphoning off his time. Joe assures her this isn't true. He points out the obvious: Keyoke and Ms. Diane have vastly different life experiences, and see the world in contrasting ways.

"You can't relate to each other," Joe says, "because y'all never lived like each other."

"Got me fucked up," Keyoke says, attempting to calm down. "Because I don't have it like I used to, and I'm not able. So that's a insult to me."

"But I was like: Ma, you good," Joe says.

"That's still a insult, though!"

"Ma. You *good.*"

He's not the little boy she needs to dress up anymore, Joe explains, but he loves and appreciates Keyoke anyway. He just wants his mother to be safe.

Keyoke says nothing as she stares at the floor. Nick tries to lower the temperature by asking if she'll be at Karr's next game. She says she doesn't have a ride and can't afford bus fare.

"I'm supposed to have me a VIP pass on my baby last year," she grumbles. "I ain't got no shirt; I ain't got nothing. Y'all know I just come home. I ain't in the fast lane no more. I'm in the slow, slow, slow, slow, *slow* lane. Fuck. It's, like, so slow here."

Nick says he'll talk to Brown. The coaches want Keyoke to be happy, and to take part in her son's success. Joe purses his lips and smiles at his mother. She shakes her head and chuckles.

"Y'all ain't even throw a n—— a bone over here," Keyoke continues, then looks at Joe. "You got some money for me?"

He leans forward and rolls down one of his crew-length socks. Inside he has a folded twenty-dollar bill that someone gave him at school. He peels off the cash and hands it over.

"This ain't even enough for no gas!" she says, and Joe laughs. "I need twenty more."

COACHES ALWAYS THOUGHT Joe would play better once his mama came home. He'd no longer have to worry, which would free his mind to play with discipline and even greater determination.

But this had been fantasy.

Instead, Joe left the apartment each morning and worried *more* than he had with Keyoke in jail. His teachers and ACT tutor caught him staring into space, and coaches continually corrected his mistakes. He blew assignments, missed signals, relayed bad information to his teammates. Though this was Karr's stretch run, Joe the team's heart and soul, Brown knew the young man's head just wasn't in it. T. Howard, the team's defensive coordinator, "dog-cussed" him so often for running toward the wrong gap or failing to attack the line correctly on a "Base Chin" blitz or going the wrong way on a play, that Howard eventually ran out of cuss words and just laughed. Still, the timing couldn't have been worse.

Brown tried to snap Joe out of it, especially on game days. Karr had, almost inexplicably, come together in the last few weeks. It helped that, for the first time all season, Karr's starting lineup—and in particular its offensive line—wasn't decimated by injuries. Center Joe Hayes had returned from his ankle sprain, left tackle Kenny Bannister was healthy and dominant, and receiver Aaron Anderson had finally gotten over his sprained knee. Rodney Johnson, a tall defensive back who'd torn his anterior cruciate ligament in the second game, was the only player actually lost for the season.

There otherwise was no magic formula or skeleton key. Brown

hadn't drastically altered the offense or indulged in any addition-by-subtraction lineup maneuvering.

If anything, it's that Brown *stopped* tinkering and just accepted something he'd actually known since training camp: that, as he'd put it, this is a "fucked-up team." More pain and immaturity than the previous three state champions, less talent and experience, no immediately discernible identity. And after the thing happened with Trent Washington, Brown finally realized that this was just a collection of busted-up souls, coaches and players alike. That *was* this team's identity. For weeks now, a coach who builds his program on a foundation of individualism had been trying to turn this group into something it wasn't. Brown was embarrassed when he finally realized how simple it had always been. Now that he stopped experimenting and just designed and called plays, accepting that the team often made mistakes early in games and then recovered, Karr found its stride.

They won three, four, five games in a row. The Cougars went on the road and beat Wossman, came home to hammer Eleanor McMain, survived a tense rivalry game against Landry-Walker.

But every game from here on was important, especially if Karr had any hope of getting home-field advantage in the state playoffs. Brown saw that as critical to his team's chances of playing in the Superdome and reaching the Class 4A championship game for the fifth consecutive year. As it was, Lakeshore High was undefeated and seemed to be a lock for the top seed—and, barring a massive upset, the championship game. Neville, whose campus is five hours away in Monroe, had one regular-season loss compared to Karr's two. That gave Neville the advantage for the number 2 seed. Brown's team could be perfect to end the regular season, win its first three playoff games, and *still* have to endure a harsh road trip. Brown wanted to avoid that at all costs. When Karr went to Monroe to play Wossman, a good team but one in a smaller classification, Karr had won despite its exhaustion. Brown had elected to go up and back in less than twenty-four hours, sprinkling in a game, walk-through, and two team meals as part of a marathon itinerary. A similar trip against Neville, an elite opponent on its home field, was the kind of scenario where championship dreams go to die.

Brown was hopeful, though not if a keystone player such as Joe was distracted. He reminded Joe that college recruiters would be watching. Nothing less than Joe's future, the dreams he'd worked so hard to make real, was on the line. Though Joe kept saying all the right things, coaches often found him staring into the bleachers before and during games, trying to find his mom.

If he found her, he'd run confidently onto the field and play as coaches hoped. If he didn't, he'd make mistakes. Brown again contemplated temporarily stripping Joe of his captaincy. A psychological reboot, perhaps, and a way to simplify a clashing set of priorities. But Nick and Norm Randall reminded Brown that this was Joe they were talking about. His jersey number and authority over teammates weren't meaningless superlatives. They were powerful symbols of the growth he'd made, and of the person he was trying to become.

Brown agreed and stood down, again resisting the temptation to tinker with a fragile kid during an especially precarious time. Brown decided to just talk to him and try shepherding him through this. Joe opened up to Brown in ways he couldn't with Keyoke, admitting he lived in constant fear that his mother would get arrested or even shot. He was nonetheless thankful for the things he learned while Keyoke had been in prison, becoming self-sufficient and learning to get along with individuals from different backgrounds. Joe secretly wondered if his mother's absence, painful and frightening as it had been, had actually been the best thing for him.

"More doors opened," he'd say. "Something could happen to my mama any day. I need to grow relationships with more people."

This included Brown and Nick, Leonard and Jamie, Cassidy and

Ms. Diane. These weren't bit players who shared Joe's world. They had fused into a support system, something he'd never had. If Keyoke made a mistake or couldn't find a solution, others could.

"Football just saved me," he said one day. "It just changed everything and gave me love. That's probably what I was missing: not enough love."

Keyoke had provided it, preparing him to exist in the world she knew. Like many single mothers, she had done the best she could despite limitations. Her style wasn't perfect. But she'd worked, nurtured, and sacrificed in a society that often makes parenthood more difficult than it should be. And, most important, she realized she wasn't equipped to push Joe to the finish line alone. In signing him up for football, submitting his name into the InspireNOLA lottery, and turning him over to Brown and Karr, Keyoke was admitting—in her way—that she needed help.

Keyoke knew her job wasn't yet complete. And now came the final, and hardest, part of her son's training: protecting him not from the world, but from his own mother's worst tendencies. She'd always said he'd have to learn to live without her, and what Joe wanted and the things he needed were sometimes in conflict.

So a few days before Karr's game against Belle Chasse, Keyoke called Brown. That was Senior Night, when Karr honors its upperclassmen, and Keyoke complained that the ceremony had been scheduled too early. She'd never existed on anyone else's schedule, and she couldn't guarantee she'd make it to Behrman Stadium by 6:30 p.m.

Brown offered to delay the event by thirty minutes. When game day arrived, Joe warmed up but kept glancing toward the bleachers. Keyoke wasn't there. The ceremony began, and the public address announcer called Leonard's name. He walked onto the field with Demetrice and Leonard II. Then came Jamie, who stood arm in arm with his parents as they posed for photographs. The other seniors followed with their relatives, standing along the Karr sideline.

At almost seven, Keyoke was nowhere to be found. Joe had badly wanted this, to smile for the camera and pretend he was like the other boys. But Keyoke never saw much use in showing her son a sanitized view of his world, or being fake, even on Senior Night.

As Joe kept searching for his mother, Ms. Diane saw him from the bleachers. She hurried down the stadium's concrete stairs, darted around the corner, dashed through a gate. She reached the sideline and slid her arm around Joe's, and whether this was right or wrong for him, they smiled and walked together as he tried, for just a moment, to be like everyone else.

CHAPTER 9

ONE FOOT OUT

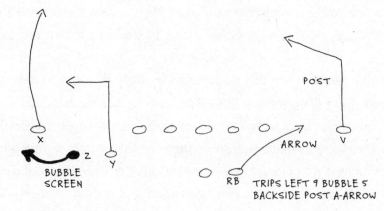

FOR ALL HIS TOUGH-GUY theatrics and hulking size, Brice Brown is actually a four-hundred-pound teddy bear. His laugh, especially when indulging his prankish side or quoting comedies such as *The Hangover*, is a high-pitched cackle. One evening while picking up food for players at the fast-food chicken joint Raising Cane's, Brown cracked himself up after getting tangled up in his own seat belt, driving onto the curb in the drive-through line, and accidentally tooting the horn of his Silverado.

He's highly intelligent and generally impatient with those who don't process information as quickly as he does, which is nearly everyone. Despite his authority, Brown truly loves being intellectually challenged. He's intrigued by history, politics, and behavioral psychology. But most everyone here would rather talk football, a subject that comes so easy to Brown that it bores him. Sometimes in the middle of a conversation about downs and distances, he'll stealthily remove his phone and fire up *Toy Blast*, the addictive iPhone game. He enjoys the dopamine hit of leveling up, but more than that, this master of self-distraction likes that it soothingly occupies his mind when there's something Brown doesn't want to deal with. He plays at restaurants and during administrative meetings. During halftime of the 2018 state championship game, with Karr narrowly leading Warren Easton High, assistant coaches were screaming, cursing, more or less losing their minds. Brown decided that his plays would either work or they wouldn't, and no amount of fretting would change that. So he found an empty chair in a breezeway, opened *Toy Blast*, and lost himself in the colorful squares.

His happy places are restaurants, of course, but also open fields with clear views of the night sky. Brown downloaded a stargazing app, and one evening after practice he pointed his phone at Vega. He called over Leonard and Karr's other two quarterbacks, and Brown considered that the star was twenty-five light-years away. The light they were all looking at, he told the teenagers, had actually been emitted seven years before Leonard was born. They oohed and ahhed, and Brown then moved the screen toward Antares, a red pulsating variable that's 554 light-years from Earth. This light had been traveling since the time of Leonardo da Vinci, and Brown thought about the fact that the star might not even *exist* anymore. Though Leonard seemed interested in all this, he was actually more fascinated by the fact that his coach seemed to have entered a cheerfully hypnotic state.

Brown can be moody, especially when he's tired, overly strained, or lost on the back roads of his own mind. On occasion he turns into the Incredible Hulk, even if many of his outbursts are artificial ways to get the attention of his players and staff. He boasts after the fact that it feels like acting. Brown likes to see how authentic his anger feels, even to him. Those closest to Brown know when he's in character, though, and when he's not. And they've learned to recognize a telltale sign of when his fury is genuine. To identify the rumbles, as it were, of a certain indisputable truth that rages within this Hulk: that you wouldn't like him when he's hangry.

For most of the last decade, Karr's coaches have adopted an unusual, and uncomfortable, tradition. Karr played Neville in the 2011 state championship game, the start of an on-field rivalry and collision of cultures. Neville is in Monroe, a blue-collar city about three hundred miles from New Orleans. That year it hammered Karr, 27–6, for Neville's tenth state title. Karr's coaches decided the loss hadn't been because of inferior talent or lax preparation. Rather, the program had somehow gotten cross with the man upstairs.

"God was punishing us," Brown would explain. He's not joking.

So the next year, then-head coach Jabbar Juluke proposed a staff-wide cleanse as a show of gratitude and fealty. Karr loosely follows a Catholic curriculum, though beyond prayer after practices and meetings, there aren't many reminders of this around the football office. But for three weeks in 2012, coaches fasted during daylight hours. When Karr and Neville met again in that year's state title game, it was Karr that hoisted the championship trophy.

The fast had worked. Or so coaches told themselves. Regardless, they kept doing it, and considering Brown enjoys social experiments, these sacrifices have grown only more intense. One year coaches agreed to eat only fruits and green vegetables for three weeks. Brown, of course, refuses to eat most plant-based foods and claims they make him sick (though not, curiously, when lettuce comes on a burger or chicken sandwich). He mostly starved himself and was generally unbearable. Another year the staff could eat seafood, so long as they omitted all other meats.

"We tried the no-cussing one," Brown recalled. "*That* didn't fucking work."

In 2019, coaches decided the team was just warped enough that drastic measures were necessary. From sunup to sundown, Monday through Wednesday, the staff could eat no animal products whatsoever. Anything but fruits, veggies, and grains were to be considered an affront to God himself.

The afternoon before Karr's homecoming game Marvin Rose kept sneaking into the coaches' office to crush granola bars. Nick Foster ate from a box of Nutri-Grain snacks with the grace and ferocity of a starving bear at a campsite. Omari Robertson sneaked to a grocery store to build a mountainous salad, and Mike Thompson pounded cough drops as if they were candy.

Brown, of course, had eaten nothing all day. As practice began, most everyone avoided him. The team's first-year medical consultant, a soft-spoken man named Will, hadn't yet learned to give the starving man a wide berth.

"You okay?" Will asked Brown. The coach stood on the sideline with his arms crossed.

"They don't want to be out here," he mumbled.

Brown watched as Leonard's passes were off target time and again. Fat and other receivers kept dropping passes or running bad routes. Joe was still making mental errors in the weeks after his mother came home. This walk-through practice, meant as a final tune-up for tomorrow night, had been scheduled for two hours. Instead, Brown sounded an air horn after thirty minutes.

"Send 'em out!" he thundered, and assistants looked at him with confusion. They ordered players off the field anyway. The execution wasn't perfect, but it hadn't been *that* bad.

Brown fumed as he lumbered toward the school. When he entered the football office, he saw players carefully removing and stowing their equipment, precisely as they'd been trained to do.

"Leave that shit!" Brown shouted. "Go home!"

He retreated into the coaches' office, plopped into a chair, stood back up. He stormed into the weight room and screamed at his assistants for, generally speaking, being terrible at life. When Brown is mad—legitimately, as is the case now—his voice deepens into a low-pitched growl that cuts through ambient sound. It is impossible to ignore.

"Ain't going to the pep rally. Ain't doing *shit*!" he said, spinning in the doorway and sitting again in the rolling chair.

Seething, Brown removed his phone and opened *Toy Blast*. He jabbed the screen with his finger and grumbled about poor habits and a lack of motivation. If players don't give a damn, he murmured, why should he? He kept playing his game, trying to self-soothe. But at least the adults here knew why Brown was ornery: he was just hungry, and his blood sugar had cratered. His mood smashed into a brick wall, then caught fire, then exploded.

Tiga gently opened the door and asked if he could bring Brown a Coke. The coach declined. Sometimes, because of stress or stubbornness or both, Brown either forgets to eat or outright refuses. This time, he instructed Tiga to prepare the 2012 uniforms for tomorrow's game. Players love playing in gleaming new threads, and pulling on old uniforms is a form of punishment. If equipment was musty or dirty, Brown said, Tiga was to avoid washing it. The pregame meal, Brown told his dutiful equipment man, was to be three fish sticks and one red potato per player. They could cancel the lavish homecoming meal previously scheduled with a local caterer. Tiga, visibly regretting having entered, agreed. Then he left as quickly as he could.

Brown was alone, joylessly popping the yellow and blue bubbles on his iPhone, muttering to himself about what sounded like revenge.

"*I'm* gonna show 'em," he said.

A FEW WEEKS EARLIER, during the long trip to Wossman High, Brown had arranged for the team to hold a brief walk-through practice on the campus of the University of Louisiana at Monroe. He often does some version of this during road trips, and the rationale is multipronged.

The obvious reason is that Karr just needs an open field to stretch its legs and practice on. The more subtle, and clever, motive is that Brown uses these visits to expose children, some of whom had never left the West Bank before playing for Karr, to a pristine and sprawling college campus. Brown schedules walking tours of quads and manicured green spaces, and he points out stately buildings and raves about their histories. These trips aren't cheap, and an interesting by-product of a cash-strapped school's success is that a deep playoff run or championship leads to additional games, which then leads to considerable cost. For instance, Karr's annual football budget is a little more than $50,000, according to athletic director Taurus "T." Howard. In 2018, Howard had to stretch that budget (and later supplement it with fund-raising efforts such as a fish fry, car wash, and T-shirt and candy drives) to rent Behrman Stadium and pay game officials for three postseason home games. The school was also responsible for transportation and food costs for about a hundred players and coaches when Karr went on the road to play Tioga, about two hundred miles away, in the second round. And when the team captured its third consecutive state championship, that meant a massive bill that set Howard's budget ablaze: roughly $47,000 for championship rings.

"It's expensive to win," says Howard, who's also the football team's defensive coordinator. "I really understand that now."

But Howard also trusts Brown, who understands the potentially life-changing value of everything from winning a state championship to just setting foot on a college campus. These are previously unfathomable achievements for some kids here, and more than Brown just making them real, he wants these experiences to feel grand. The team eats pregame meals at either the campus dining hall or a nearby buffet, with hungry kids loading plate after plate just because they can. If the trip requires an overnight stay, Brown pushes Howard to spring for the Hilton or a Marriott. Howard never says no.

"We're gonna figure out how to do it," he says. "It's my job to make sure we get what we need."

The purpose of this, other than giving Howard a headache, isn't opulence. It is to begin demystifying the world beyond a problematic, if familiar, New Orleans. It's also to incentivize a future escape. On this side of the Mississippi River, according to Brown, is an unkempt and dangerous land. Players needn't look beyond Karr's dank football office, with its peeling paint and dilapidated equipment, for daily reminders of a message their coach wants them to receive.

Across the river, now a little less foreign, is a bountiful landscape of peace, comfort, and possibility. There are no gunshots there. No hunger. The pillows are fluffy, the sheets clean. Brown wants to entice them to get out of New Orleans, fall in love with life—or even the *idea* of life—elsewhere, and never come back. It's not that he cares so little for the young men that good-bye means nothing. It is that he cares enough, in fact, to admit good-bye might save their lives.

It is an elaborate, and convincing, display. But the children are neither old nor well traveled enough to recognize the irony in this part of their coach's mission.

Nearly two decades ago, an ambitious young man from Algiers used football as a springboard out of New Orleans. It was, as it's often put in places like this, his way out. But after three years at Grambling State, young Brice Brown felt an overwhelming pull, and he did the one thing he'd later implore the next generation to never do. He went home.

Over the years Brown has had opportunities to move on and chase his dreams elsewhere. He always said no. At first it was because he had so much authority in his midtwenties. Juluke let him design his own version of the "Tiger Stretch" offense he'd learned at Grambling. Then it was because Brown was named head coach. Then because he was too successful, too important to the Karr machine, afforded too much deference and control. He bowed to no one. Not the principal or the charter CEO or politicians. Saints coach Sean Payton and then-mayor Mitch Landrieu knew Brown's name. How do you walk away from that?

Then Guy and Tonka died, and Brown's objective changed. So did what he valued. He saw the dead men's faces in young players he'd grown to care about. He couldn't push them into the world without further preparation. So no matter his accomplishments, no matter the wins and championships, Brown's task felt incomplete. It was also just beginning.

At first there was Racey McMath, a star wide receiver. If Brown could get Racey out of New Orleans, perhaps now he'd be ready to move on. But then Racey got a scholarship to Louisiana State, and there was a hotheaded running back named Ronnie Jackson a year behind him. Maybe if Brown got Ronnie out, then he could go, too.

Ronnie was a challenge, maybe the biggest of Brown's career. He was talented like Tonka, charismatic like Guy. He quit every team he'd ever played on. Even at Karr, he skipped practice to smoke weed, and some weeks he'd march in and announce he was done with football. He wanted help signing up for trucking school or advice as he applied for a job.

"Get the hell out of my face," Brown told him. "You don't get to determine when you're finished."

His point was that, by then, others had a stake in Ronnie's future. They cared about him, his survival and success. Brown had found that young people, here and perhaps elsewhere, get overwhelmed and stressed out when authority figures tell them they can and should be anything. The message may be well-intentioned and even true in theory, but Brown discovered that kids do better when they're given *fewer* options, not more. Pick this or that, not this or a dozen possible thats.

When Ronnie realized Brown would only help him on the coach's binary terms, he kept coming back, even if it was to pick another argument. Whatever it takes, after all. Brown brought Ronnie food when he was hungry, gave him a ride when he needed to go somewhere, argued or provided advice depending on what the kid needed. Sometimes they got into shouting matches that rattled the office door. Ronnie toured campuses during Karr road trips, and Brown personally drove him to visit other schools in Kentucky and Texas. They won three state championships together. Ronnie wasn't just a team captain and Karr man. He was on track to be Brown's greatest success story. Eventually a recruiter from the University of Texas at San Antonio called and offered Ronnie a scholarship—his way out. Off Ronnie went, across the bridge and gone from Louisiana.

At last, Brown's work was finished. He could indulge his own dreams and try calling plays for a school where the windows aren't cracked and the kids don't go hungry. A Power Five coach offered Brown a dream job, and he decided to take it. He told some people of his decision, Ronnie included. The young man wasn't happy for his former coach. He was angry.

"You can't fucking leave," he told Brown. Who would buy school clothes for disadvantaged kids? Who'd bring them food or provide counsel? Ronnie was right. Brown couldn't do it, so he turned down the chance of a lifetime. Then, early in 2019, UT San Antonio made overtures to Brown. He could be the Roadrunners' offensive coordinator, call plays, return to Ronnie's side.

Brown again said no. Then, a few weeks later, Grambling called. Brown's alma mater wanted him to join the staff and leave New Orleans once again, perhaps this time for good. Brown talked himself into it, then he returned to the Karr football office and changed his mind. Though their names were different—Leonard and Joe and Leonte and Fat—what he saw in their faces wasn't. Brown still saw Tonka and Guy, the young men he hadn't saved. He could change that with the kids here, looking up at him. Though the itch remained strong to bring his offense and philosophy to the college ranks, he called Grambling's head coach and said he couldn't do it. At least not yet.

As the months and years pass, Brown has thought often about this quandary. If he spends his entire career at Karr, he'll win championships and provide a valuable public service to an underserved community of youngsters. But he'll be unfulfilled, underpaid, struggling to sleep as he worries or wonders if he'd really been destined to be "just" a high school coach. If he leaves for another job, he'll test himself on a grander stage and see what his mind is truly capable of. But if a kid from Karr gets shot, especially a kid he once coached and cared about, Brown knows he'd never forgive himself.

"I'm damned," he says one Saturday afternoon after driving to LSU to visit Racey. He's one of several players Brown spends his downtime checking in on and supporting after they've left Karr. "And that's just the truth."

During that road trip to Monroe in October 2019, players and coaches pile into two motor coaches and complete the entire trip in a penny-pinching but exhausting twenty-one hours. Brown snuggles up with a pillow in a row to himself, but he doesn't sleep. As usual, his mind races.

At one point Nick, sitting in the row next to Brown, realizes something. Over all these years, Karr has visited more than a half-dozen colleges. But never Grambling.

"You don't think the kids wanna see where their coach went to school?" he asks Brown. The big man shrugs and insists the day's schedule is set. The trip's shoestring budget has been approved.

Nick doesn't buy it. Brown still bows to no one and can alter the schedule any time, and Nick knows the team is scheduled to have lunch in West Monroe at a Golden Corral, which can't be far from Grambling.

Brown closes his eyes and tries to get comfortable. The truth is, he hasn't set foot on Grambling's campus in years. It has nothing to do with logistics or the school's isolation. It's because visiting, inspiring as it might've once been to the young man from Algiers, is now a reminder of what Brown *hasn't* accomplished, and of the decision he made years ago to come home.

Nick pulls up a map on his phone.

"Thirty-five miles," he says, turning the display toward his boss. Maybe a quick detour?

Brown nestles deeper into his pillow.

"Maybe next time," he says.

NOT LONG AFTER the Wossman game, when Brown's doubts in the season and himself were most intense, three seemingly unrelated events threatened to crumble Karr's foundation. The first, and most frightening, was the on-field incident involving Trent Washington.

Nick noticed unmistakable signals of Brown's anxiety. He seemed unusually distant and isolated. If coaches gathered to crack jokes or talk shit after practice, or if a dance party broke out before a game, Brown could usually be found alone. Nick believed Brown was having a harder time opening up to kids. He wondered if the boss had begun putting emotional distance between himself and the players, preparing to make a move. Work seemed unsatisfying to Brown, and he was looking older and more tired. Part of that was the normal rigors of a hard season. But there had been nothing normal about what happened with Trent, which had legitimately scared Brown and Nick. As the days and weeks passed, it became clear two men used to controlling this tiny universe were losing their grips.

The next was when Norm Randall, a Karr man if there ever was one, privately told Brown he'd soon be stepping away. Like most assistant coaches here, Norm has a day job, along with a wife and two sons. His football stipend pays him about $18,500 a year. As Norm's responsibilities expanded as an information technology consultant at the Ernest N. Morial Convention Center, it was becoming increasingly obvious that coaching Karr's special teams and defensive line was a hobby, not a career.

He'd been offered an assignment requiring weekly travel to work trade shows in Orlando and San Francisco. If he accepted, Norm would earn in a few weeks what he made all season coaching football. But he'd be gone during the week throughout most of November and December, Karr's stretch run and most of the playoffs. He was an essential part of the coaching staff, a skilled and honest teacher of the game's finer points. More than that, if Brown was the program's brain and Nick its muscle, Norm was the team's conscience. He had deep and meaningful conversations with players about race and identity and purpose, and regardless of a player's athletic ability, Norm challenged them to think beyond a lottery-ticket career in sports or hip-hop. He encouraged them to learn a musical instrument, a foreign language, computer programming and code.

"I'm just trying to tell them: the world is so big," Norm said one afternoon at the school. "It's little shit: Kids don't want to get clowned, but maybe that's okay. It's okay to be a regular student and go play music, go work on your computer, go read a book—shit that normal Black kids don't do."

Norm told Brown he was conflicted. As he'd told Chris D months earlier, Brown said he shouldn't be. He advised Norm to do what's best for his family and go. Karr would figure it out, or maybe it wouldn't. Who cares? Brown said. It's football.

The third event in the sequence was the most subtle, appearing at first to have nothing to do with Karr. St. Augustine High is an all-boys, predominantly Black parochial school in New Orleans's Seventh Ward.

Its football program, recently overshadowed in Louisiana's "Catholic League" by giants such as John Curtis and Catholic High, is nonetheless among the state's most prestigious programs. NFL stars Tyrann Mathieu and Leonard Fournette came of age playing for the Purple Knights, and they're among a loyal alumni base that often recites the school's goose-bump-inducing motto, an expression of Black strength: "Rise, sons of the gold and purple."

Following St. Aug's loss against Brother Martin on October 4, a video apparently taken before the game made its way onto social media. The footage is blurry, but a Black assistant coach can be seen and heard leading a chant with players in the locker room: "I got two hands, two pads; knock a n——'s shit loose!"

The video went viral, and national media outlets reported on it along with the school's response. Unlike other New Orleans high schools, St. Aug's curriculum and culture are strictly tied to the Catholic Church and its campus ministry. It offers a four-year theology program, and students attend Mass at the school once a month. Five Josephite priests serve on St. Aug's board of directors, and the school has a chief religious officer. After the locker room video leaked, St. Aug issued a statement in which the school's president and chief executive said he was "shocked and embarrassed" by the use of "indefensible" language. Head coach Nathaniel Jones and two of his assistant coaches were fired. Jones, who had been Karr's head coach before leaving the school in 2015, would claim he hadn't been in the locker room during the chant. In a wrongful termination and defamation lawsuit, which asked for $6.5 million in damages but which a federal judge later dismissed, Jones said he never uses the N-word and in fact hasn't used profanity since 1997.

Immediately following Jones's ouster, St. Aug athletic director Barret Rey formed a list of possible successors. A former college baseball player and coach, Rey added an ambitious candidate to that list: Brice Brown. Rey knew prying Brown from his high school alma mater, a Louisiana football power, was unlikely. But what did he have to lose?

What Rey couldn't know was that Brown had again been thinking more about a new job. St. Aug was, at best, a lateral move and wasn't the college opportunity Brown and Chris D used to discuss. Karr would be moving to a state-of-the-art new campus the following school year, but Brown didn't like that InspireNOLA hadn't so much as asked him to share ideas for the football facility and practice field. Chris D had left the program, and now Norm was stepping aside, too. Nick remained committed to Karr football, but he was increasingly distracted by personal matters. Nick, who has two children, went months between jobs when he lost his teaching position at a school on the East Bank. Though he made extra money driving for rideshare companies, he has diabetes and no longer had health insurance to help defray the cost of insulin. To further complicate matters, the health of Nick's father, Ethridge, was eroding fast. Most nights Nick raced out of the football office to help get his dad to bed.

The Karr band, it seemed, was breaking up. But nothing had convinced Brown he needed a change of scenery like the episode with Trent. Brown suggested before the season that kids seemed to be less willing to buy into his message. He'd second-guessed himself and his program's durability after those two losses early in the season, and like an aging pitcher, Brown worried he might be losing his fastball. To him, Trent—and the fact that coaches hadn't seen any of it coming— was confirmation.

So when Rey called to ask Brown if he'd meet to discuss the opening at St. Aug, he couldn't believe Brown said yes.

"This might get interesting," Rey told his fiancée after the call.

The next week they met at a pizza joint near Karr, and Brown was serious enough that he brought Nick along. Any job for Brown would be contingent on positions for several important assistant coaches. As the conversation advanced, Brown asked for things, and Rey kept saying yes. Rey talked about the Black experience, the time he clashed with white police officers outside his mother's front door and going on to play for Southern University, a historically Black school in Baton Rouge. He told Brown about coaching baseball at Grambling, then Alcorn State when a kid named Tonka George played football there. A skilled and perceptive recruiter, Rey noticed when Brown's attention drifted when the talk turned to football. So he pivoted. He brought up a love for reality television shows such as *Pawn Stars* and *American Pickers*, where some expected treasure could pass through your door any time. Brown told him about his love of history, war movies, and this app he just downloaded.

When they finished dinner and walked outside, Brown opened SkyView Lite on his iPhone and lifted the display toward the heavens. There, shining in the distance, were Saturn and Jupiter. A bit farther away were the stars Betelgeuse and Sirius and Canopus. Sensing an opportunity, Rey said he'd download the app for himself.

They parted ways, and if Brown was intrigued, Nick was sold. *This* was the move they'd been waiting for: a school rich with tradition and resources. This, Nick said, would spring them toward the big time. They agreed to keep talking about it, though Brown insisted a final decision wait until after Karr's season.

A short time later, the friends returned to work and pretended their eyes weren't wandering. There were still a hundred vulnerable souls in here, a hundred little Tonkas and Guys. There were still games to win, scholarships to secure, futures to plot.

Weeks passed. Rey kept calling, and Brown kept answering, engaging, and imagining. One day near the end of the regular season, Brown takes his usual place in the rear of the weight room, behind the back extension platform. He invites Norm to the front, and Dany'e hops up and takes his usual place.

"Where my *n——s* at?!" Dany'e says, punching the air. Nobody winces at the word's use here. It's just a call to order.

"Uhh-*UHH*!" the other players reply.

Norm stands between two weight racks and begins.

"Some of you know," he says, "there's this thing called life."

Norm vows he won't break down, though nobody believes that. If Brown keeps the enormity of his emotions at bay, Norm feels and considers every ounce of his. He explains why he's moving on, that it's just something he has to do. Coaching, at least at this level, is a young man's game. But he has spent nearly twenty years here, watching kids become men and players become coaches. One of those is Noel Ellis Jr., a twenty-five-year-old former high school All-American who'd grown up and will now step in as special teams coach.

"You guys are in great hands," Norm says. "I don't want you to think that I left you, I abandoned you, nothing fuckin' like that."

He pauses to address a lump gathering in his throat. He steels himself by cussing through it.

"If you think you fuckin' need me to go do your fuckin' job," he says, "you are sadly fuckin' mistaken."

Some of the young men are nodding. A few are crying. Brown listens, staring into space as a longtime assistant says farewell.

"Karr men? Karr men stick together," Norm says, words that finally overwhelm him. His eyes fill. "I know y'all gonna get the fuckin' job done."

He pauses again.

"If you don't get the job done, that's life," he continues. "But don't ever hold your head down. No matter what you accomplish, no matter how long it lasts, a career in football almost never ends the way you hope."

Brown, his eyes wide up till now as the machinery in his brain cranks, snaps to attention. These words feel relatable.

"In fact, almost nothing at all does," Norm says as his boss stands behind him, pursing his lips and nodding.

BY THE TIME homecoming week arrived, Brown was fielding almost daily overtures from Rey. St. Aug wanted him. Bad. And it was nice to feel wanted.

Nick is pushing Brown to go. Mike, whom Brown would choose over Omari as a member of his prospective new coaching staff, prefers to stay at Karr.

Brown called Chris D and asked for his opinion. Was this a change just for the sake of change? A career killer? Or precisely what Brown needed? Chris D thought Brown could do better, especially if he's patient. But he also knew his old boss had accomplished everything he'd hoped to at Karr.

He could hear in Brown's voice that he was worn down. He was leaving the football office earlier than he used to, socializing less, even skipping the dinners he loves. Early in the season, Brown plucked the gray strands that sprung from his beard. Now there were so many that he didn't bother.

He sometimes wore the same clothes day after day. He went months between haircuts. He told Chris D that he longed for sleep, explaining on a Saturday morning that a player had called the previous night at 3:42 a.m. An argument between the player and his father had grown explosive. Brown intervened and had never gone back to bed.

The possibility of Chris D returning, no matter how unlikely, temporarily buoyed him. Brown murmured aloud about flying him to New Orleans during the playoffs to be an offensive line consultant. The truth was he just wanted to see his friend.

"I love it there . . ." Chris D said during one of those conversations.

"But it's over," Brown said.

"For me it's over."

When Chris D probed Brown about St. Aug, the big man demurred. He just had to get through the next game, the next practice, the next day. Brown is a man with so many responsibilities, almost all of them organized in his mind and competing for attention and priority. Brown's truck needs repairs. Fat needs new clothes. There is a game against Helen Cox to prepare for. Brown has media responsibilities in advance of homecoming and the playoffs. He needs to talk to Joe about college. He hasn't checked in on Racey or Ronnie for a while. There's more. Much more.

"Just shit on top of shit," Brown says. He insists that once these tasks are complete, he'll finally have a chance to think about himself, St. Aug, and whatever lay ahead.

But Chris D knows fixable crises are just one more way Brown distracts himself—a wall of responsibility shielding him from anxiety about his future. After the fallout with Trent and the day-to-day psychological maintenance of players such as Joe, Brown isn't driven so much by ambition anymore. Instead, his own motivation is escape. Sometimes Chris D, no longer Brown's employee, reminded him that life isn't like this everywhere. Almost nobody manages this much, works this hard, worries so much. Certainly not in college football. At Virginia-Wise, Chris D told Brown, he's a coach, not everybody's guardian angel. He focuses on the game, a bottomless world of recruiting and play design and game planning, around the clock. All day, every day. Chris D has time to lift weights and run a few miles each day. He never forgets to eat. He sleeps like a baby.

"It's something that we always talked about," Brown says.

They imagine working together again someday. Perhaps when that day comes, Brown will work for Chris D and serve as his enforcer and follow his rules. They laugh at the possibility. After a moment, Brown's smile fades.

"My window is getting smaller," he says.

Not long after this conversation, Brown notices that texts have collected on his phone. Messages from players and assistants, which means more problems to solve. One of the texts, though, is from Rey. **Clear skies**, it reads, **full of stars and planets.**

IT'S CLOSE TO NOON on homecoming Thursday, and Brown is sitting alone in the Karr cafeteria, brooding. Thursday falls outside the coaches' weekly fasting period, though for one reason or a hundred, Brown hasn't eaten.

Tiga approaches with a plate of fried chicken. Brown grimaces but accepts it. Then he barks at Tiga for microwaving it too long. He dives in, anyway, starting with a wing.

A few minutes later, as if by magic, Brown is almost bubbly. He's talking about the evening's contest against Helen Cox. He's looking forward to the playoffs starting in eight days, and this week Leonard reminded Brown of his uncanny ability to process and retain information.

"They amaze me," he says of his quarterbacks. Brown's blood sugar has normalized. For the moment, the Hulk is gone.

After vowing last night to punish players for a lackluster practice, Brown settled down. He canceled nothing. The caterer delivered a feast as scheduled, and when students gather in the gymnasium for the afternoon's pep rally, captains and seniors will be introduced to thunderous applause.

Brown didn't back off everything, though. A snarling dog, hungry or not, must occasionally follow through with a threat to bite if he's to be taken seriously. Players will indeed wear uniforms from 2012 during tonight's game, though they've been laundered as normal. Brown says Karr kids respond strongly to shiny, new equipment. Some of them rarely get new clothes at home. They wear hand-me-downs or items from thrift stores. So unusual as this punishment may be, it's also an effective, and ultimately harmless, psychological reset.

Brown also has a plan for getting Fat's attention. Though he is Karr's most explosive receiver, especially on downfield routes, lately Fat has been dropping passes. He's clearly distracted, but Brown can't just ignore it. He plans to hit the kid where it hurts, while having a little fun in the process.

As the pep rally begins and players are occupied, Brown dispatches Tiga to the locker room. He is to remove the number 2 jersey and Fat's helmet from his locker before hiding them in Brown's office. Tiga is unflinchingly loyal, an intense face offset by his whisper-soft voice and adorned with cornrows clipped at the ends by white cowrie shells. But he's not always as exacting as Brown likes. He stuffs the jersey into a file cabinet but leaves Fat's helmet on the love seat facing Brown's desk, forgets about it, and leaves.

Fat and Brown have become close lately, and most evenings Brown gives him a ride home. Not only does the kid like to eat, he's also a lovable boundary pusher. Brown is a devout individualist, and Fat—loud in both personality and appearance—is truly one of a kind. Though Fat's training camp throwdown with Omari had been unpleasant, it had served a purpose while also impressing Brown. The kid stood up for himself and literally fought for his jersey. The coach likes boldness in players, especially his stars, but this instinct must also be harnessed. Fat has a reputation for speaking or acting without thinking, and recently Brown has been working with him on that. He assigns him newspaper articles to read, for instance, to learn what to say, and not say, to a reporter before and after games. On occasion they talk about the things Fat would like to tell his bi-ological father, from whom Fat is estranged. One day in Pride Panel, where there are no secrets, Brown asked Fat to tell his story. Joe had shared his painful experience after receiving the eviction notice. Now it was Fat's turn.

"My daddy just fucked up," Fat said with a shrug. Brown turned it into a lesson on the importance of forgiveness, and Fat would add later that, as a result of his speech, "now everybody is trying to repair relationships."

On this day, Fat walks into the locker room after the pep rally and discovers his gear missing. Rather than report this to Omari, his position coach, or perhaps Tiga, Fat sets off looking for it. The football office is usually empty during early afternoons, and as a captain, Fat can theoretically come and go as he pleases.

He walks in, combs the weight room and the assistants' office, then peers through the window of Brown's locked office door. There's his helmet. He somehow jimmies open the door, retrieves his helmet, and heads back into the locker room. A number 81 jersey has been placed in his locker, and he heads off again, this time in search of Brown.

"Stop playing hide-and-seek!" Fat says, smiling, because he knows he's being messed with. Brown can barely contain his glee.

"I don't know where it's at, dog," the coach says, stifling a cackle. He's a terrible liar. "I really don't."

Time passes, and Fat joins his teammates to dress for tonight's game. He refuses to put on the 81, which is good, because that's what Brown wants him to do. If Fat acquiesces and puts on the replacement jersey, that's the one he'll wear against Helen Cox. As Leonard learned months earlier, surrender is the most unforgivable crime in Judge Brice Brown's courtroom.

"Where's it at?" Fat yells toward his coach as players head toward school buses.

"On your back," Brown says without looking at him.

"That's not me!"

Brown finally laughs before whispering something to Mike. He is to slip into Brown's office, grab the 2 jersey, and stuff it into a duffel bag. The assistant coach does as he's told, though Omari rolls his eyes. He thinks mind games like this, especially this close to game time, are pointless.

Brown, still in a good mood, is unbowed. He notices a torn-open bag of hot dog buns near a storage room. This elicits a winding anecdote about "Meatball," the legendary (and possibly imaginary) rat that makes its home in the crumbling walls of Karr's football office. Nobody ever sees "Meatball," other than Marv when he hasn't taken his medication, though everyone insists the monster weighs twenty pounds. Maybe thirty.

How could Brown leave all this? So maybe the king lives in a busted-up castle and is surrounded by a staff of loyalists and madmen. He's still a damn king.

A few minutes later, Brown climbs into the passenger seat of his dimpled royal carriage. Marv has already taken his usual place in the back seat, and Officer Pat settles in behind the wheel. Asked if he's armed, Pat smiles and pats his leg. They set off, across the field and through the back gate. Brown searches YouTube for his game-day song. He hits play, filling the Silverado's interior with the sound of strengthening applause, which gives way to drums and the soft strums of an electric guitar. Then the Mississippi Mass Choir's mighty soloist, Mosie Burks, takes over.

> *Sometimes my burdens press me down*
> *I'm not tired yet.*
> *Sometimes I hasten to higher ground*
> *I'm not tired yet.*

As Officer Pat drives toward the stadium, following the newly assigned police escort, Brown taps his fingers on the armrest and quietly mouths the song's lyrics.

Sometime I can hardly see my way
I'm not tired yet.
So I get on my knees and I begin to pray
I'm not tired yet.

The coach bobs his head as the chorus hits and the rest of the choir joins. So does Brown.

"Nooo!" he bellows. "I'm not tired *yet!*"

The convoy arrives at Behrman Stadium, and after Brown's usual tradition of a few moments alone in the truck, he steps out and ambles toward the sideline. He passes Baylon, Norm's older son, playing catch on the field. He's arguing with another boy about which of them will someday play quarterback for Karr and be a captain.

In the stands, Leonard II has already staked out his premium seats on the fifty-yard line, and the Ticket Man is surrounded by nearly a dozen family members. Rhonda George has slipped through a gate and is standing on the field delivering hugs and leftovers from a pot of gumbo from last weekend. In her pocket are purple bracelets embossed with #LongLive5, and she wants to give one to running back Kevin Marigny, who's on the field warming up. Brown notices Rhonda and walks over, accepting his hug and slipping Kevin's bracelet in his pocket. He says he'll make sure Kevin gets it before the game.

Usually impatient before kickoff, Brown stands and breathes in his surroundings. He's living in the present as usual, though for once it seems a healthy act of appreciation rather than yet another escape. Maybe, as he stands here, Brown is coming to terms with the fact that, after nearly two decades of Karr homecomings, this one might be his last.

"I find myself taking more moments," he says, "to soak it all in."

Fat notices him standing there absorbing, and after catching warm-up pregame passes in a white T-shirt instead of the 81 jersey, he jogs off the field. Brown has already instructed Mike to give the kid his damn number 2 jersey back just before "The Rock." But Fat doesn't know that yet.

"Hey, dog," the young receiver calls toward his head coach. Like most everyone else at the stadium, Fat has no idea Brown isn't just waiting for kickoff like usual. He's standing at a life and career crossroads. "What we gonna do?"

CHAPTER 10

PENUMBRA

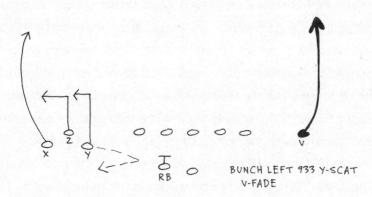

BUNCH LEFT 933 Y-SCAT
V-FADE

Tomorrow, after one more practice and one last meeting, the play-offs start. Usually Karr coaches joke that this is when the real season begins. The nine games that compose the regular season, they like to say, are merely a series of tune-ups that set the final, more meaningful chessboard.

But today they're not saying that. Because of Karr's two losses, it is the number three seed in the Class 4A playoffs, its lowest ranking since 2015. Lakeshore High, which is technically in the New Orleans area but feels a world away on the north side of Lake Pontchartrain, is the top seed. The Titans went undefeated and stomped opponents by nearly thirty-two points per game. Neville, whose path always seems to cross with Karr's this time of year, is number two and therefore possesses home-field advantage throughout the playoffs. Unless Neville loses, which seems unlikely, Karr is almost certainly heading to Monroe for the semifinal round. Considering the team's sleepy performance in October when it made a similar trip to play Wossman, Brown doesn't exactly like his team's chances if that were to occur.

Regardless, all that starts tomorrow. Today the coaches are packed into the assistants' office, and perhaps to conceal their concerns or just procrastinate, they're killing time. They're talking trash and trading war stories. Remember the playoff game in 2015, when Karr upset Franklinton? Everyone celebrated so hard that they turned the locker room into a dance club, and Franklinton's golf cart may or may not have sustained $5,000 worth of damage. What about the trip to Leesville, when it was raining and Brown refused to leave the bus because, not unlike a house cat, he hates being wet? Or the night at Cecilia, when Brown accidentally got bug spray in his mouth and panicked, then retreated into the forest to make himself vomit?

Remember "Big Cat"? The coaches pause, thinking about it. They shake their heads. Stupid, glorious, horrible "Big Cat."

Years ago, Brown heard about an unusual drill being used by Louisiana State University's football team. Coaches there liked to get everyone's blood pumping before practice, so every day they'd draft two players—one from the Tigers' offense, the other from the defense—and pit them against each other in an invisible sumo ring. A whistle would blow, and the players would break from their three-point stances and collide. One would inevitably tackle the other or push him out of the ring, asserting himself as, well, the day's big cat.

Football fields aren't always the most sensible or mature places, especially when testosterone-fueled men are involved. But regardless, Brown loved the drill and brought it back to Karr—albeit with some modifications. For one, he preferred "Big Cat" to occur before games instead of practices. He also didn't limit it to players. Because there was usually some disagreement simmering among coaches, Brown gave his staffers the week to work things out. If they couldn't, then on the sideline before the next game, Brown would point toward, say, defensive backs coach Shakiel Smith and defensive line coach Dwayne Mitchell, and tell them to come on down.

They'd lean into a three-point stance, Brown would blow his whistle, and the two rams would do battle. With everyone cheering and backing a preferred gladiator, a victor would eventually emerge. The kids loved it. One position group had bragging rights. Adrenaline soared. Staff tension had, in a very Karr way, been dealt with.

Sitting here now, Brown suggests it may be time to bring back "Big Cat." A cold snap has pushed temperatures into the forties, so maybe that'd be a good way to bring a little heat to the Karr sideline. Brown points out that Mike Thompson and Omari Robertson, the team's wide receivers coaches, would be intriguing combatants. Not only have they been disagreeing lately, but they're also different in most every way.

Mike smiles and shakes his head. He's up for it if Omari is. Working out some differences in a cloud of masculinity, ego, and the whip of Mike's dreadlocks would be quite a sight. But Omari, sitting on a desk platform, is expressionless.

"I'm not doing that shit," he says flatly.

The other assistants laugh. It's just a joke, Omari; lighten up.

"You haven't done it yet," Brown says.

Omari pushes himself off the desk and steps toward the office door.

"And I'm *not*," he says, leaving without another word.

WHEN OMARI WAS LITTLE, he'd go on walks around New Orleans East with his father. Clyde Robertson's success had been self-made, and he was a history professor with a doctorate from Tulane. On these mornings, their classroom was the neighborhood. The curriculum was pride.

Though Omari had a lighter skin tone than his dad, he otherwise looked just like him. Talked like him. Made the same facial expressions. The shopkeepers smiled when the father and son entered, and they greeted the eight-year-old as "Little Clyde." At the time Omari loved it. His father didn't.

"Tell them your name," he'd scold as they headed home, down treelined streets as white neighbors walked their dogs. Nothing is more precious than a person's identity, because when everything else is stripped away, that's the last thing standing.

This was only the beginning of Omari's lifelong education. His father supplemented it by challenging him to suppertime debates about postcolonialism and class discrimination. Omari's grandparents had attended segregated schools in Louisiana, and Clyde invited them to explain that their sacrifices and fear made it possible for Omari to attend a Montessori academy and tae kwon do lessons. The young man came home some days to discover books, such as *The Mis-Education of the Negro* and *Countering the Conspiracy to Destroy Black Boys*, waiting for him. Omari wasn't just exposed to America's dark history of exploiting, culturally indoctrinating, and attacking its Black men. He came of age surrounded by conversations about social injustice and cautionary tales. Eventually this hardened into a deep skepticism of anyone who might be scheming to break him.

Then Katrina made landfall in August 2005, bending the palm trees along Lake Pontchartrain with 145-mph winds and dumping 2.3 trillion gallons of rainwater onto Louisiana. New Orleans East, an upper-middle-class Black enclave, had largely been developed in the decades after World War II as part of efforts to decentralize the downtown area and keep the city segregated. It had also been built on wetlands protected by what was seen in the late nineteenth century as a marvel of engineering: New Orleans's levee and drainage system.

The dreadful irony of this system, and New Orleanians' faith in it, was that constructing those levees came as a result of *lowering* the terrain of a city that famously sits below sea level. The soil that constructs a man-made protective mountain has to come from somewhere, and much of it had been excavated from the lakefront (and, at the time, sparsely occupied) grounds of what would become New Orleans East. Decades later, many residents would be thrilled to get a home of their own. They had no idea they were moving into the lower rim of a bowl—some parts of which, thanks also to continually rising water levels, are now believed to sit between eight and twelve feet below sea level.

Omari, like thousands of traumatized New Orleanians, would vividly remember his family's hurry to escape Katrina. Their home, a half mile from the lakefront, sat in a lower well of that bowl. Omari would recall seeing the moon shining brightly through a pair of tall trees, and the fourteen-year-old couldn't square how a storm was approaching with the sky so calm. They packed what they could and headed to Baton Rouge, and the next day Omari turned on the television to see his city battered and its residents tearing the rest of it apart. The federal government had largely left New Orleans for dead.

When Omari came home more than a year later, after relocating again to Atlanta, the carpet in his bedroom still squished. His clothes and sneakers had mold on them, and photographs were softened and torn. The trees that'd framed the moon months earlier were gone.

The Robertsons rebuilt on the same tract they'd called home for years. Before the storm Omari had been accepted to Edna Karr Magnet School, where admission required its largely gifted and talented students to pass a written test. But with Karr recommissioned as a citywide charter school, Omari would now cross the river into a very different environment. Even for a young Black man, it felt unfamiliar.

Omari met Shakiel Smith first. Long before they'd coach together on Brown's staff, they were football teammates—Omari a wide receiver, Shak a cornerback—who lined up against each other in practice.

Shak had a thick Afro and dark skin, and when he spoke Omari could barely understand him. He cursed almost constantly and used slang Omari had rarely heard. Shak would be similarly fascinated by his new friend. Omari's hair was short, his diction polished. He glided across the practice field and through Karr's hallways—shoulders back, eyes down—as if he'd never experienced a bad day.

Though football was a melting pot, Omari nonetheless stood out. Shak introduced Omari to fellow defensive back Jordan Sullen, who'd grown up in the Cut-Off, where he frequently heard gunshots and saw blood. Omari had never seen that New Orleans, and so on top of his manner and speech and demeanor, this made him noticeably different.

"We would clown him just because we were clowns," Munchie Legaux, Omari's quarterback, would say later. "He's so soft-spoken and laid-back and got nothing but wild fucking beasts around him."

Indeed Omari had a carefree way, and for reasons that'd confuse him even decades later, this rubbed people raw. Brown, then an assistant coach who oversaw Karr's offense when Omari played, seemed confounded by his too-cool demeanor. Jordan called him a "pretty boy" who'd never felt adversity and couldn't be counted on if a fight broke out. Shak made fun of him because he talked like a professor, not a Karr kid. Usually it was meant in good fun.

But sometimes the friends really wanted to piss Omari off, so they'd bring up his skin tone.

"That's some real light-skinned shit you just did," Jordan says he used to tell Omari if he did something that felt disloyal.

Others asked Omari, and occasionally still do, if he's biracial. He'd roll his eyes and say he's as Black as they are. Friends picked on him for living a plush life, pouncing on the fact he'd never experienced the horrors they had. They ribbed him because Omari's parents are married and hold college degrees.

He tried, at least on the surface, to shake it off. But sometimes he came home and seemed withdrawn. Clyde Robertson again told him to stand his ground, to be proud of who he is, to resist the urge to conform. His differences weren't a weakness. They're what make him unique. They could also make him powerful—as long as he retained his pride and never let anyone see him sweat.

Omari returned to school and the football field. Shak and Jordan would later be named team captains at Karr. His friends and teammates kept trying to toughen him up. Maybe then Omari could be a captain, too. Other times they'd ridicule him, pointing out the boujee-ass way he spoke, thought, and carried himself. He was like Braxton P. Hartnabrig, the prim-and-proper sidekick on *The Jamie Foxx Show*. So that's what they called him. He was rich, sheltered, pampered.

He was Braxton.

But he wouldn't answer to that. He never lost his temper. He never got into a fight. He just calmly told them, again and again, his name is Omari.

ONE DAY AT PRACTICE, wide receiver Darrell Hills kept running the wrong route. Leonard and Fat tried reminding him of the assignment, and at last he got it right. But when Leonard's pass reached him, Darrell dropped it.

Brown went ballistic.

"Not your day, bitch!" he yelled at the kid. Nick Foster screamed at Darrell, following him as he jogged back toward the huddle with his eyes down. He kept doing so as Darrell stood alone with his hands on his hips. This can be difficult to watch and is almost certainly uncomfortable to experience. But coaches here insist that this is just another way of making players confront adversity. The sooner they do, the quicker everyone can move on—and, to hear coaches tell it, the better off the kid is.

A moment after these exchanges, Omari walked over and put his arm around Darrell.

"Hey, look," he said. "Don't even worry about it."

Brown and Nick rolled their eyes and would later accuse Omari of coddling a receiver they'd diagnosed as unreliable. Darrell was having a bad practice, and when this happens, he struggles to shake off his mistakes. On a football field, as in life, it's possible for this response to turn small problems into big ones. And most of Darrell's coaches believed he needed to develop thicker skin. Omari, though, opted for reassurance. The next time Darrell ran the play, he ran the route flawlessly and caught the pass.

This otherwise unmemorable scene during a midweek practice raised several questions. Had Omari's more delicate touch, despite the scorn it elicited from his peers, actually worked? After all, the nerve center of Brown's philosophy is that people, here and virtually everywhere, respond to wholly different stimuli and approaches depending on their physical and emotional needs. Brown's staff is built to address these needs using diverse specialties and viewpoints, from proper tackling technique to the obvious perspective differences of, say, Chris D and Alan Boyd.

The other, more big-picture question: Regardless of Brown's success, not just in winning championships but in reprogramming players, is there an alternative to his harsh, profane, possibly draconian process?

Brown and Omari have different answers to this question. That is the root of a growing tension between them.

Omari is very much a Karr man, but because he has yet to fully embrace the Karr Method, Brown sometimes wonders if he has a future here. In brainstorming which of his staffers he'd take with him if he accepts the job at St. Aug, he settled on Nick, Norm Randall, and Mike. But not Omari. In fact when Norm stepped away from coaching late in the season, Brown used it as an opportunity to talk about the inevitability of staff turnover and the fact that Brown himself wouldn't be here forever. "Your replacement is in the room," Brown says often. "Even mine."

In front of the entire team, he singled out Nick, Norm, and twenty-five-year-old Noel Ellis Jr. as possible successors as head coach. Asked later why he'd omitted Omari's name, Brown suggested the young coach was entitled and stubborn; Brown joked that elevating Omari to head coach would leave the program "in ruins."

For his part, Omari believes conforming would be more than just pleasing his boss and ignoring his instincts. It'd be a betrayal of the thing he holds most precious: his identity. He is who he is, like him or not, and he doesn't plan to change. The preseason fight with Fat had embarrassed Omari, and not only because he'd lost his temper with a sixteen-year-old. He'd felt manipulated by Brown, whom he blamed for setting the events in motion. He vowed to never let his boss use him as a pawn ever again.

"That was it for sure," Omari says. "I'm like: 'Man, I'm not doing that no more.' Because it didn't make sense! He gave the jersey right back to him. He ain't about to hang me on no string like no puppet."

It's hard to know who's right, or whether they both are. Indeed Brown sometimes regrets his explosions with players and coaches and wishes he'd been more tactful. Other coaches wince at the language Brown uses and wonder (though not to Brown's face) if there's a different way. These are kids, after all, and though the results on and off the field speak for themselves, the beginning of the playoffs is about reflection—what worked, what didn't. This seems as good a time as any to consider the questions Omari raises.

Brown insists this is just how kids here must be addressed. Politeness, he says, might work at John Curtis, where players are removed from the practice field if they're heard using profanity. Brown does not believe a soft touch works here and is often interpreted as a show of weakness.

"You *have* to speak their language," he says. "If you tell them to 'Please go get that water bottle, Joe, when you get a moment,' they'll walk all over you. Now, if you tell them: 'Go get the fucking water bottle,' they'll go get the fucking water bottle."

Brown uses Joe in this example deliberately, because the young linebacker is actually the perfect test case. Though Brown doesn't agree with all of Keyoke's techniques, she didn't ignore the realities that surrounded her son. She confronted them. Trent Washington's mother, on the other hand, tried to avoid making her son angry and uncomfortable. Joe went his way, and Trent went his. Brown doesn't think the results are coincidence, and might in fact prove his ultimate point: Karr kids can be neither babied nor pitied. They must, at all times, be given the real.

Omari rejects this. He played for, and coached with, pushovers and tyrants—men with vastly different approaches. Some were effective; others weren't. At Southern University, the historically Black school where Omari played wide receiver, his easygoing position coach whom he greatly admired, Eric Dooley, never used profanity and greeted players with Bible verses. Dooley was respected by his players because he showed them how they might choose to act off the field—with a calm, peaceful spirit, humility, integrity, and self-respect. This resonated with Omari. Players can't take all that yelling and screaming and cussing with them to the grocery store or the office. There are benefits to showing kids how to approach football the way they might approach any other situation. Omari believes there are many ways to reach, and teach, a child. And regardless of what's been working at Karr, he says, there is no gospel.

"I've taken a mixture of everybody I've had as a coach," Omari says, "and I've tried to put it into what I'm doing. My biggest thing when I started doing this was to not be the coach I didn't like."

Brown is smart enough to understand that, and in exposing players to restaurants and hotels, it's obvious he believes in some of the same things Omari does. But he and Omari have simply never had that conversation, and this seems incongruent with honest conversation being one of the program's core tenets. Brown has never invited Omari into his office to compare and contrast their experiences and philosophies, and in general to just hash this out. They've never had their verbal "Big Cat" showdown, even though Brown thinks highly of Omari's potential—if he'd just make some adjustments.

"Omari is going to be a great coach," Brown says. "He doesn't wanna take the initiative of *now*. He wants to keep saying: 'It's gonna come with time; it's coming.' He don't want to grab the bull by the horns."

Similarly, Omari has never explicitly stood up to Brown, told him to back off, invited him to kindly go fuck himself if he doesn't like his style. The boss might actually respect him for it. Some of Brown's favorite people, after all, are hotheads who challenge him.

Then again, the men seem different in many ways. Some of the same assumptions that made Omari an outlier in his youth now push him to the outer edge of the Karr staff's social circle. Whether or not it's intentional, Omari can sometimes project an above-it-all quality. He lives and teaches across the river, and he has sculpted arms he frequently shows off by wearing sleeveless shirts. His thin goatee and thoughtful eyes highlight a professorial face that colleagues occasionally read as projecting aloofness. He drives a Nissan Altima, reliable and safe, which Munchie still relentlessly ridicules him for because it "looks like a baby mama car."

But Omari and Brown also have plenty in common, most notably their striking intellects, strong wills, and a shared history of deep emotional pain. They've never talked about that, either. Nor have they the fact that Omari is one of several former Karr players on the coaching staff. Ronald Davis, Shak, Dwayne, and Omari all played together in those post-Katrina melting pot teams and are helping to mold the next generation. But Omari is unique in a quietly meaningful way: he's the only staff member who actually played for Brown's offense.

This again brings up several questions. Is this why Omari, proud as he is, craves Brown's approval? When Brown texted Omari shortly after the 2018 state championship, thanking him for his efforts with Karr's most important position group, this brought Omari as much fulfillment as did the championship itself.

The other, more big-picture question: Is it possible Brown, who's only six years older than Omari, still views him as a kid he can break and rebuild in a different image? Is this why Brown can't seem to accept him as a peer, and as he is?

Driving one evening to a radio appearance in the New Orleans suburb of Harahan, Brown is asked about this directly. He has never thought of it this way, he says. As a student of lifelong improvement, he thinks about it for a long time.

"I gotta work on that," he finally says.

KARR MAKES EASY WORK of Cecelia in the playoffs' first round. Though, because of a byzantine Louisiana high school playoff rule, Karr will not play its second-round game at Behrman Stadium. G.W. Carver High is the number nineteen seed in the Class 4A bracket, and it defeated fourteenth-seeded Franklinton. The Louisiana High School Sports Association rewards upsets and encourages parity, so Carver will host the heavily favored Karr at Joe W. Brown Park in New Orleans East.

This is a road game for Karr, but it's a homecoming for Omari. After college and a graduate assistantship on Southern's football staff, he moved back into the same three-bedroom house his parents have owned since 1999. But the neighborhood felt nothing like the one Omari remembered.

Many of the white residents were gone, and Kenilworth Mall had been shuttered. A year after the storm, the New Orleans housing authority decided to tear down four of the city's largest and most notorious housing projects. The Fischer Housing Development, the grisly site of the "Algiers 7" ordeal nearly three decades earlier, was among them. At least on paper, decentralizing poverty while dismantling hives of drug use, crime, and heartache seemed like a fine idea.

"The most exciting urban opportunity since San Francisco in 1906," the author and academic James K. Glassman wrote in January 2006. After a devastating earthquake in Northern California nearly destroyed the city, San Francisco rebuilt as an efficient and modern metropolis. City officials provided immediate housing for displaced residents, offered competitive wages to work in the cleanup effort, even handed out free food and tobacco.

In New Orleans, though, the city council voted unanimously to tear down some forty-five hundred low-income housing units. Almost all of them were occupied by Black residents. A public hearing included several protesters being forcibly removed and others pepper sprayed and Tasered. Residents of those units would be locked out of their homes, prohibited from retrieving their belongings, and given a voucher for a new home that hadn't yet been built. Only one in ten of those units was actually replaced. If vouchers were honored at all by landlords, rents were on average 35 percent higher and no longer included the cost of utilities.

While displaced residents waited, hundreds sought shelter with friends and relatives in middle-class Black neighborhoods such as New Orleans East. Vagrancy and crime followed, underscoring that it's not buildings that cause a city's decay. It's desperate people who seek shortcuts in a system that tries to cut just as many corners. Longtime residents of the East came to routinely witness drug deals and the mating of stray dogs on the sidewalk. The Robertsons refused to abandon their home and neighborhood, and Omari heard gunshots in his neighborhood for the first time. He gradually got used to it. When his car was broken into, he says, police didn't arrive for nine hours.

Omari tried to avoid home, preferring to focus on his teaching and coaching career. Brown had initially passed Omari over for a job at Karr, adding a layer of resentment, so he took a position coaching wide receivers at Carver. He didn't berate players if they made a mistake during games. He talked to them. Asked what had happened, and what they needed from him.

"Doing that in the heat of the battle would do nothing for the player but make him worse," Omari would say. Practices, though, were fair game for harsh corrections.

One day, a receiver named Keyon Clark was half-assing it during drills. Omari walked over, and in his smooth-as-silk cadence, calmly asked Keyon why he was wasting everyone's time. That got Keyon's attention, and Omari explained that it wasn't talent alone that elevated an athlete. It was hard work. It had gotten Omari to Southern, and it could lift Keyon out of the Seventh Ward and into the college ranks.

They grew closer, and sometimes Omari drove Keyon home. He bought him lunch or dinner, and they talked—sometimes about the future, but just as often the past. They shared memories of life after Katrina, and Omari talked about his changing neighborhood and the erosion of his feelings of security. They talked about identity and how nobody will protect it more than you.

Keyon was smart and ambitious, but more than that he was funny. He made Omari laugh so hard that he could feel the humor rattling his bones. Talented, too. When Carver and Karr met in the second round of the 2017 playoffs, Keyon was a senior who entered the game with eleven touchdown catches. That evening Omari was on the Behrman Stadium sideline wearing Carver's orange and green, wishing for an upset to stick up Brown's ass. And indeed the Rams had a lead with two minutes, thirty-seven seconds to play. Then Skyler Perry, Karr's quarterback and Brown's protégé, hit Anthony Spurlock for a fifty-four-yard touchdown pass, and a few minutes later Omari walked across the field to congratulate his old coach and shake his hand.

Four months later, Brown visited the East Bank and Andrew H. Wilson charter school, where Omari teaches special education. He asked Omari to come by Karr after work, and Brown planned to offer the young coach a job. Omari crossed the river, met with Brown, and couldn't say no. He'd join Karr, teach the next generation, and, yes, learn from an offensive mastermind such as Brown.

He nonetheless kept up with his old players, including Keyon after he enrolled at nearby Delgado Community College and kept training to play college football. Omari was scrolling through Twitter one evening in June 2019, when something caught his attention.

Hours earlier, Keyon had posted a live video singing as he and the rest of New Orleans celebrated the Pelicans' surprising win in the NBA draft lottery. They would select Zion Williamson, a once-in-a-generation player, and Keyon retweeted two interviews about Williamson's potential. Then he headed to a playground in Metairie to play basketball with his older brother.

Omari then saw tweets about a triple shooting, and about Keyon. Panicked, Omari climbed into his Altima and sped toward Metairie. He told himself this couldn't be happening. Not to Keyon.

When Omari arrived, though, he learned a horrible truth. Keyon and Darrell "DJ" Clark, who played wide receiver at Grambling State, had been waiting for their ride home when someone approached and started shooting into a crowd. DJ and another victim had been shot but would survive. A single bullet had pierced Keyon's chest.

Omari pushed toward the police tape, the first time he'd been at a scene like this. He'd arrived just in time to see Keyon, his nineteen-year-old former player and friend, being zipped into a body bag.

KEYON CLARK DIED exactly one month before Karr reported to Thibodaux, Louisiana, for training camp to begin preparing for the 2019 season. (That same July, Jefferson Parish Sheriff's Office deputies approached a suspect in Keyon's murder and shot the twenty-four-year-old man dead, saying he'd reached for a gun, before making an arrest. JPSO deputies do not wear body cameras.) One month before Omari sat quietly in a chair as Brown and Nick confronted Fat for supposedly rolling his digs. One month before Fat stalked upstairs, slid on the number 2 jersey, and effectively dared his position coach to do something about it.

Omari, perhaps understandably given the trauma he'd endured, exploded. As the hours and days passed and the emotions settled, the thing Omari regretted most wasn't that he'd let himself be used. It was that he hadn't yet realized that Fat, with his big personality and bleached twists, wasn't refusing to surrender his jersey. He was holding on to an important piece of his identity. And Omari, later seeing himself in the kid, had physically tried to take it from him.

"He wants to be loved. He wants to be liked, and he . . ." the coach would say over breakfast a short time later.

Omari pauses, choosing his words carefully.

"It's not like I was begging or *he's* begging to be liked," he continues. "We're just doing what we do naturally. It's either good enough or it ain't."

They all tried to move on, and eventually did. Or mostly did. Omari's colleagues sensed a persistent guardedness in him and wondered if Keyon's death had damaged Omari more than he'd let on. Or maybe more than even he realized.

Usually after practices, when the rest of the staff yukked it up in the coaches' office, Omari left to see his girlfriend. When Dany'e Brooks called some weekends, indicating he wanted company or needed food,

Omari didn't take the hint. When Fat went to tour the University of Alabama, it wasn't Omari who drove him to Tuscaloosa. It was Brown, who by then had gotten close to Fat in a way that his position coach had not.

"Hey, your daddy here," Brown joked to Darrell one afternoon when Omari walked in.

"I'm *not* his daddy," Omari fired back at his boss. Was this an attempt at establishing boundaries between a coach and his players, or a way to protect himself by maintaining emotional distance? "I don't give a fuck about none of that shit."

Omari kept most of those thoughts to himself, and Brown didn't press him on it. They tried to bury themselves in the season's hum and let the routine occupy their minds. When the young woman ran onto the field and threatened Trent Washington, that made routine impossible and forced everyone to reevaluate their surroundings and approaches. Brown and Mike Thompson agonized not only over what happened but what *could've* happened. Mike, still struggling with it a month later, would say that the day you stop trying to save a kid is the day you should get out of coaching.

He learned that from Brown, who responded to Tonka's murder by growing closer to his players and, in many ways, sacrificing his own life in order to redirect or even save theirs. But though Brown and Omari now belonged to the same gruesome club, each having lost a player they'd grown fond of, their responses to such traumas further illustrated their differences.

Months after Keyon's death, Omari sat in the library at Andrew H. Wilson Charter School. He'd say coaching is what he does, not who he is. He cares about players, but this has limits. After all, he'll say, coaches tried to save Trent. But he'd rejected their guidance, it wasn't being reinforced at home, and the kid had carried on looking for trouble.

"I just don't have time for that shit," Omari says. "You can't save them all."

IT'S TIME TO LEAVE for Carver, though the truth is, that time was ten minutes ago. Brown likes to plan everything to the minute, but sometimes one of the school bus drivers runs late. Sometimes players are left waiting in the parking lot until she arrives, and sometimes Brown is sitting in his truck grumbling to himself as he watches the scene unfold.

A believer in omens, Brown doesn't like what this foretells for the evening. He plays the fifteen-minute version of "I'm Not Tired Yet," and when it's finished, he plays it again.

The driver arrives, Marv leans out the rear window to scream at her, and at last Officer Pat hits the gas. Now Brown can't find his coaching whistle. Because Joe W. Brown Park was built on marshland, Brown worries he didn't bring enough bug spray. The truck, and the police escort and school buses, hits traffic as the convoy attempts to pass near downtown New Orleans.

It's a mess. Brown lets out a loud, exaggerated sigh.

Marv, apparently trying to help, rolls down his window and continues screaming profanities at other drivers. This truck could just as easily be headed for an insane asylum. When Marv pushes his shoulders through the open window and is more outside the truck than in it, Brown decides this has reached a hilarious point of ridiculousness.

He laughs, eventually the truck arrives in plenty of time, and Brown even discovers his whistle buried under food wrappers in the back seat. Things are looking up, though when he reaches the bench on the sideline, he sees Omari and frowns. He isn't doing anything remarkable, just standing on the field during warm-ups. But as Brown's most natural foil and the staff's resident buzzkill, he doesn't have to do or say much to get on his boss's nerves.

"Look at him," Brown says. "Just watch him."

Kickoff approaches, players gather for "The Rock," and a moment after Karr players run onto the field, Carver's band attempts some psychological warfare by playing its own version of the song. One Karr player starts to sway, and an assistant coach shoves him and reminds him that time has passed.

Brown spent this week reminding players that this won't be a matchup of similarly talented teams. It'll be decided by discipline. If the game devolves into a free-for-all, Carver could pull the upset.

"The only person that can beat y'all," he said, "is yourself."

Indeed there are neither free-for-alls nor fulfilled omens tonight, at least none strong enough to overtake Karr when it's hitting a groove. Leonard aced his weekly test and is pitch-perfect, Leonte is powerful and fast, Joe seems to be playing without pressure because Keyoke has friends in the East and came with them to the game. Karr will go on to chew up Carver, 46–13, and though the performance is lopsided, it's not perfect.

Fat catches a deep pass in the first half and runs into the end zone with a smile. But a little before halftime, he mishandles an easy pass— his third drop of the game. Brown had noticed Carver in Cover 1 man-free and called a favorite hack for that defense. It's a fade route, a play that shows off Leonard's touch and highlights the speed, size, and hands of his most dynamic receiver.

But Leonard's pass, which is dead-on accurate, again slips out of Fat's hands. After the horn sounds to end the first half, Brown slams his headset to the turf and stares Fat down. He follows the young receiver to the end zone, where players are sitting on the ground and forming a semicircle, and now Brown is screaming.

"You can fucking bet you'll never get *that* fucking call again!" he shouts as Fat looks away.

Omari takes a breath as Brown parades by.

"You can fucking *BET*!" he's still saying.

Alan Boyd addresses the receivers first, cursing and screaming, and maybe ten seconds elapse before he's red-faced. Brown can hear Boyd's theatrics, a master class in the Karr Method, and Brown looks on with what appears to be approval.

"Fucking inside placement on a fucking Z-spot," Boyd says, referring to a stemmed curl route assignment that the slot receiver botched. "What the *fuck* you doing?"

Boyd storms off, though he's not quite finished.

"I didn't fucking come here for this bullshit!" he says. "That's my fucking halftime fucking speech. Ain't fucking small shit. It's a fucking real game! Go home if you don't fucking score!"

Now it's Omari's turn. He begins with an anecdote about former NBA legend Allen Iverson, whose nickname was "The Answer." Omari challenges players to avoid raising questions for Karr and instead be the team's answer. Boyd, meanwhile, is still yelling a few yards away.

"Damn!" he says. "Fuck!"

Omari ignores Boyd, and he knows he has to confront Fat about the dropped pass. Standing just outside the circle, Omari looks into the young man's eyes and shrugs.

"Just make the fucking play," he says without raising his voice. Fat smiles and nods, as if to agree with his coach that sometimes it really is that simple.

Karr players pass the school's gymnasium as they head toward an evening football practice at Behrman Stadium. When gunshots rang out during a basketball game in February 2017, boys basketball coach Taurus "T." Howard was told to continue the game, ignoring the familiar sound and the fact that two young men were bleeding to death in the school's parking lot.

At Karr, almost nothing happens without premeditation and thought: from the synchronized way players turn toward coaches before a play, to the right way to stand for the national anthem, to how to assemble on the sideline.

Brice Brown is the architect of the Karr program and a constant for many of the kids here—a massive boulder in a river of young lives. But facing a current this strong, the thirty-four-year-old coach could pass for a decade older.

The Cougars' best wide receiver is Destyn Hill, though years after he was a chubby offensive lineman in park ball, most everyone still refers to the slim and free-spirited junior as "Fat."

Leonte Richardson is a passionate senior running back who lines up for every play as if it could be his last. Though his theatrics sometimes draw eye rolls from coaches, Leonte is driven to leave his mark on the Karr program, and his deepest fear is being forgotten.

Quarterback Leonard Kelly III is the key to Brown's fearsome spread offense. His agility and intelligence helped Karr win its third straight Louisiana state championship, but coaches fear that Leonard's immaturity could be what keeps the team from winning its fourth.

Joe Thomas witnessed his first murder when he was eight years old, and he spent years as the lookout for his mother, Keyoke, who worked street corners in New Orleans and Houston. Now a senior linebacker and the Karr team's protector, Joe is striving toward a very different future—one he has seen only in movies.

Wide receivers coach Mike Thompson reviews a rushing play with players during a Karr football practice at Behrman Stadium. Though Brown's highly complex offensive plays often come easy to him, that's not always true for players, or even some of his assistant coaches.

Nick Foster isn't just Karr's running backs coach. He is the program's enforcer and, after coming of age alternating between the right and wrong sides of the law, found purpose in coaching and is perhaps Brown's greatest success story.

Omari Robertson, who coaches Karr's outside wide receivers, is a Karr Man through and through. But he and Brown clash over Omari's refusal to fully adopt the Karr Method. When other coaches try to draw toughness out of sensitive players, such as versatile receiver Aaron Anderson, seen here wearing number 4, Omari instead shows compassion. *Photo courtesy of Shandrell Briscoe, InspireNOLA Charter Schools.*

Karr's quarterbacks endure grueling game planning sessions each week as they search for vulnerabilities in the next opponent's defense. The day before each game, Brown provides a written test to, left to right, backup A.J. Samuel, reserve Khamani Simmons, and Leonard to quiz them on coverages, defensive leverage, and possible adjustments before and after the snap.

Karr's cramped weight room isn't just the program's hub and primary meeting space. Its four purple walls also represent a safe haven for the hundred or so young men who file in here each day. In exchange for mentorship, love, and the chance to win championships, coaches expect players to show their gratitude with honesty and, during practices and games, by giving everything they've got.

Running back Kevin Marigny wears a message on his hip pad, just his way of remembering someone he lost. Most everyone at Karr knows loss all too well, and in 2018, Brown asked players and coaches to raise their hands if they didn't know someone who'd been shot. Nobody raised their hand.

When the football office doors open for the first time each spring, coaches have no idea who will stream through or what each young man needs. The staff sometimes spends years learning whether a kid benefits most from toughness or love, or some combination of the two.

The pressure at Karr is enormous, and if success serves as an incentive for players, it is often burdensome for Brown. Each day everyone walks past the school's massive trophy case, not just a glimpse of the football team's recent past, but a reminder that extraordinary performance is the expectation.

Kids make their way to the football office immediately after school, and Karr's coaching staff occupies them for hours: meetings, conditioning, practice, speeches. Usually everyone heads home after sunset, and when the young men here scatter throughout New Orleans, that's when Brown worries. It's not uncommon for him to drive around the city and call player after player, just so he can sleep knowing everyone is still alive.

CHAPTER 11

CRABS IN A BUCKET

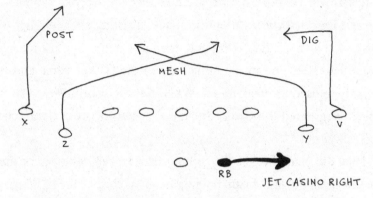

KEYOKE CAME TO THE school today, looking for a fight. She and Joe had gotten into it again, this time because Keyoke offered Joe a few dollars. He'd waved it off. She erupted. He'd damn sure take whatever Ms. Diane, or Cassidy, or Brown was offering, she said.

They screamed, cursed, made threats. In the moment Joe hadn't considered this wasn't his mother being jealous and wasn't just cash she was pushing. It was a token of her dwindling, and frequently threatened, sense of usefulness. Always amplifying the volume, she accused him of being something she hated: phony.

"Joe, you faking it to make it, huh?" she said. Joe stormed out.

These last few weeks had been taxing. He and his mother were still trying to establish equilibrium, and there were good days and bad. For the first time in Keyoke's life, she had a real job. She'd passed a certification test to cook in a commercial kitchen, and a temp agency placed her in a job at a nursing home. She was up early and came home exhausted. Usually she and Joe didn't see each other. When they did, both were fried and had short fuses. But Keyoke was bona fide. She had a paycheck, meager as it was, and she didn't understand why her money was no longer good enough for Joe.

The next day she showed up at Karr and demanded a meeting with Brown. He agreed, and Joe joined them. Keyoke ranted, and Joe cried. At first she went on the attack, insisting she's tougher than Joe and that her "dick is bigger" than her son's. She claimed Ms. Diane had been "mean-mugging" her at the Carver game and that Cassidy refused to speak to her. When Keyoke was finished venting, Brown suggested the two of them go for a walk around the school and talk it out.

They did, and after maybe an hour Brown went looking for them. He saw them down the hall, holding hands as they walked. "I ought to bust you in your head," she told Joe with a smile, and Brown realized this was just the volatile way they communicated. Whatever they'd said, however Keyoke had lowered the temperature, she hadn't been comfortable doing so in front of Brown.

After she went home, Brown offered to talk to Joe about what just happened, and about the various stresses he must be feeling. But Joe said he'd rather focus on the day's practice. He walked outside and stood in a breezeway that connects the main part of the school to the football office. Players would be arriving soon.

"Go, big B, hurry up," Joe said to one freshman taking his time.

"You're running late," he told another player.

Brown believed Joe wasn't just anxious about his mother. He was nervous because, no matter what happened in the final three weeks of the playoffs, football season would be ending. Similar to his mother's relationship with money, Karr football wasn't just a sport to Joe. It was a delicate symbol of his new identity, and one that'd be slipping away no matter what.

In these halls, on that field, in this breezeway, he was a captain. A *giant*. If he told a freshman teammate to move faster, usually he did. But what about after the season? He'd be just another kid without a plan for the future.

When he and Brown talked about college, Joe made it clear he had no idea what campus life was like or even how to submit an application. His vision of college was limited to Karr's brief tours and what he'd seen in the movies. His friends on the team were being recruited to play college football, but Joe wasn't.

Brown knew another hard conversation lay ahead. Maybe several. For now, Joe was outside, alone. And he hated being alone.

"*Move*," he ordered another freshman. The kid ignored him. Joe approached, wrapped his left arm around the freshman's neck, and whispered in his ear.

"Oh, you wanna be different, huh?" he said.

The freshman told him he gets it already, and to leave him alone. Joe, usually calm but rubbed raw, responded by punching the kid in the chest.

NOT LONG AGO, it had been Joe who sometimes got a proverbial fist to the chest. He ran through the halls and ignored teachers' instructions. Immediately after the 2018 state championship, Joe had disappeared from the sideline to dance with someone not associated with Karr. A teammate interrupted their celebration and physically pulled him back toward the team.

Usually it was Ronnie Jackson attempting to shepherd the strays back to the flock. He had grown up under tough circumstances and risen to the captain's line, earning the respect of his younger teammates. Most everyone here, Joe included, wanted to be just like Ronnie.

He wasn't just Brown's most impressive reclamation project. He was Karr's ultimate triumph. On the field, he was the team's brightest star and the player who wore the number 2. Off the field he rode in Brown's truck, went to dinner with him, had food and equipment delivered to his door. He was, in every way, "Action Jackson."

This was an image Brown encouraged, and more than anything the coaches did or said, examples such as Ronnie were the staff's secret weapon to getting other kids' attention. He was the starting running back, a team leader, a celebrity. A *giant*.

When Ronnie gave Joe his cell-phone number, the kid couldn't believe it. When he texted Joe or called him, he made sure to respond immediately. When Ronnie pulled him aside after losing his temper, Joe always listened.

"You trippin', just calm down," Ronnie found himself telling Joe often. Just cool off. Consider your actions. *Never* just react. Racey Mc-Math and Dai'Jean Dixon had done the same things for him. It's just an unspoken, barely visible—but integral—part of the Karr machine and the high-test mystique that fuels it.

Ronnie rarely said anything about how often he quit the team, or how many times Brown threatened to cut him. If his mission is as stark as life and death, then his program is built on a pass-fail system. Ronnie constantly tested boundaries and searched for gray areas and weak points. Joe, in one significant contrast, has adopted Brown's teachings to an eye-rollingly literal degree.

"He's *so* programmed," Norm Randall would say. Even teammates make fun of Joe for his robotic adherence to Brown's method and point out that in a landscape packed with big personalities and singsong names—*Munchie Legaux! Destin Refuge! Ronnie Jackson!*—someone named Joe Thomas stands out for being remarkably vanilla.

Ronnie rarely told Joe, or anyone else, about the uncle confined to a wheelchair after a bullet tore into his belly. Or how, when Ronnie attended family reunions, he was almost always the only male in attendance between the ages of sixteen and fifty. Or the fact that Ronnie's mother, Lisa, earnestly believed the men in her family had a curse on them.

Ronnie shielded his teammates and most everyone else from the backbreaking pressure he felt. He wasn't just supposed to survive or even make it to college. His family expected him not only to play college football, reach the NFL, become a millionaire. He was going to lift everyone up. Ronnie was an entire family's beacon.

"You have come a long way, baby," Lisa told him one Sunday, when the entire family gathers for shrimp pasta, fried chicken, and conversation.

Lisa was sitting at the foot of Ronnie's bed, and at one point there were four generations of relatives packed into the room Ronnie shared with a cousin. Because Ronnie's older sister Jasmine is pregnant, a fifth generation was on the way.

"He's the only one that made it," another sister, Kijha, says.

"You're going to be really something," Ronnie's great-grandmother, Suzie, says.

While they're fawning over him and imagining his future and its effect on theirs, Ronnie doesn't say much. He keeps some truths from his family, too. It's hard being everyone's champion, especially when you're eighteen and play a sport and live in a city where futures change in an instant.

He doesn't tell them that, not long ago, a stranger followed Ronnie and a friend before pointing a gun at them. Or that, in 2017, he was one of two dozen Karr players at a "teen party" near Tulane University. Alcohol- and drug-free, these gatherings are advertised as safe spaces for young people to dance, cut loose, and have fun. But a car drove by and an occupant opened fire.

A former Karr assistant coach, Noel Ellis Sr., was earning extra money that night working security. He contacted Chris D, who then sent a late-night text to Brown.

They're shooting, the text read. Panicked and flashing back to that Friday night when Tonka died, Brown jolted out of bed and tried calling Ronnie. It went straight to voice mail. For hours, most of Karr's coaches had no idea whether Ronnie, their own champion, was alive or dead. He wasn't great at answering his phone under normal circumstances, but this time, his battery was drained.

Ronnie would tell them later that he'd hidden until the shooting stopped. In the pandemonium he'd stepped over a victim, before hearing Ellis calling for him. He ran toward the coach's car, got in, and everyone from Karr drove away still breathing. But in the evening's aftermath, Ronnie decided he could no longer socialize as a normal high school student. He was too recognizable. There was too much at stake. He refused to walk anywhere or accept rides from anyone not associated with the football team. Even as a senior, usually he just stayed home.

Ronnie's family, like so many of his teammates, think everything just comes easy to him. He was blessed, and he will therefore share the fruits of those blessings with them. On this Sunday afternoon, though, he can hold his tongue no longer.

"You gotta hide," he says. "In New Orleans, they don't care if you run the ball good. They don't care nothing about that."

His grandmother, Darlene, is more honest about Ronnie's circumstances than everyone else in this room. She lives in constant fear that her grandson will be gunned down. Recently she had to choose between paying for Ronnie's cell-phone bill or her cable, and because she cannot bear the thought of worrying for him and being unable to hear his voice, Darlene hasn't watched television in weeks.

"These little boys are so jealous of him because he's doing good," she says. "They'll kill him."

Jasmine, sitting on Ronnie's bed and supporting her lower back with his pillow, looks up.

"Just to see him not make it?" she asks.

"They don't want to see him make it," Darlene says.

Ronnie's sister shakes her head. Even in a city where people get shot all the time, this almost feels too unbelievable to be true.

"Everyone down here is so prideful," Jasmine says.

PUNCHING THE FRESHMAN led to another conversation between Joe and Brown. The coach had no choice but to discipline his team captain and a young man he saw almost as family.

Brown knew Joe was upset. But he had acted without thinking, and around here that can get you killed.

"There's another way," Brown told him. "That's the *typical* way."

Joe promised he'd do better, but he'd nonetheless be benched for the first half of the next playoff game. Instead of wearing number 7, he'd play in the number 30. Fighting tears, Joe accepted his punishment.

He went home, attempted to stay on Keyoke's good side, tried to understand her and the stress she, too, was under. But his worries outweighed his sympathy, especially knowing his mother's associations with money. If Joe asked his mother for cash and her pockets were empty, Keyoke had a proven way to refill them. That's another reason he'd said no when she offered him a few dollars.

"I'm your son," he told her. "I know what's going on. I don't need everything now."

As much as anything, Joe tried to distract himself from worrying about his future. It felt impossible. Fat and Tygee Hill, the team's man-child sophomore defensive tackle, were already collecting scholarship offers from elite college football programs. Jamie was approaching a final decision between Arkansas and Louisville, still hoping a blueblood program would offer him late in the process and sweep him off his feet. Leonard was being courted by Nicholls State and Northwestern State. It seemed as if everyone was sorting out their college plans. Everyone but Joe.

Discussing the end made him anxious, and coaches noticed he was quieter than usual. If Leonard or Jamie said something about the season ending, or their final game at Behrman, or swaying to "The Rock" for the last time, Joe demanded they change the subject.

"I don't want to hear about that shit right now," Jamie would recall Joe saying. Sometimes Joe would accuse his wistful friends of getting soft. "He don't let it get there because he knows he's gonna get emotional, too."

But Joe wasn't the only one worried about the uncertainty of his future. Brown and Norm feared the next three games could be life or death for a kid on the razor's edge. He had given himself completely to the program, in effect choosing this path over his mother's. Joe had come further than perhaps anyone, including Ronnie. His hard work and sacrifice had so far been rewarded. If the ultimate reward eluded him, though . . . well, Norm didn't like thinking about that.

"There's a battle coming," he'd say a few weeks before beginning his consulting contract. "Brice keeps talking about *getting* him somewhere. But if you don't; if he *can't* get somewhere . . ."

Norm pauses and shakes his head.

"We might lose him," he says in a tone that, for him, is uncharacteristically soft. "It's all or nothing. And it's tough. I'm scared of Signing Day. If he don't sign, what's gonna happen? He's not gonna be able to stand up there and watch those guys sign. He doesn't have a choice. He'll be at that house or he'll be doing whatever, saying: 'Maybe my mom was right.' Ronnie had uncles, a grandma. That's what scares me: He might say, 'Fuck this shit.' There is no 401(k) plan in their house. It's this or the streets."

Despite its popularity and media coverage, college football recruiting is a widely misunderstood construct. Top players such as Fat and
Tygee begin attracting attention and even scholarship offers in eighth
or ninth grade. Such four- and five-star prospects represent the first
links in a supply chain that fuels the $4.1 billion college sports indus-
try and largely drives the subscription-based recruiting news websites
that reveal only the tip of a massive iceberg. If, say, Jamie is the top
cornerback recruit for Arkansas and Louisville in the class of 2020, the
school he *doesn't* choose will still sign a corner—in this hypothetical its
second or third or fourth choice. The elite programs usually gobble up
the top-ranked players, then the second-tier power conference schools
scramble to collect the best of the players left.

This continues down the chain, where lower-ranked players such
as Leonard—smart and talented but undersized at five foot ten—have
the option of either walking on at a larger school to play without a
scholarship, or choosing among smaller-conference programs that
might offer a full ride. Below that are Division II and Division III
schools, then those within the National Association of Intercollegiate
Athletics and junior colleges. The smaller the schools, the longer it
takes for them to find players who'd been passed over elsewhere to
fill their rosters. There is little coverage of the one- or "zero-star" kids
who, in actuality, are the true lifeblood of college football. Each year
more than ten thousand new players join nearly nine hundred college
football teams on various levels, and a surprising number of those
shotgun marriages take place in the days—and sometimes hours—
before Signing Day.

For various reasons, Joe represents the final link of the chain. There's
no question he has the ability and leadership skills to play college
football—somewhere. And those smaller schools, who rarely bother
recruiting ranked players, must take a chance on unknown commodi-
ties to fill their rosters. They rely on word of mouth from high school

coaches, self-promotional efforts by the players themselves, and most of all, highlight videos from games.

Fat has spent years hyping himself on social media, and after Karr games, Leonard and Leonte often share news coverage and highlights from their performances. Each of those players has a page on Hudl, the network that hosts prospect videos and statistics, such as height, weight, and grade-point average. Joe has no Hudl page, and no idea how to assemble one.

He plays inside linebacker, a position that in Karr's defense rarely generates jaw-dropping sacks, interceptions, or game-saving tackles. Joe's assignment is nonetheless an essential one: he is to patrol the center of the field and act as a wall to stop rushers up the middle. But even when he's doing his job and displaying his value to the defense, video of his play isn't exactly exciting. He rarely shows emotion or celebration, which can signal passion to recruiters. He is muscular but undersized at five foot eleven and 215 pounds.

Joe, in other words, is a perfect candidate to fall through the cracks of a college football system that actually wants him. But it still needs help finding him.

Brown has promised to do all he can, but the best and worst parts of Joe are his pride. He refuses to ask teammates to mention him to recruiters, to ask coaches to help him build a Hudl page or help him understand where he stands in the college football ecosystem. He won't even ask teachers to assist him in filling out a college application.

More troubling, he is confused by the college process and hasn't so much as asked Brown to explain it. Brown is waiting for Joe to take the initiative on these tasks, an essential show of ownership and independence. But it's December. Signing Day is two months away.

Instead, Joe has been telling his teammates the same thing he tells his mother: he's just fine. He tells them programs from tiny Prairie View A&M to mighty Alabama have contacted him. The teammates are skeptical of this, and on the way to a seafood restaurant one evening, Fat told Brown that Joe seems to have no idea what he's talking about.

Brown issued a long sigh. If Joe had any chance of using football to get out, Brown knew several more hard conversations awaited. And that they were both running out of time.

THERE'S ANOTHER UNSPOKEN TRUTH of living in New Orleans and playing football for Karr: just because you get out, doesn't mean you stay out.

In late summer 2019, Ronnie's phone rang. A few months earlier, he had signed a scholarship agreement to play at the University of Texas at San Antonio. He was in his dorm room when he answered the phone, heard his mother's voice, tried to make sense of her words.

"Jas just got shot," Lisa told him.

Ronnie's older sister, who months earlier sat on his bed while carrying a baby girl, had been shot in the head. She was in a New Orleans hospital, clinging to life. Lisa Jackson had no idea if her daughter would live or die.

Ronnie hung up and, in a cloud of shock, picked up his football cleats. He asked two friends to join him for an emergency workout, declining to say why. They spent an hour or two on the practice field, but Ronnie's mind kept drifting, imagining the worst. He had to go home.

He called his coach and explained what'd happened. The coach told him to remain calm, try to focus on his responsibilities at school, and establish a plan. Ronnie interpreted this as his coach encouraging him to choose football over family. Ronnie nonetheless called a friend in Houston and asked him to pick him up in San Antonio. He had to get to New Orleans.

"When football is a business . . ." Ronnie would say later, trailing off. "I felt like football ain't that serious that I can't go visit my people."

So Ronnie told himself during the long ride that he was finished at UT San Antonio. Maybe with football altogether. Everything he'd worked for, poof, just gone. He arrived at a New Orleans hospital and found Jasmine's head covered in bandages. He struggled to look at her, and he collected only particles of a story he was unsure he wanted to know. Something about a dispute between two men, and somehow Jasmine had found herself caught in a literal cross fire.

At first, Ronnie felt an overwhelming wave of anger, then a need for vengeance. *Action Jackson* had to do something, and that something was putting his hands on a gun, hunting down the man responsible for this, and letting a bullet and God sort out the rest.

But then he paused. He reminded himself of words he'd heard from coaches and shared with teammates: *just calm down.* Revenge was pointless, and even if the man who'd put Jasmine in this hospital bed was snuffed out, it wouldn't erase what had happened. If Ronnie got locked up or killed, Lisa might be dealing with the loss of two children.

"I had to use my head," Ronnie said. "Freshman-year-of-high-school Ronnie, that most definitely—I probably would've tried to kill him. I ain't even gonna lie to you. I was that much of a hothead. I wasn't thinking."

Time passed, and Jasmine woke up. Ronnie would recall a doctor telling the family it was a miracle. The bullet had entered the back of her skull from the right side, close to her ear. A few millimeters to the left or right, and she would've suffered irreversible brain damage, or worse. As it was, she'd been lucky; soon she'd be discharged, go home, begin the march back toward being a young mother who took college classes.

Ronnie was relieved, but so many thoughts had pooled in his mind. He stuck with his decision to quit football, though. When word of this spread, Ronnie's phone started ringing. Brown was calling, and so was Nick Foster. He knew what they'd say. Ronnie declined the calls, sending them to voice mail. He never listened to their messages.

The days dragged by, and Ronnie began hearing rumors about himself. That he'd failed out of school. Couldn't handle college life or big-time football. He was selling drugs now. What a shame. So much talent.

"Fucked me up," Ronnie would say. "I really started realizing what Coach Brice used to say: a pat on the back is really six inches from a kick in the ass."

His phone kept ringing, and some days it was Fat calling. At least once it was Joe. Aaron Anderson sent him encouraging messages on social media. One day Ronnie looked at his phone and saw the number of Tonya Allen, an administrator at Karr. For reasons he'd struggle to explain, Ronnie answered but heard an unexpected voice.

"Bitch, I *know* you seen me calling your phone," Brown said. Perhaps for the first time since learning about Jasmine's injuries, Ronnie smiled. He talked with his old coach, who reminded him he'd never give up on him. He was there for whatever he needed: guidance, a sounding board, anything.

Brown kept talking, and these conversations made him acknowledge several things. The first was that Ronnie was like a son to him, perhaps the closest he'll ever have to a child of his own. Their relationship was explosive, but it was precious. His other realization is that, like a son, Brown's social contract with Ronnie hadn't expired when he'd left Karr. For better or worse, their bond was for life.

"I don't think my job can ever be done with him," Brown said.

Eventually they agreed Ronnie belonged in school. He was the champion not just to his family but so many little Ronnies and Joes in the Karr program, on the West Bank, in New Orleans. *You don't get to determine when you're finished*, Brown had once told him. With so many people still looking to him, and whether Ronnie liked it or not, this was still true.

Brown called Tim Rebowe, the head football coach at Nicholls State. He explained the situation, and Ronnie. Rebowe didn't need another running back, but he agreed to make space for Ronnie.

Now nineteen, Ronnie enrolled at Nicholls and took classes. He told almost no one. He made no announcement on social media. When he stood on the sideline at Karr games, he wore no Colonels apparel. If a stranger asked what he was up to now, Ronnie lied, saying he was still figuring it out.

He didn't care if his cryptic answers inflamed chatter about his supposed involvement in something nefarious. He didn't correct them, but Ronnie told the truth to some people. Joe was one of them. Brown taught him to never lie to a Karr man. In fact, Ronnie was just as honest with Joe about other things.

One was that he'd learned New Orleans isn't just a city. It's a state of mind and a culture, and more than that, it is home. Detaching from it is harder than just signing a scholarship and driving away. It involves saying good-bye to the people who love you, those who *made* you, because Ronnie learned when he came home that even some relatives seemed happy he'd washed out. They care for him, sure. But the more he succeeds, the more it highlights their own failures.

"New Orleans," Ronnie says, "is like crabs in a bucket. Every time that crab about to go out, something just pull it back in; 'If I can't leave, you can't leave.'"

But he says the shooting, and its aftermath, taught him the secret to escaping the bucket: Alert none of the other crabs and just go. Stop caring what they think or say. This is easier said than done, of course, and perhaps Ronnie is fooling himself. But he insists that the time is coming for him to make a move. He says he hopes his mother will come with him.

If she doesn't . . .

"You gotta sacrifice sometimes," he says. "Ain't nothing down here for us. We been here too long, and it's the same old stuff that's going on."

Sitting behind Brown's desk during a visit home from Thibodaux, Ronnie pauses. He stares into space, contemplating the uncertainty and promise of a blank future. There is no curse on the men in his family. Just that they were born in a place where Black men die young.

"It's too wild out here," he says. "Me? Nah, I'm out. I'm just gonna be gone."

BROWN'S JOB IS NEVER DONE, and this is a burden that doesn't just exhaust him. It corrodes him. If there wasn't a crisis today, that only means the one tomorrow will be worse. The bill for joy and satisfaction always come due, which is why Brown tries to avoid feeling those things. He has decided that he can never let his guard down. He can never stop coaching, teaching, rehabilitating.

He certainly can't take a day off. If Keyoke calls again, saying she needs to talk, Brown can never say no. He can never ask her to wait.

Everything here feels urgent, and though there are many things competing for Brown's attention, today's top priority is talking to Joe about life after Karr. So this morning he calls Joe's study hall teacher and summons him to the football office. He walks in to find Brown sitting in a rolling chair, and he pushes another one to Joe.

"Who's been hitting you up?" Brown asks.

"Uh, one of the camps I went to, Coach Brennan said they called him," Joe says. He's referring to linebackers coach Brennan Harris. "Houston. He told me Bama called him."

"Which Bama?"

"*Ala*bama."

Brown smiles. He doesn't want to crush the kid's spirit, but there's no way this is true. For more than a dozen years, Alabama has been college football's top program. Coach Nick Saban has won seven national championships and has built his program into a colossus that draws in the country's best of the best high school recruits. Brown provides a brief explainer of the college football landscape, focusing on the major-conference Football Bowl Subdivision and the smaller-school Football Championship Subdivision. It's immediately clear Joe has never considered the intricacy of this sport and its vast web of levels.

"Alabama is the highest level of football other than the NFL," Brown says. "Houston is, probably—I would say probably—four conferences underneath them. So that's still a high level. You see what I'm saying?"

Joe nods.

"So how you feel if you don't get that offer from Houston?" Brown says.

A moment passes, and Joe clicks his teeth the way his mother does when she's uncomfortable.

"Then I didn't do good, fuck," he says. He shakes his head. "Ahhh, I just, like—I ain't work hard enough."

Brown chuckles. There's something both charming and frustrating about the black-and-white way Joe views a complicated world. Playing college football anywhere would be an incredible achievement, especially considering a few months ago he was hiding in abandoned houses to avoid an ambush. But to him, anything short of a top program represents failure.

"When I get to where I'm going," Joe says, "I'll just work harder."

Brown says that the point of playing college football isn't the football. It's the college. And it'd be free. He says a scholarship can be worth six figures, especially when factoring in housing and meals alongside tuition and fees.

"Your mama don't have to pay for it," Brown says, and Joe looks up.

This means she'd have one less reason to drift outside. "You're looking at that shit backwards."

Nick walks in and overhears their conversation. He reminds Joe that Brown went to Grambling, and Nick went to the University of Alabama at Birmingham. Both were smaller schools, and in fact both players had no scholarship. They were walk-ons.

"That Alabama thing far-fetched," Brown says. "You know that."

Sitting on a table, Nick looks up.

"You think you're going to *Bama*?" he says. "You're good, but bitch . . ."

Joe laughs, and his lips stretch around his braces.

"Juluke used to tell me the same shit," Nick says. "You couldn't tell me I couldn't play at LSU: 'You ain't this. You ain't fast enough.'"

"It's real," Brown says.

"That shit is a real business," Nick says.

They discuss the possibility of Joe walking on somewhere, though the coaches agree that should be a worst-case scenario. A scholarship is very much a possibility, though Brown points out that Joe can't keep punching other teammates and getting himself benched.

"The easiest route to getting all that," Brown says, "is going to the state championship, when all those suites is full with scouts. Then they all just get a chance to see you, and they're looking for new talent that's under the radar."

Joe nods, though he still looks overwhelmed by all this.

"You got any questions?" Brown asks.

"I'm straight," Joe says.

"Not one question. What'd your mama cook this weekend?"

Joe says she stayed out of the kitchen. Instead Keyoke spent the weekend at the Fischer Development Neighborhood, a place that's familiar and comfortable to her, attending a second line and visiting old friends. Joe was at Ms. Diane's, trying to relax but mostly worrying.

"How you balancing all that shit?" Brown says.

Joe shrugs, saying the last few days have been better. Or at least simpler. Cassidy is in Paris with her family, so Joe has had fewer distractions and could spend more time at home.

"Oh, Par-*ee*," Nick says, and for a moment they imagine Keyoke exploding into the Louvre and demanding to see the *Mona* fucking *Lisa*.

They laugh, and a moment later, Joe thanks his coaches and heads back to study hall. Brown and Nick look at each other.

"She's *gonna* go back out there," Nick says. He believes that without Joe here, Keyoke might find it easier to fall into old habits.

Brown shakes his head. Part of him wants Joe to get as far from this as possible. But with a crisis seemingly unavoidable, at some point Joe will require support. In that case, closer is better. Perhaps Joe can join Ronnie at Nicholls State and, more than just playing together, the two of them keep each other going.

The coaches cannot know what is right, or whether Joe will go to college at all. Some projects are simply too daunting, some children too broken. Even if Joe is offered a scholarship, can he overpower the stresses he's facing and break free of the tentacles gripping him? Perhaps he will. Perhaps he'll go and thrive. But his ultimate success, and in some ways the efficacy of Brown's program, depends not on a difficult question but an impossible one: Can Joe do what Tonka couldn't, and Ronnie hasn't, and leave his mother behind?

Brown sighs, lamenting the wretched truth that a kid can be born into a place—a home, a city, a nation—where choosing between success and family is sometimes necessary. With the Fischer in one direction and Paris in the other, which of Joe's two lives would pull stronger? He used to forgo sleep to avoid nightmares about his mother, so what might he do if something real happens and that dreaded phone call someday comes?

"He would get the same feeling Ronnie got," Brown says. He worries Joe might fall victim to instinct and, seeking vengeance, resort to violence. Just think about how he reacted a few days earlier when the freshman disrespected him.

"I think he wouldn't do it," Nick says.

"I don't know."

"He's got a conscience, Coach."

LITTLE SHIT

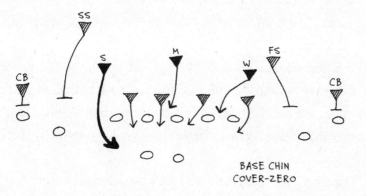

BASE CHIN
COVER-ZERO

If KARR WON ITS third-round playoff game, setting up what felt like an inevitable showdown against Neville, Brown had no idea what he'd say to the team.

Maybe the football gods would spare him. Not just the five-hour bus ride to Monroe and a rematch of schools that have met six times in the last eight postseasons. Brown had also been dreading the pressure of trying to convince players they could finally beat a talented, well-coached, predominantly white team. Brown wasn't so sure himself.

But, no, some higher power wouldn't let him off easily. Leonard had been too sharp in practice and too smart picking apart Breaux Bridge's defense. He had a perfect score on his written test, and Leonard would complete his first ten passes in a 51–14 victory. He accounted for all seven Karr touchdowns. In the truck after the game, Brown maintained hope he could avoid a challenging address back at the school. Marv was in the back seat checking scores on his phone, and Brown perked up after Marv announced Westgate High was leading Neville in the fourth quarter. He sank back in his seat when Neville went ahead, 26–24, then got the final defensive stop.

Officer Pat parked Brown's truck, and the coach climbed out and headed inside. He decided to just wing it. There was a chance this would be his final speech to Karr's seniors. Downing the second of two Cokes in his office, Brown could hear players filtering into the weight room.

He lumbered past his desk, through the assistants' office, toward his makeshift lectern. Leaning against the back extension platform, Brown drew a breath. A cluster of Karr alumni had attended tonight's game, many of them wearing apparel with college logos. This is how he began.

"The old players come back and see y'all making the same mistakes they once made," he says. "Getting the same cussin'-out they used to get."

This group, though, was different. Virtually every player here had won a state championship. That's a weakness, not a strength, when you're trying to win one more. Earlier this season, the team had expected to win games without putting in the work. Now it couldn't bear the thought of losing them.

"The same thing we're telling y'all," Brown continues, "*they* trying to tell y'all, too: 'Man, y'all gotta go back and win this shit. Y'all *gotta* keep doing it.'"

He pauses.

"To win four straight state championships in 4A—a public school in New Orleans, don't got shit," Brown says. "Hundred percent Black people on the team. You know, I'm gonna say it: a hundred percent *n——s*. Don't got a pot to piss in. Don't got a window to throw it out.

Most of us in here living below the poverty line. Most of us in here got fucked-up households, got fucked-up situations."

He smiles. It'd be so easy for the young men here to give up. That's the predictable response, the one many outsiders see as typical of a team from a place like this.

"How many people in here got fucked-up shit going on?" Brown says.

Most every hand goes up. The coach raises his hand, too.

"They say God never put more on you than you can handle," he says. "That's why he put this here before you. You don't have *time* for emotion. Don't have *time* to worry about circumstances at home. What you *do* have is another opportunity to make your family proud. Another opportunity so you can play on the highest stage in Louisiana, to show that you're the best. Not *talk* about being the best. But show that you're the best."

The heads are nodding now. Winning isn't just an incentive here. It's an equalizer. It erases who you were and announces who you are today. What you've become. It commands respect and shuts mouths. Leonard, sitting on the floor, is looking up into his coach's eyes.

"It's gonna be ten thousand people there, hollering that shit all night—*Ne . . . ville, Ne . . . ville*—in they spot," Brown says. "But what's gonna be special to you? When you shut 'em up. Not in what you say. But in what you do."

He's good at this, pausing as he speaks. He punches certain words and phrases for emphasis, a foulmouthed Baptist preacher in sweatpants.

"What it's gonna take to go up there and beat them on Friday night is a hundred percent. A hundred per*cent*," Brown says. "Or you know what's gonna happen? You're gonna leave just like you left Baton Rouge Catholic, with that look on your face. You're gonna leave out the stadium just like you did against John Curtis, with that look on your face."

He establishes eye contact with each of Karr's captains.

"When you gonna stop doubting yourself?" Brown says. "When are you gonna be a motherfucker and stand up there and say: 'Man, *fuck* Neville'?"

Players are smiling. Having worked up a sweat, the coach takes another breath.

"You've got one . . . mother . . . fucker in your way. Can't go around 'em. Can't go under 'em," he says. "You gotta go through 'em. Everybody understand that?"

"Yes, Coach," the players say back.

"Don't be typical," Brown says in closing. "You know how I feel about that shit."

THREE HUNDRED MILES north and west, the celebration was on. Karr and Neville had gotten to know each other well over the last decade. But in nearly thirty years of varsity football, Karr had never played at Neville's Bill Ruple Stadium.

As soon as the match was set, worshipers at First United Methodist Church in Monroe began planning a catered dinner for Neville's players and coaches. Whispers circulated about a midweek cookout, and a law office and optometrist put up signs wishing the team luck. Neil Shaw, the Tigers' radio voice, hacked through a thicket of emotions and started preparing for his midweek call-in show with head coach Mickey McCarty.

"We treasured the chance to get revenge," Shaw would say in an interview. "I hate that word. To get redemption."

Fifty-one weeks earlier, Neville had made the long trip to Behrman Stadium for a state semifinal game. The drive was hellish, the atmosphere intimidating, the culture shock unmistakable. Ouachita Parish's population is nearly two-thirds white, and in 2010, Florida

State University found that Monroe was the thirteenth-most-segregated city in the United States. They mill rice and make aluminum here and send conservative politicians to the state house and US Capitol. At least traditionally, it's not exactly a panacea of Black opportunity. In 2016, a district court examined a culture of lingering racial segregation within Monroe's schools. Black students at Neville, for instance, were five times less likely to be enrolled in gifted and talented courses compared with whites, and seven times less likely to take an advanced placement test.

Shaw, the radio voice, is sixty-four and white. He says he felt uncomfortable at Behrman from the moment he arrived. The fans near the press box were "very vocal," he says, leading him to perform the broadcast on a folding table near an exit. He shared his safety concerns with security personnel before the game and let them know he's had some law enforcement training. He nonetheless made his wife and their Yorkshire terrier stay in the truck. Shaw would say later that he heard multiple gunshots during the game.

"They don't sound like they do in the movies," he says. Karr beat Neville, 25–13, before winning its third consecutive state title a week later.

But that was ancient history. The big, bad team from Algiers would now face a shock of its own. Karr wasn't used to facing a defense like Neville's, and quarterback Andrew Brister is six four and two hundred pounds. Because of his NFL genes and experience running Neville's spread, he won't be intimidated by the grandness of Friday's stage.

"We're not intimidated by anything," corrects the young man's father, former NFL quarterback Bubby Brister.

Neville fans toasted the long-overdue reckoning that awaited. After all these years, Karr was finally about to learn what Monroe, and Neville, are made of.

Not long after Brown's address to players, he went to see athletic director Taurus "T." Howard. By now Brown knew his team's strengths and weaknesses. He had in fact tested them.

When he'd scheduled the game against Wossman, whose campus is about four miles from Neville's, it was to see how players and coaches handled doing the entire trip in a day. Karr won, but Brown saw a team that was lethargic and sloppy.

"Coach, look," he therefore told Howard. "This ain't a team that can go up there day-of."

If Karr had any chance of upsetting Neville, coaches needed to simulate routine and provide players with adequate rest. Maybe a few rewards. That would require Howard to dig deep into the athletic department budget: two luxury motor coaches ($9,100 for the trip), Howard estimated, and a bloc of hotel rooms in Monroe ($10,000 for the night).

Though Howard didn't yet know where that money would come from, he told Brown to consider it done. He'd later say Karr had a few extra dollars in its savings account and that the charter network, InspireNOLA, assumed some travel costs. Howard has a quiet voice and an easygoing demeanor, but in truth he's a political shark. "We gotta do this for the kids," he'd recall imploring Jamar McKneely, InspireNOLA's chief executive.

With that off Brown's plate, he could focus on preparing for the game itself. He spent most of Saturday alone with his iPad in his cramped office, studying footage from each of Neville's games this season. What he saw didn't exactly lift his spirits. McCarty's defense uses five defensive backs and often operates out of Cover 6, a highly sophisticated structure that splits the field in half. One side is in a zone, usually Cover 4, and the other in Cover 2. It has weaknesses, just like any defense, but Brown struggled to positively identify Neville's tells. The more notes he typed, the more his observations seemed to contradict themselves.

```
1ST PRIORITY WILL BE OUTSIDE ZONE
NOW/RPO IS 2ND PRIORITY DEPENDING ON LEVERAGE
    AND FRONT
PRIORITY WILL CHANGE
```

Then he had an idea. Sometimes Brown saves an offensive play or formation all season until the moment—and opponent—is right. Ten weeks after conjuring his modified "Z-hunt," in which Fat runs a deep post following a pre-snap motion designed to flummox defensive backs, Brown still hasn't called the play in a game. This reminded him that McCarty almost certainly holds back some plays, too.

So he opened one more video, this one from the game at Behrman fifty-one weeks earlier. And there it was. Neville in its usual Cover 6, with cornerbacks often "bracketing," or double-teaming, Karr's two best receivers in man coverage. Plays such as "Z-hunt," which rely on pre-snap confusion, can help with that because cornerbacks aren't certain who they're supposed to cover. Brown also found that the footwork of Neville's "rover," a cornerback given the freedom to roam around the field and improvise, was a bad poker player. His feet often revealed the entire defense's intentions. If the rover was flat-footed, that usually tipped off a blitz that would slow down the read-option game, a cornerstone of Karr's rushing attack. But if the rover leaned forward, that signaled he would drop into coverage. Neville's defense in general had struggled with Karr's up-tempo plays in last year's game. Exhaustion, especially coupled with panic, can be an offense's friend.

Brown could work with that. He kept watching, made more notes, ultimately decided victory would come down to two things. The first was that this would be a match between two chess masters. Brown's plays would require an extra layer of deception and would rely more than usual on timing. The second was more stark: Leonard, in the biggest game of his life, would have to be near perfect.

When Leonard walked into the football office at 7:15 on Monday morning, Brown handed him a final draft of the game plan. The three-page document consisted of 1,049 words, fifty-four plays, and eight new offensive concepts. Leonard, usually expected to throw the ball no more than 2.5 seconds after the snap, must release it in 2.3 seconds to stay ahead of Neville's pass rush.

Brown had included hints, signals, observations. He'd listed several of them in bold.

```
TAKE CHANCES IN JET FORMATION
KEEP TEMPO HIGH
READ THE ROVER DO NOT CHOOSE IN PRE SNAP
   WHETHER TO GIVE OR PULL READ IT!!
```

Leonard had less than forty-eight hours to memorize everything. Because Karr would be leaving for Monroe on Thursday morning, he and the offense would have three days to practice instead of four. Leonard started preparing immediately, studying the tiny print on three densely filled pages.

On the bottom of each one, Brown had included a message: "YOU ARE ONLY AS GOOD AS YOUR LAST PLAY."

FRIDAY'S COLLISION BETWEEN the two Louisianas would be a battle of wits and, at its core, Brown's intricate offense against McCarty's highly advanced defense. But the true matchup would be perception versus reality: city against country, rich against poor.

Neville seemed to be leaning hard into these differences. Though the team roster has a high number of Black players, Karr doesn't know that. And used correctly, contrast and intimidation can be powerful weapons of their own, especially in making an opponent feel out of sorts. McCarty likes to take visiting coaches and administrators for pregame tours of his lavish facilities. Tours begin with the stadium's stately wrought-iron fencing, which happens to be festooned with eighteen championship and runner-up banners. It continues into Neville's sprawling locker room and state-of-the-art weight room before ending at McCarty's office, whose balcony overlooks the five-thousand-seat stadium and its all-weather field turf.

Karr would be greeted to similar hospitality, along with a stadium playlist that before the game would include suburban favorites from Three Dog Night and Counting Crows. Just before kickoff, the Band of Heathens' alt-country version of "Hurricane" would blare sedately through the speakers.

The high black water, a devil's daughter
She's hard, she's cold, and she's mean.
But nobody taught her, it takes a lot of water
To wash away New Orleans.

There would, of course, be one last surprise. Nearly three months earlier, the Monroe County School Board hadn't just approved the construction of a massive video scoreboard at Ruple Stadium. It had agreed to front the $558,664 to build it, with Neville agreeing to reimburse the board for its crown jewel.

It had been finished a few weeks earlier. But it hadn't been turned on in a game yet. On Friday, shortly before Karr arrived, it would be.

THE EVENING BEFORE Karr hits the road, Brown calls Leonard toward the sideline. Then they go for a walk around the field. The debacle at Catholic, Brown tells him, had been painful. But it'd been the best thing that happened to Leonard and the team.

At the time, he hadn't been preparing as diligently as Brown wanted him to. He skipped over the tiny details—the "little shit," Karr's coaches call it—that make a quarterback successful here: reading defenses and taking his time before the snap to outwit opponents.

He'd grown up, and Brown says he's thankful—maybe not for the episode itself, but in how Leonard had responded.

"I hope you don't think that I'm belittling you," Brown says. "I want the best out of everybody. I can't tell you why I'm like that. I want the best every time. Maybe it's because I'm giving you *my* best."

The next morning, players and coaches board the two luxury buses Howard had reserved, one for offense and the other for defense. Off they go.

Their first stop is Wossman High, where Karr holds a brief walk-through and Leonard looks sharp. Then the buses continue to the Hilton Garden Inn west of Monroe. There's Christmas music playing in the lobby, and players howl about the flat-screen TVs in their rooms. Brown is unable to reserve a space large enough for a team meeting, so he assembles everyone in a hallway near the elevators. This isn't a vacation, he tells them. It's a business trip. There is to be no nonsense after lights-out.

"If you're in the hall and I catch you," he says, "you're done."

Joe nods, looking into the eyes of a few known loudmouths.

"Got you," he says, making sure coaches hear him.

"Don't forget why you're here," Brown says as three newly checked-in guests wait with their luggage for the meeting to end and the bottleneck to clear. "The reason why you're here today, right here, is so you can kick their ass tomorrow."

It's near dinnertime, and Brown instructs players to be on the buses by 5:59 p.m. They'll be leaving at 6:00. Brown can be a bit obsessive on the details, especially when the stakes are this high. So to drive that point home, he insisted that the bus company assign a former Karr football player to drive the offense's bus. This was partly because he'd lost faith in bus drivers after the Trent Washington ordeal and the tardy departure before the Carver playoff game. But it also allowed Brown to make a point to his players. The driver was behind the wheel at 5:54.

He steers toward Golden Corral, and if across town the video board and artificial turf symbolize abundance, to Karr kids it's the promise of an overstuffed belly. Indeed when the buses stop and the team off-loads, players don't just approach the food stations inside. They attack them.

"Fucking scavengers," Brown mutters to himself. When he surveys the gastronomical landscape for himself, he frowns.

He nonetheless fills a plate with popcorn shrimp, white rice, and macaroni and cheese before announcing at his table that he has no appetite. Noel Ellis Jr., the team's slim and newly minted special teams coach, playfully offers to bring Brown a salad.

"You want me to be sick?" the coach asks. He says his body would "reject" the vegetables as foreign objects.

Brown quietly calls over Leonte and asks him to load up another plate. Bring him the same items, but this time, don't let the foods touch. Leonte looks at him with confusion, but it's his coach, so he obliges. While Brown waits, he grimaces as other kids pass with plates packed with all manner of creative delights: a tortilla loaded with gummy bears, leaning towers of soft serve topped with bacon. Personalization and oddities are perhaps part of the Corral's charm, but Brown isn't feeling it.

His mind is bound up. Thoughts about McCarty's strategy crash into those about Leonard's readiness for tomorrow. Brown keeps saying he's fine. Really. But he's quiet, and when Leonte returns with a plate carefully arranged with three islands of food, Brown thanks him but pushes the plate forward after a single bite. He suggests ordering a pizza back at the hotel. Maybe some wings, too.

Eventually it's time to reboard the buses, and the kids are loudly talking and laughing. Marv suggests this is a good sign for tomorrow, a signal that players are relaxed. But Fat speaks for everyone when he begs Leonte, singing in a blood-curdling falsetto, to be quiet for the love of God.

At the hotel Brown stops at the front desk to investigate the local pizza situation. When the clerk recommends a place with a good Hawaiian pie, delivered piping hot with pineapple and ham, Brown wrinkles his nose and heads toward the elevator. He opens the door to his suite, plops into a desk chair, and opens his laptop to study more Neville film.

What has he missed? He's leaning forward when there's a knock at the door. Leonard doesn't wait before walking in and taking his place on a love seat. Backup quarterbacks A.J. Samuel and Khamani Simmons wedge in next to him.

This is the week's final quarterbacks meeting, which always ends with Brown distributing his weekly written test. Since the Catholic game Leonard hasn't scored below a 90.

"Y'all ready?" Brown asks. A.J., an eager and perceptive freshman, says he is. "You might have to be, the way Leonard has been looking."

Leonard smiles. His coach's test has already begun.

"My last play was very awesome today," he says. "It's gonna be excellent tomorrow."

Brown purses his lips but begins reviewing the game plan. What does it mean if the boundary cornerback shows inside leverage against Karr's outside "V" receiver? That he's likely blitzing, Leonard says. What's the call if the rover is standing flat-footed when the defense shows Cover 2 man? It means bring the slot to the "jet" motion, Leonard says, and plan to throw a quick screen to the opposite side. Leonte will be a blocker in every passing play but which one? "Casino," Leonard says, because Leonte becomes the primary receiver on that play. There's another knock at the door, and this time Omari Robertson and Mike Thompson enter. Usually Omari skips meetings like this, and Brown shoots him a surprised look.

"Gotta be on my p's and q's," Omari says. He sits on the carpet and the session proceeds. No matter how hard Brown tries to trip Leonard up, the quarterback doesn't miss. Brown drops his notes and shuts his laptop.

"I ain't got no test for you," he says. "Your test is tomorrow."

Leonard nods.

"We will pass," he says. "You got faith?"

"You wouldn't be behind the center," Brown says.

"That's all I need to hear."

Leonard, A.J., and Khamani stand and head through the door and into the hallway. Just before the door closes, Leonard presses his face toward the opening.

"Good luck," he whispers, and Brown smiles for maybe the first time all week.

LOCALS LOOK UP as two luxury buses pass slowly along Forsythe Avenue. Their eyes follow the massive vehicles as they back in through a gate before stopping. They watch as a hundred men and boys from a distant land step onto the dirt and say nothing. The players silently and methodically form two lines.

Then they see the visitors march forward, each player holding his shoulder pads and helmet, and disappear through a locker room door. For the next little while, the visitors will be hidden from view.

The team's coach won't, though. Brown wears a large purple shirt with a massive *K* on the front as he steps slowly onto the field and finds an empty bench. His eyes are curious, too. He looks up and admires the video board whose yellow numbers count down to kickoff. He marvels at the extravagances surrounding him.

When he looks across the field, he sees Karr's principal, Dr. Chauncey Nash, walking toward him. Nash has just returned from a tour of Neville's facilities, and the experience seems to have had its intended effect. Nash is shaking his head in amazement.

"Two different worlds out here, Doc," Brown tells him. "Two similar programs, two different worlds."

"Mm-hmm," Nash says.

"You got the life of privilege, and you got the life of nothing."

Nash didn't just fly unknowingly into McCarty's web. He's involved in the planning of Karr's new campus, scheduled to open about a year from now. He's always on the lookout for inspiration. Brown has dropped hints about wanting a more spacious locker room and an indoor practice facility. He doesn't expect to get either of those, though perhaps as his negotiations advance with St. Aug, he'll be asked to share a few ideas.

"You saw the weight room?" Brown asks.

"I took pictures!" says Nash, who offers his phone to the coach.

Brown swipes through the photos and is nearly overcome with envy.

"Oh! *Why* are we looking at this shit?" he says, taking one last look anyway.

Through a tunnel behind Brown, a skull-rattling dance party has begun in the Karr locker room. A freshman flips the lights off and on, Leonte stands on a bench and dances to Meek Mill's "Dreams and Nightmares," and Leonard punches the air in time with the beat. Tiga stalks through in his light-up Guy Fawkes mask, and Joe seems particularly—if a bit unusually—fired up. He's standing alone in an open doorway, hollering into the evening air.

A few minutes later, the team has pushed into the tunnel behind Tiga, who pretends to hold back this assembly of lunatics. Karr's players run onto the field, Joe in the front and Leonard in the rear, passing men dressed in half-zip sweaters and ball caps adorned with college logos. Joe warms up in front of recruiters from Grambling State and Northwestern State, though they don't seem to notice him.

The representative of Northwestern State has driven the ninety miles from Natchitoches to see a different player. At one point he notices Brown sitting alone and walks over.

"You looking to close the deal on Leonard?" Brown asks, and the recruiter looks at him with a guilty-as-charged grin.

"I think it's a no-brainer," the Northwestern State coach says. Brown says he isn't involved in Leonard's college decision, and as the man keeps talking and explaining and selling, Brown unlocks his phone and pretends to listen while he plays a covert game of *Toy Blast*.

A cluster of Neville players, most of them Black, gathers near the Karr sideline to chant and get their adrenaline flowing. Tikey Reese, a senior defensive tackle, waves his teammates toward him for a final message.

"Hey! Fuck them boys on three," Reese says. "One, two, three!"

"Fuck them boys!" his teammates say.

A few yards away, Fat and Leonte are standing near midfield. Fat squats to take imaginary photos of Leonte in the Heisman Trophy pose and flexing his arms.

"Hey, let's go!" Fat says. "It's about that time."

Indeed the yellow numbers on the video board have counted almost all the way down, and the low brass section of Karr's marching band issues a concert F to D. That signals players to gather for "The Rock." Joe keeps lurching forward, visibly eager, and a coach holds him by his waistband. His teammates stand near the end zone, several of them saying "New Orleans!" again and again, and when the drums kick in, players link arms in the shadow of the dazzling scoreboard. The tempo quickens and players run onto the field, the arrival—in recent years, anyway—of Class 4A's kings.

Maybe fifty yards away, the home team bursts through a paper banner. The Neville faithful erupts. Then, a few moments later, the time for preparing and thinking and theatricality has passed. These football and cultural forces will meet at last in this hadron collider. And with each team lined up, waiting to face its counterpart, Neville's kicker jogs toward a teed-up football and boots it into the air.

NORM RANDALL is in a Fairfield Inn eight hundred miles away, listening to a web stream of Neil Shaw's broadcast. He hears the drop in Shaw's voice when Karr marches deep into Neville territory on its first possession. He hears it lift and race and grow louder when wide receiver Reynaud Shields fumbles three yards from the end zone. Neville recovers and immediately scores a touchdown.

Norm feels his heart sink.

"Y'all can beat the other Black kids," he'd say later. "But can you beat the white ones?"

A few minutes later, Leonte fumbles. An official flags Karr for having too many players on the field. Then a false start. Kevin Marigny, Karr's running back for speed plays, fumbles near the goal line. Another Karr penalty. Another Neville touchdown. Five minutes into the first quarter, it's 14–0.

It's happening, Norm would recall thinking. *Again.*

Joe sits on a cylindrical cooler and tries to fight off strengthening feelings of despair. This is a disastrous start. Players are quiet on the sideline. Brown and Leonard are discussing something, and they're the only ones who don't look panicked. Brown keeps noticing something in Neville's defense. He tells Leonard to prepare for a play Brown has never called.

When the offense lines up in trips formation, three receivers to Leonard's left, the quarterback pauses. He notices Neville's rover, Kareem Moore, drifting toward the line of scrimmage. He's flat-footed.

Leonard looks toward the sideline and he sees Nick Foster signaling Brown's updated call: "Trips left Y-scat Z-hunt." The opposing defense and moment are worthy. It's time. The receivers adjust their alignment, and Leonard puts the inside receiver, Fat, in motion. Neville's defenders look confused, and they're trying to communicate and decide which of the receivers they're supposed to . . .

Leonard snaps the ball, Fat sprints forward, and the corner knows he can't keep up in man coverage. The safety races over to help, but it's a mismatch. Leonard plants his feet and launches the ball nearly fifty yards in the air. Fat cuts toward the center of the field, where he can see the ball floating to his right. Running at full speed, he gets to it just in time for the catch and a huge gain. On the next play, with Neville gassed, Leonard fakes a handoff to Leonte before running eighteen yards for a touchdown.

"Keep fighting!" Joe yells, having departed the cooler. Now he's stalking up the sideline.

Though Brister passes for another touchdown on a wheel route, a signature play Karr's defense has been preparing to stop all week, Leonard remains unfazed. He scrambles away from Neville's pass rush and finds Darrell Hills on a deep comeback, then Darrell again on a slant, then Fat near the sideline. He hands off to Leonte for Karr's second touchdown. He scrambles to his right before passing to Aaron Anderson for the team's third score. Karr misses the extra point, and just before the second quarter ends, it's penalized once again for a personal foul.

It's 21–20 at halftime, and this game is a chaotic, thrilling mess. But the team from New Orleans is coming together, shaking off adversity, charging back. One thing it's not doing is accepting defeat, as it did against John Curtis. It's not folding, as it did against Catholic. It's not submitting to some deep-seated fear of inadequacy, as Norm believes Karr players sometimes do against schools like this.

Instead, players are energized as the half ends. The visitors' locker room, like most everything at Neville, is luxurious and spacious: one room for the offense, another for the defense. Each player plops into his own stall.

"Take a deep breath," Omari says.

"Make the impossible fucking possible!" Thompson says.

In a hallway connecting the two rooms, Howard is calmly sharing his analysis. In this cocktail of steam and noise and stink and worry, Karr's athletic director and defensive coordinator is speaking barely above a whisper. As usual, he's the program's designated pragmatist.

"We're fucking faster than them. We're stronger than them. We're *better* than them," Howard says. Then he shrugs. "Just shut they fucking ass down and we on to the dome."

Easier said than done, especially against an offense as explosive as Neville's. But one defensive player is living proof that anything is possible.

Joe pushes through the door separating Karr's two locker rooms. He sees his offensive teammates leaning forward with their faces showing a mix of exhaustion and concern. Thompson and offensive line coach Ronald Davis are screaming, and Alan Boyd's face is still red following his ear-splitting remarks to receivers. Leonte, who was tackled hard and hurt his leg, is muttering about his fumble. Fat makes the sign of the cross.

Joe approaches the linemen first, looking into each player's eyes.

"We got y'all, brother," he says in a matter-of-fact tone. He slaps each teammate's hand before heading toward the running backs. "We got y'all."

He makes his way around the room, addressing every teammate. He ends with the receivers: Reynaud, Darrell, Aaron, Fat.

"We got y'all," Joe keeps saying. Behind a row of lockers, Leonard and Brown are studying footage from the first half on an iPad. When Joe approaches, Leonard looks up and the old friends make eye contact. They touch hands, the linebacker repeats his promise to Karr's quarterback, and in a moment it'll be time to jog back outside and get back to work.

ANDREW BRISTER may not have been intimidated, as his father insisted, but he was overpowered. Karr's defense had spent a week studying and preparing for him. But at some moment in the first half the kids from New Orleans started to believe: not just that Brister couldn't beat them—but that no one could.

Self-worth is both the most difficult and most essential thing Brown and his assistants try to instill in this yearly assemblage of damaged souls. It comes slowly under normal circumstances. This group, perhaps tougher to unify than usual, was the challenge of Brown's life: a thoroughbred like Leonard had to be tamed; a church mouse like Joe had to learn to trust.

Shortly after the second half began, Joe beat the tight end and forced Brister to hurry and overthrow his pass to an open receiver. A few plays after that, T. Howard called a risky play of his own: "Base chin cover-zero." It's a blitz that sends all three linebackers after the quarterback and leaves defensive backs alone to prevent a big play. Joe's responsibility is to come around the left edge and attack. When Brister snapped the ball, Joe ran past a blocker and got Brister in his sights. He chases him, arrives, and sacks Brister near Neville's end zone. Then, like a cougar, he drops to all fours and crawled across that expensive turf. The college recruiters had no choice but to notice now, and neither did at least one member of the Neville radio team.

"It rubbed me the wrong way," Shaw would say later. "And, quite frankly, I was not completely surprised."

Leonard, though, surprised everyone but himself. At one point he sidestepped a rusher, ran to his left on a run-pass option, and delivered a perfect throw near the sideline to Aaron. He evaluated Neville's defense near the goal line, noticed a possible tell, and sent Fat in pre-snap "jet" motion to confirm it. Then, with the ball in his hands, Leonard ran through a hole he knew would be there, right into the end zone.

He later broke to his left and found Fat open near the sideline for another score, pirouetted through Neville's defense to find Aaron up the field, stepped through the secondary for Leonard's second rushing touchdown run and a 40–21 lead.

By then Leonard II, who had rented a van and driven through the night to Monroe, had sneaked onto the field wearing a FOOTBALL DAD T-shirt. He broadcast the game's final minutes on Facebook Live and started celebrating that he, not Bubby Brister, was the winning quarterback's daddy. Eventually he found his son on the sideline and wrapped him in a hug. Maybe it takes privilege to take down privilege, but tonight at least, Leonard never blinked when he looked advantage in the eye.

"We *can* get on the same level as them," Norm, listening from Orlando, would recall thinking. "'You're not dumb.' I think our kids need to hear that."

Regardless of the how and why, Karr's defense allowed zero points in the second half. It had done what Howard hoped and had in fact challenged players to do at halftime: beating Neville's size advantage on offense with speed. Jamie intercepted Brister late in the second half, Destin Refuge broke up another pass, Dylan Smith and Tory Morgan kept pushing into the backfield and causing problems. Joe was the first teammate to celebrate with each of them.

Indeed Joe's defense had handled its business, easing whatever burden Leonard might've felt over the game's final minutes. It didn't look as though he felt any, though, considering he'd end up passing for 304 yards and accounting for five total touchdowns.

If this wasn't perfect, it'll do until he is.

Leonard's last play, considering Brown's emphasis on it, was a quarterback kneel to secure Karr's fifth consecutive trip to the state championship game. Receivers and blockers surrounded their quarterback, and together they danced and hopped and shouted as they returned to the sideline.

"Back to the dome!" Nick kept yelling.

"Fuuuuuuck, my leg," Leonte kept moaning.

"My job's not done," said Joe, who kept not smiling.

Leonard, for his part, had no intention of stifling his emotions or immediately looking ahead. He ran toward Brown, after what might've been the finest strategic performance of his coaching career, and hugged him. Then Leonard made his too-serious coach smile by rubbing that big, purple-clad belly. And after a few minutes of celebration on Neville's home field, the Black team from the forgotten corner of a broken city wasn't so silent when it climbed back aboard the two idling buses to begin the long ride home.

CHAPTER 13

GOOD LUCK

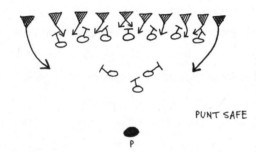

PUNT SAFE

Brown believes there's always a cost to victory, which explains his insistence that no one should allow their emotions to get too high or too low. To him, the party is never worth the hangover. In fact there's a part of Brown that seems to believe self-satisfaction actually *causes* catastrophe, or at least exacerbates it.

So when Karr won the 2018 state championship in a thriller against cross-town rival Warren Easton High, Brown had retreated silently into the locker room as players and assistants celebrated on the Superdome turf. There were no sighs of relief or promises to reward himself for ten months of hell. That night at the football office, after winning his third consecutive state championship, Brown drank his two Powerades and left the football office alone.

Just like that, the season was over. Another senior class had reached its finish line. There was no game to plan for, no practice to oversee, nothing—and nobody—to correct. Players still encounter Brown in Karr's hallways, but they're no longer required to follow his rules. The off-season is a chance for Brown to catch his breath, sure, but it's also a time he feels powerless and adrift. He goes home, turns on the TV, tries to sleep. He pretends to not worry.

Without a schedule or day-to-day football responsibilities and oversight from coaches, kids are free to wander. Brown has limited control over this community he feels called to protect, and for the next few months, his tribe will be vulnerable.

It's not yet time to think about that, but it soon will be. He'll be faced with the thoughts he has set aside, such as changes he'll make to the coaching staff, ways he'll upgrade his program, Karr's new campus, and his own future. The season's last game is a conclusion. But for Brown, it's a countdown clock that restarts immediately, with an entirely new and intense set of stressors.

On the bus ride back from Neville, Brown can feel his anxiety building. He has been avoiding making a decision about leaving Karr for St. Aug. But in the opposite row, Nick Foster is leaning against a window. He keeps clearing his throat and pressing fingers into his eyes. Nick says he's fine, but Brown knows he's not.

It has been hours since Nick ate anything, and his blood sugar has plummeted—a possible health emergency for someone with diabetes. Nick's new teaching job requires thirty days of employment before his health insurance kicks in, and he's among many Americans who wrestle with an agonizing choice: pay out of pocket for expensive medication, or deal with other financial responsibilities and just hope for the best?

Brown, always the protector, knows Nick's salary would increase if they go to St. Aug. His benefits would improve. It's something for him to consider. Just not yet.

For now, Brown tells Nick he'll pay for a damn vial of insulin. But it's late, and pharmacies are closed. So Brown comes up with a clever, and very Louisiana, solution. He tells the bus driver to floor it to the nearest Popeye's. When the vehicle pulls in, Brown dispatches Marv to run inside, ferry back a few handheld pies, and bring poor Nick back to life.

At least at this moment, there's nothing in the world more important.

HE FILLED EVERY WAKING HOUR of championship week with something, a reliable way to occupy his mind. Brown personally handled ticket requests from players' parents. He said yes to every interview request from the news media.

Karr would face a rematch against Easton, which upset top-seeded Lakeshore in a semifinal thriller. Brown knew this opponent better than any other. The teams had met three months earlier during the regular season, a 38–12 Karr victory, and these games had the feel of a reunion. In September's meeting at New Orleans's City Park, fans of both teams huddled under tailgating tents to load plates with Karr principal Chauncey Nash's pulled pork and assistant principal Wilfred Wright's fried catfish. Easton's head coach and both coordinators were Karr men, and though they respected and had great affection for Brown, they also saw validation in whooping the big man's ass.

"It's like, man, just to *show* him," said Munchie Legaux, Brown's old quarterback from a dozen years earlier. Now he runs a similar version of the spread as Easton's offensive coordinator. "I can't even explain how bad I want to beat him."

Regardless, there wouldn't be many surprises when the teams squared off Saturday afternoon. But that didn't stop Brown from combing through defensive footage from Easton's previous fourteen games.

"The iPad gonna tell it all," Brown kept saying, though in truth it was just something to do.

If anything, Easton had made it this far because of the remarkable growth of its offense. Two weeks before the season, starting quarterback Stephen Banford Jr. abruptly, and surprisingly, told coaches he'd be transferring to Belle Chasse High on the West Bank. That left Easton, two years removed from Lance LeGendre's star turn on a Netflix docuseries, without a quarterback. So head coach Jerry Phillips moved free safety Dayshawn Holmes to a position he hadn't played since park ball, and Munchie redrew his pass-heavy playbook to highlight Holmes's ability as a rusher.

Easton started 3–3, including that four-touchdown loss to Karr, but afterward something clicked. The team scored an average of fifty points in its last seven games before the championship.

But Brown had no interest in, and little understanding of, how to stop Munchie's offense. That was T. Howard's job. Defense has always been boring to Brown, other than how easy it is to weaken and ultimately defeat it. In Brown's mind, he has already mastered Easton coordinator Noel Ellis Sr.'s "gap integrity" defense. After all, Ellis had been Karr's defensive line coach until recently, so Brown and Leonard went against some version of this attack every day. Brown knew Ellis likes to plug rushing lanes and disrupt the quarterback's timing, just as Ellis knew Brown's offense is built on pre-snap signals, confusion, and the athleticism of slot receivers.

"It ain't no secret, man," Ellis would say. "Brice know what I'm doing; I know what he's doing. We're not gonna trick 'em."

Where Neville's defense was centered on the versatility and unpredictability of its secondary, Easton relied on pressure at the line of scrimmage. Ellis knew disruption would be critical to stopping Leonard, though that's not the offensive player Easton's game plan would focus on. Not Fat or Leonte, either. Instead, Ellis spent all week harping on the emotional vulnerability of Aaron Anderson, Karr's skilled but inexperienced wide receiver. Aaron is only a tenth grader, but he is supernaturally talented and is the team's best multitool. Though Aaron is most lethal as a fast and disciplined route runner, he also lines up sometimes as a rusher in the "jet" formation. He is also Karr's primary kick returner and its punter.

Ellis, though, wanted Easton's cornerbacks to engage Aaron immediately after the snap. After *every* snap. In part because of his youth, but more because of a sensitive demeanor, Aaron doesn't yet possess the thick skin most of his coaches demand. If he makes a mistake, Aaron often sulks and makes more mistakes. He'll draw penalties, drop passes, even throw the occasional punch at an opponent. Ellis knew this from his days at Karr, and he told Easton's defenders to get in his face, be physical, make him almost afraid to touch the ball. If Easton couldn't weaken Karr by psychologically taking Aaron out of play, Ellis doubted his team had much chance.

Brown wouldn't learn of Ellis's specific plan until Saturday. Besides, he figured that Leonard's preparation and ability were again the key to victory. Easton typically played only three coverages, none of them particularly complex. Its blitz tells were easily recognizable, and all Leonard had to do was locate the "rover" before the snap, translate what Easton was signaling, and keep his cool. "POISE AND COMPOSURE," Brown wrote on his game plan as Leonard's top priority.

A week after Brown pored over Neville footage and spent days second-guessing his interpretations, prep for Easton was barely a challenge at all. And that, in some ways, was a letdown. Practices had been mostly smooth, and where's the adventure in that?

Brown was so desperate for a puzzle, for something to fix, that he picked on Leonard as though it were the season's first week. During a midweek practice at Tulane University, Leonard read Karr's defense and identified a likely blitz. He "free-released" Leonte, anyway, assigning him to run a receiving route instead of remaining in the backfield to act as an emergency blocker. This had been a mistake. A minor one, but a mistake nonetheless.

"You still don't know what the fuck you doing!" Brown boomed from the sideline. Leonard turned and shrugged at what seemed like an overreaction.

Brown huffed at Leonte as he performed exaggerated knee lifts between plays, rolled his eyes at Joe as he called out warm-up cadences for the last time, grumped at Omari Robertson for going too easy on receivers during practice.

"It's been a pleasure," Omari told his position group a moment after Brown sounded his little air horn.

"You don't even know how to line up!" Brown interjected.

Brown was just moody and impatient, and by now most everyone recognized that as a by-product of his nerves. The days passed, and the coach kept looking for ways to busy his mind, before the season ended and the future came flooding in.

He played so much *Toy Blast* that he reached level 3,273. He tried to sleep, and when that failed, he stayed up late and rewatched *Colombiana*. He scribbled twenty possible successors to "Good luck," his ubiquitous catchall and the Aaron Anderson of phrases. "Good for you" and the slightly less condescending "God bless you" emerged as early favorites.

When none of it worked and his mind kept churning, Brown decided to call in a reliable old friend. He went to his closet and removed the hoodie from Tonka's senior year. The purple fabric was faded and worn. When Brown put it on, his elbows pushed though gaping holes in the sleeves, though after a decade it was more ThunderShirt than high fashion. It would follow him throughout the week, during a walk-through at Behrman Stadium and the practice at Tulane and a team lunch at Boomtown Casino, where Karr's principal tried to butter Brown up—and perhaps get him to turn down St. Aug—by promising a steak dinner. Brown ignored him, and day after day he nestled in and let the hoodie wrap him in a warm hug of security.

BY GAME DAY, Brown had made himself a promise: if Karr beat Easton, he was entitled to a reward. Though not with a new car, as some assistants were proposing, or a bountiful meal. Instead, he would turn off his television, silence his phone, and sleep in the next day.

He had spent ten fitful months falling into bed with his phone next to him, in case a player or coach needed something. He was usually up by 6:00, at the school by 6:30, in a meeting with his quarterbacks by 7:15. Even today, when he wasn't due at the school until around 11:00, Brown had set an alarm for 6:45 so he could call several players and remind them to be at an ACT prep session. He'd estimate that, during the season, he averages about four hours' sleep.

Brown picked up Tiga, and Brown bought both of them a Popeye's three-piece before heading to the school. Leonard and Joe are the first players to arrive, and each pokes his head into the assistant coaches' office to say hello to Brown.

He ignores them, too, leaning back in his chair and imagining Easton's defensive tactics and his answers. Like an actor reciting his lines one final time before the call to the stage, Brown is staring blankly at the television and playing out the game in his mind.

Easton's free safety drops deep, tipping off Cover 2 zone? *A quick out to Aaron.* The rover steps forward to confirm Cover 4 match? *Shift to "Hammer Sledge" and dump the ball to Leonte.* Both safeties step forward, indicating an all-out blitz? *Call "Jet-Stack 83–73," sending Fat on a deep post.*

In Brown's mind, he can see it: the blitz, Leonard's imaginary throw, the ball landing right in Fat's breadbasket.

Boom. Touchdown.

When Brown emerges from his trance, the weight room is full of players and assistant coaches. He scans the faces and makes fun of Omari, dressed in a black sweater showing the collar of his dress shirt, white hat, and sneakers. Just a few minutes ago, the football office was quiet as a library. Now it's loud, raucous, teeming with energy and anticipation.

"Let's get it, let's get it, let's get it!" players chant as they push into a tight cluster and clap.

Joe sits on his captain's bench with his headphones on. Fat leans back and scrolls through his social media feeds. Leonard keeps taking big gulps from a gallon jug of water. Leonte is stalking through the weight room, barking orders at teammates. Wide receivers coach Alan Boyd, who's just as much of a hothead as Karr's senior running back, steps in his path.

"It's fucking real now," Boyd says, bumping his chest into Leonte's. "Don't be scared of being successful."

"Fuck being scared," Leonte says.

Brown checks the time on his phone and, in that sound-piercing monotone, announces it's time to go. Players grab their helmets and funnel into a hallway, through the school's decrepit auxiliary locker room, through a doorway and into the early afternoon air. The buses are here.

Coaches shepherd them toward the parking lot, and Brown is the last to leave. He locks doors and turns off lights before heading off.

"The final curtain call," he says. Brown pats his pockets and realizes that, shit, he has again misplaced his whistle.

He returns to search his desk, the pockets of his spare pants, his neck to make sure he's not wearing it.

"Coach, you need something?" a school employee asks.

"No," Brown says with a laugh. It's too late now.

"A prayer?"

"Could always use a prayer."

Brown walks outside to search his truck, and Marv suggests borrowing an assistant's whistle. Brown frowns at him. He has no intention of trusting Omari or Mike Thompson with something so important.

"Can't leave nothing to chance," Brown says. A moment later, he discovers the whistle under a stack of papers. Finally it's time to leave, and the buses pass through the gates and start toward the Superdome.

Brown climbs into the passenger seat of his Silverado, Officer Pat turns the key, and Marv starts chattering about the lovely day he once spent with a prostitute in Vietnam. Brown snickers as he thumbs letters into a YouTube search box and hits play, which fills the pickup's cabin with the familiar sound of drums, a guitar, and an organ.

"Let her sing, man!" Marv calls out, and as Pat crosses the grass and turns onto Somerset Drive, that's precisely what the silver-haired woman does.

Been working for Jesus a long time
I'm not tired yet.
Been running for Jesus a long time
I'm not tired yet.

Mosie Burks's towering voice fills the air as Officer Pat accelerates in front of the lead vehicle in Karr's police escort. Brown bobs his head along with the claps of the Mississippi Mass Choir, looking through the window as the scenery passes. To the right is Karr's new campus, still under construction, and a few blocks up General De Gaulle Drive are the turnoffs for Behrman Stadium, Tiga's house, and Joe's apartment. To the left is the gas station Tonka visited three and a half years ago.

Noooo! I'm not tired yet!
No!
Noooo! I'm not tired yet!
No, no, no!

Brown chews his fingernails as the truck approaches the Crescent City Connection, the bridge that links the real New Orleans to the one everyone knows. Ahead, past a curve, is the downtown skyline: the three spires of St. Louis Cathedral, the rooftops of the French Quarter, the white curve of the Superdome roof.

Invisible to the naked eye are the young lives unfolding here, the little Tonkas and Ronnies and Joes, and some will come to know purpose and many others will not. Some mamas will cheer, others will mourn. Rhonda George, who's done both, is making her way to the same building as Brown's Silverado, and somewhere out there is Rayell Johnson and the man or men they both seek.

Running by day
(Running for Jesus)
And by night
(Running for Jesus)
Keep on running!

Officer Pat gases it to the bridge, and Brown reflects on the progress of the last few months. Joe, the wild child, is now the ultimate Karr man. Leonte, the reactionary, is now a mentor who pulls youngsters away for quiet chats—and who, by keeping calm when the young woman ran onto the field to confront Trent Washington weeks earlier, might've saved the team from catastrophe. Fat, so insecure just five months ago, has grown into Brown's favorite source of comedy.

Is this the coach's magnum opus? Or just something Brown and his staff do every year?

It's difficult to know, and that'll remain true long past today. For now, the truck heads west and the Mississippi is flowing nearly two hundred feet below. Brown stares through the glass, saying nothing as the music plays and these hundred or so denizens of a twisted little universe cross the river together one last time.

WHEN THEY ALL ARRIVE and start to unload, Brown delivers the season's final surprise. In his week of mental toiling, he'd thought about the 2013 state championship game. All-American Devante "Speedy" Noil highlighted Karr's star-studded, and largely college-bound roster.

But following a disastrous fourth quarter, that loaded Karr team—which had outscored opponents 163–13 in four previous playoff games—lost to East Jefferson, 38–28. Speedy fumbled, and quarterback Kerry Taylor threw two interceptions. It was so bad that Brown could explain the loss only one way: it had been bad luck. Maybe even a curse.

Either way, the deep purple jerseys and yellow pants would collect dust in Karr's football storage room. That is, until a few days ago, when Brown told Tiga to prepare those dank uniforms for Saturday. He'd say it was the only way to test his theory, and the hardiness of Karr's players. A more likely explanation is that Brown was just bored and wanted to liven things up.

Regardless, Joe does as instructed, pulling on his purple number 7 jersey in Locker Room 2. Leonard sits in his stall and dresses in silence. Jamie, who earlier today announced on Twitter that he was committing to play for the University of Louisville, scrolls his feed to gauge the reaction. Underclassmen ask if they can crawl on the turf during the season's final performance of "The Rock." Leonard looks up.

"Captains only," he says, pointing out the underclassmen can "run like monsters."

"Fuck that," an assistant coach says. "Everybody crawls."

Nick and Mike each step into a corridor to make a pregame phone call. Nick's father, ill for about a year, has recently taken a turn for the worse. Everyone in the family knows the end is approaching. Nick almost didn't coach today, but when choosing between your family and your calling, there's no right answer. He calls his brother to ask how their dad is doing.

Mike heads around a corner and initiates a FaceTime call. It's not a relative he's calling, though Mike feels a similar bond. The call connects, and a moment later a familiar face appears on the display.

"Can I come back?" Trent Washington asks his former position coach.

Now two months after the postgame incident at Behrman, Mike has gone back on his pledge to move on from Trent. *He's really a good kid,* he'd said a few days afterward, and this notion never left him. Mike hadn't stopped by Trent's house, but he does call sometimes to check in. He encourages him to complete his classwork and to pray. Trent has been spending most of his time at home, trying to stay out of trouble in the weeks after he was charged with attempted murder. Recently a court appearance was rescheduled, and Trent's mother, Gwen, would say she'd spent nearly $10,000 on legal fees. She was planning to put her house up for sale and had considered quitting her job and moving to Dallas with Trent.

Mike cared for the kid and knew he still loved football. Days like this were hardest. Trent wanted to be at the Superdome with his teammates. But when he asked if he could eventually return to the team, Mike couldn't say yes. He also didn't say no.

"Do you miss football?" Mike says during their FaceTime call. The sixteen-year-old says he does, though his words and actions haven't always been in alignment. "How *much* do you miss it?"

The coaches end their calls, and the time is coming to leave the locker room and walk onto the turf. This is the moment Brown and his assistants sell: not just all season but for years—the payoff for all these sacrifices, the reward for all that work. Though players here have gotten used to this feeling, there's always someone walking through the tunnel for the first time. And the last.

Nick is waiting as players depart the locker room and, like usual, form two lines: offense and defense. He slaps each player's hands and relays messages that seem personalized.

"Light the fuckin' scoreboard up," he tells Fat.

"It's about pride," he says to Leonard.

"Make memories," he tells Leonte.

Now it's the defense's turn. Joe is in the front of the line, and beyond a dark curtain, Ms. Diane is in the stands and Keyoke is in the stadium . . . somewhere. The first mellow beats and synth chords of "In the Air Tonight" can be heard blaring through the Superdome's thundering speakers. Jamie puts his hand on Joe's helmet as the friends prepare for one last ride. Joe nods and bites down on his mouthpiece, saying nothing as he approaches Nick.

"Make 'em know your fuckin' name," he tells Joe, slapping his hands.

It's STILL EARLY in the game, but Leonard seems rattled. He doesn't seem to trust his own eyes, or himself. Brown yells at him for missing his first three passes and never seeing a receiver who's wide open. Leonard keeps checking the sideline for direction. He runs up the middle, attempts a lateral to Aaron, and fumbles.

"It looks like we haven't practiced one goddamn day!" Brown yells.

Just as Leonard's composure inspired his teammates at Neville, his nerves seem contagious against Easton. Karr whiffs on a kickoff to allow a touchdown, and Joe gets fooled on the two-point conversion. Phillips, the Eagles' head coach, also calls plays on special teams. Munchie has a formation known as the "swinging gate," in which the field-goal team initially lines up for an extra point. Then, six players split toward the sideline and leave the remaining five near the ball.

Something that seems directly lifted from the Brice Brown handbook, it's designed to confound a defense and cause panic. That's precisely what happens. De'juan Kennedy, a senior safety for Easton, tosses away a kicking tee before gesturing toward the center. Kennedy takes the snap, Joe has no idea which way the ball is going, or who even has it. He barely gets a hand on Kennedy as he runs into the end zone.

"Fucking *soft!*" Brown screams.

No one, though, looks as out of sorts as Aaron. Easton's defenders have pressured him, as Ellis's game plan directed. Aaron loses control of the ball during a kickoff return, and Easton recovers his fumble. He lets an easy pass slide through his hands, and in the second quarter, Aaron shows his remarkable athleticism with a long punt return— before fumbling again near the sideline.

Teammates and assistant coaches confront the shell-shocked youngster, who tries to look away. He says nothing when Dennis Lore, a former longtime Karr assistant, grabs his facemask. Aaron is silent when Nick stalks over and looks him in the eye.

"Sit on the fucking bench if you can't hold on to the ball!" he says.

Omari tries a different tack. He approaches Aaron, who's having the worst game of his young career, and puts his arm around him. Omari leads him away from his teammates, an attempt at calming the young man down.

Leonard, meanwhile, seems to be settling in. He reads Easton's 4–2–5 coverage, looks toward the sideline, and changes the play. Instead of passing, Leonard hands off to Leonte, who runs fifty yards before dramatically extending the ball across the goal line for a touchdown. Fat sprints over and chest bumps Leonte, and a moment later, junior defensive back Destin Refuge returns an interception for a touchdown. Though Karr is in control at halftime, leading 29–14, Brown nonetheless suspects something isn't right.

Brown, somewhere between a social scientist and self-torturing anarchist, wants to see if he's correct. He calls "Twist," a variation of the high-low pass Brown called against Catholic. That time it led to Leonard ignoring his progressions, throwing an interception, and getting himself benched. It was such a painful sequence that Brown went nine games without calling the play.

This time, it has a chance to put Easton away. Nick relays the signal to Leonard, who lines up on fourth down and evaluates the defense. He takes the snap and eyes the nickel corner, whose actions immediately after the snap will reveal the open receiver: either Aaron running an over route or Darrell Hills on a deep comeback. Fat will also be running an over route, but he's a decoy who's supposed to draw the safety away from Aaron. Leonard snaps the ball and reads the defense. Darrell is alone near the sideline, but Leonard freezes, he scrambles, and Easton defensive lineman Sidney Humble knocks the ball out of Leonard's hand to force a fumble.

Though the half ends and the mistake is ultimately harmless, it reinforces to Brown that there's some bad juju unfolding here. Maybe assigning the supposedly cursed purple uniforms was a step too far. Regardless, the team heads to the locker room, where Brown erupts.

"This shit is ridiculous, man," he says. "Where my iPad?"

He suggests this team, like the one that lost to East Jefferson in 2013, lacks a killer instinct. He says this is the worst game of Leonard's life. He wonders aloud about replacing Leonard with backup quarterback A.J. Samuel. He's just talking, working out the kinks in his mind.

Leonard knows this. As he did at Catholic, he says nothing and keeps his eyes fixed on the iPad screen. He doesn't react to Brown's ravings. But Aaron is two years younger, and he sheepishly glances at Brown from across the locker room. Omari is still talking to him, and Brown and Nick are privately debating removing Aaron from the game.

Easton starts the second half by covering sixty-two yards in two plays, including running back Ashaad Clayton knifing through Karr's defense for a thirty-yard touchdown. Leonard, who finds a newly confident Aaron for a deep pass, responds by leading a scoring drive of his own. Karr is leading, 35–22.

Another touchdown by Clayton, who shows why he'll be playing for the University of Colorado and is the sixth-ranked senior in Louisiana. With Karr cradling a 35–28 lead in the fourth quarter, Aaron picks up Easton's kickoff, turns upfield with a move that signals his dazzling potential, avoids a defender, and . . .

The ball comes out. Aaron's fourth fumble, and Easton falls on it. Teammates can't believe it. Leonard is pacing, and Leonte is shouting. Aaron is sitting on the bench alone. This time, even Omari keeps his distance. Brown is expressionless, walking with his hands clasped behind his back.

When a talented youngster is struggling and overwhelmed, even NFL coaches and Fortune 500 managers struggle with the best way forward. Though the solution may seem obvious, benching someone as special as Aaron is never simple. Sure, it may prevent another turnover and secure a victory today. But he's in tenth grade, a critical piece of Karr's future, a young man who—not unlike Trent Washington—has physical gifts, confidence issues, and emotional boundaries that remain undeveloped.

This is a football game, yes. But Aaron is a kid. Whatever happens next could stick with him forever.

Brown opts to send Aaron back in. It's a massive risk, and even the assistant coaches are skeptical. Brown, though, cares about Aaron and wants to show he believes in him. But he's also someone who thinks Karr's uniforms may be cursed. One time Brown suggested that, if a doctor told him one more Coke would kill him, he'd drink it just to see if the doctor was right.

He's just a psychological adventurer, that's all. And for reasons large and small, Brown just wants to see what happens.

It's the fourth quarter, and Leonard sees Easton showing Cover 4 match. So many options. He looks excited, almost jittery, and steals a glance toward the sideline. Brown points two index fingers at Leonard: stick with the called play.

The rover backpedals, confirming Leonard's read. The defense is designed to form a wall that prevents a deep pass while also shutting down underneath routes. But about twenty yards downfield, there's a small area that's vulnerable near the sideline. Leonard calls for the snap, and Aaron sprints forward from the slot position. The cornerback can't keep up, and the safety has drifted to his right in case Aaron is running a vertical route. But Aaron, running a corner post, makes a diagonal cut toward the sideline. There's no defender within ten yards. Leonard sees this sequence developing and has already released the ball, and a moment later it's in Aaron's hands. He wraps both arms around the ball and steps out of bounds for a twenty-six-yard gain.

Less than eight minutes to play, and one more Karr touchdown could secure victory. Brown gears down his strategy, wanting to run time off the clock. Leonte runs up the middle, then Leonard completes a short pass to Fat.

It's first and goal. Seven yards to ball game. Leonte again runs, this time for three yards. And again for one. Leonard runs forward on a quarterback draw, reaching the one-yard line. Brown signals for a draw play to Leonte on fourth down, and he takes the handoff, leaps forward and flips, ass over teakettle, onto the field.

But short of the goal line. It's a turnover on downs; Easton's ball. Less than four minutes to play. Munchie, channeling some things he learned long ago, confuses T. Howard and Karr's defense by sending out a formation with two tight ends. Brown, as always preferring speed over power, has only used a tight end in one game as a head coach.

"I'm not gonna say I have *all* his secrets," Munchie would say. But he designed this play with Karr, and Brown, in mind. Munchie's power plays bruise Karr's defense, allowing Easton to reach midfield in less than two minutes.

He notices Karr in Cover 3 and calls a skinny post. Holmes completes it for a first down, into Karr territory. A penalty for grabbing Holmes's facemask moves the ball inside the twenty. There's less than ninety seconds to play.

Brown is pacing. Howard is yelling instructions into his headset. Leonte has turned toward the crowd, unable to watch. He doesn't see Holmes running to his right, past Joe, through Karr defenders, into the end zone for a seven-yard touchdown. Karr leads, 35–34, with one minute, nine seconds left.

Phillips, though, isn't playing for overtime. He signals his intentions for another two-point conversion. Easton is going for the win. Munchie calls in his play, a similar version of the "swinging gate" concept from earlier. Six players again split out wide, and Kennedy tosses the tee. Karr defenders scramble to get set and identify their assignments. Jamie and Joe line up between the two clusters, and Joe crouches and leans forward as Kennedy runs toward Sedrick Van Pran, Easton's six-foot-four, 285-pound center. Van Pran, the nation's top recruit at his position, snaps the ball—only instead of tossing it between his legs, he flips it to his left, where receiver Jewell Holmes is waiting behind five blockers.

Joe, a goalkeeper attempting to defend a penalty kick, must commit to one direction. And he chooses the wrong one. He starts forward, toward Kennedy, who was a decoy. Joe sees the ball floating and changes directions.

Jewell Holmes plows into defensive end Josh Randall and stiff-arms him. This collision lasts maybe a half second, but it's enough time for Joe to outrun five Karr defenders and reach Holmes. Randall is still holding on, trying to keep Holmes short of the goal line. But he's losing his grip. Joe arrives just in time, from the perfect angle, pushing Holmes away from the goal line and to his left.

Having lost his balance from Joe's hit, Holmes tries to maintain his footing but cannot. He falls on his side at the two-yard line, short of the goal line. This entire sequence, from snap to tackle, takes 4.3 seconds. Josh hops off the field in celebration, and Jamie consoles Van Pran, who's pounding the turf in frustration. Joe jogs to the sideline as if his tackle had been no more important than a takedown during some practice in August.

Always mirroring not just Brown's instructions but his behavior, Joe avoids getting too high or too low. He watches the replay on the Superdome's video board, hands on his hips, refusing to smile.

"I don't show emotion," he says while his teammates celebrate. At least this time, Joe's caution is justified.

He watches as Easton recovers its onside kick, as Karr's Jacob Livas intercepts a deep pass from Dayshawn Holmes, as Jacob—who's swarmed by jubilant teammates—draws a flag for unsportsmanlike conduct. Instead of Karr taking possession on its four-yard line, space for Leonard to take a knee, it'll now start two yards from its own goal line. Virtually any mistake would be a disaster, and a safety will give Easton a 36–35 lead. Karr, in other words, is sixty-one seconds from glory; six feet from despair.

Joe scolds Jacob, who in a single sequence has both preserved and endangered his team's championship hopes. Leonard walks slowly as he takes his place in the backfield. Ellis knows Brown won't be calling anything aggressive; this drive is about nothing more than killing the clock and avoiding a turnover. What he doesn't know is that Karr hasn't practiced a quarterback sneak, or had the quarterback line up under center, all year. In this case, Brown figured practicing one play under center would just confuse players.

Then again, it'd sure come in handy about now.

On first down, Leonard runs a draw up the middle, gains one yard, uses five seconds. Easton takes a time-out. Leonard runs another draw on second down, collides with his own blocker, and is driven back to the two. Another time-out, Easton's last. Now it's third down. The last play Brown will ever call for Leonard is "Raven right green": a basic draw in which he is to run between the left guard and left tackle. There's no pre-snap motion, no audible, no trickery. Just a rush up the gut.

The result is just as unremarkable, a gain of just five yards. But Easton has no more time-outs, and the seconds tick away. Leonard walks off the field, and he and Brown make eye contact. After Karr takes a time-out, there are nine seconds left. It's fourth down. Karr has to punt, and it need not be perfect. The punter just has to kick the ball away and avoid a safety, a block, or a fumble. Just don't make a mistake. Easy enough.

The punter, of course, is Aaron Anderson.

"Go get it," Phillips would recall saying into his headset. He instructs his punt-block unit to be aggressive. Easton's championship hopes depend on it.

Aaron jogs deep into his own end zone, a yard from a white stripe. If he steps out of bounds, if the snap flies over his head or bounces to him, if a rusher tackles Aaron or deflects the punt, if he mishandles the ball—Easton wins. Three Karr up-backs wait as emergency blockers. Karr calls it "Punt safe," though nobody feels especially safe this close to the end zone. Here comes the snap.

One Mississippi.

The ball wobbles toward Aaron, drifting as if in slow motion. He catches it, though it's sideways in his hands. He adjusts it.

Two Mississippi.

He takes a step forward, and Easton cornerback Altoine Taylor has broken free. Dylan Smith, a Karr captain who's normally a linebacker, is one of the up-backs. He drifts to his right to get in Taylor's path. But nobody blocks Ramond Stevens, who's sprinting toward Aaron's left side.

Three Mississippi.

Taylor and Stevens are in the end zone. Aaron takes a second step forward, and the rushers are within a few feet. He releases the ball, which floats slowly toward the ground as Aaron's right leg swings up. His foot makes contact an instant before Taylor arrives—sending the ball up, out of the end zone, toward midfield.

Four Mississippi . . . five Mississippi . . .

Jewell Holmes, who is under strict orders to secure a fair catch to preserve whatever time remains, panics. He allows the ball to bounce off the turf before trying to field it. It tumbles in and out of his hands, trickling behind him. It's a live ball.

Six Mississippi, seven Mississippi, eight Mississippi . . .

Easton's De'Kunta Mason Jr. scoops up the loose ball near midfield, and Joe dives toward him but misses. Dany'e doesn't, though, grabbing Mason's jersey and holding on, twisting, as Mason's knee touches the ground.

Nine Mississippi. Joe looks at the scoreboard, which reads 00:00. It's over. Karr players run toward the sideline, and Joe drops to one knee before crumbling to the turf. His teammates are celebrating, swarming, hollering—but the end of Joe's season resembles its beginning. The young man is out there alone. His eyes flood, and he turns onto his back.

He hates being by himself, and after so many months and years together, his teammates know this. Five of them surround Joe Thomas, the kid from nowhere, and tell him—the captain, the protector—he's a state fucking champion. He did it. They did it. The teammates pull Joe to his feet and do not leave his side.

Fat is skipping around the field, pointing at the sky. He recognizes Aaron walking without his helmet near midfield. He approaches the young receiver and they each drop to a knee. Fat speaks into the kid's ear, and they cry together before Fat wraps Aaron in a hug. Leonte is hollering and cursing and bumping into anyone and everyone. Leonard is running in circles with his arms extended, Karr's Superman having done just enough to save the day.

"MVP! MVP!" Leonard's teammates are chanting.

A few yards away, Norm Randall is standing with Baylon and Liam, his two sons. Their daddy returned from Orlando a few days prior and is posing with his boys today. "Hold your four fingers out," he tells them over the sound of the marching band's drums and horns. They extend their fingers and smile as the photo snaps, and a memory is forever preserved.

Noel Ellis Sr., Easton's defensive coordinator, hugs Noel Jr., his son and Karr's first-year assistant coach. Joe finds Cassidy, his girlfriend and a Karr cheerleader, before looking for his mother in the stands. He locates only Ms. Diane, and he reaches up past a barrier and touches her fingers.

Brown, who rarely celebrates anything, daps up Munchie, then Omari, and hugs another Karr staffer. Brown conducts interviews and keeps trading congratulations, and eventually he ambles toward the tunnel. There's a strange expression on his face.

He looks happy.

Brown passes through the curtain, and a wave of emotions overwhelms his defenses and crashes into him. Relief. Joy. Pride. He can avoid them no longer, and steps into a corridor and sees a familiar face. It's his mother, and to her Brown isn't a coach or a fledgling football legend or a wily hacker. He's not a man whose life, altered by tragedy, is now devoted to providing purpose to young Black men.

He's her son. She hugs him and says he's proud of him. He issues an embarrassed smile.

Brown continues to a row of chairs outside the Superdome's media room. Phillips, the Easton coach, and five of his players are trying to explain what they experienced.

"If he makes that block . . ." Phillips is saying of the failed two-point conversion.

The Easton contingent exits, and Brown follows Leonard, Aaron, and defensive back Destin Refuge to a small table. Leonard II, always with the best seat in the house, has sneaked into the press room and is holding a cold drink. He listens to his son describing Brown as a "cool dude" and his experience "very special" and the championship "a blessing."

Podium talk. A master class in it.

When it's Brown's turn, a reporter asks him about St. Aug. After four championships in a row, what more can Brown accomplish at Karr?

He first claims he hasn't thought about it, which is only partially true. He's been saying since before the season that this is likely his final year here. Nick, who followed Brown into the press room, perks up. He's more interested than anyone in what his old friend has to say. He knows the perpetually honest Brown is no good at podium talk, and perhaps he'll tip his hand.

"You never know," Brown says. And in his case, that's mostly true. He'll begin considering his options in earnest tomorrow.

The news conference ends, the three Karr players head toward the locker room, and Brown and Nick walk together through the corridor. They squeeze past the performing Karr marching band, accept more congratulations, and eventually reach Locker Room 2. Maybe it's just muscle memory, but Brown is still coaching: issuing instructions in that hard-boiled tone.

"Make sure your jersey's in your bag," he says.

When everyone's things are packed, Mike blows a whistle and Brown stands near an empty locker near the corner. A few hours earlier, this is where he told Leonard it was the worst game of his career. It wasn't the best, but it's nonetheless one he'll remember more than others.

"Hey, look," Brown says, beginning another speech he has barely thought about. "Here's why you won the game: you played hard, you played smart, you played together."

Leonard listens from a far corner of the locker room, Fat is near the back, and Leonte is looking up from the center. Joe is kneeling in the front row, and his eyes are red from crying. He's listening to his now-former coach.

"That's all we asking you to do," Brown says. "When your back get against the wall, that your best come out you."

This is a group that's felt cornered all season. Maybe longer. Maybe forever. Brown reaches into the locker and picks up the state championship trophy. He lifts the hefty wood plaque near his head.

"This trophy right here symbolize all that," he says. "The one thing it do symbolize is finishing. It's finishing. Because if you remember that first game, when we lost to John Curtis—what they said?"

He pauses.

"'Oh, Karr done. They washed up,'" he says. "'Catholic blew us out. 'That's not the same Karr team. They need Ronnie Jackson.'"

Nobody actually said this. It's unlikely anyone even thought it, unless it was Brown himself.

"That's what they said?" he says. "So what got you here? *Finish.* Finish! Now you tell me another team that could win four in a row!"

"Nobody!" the players yell back at him, and they cheer.

Brown takes a breath. Still in celebration mode, he's already looking forward to the future. There are underclassmen in this cramped room, hoping to make their names and write their legacies. Perhaps Brown isn't finished writing his. Only J.T. Curtis, who's been coaching football in Louisiana for half a century, has won five straight state championships. It's a streak that feels untouchable. It did, anyway, before today.

"Two weeks from now," Brown says, "people gonna forget about this. Two weeks from now, you know what they're gonna be saying? 'They ain't gonna do it next year. Ain't gonna do it next year.'"

He smiles and again holds up the trophy.

"Well, I got two words for them for next year," he says.

"Fuck . . ." a few players start to say.

"Good luck," Brown says.

A DARK FOG HAS SETTLED over the city by the time Karr leaves the dome, and Brown climbs into the passenger seat of his pickup and plays his lucky song.

I gotta keep on running
No, I'm not tired yet.

Brown hums along, but in truth he's exhausted. All the game planning, problem solving, and crisis management has collided into this moment and given him a headache. He'd allowed himself to celebrate, and maybe a pounding skull is the worst of the hangover. He hopes it is.

Officer Pat accelerates through yellow lights, and Brown closes his eyes and massages his forehead. The truck cuts through the mist and returns to the West Bank. There'll be parties tonight, first at the school and then at an assistant coach's house, then another in the French Quarter. Brown won't be attending. He has a date with his bed, and right now he feels like sleeping for a month.

The truck heads through Karr's back gate, crosses the field, and stops just outside the football office. Brown steps outside and limps up a ramp. Marv is a few steps behind.

"Meatball," he announces, "we won it again, baby!"

Brown says nothing, knowing there's work left in closing out a season. He heads into the storage room, where the supposedly cursed 2013 uniforms spent six dusty years. He begins removing a cart for helmets and a rack for shoulder pads. By the time he's finished, players are clogging the weight room's entryway. Brown motions for the captains to enter first and hand their jerseys to assistant coach Dwayne Mitchell. He'll carefully stack each one over the lip of a laundry bin, and over the coming days and weeks, Tiga will begin laundering and restoring them.

Joe and Leonte and Fat walk in, doing as instructed. Slowly the number 7 and number 5 and number 2 disappear, just another purple layer in a stack of dirty clothes. Jamie and Leonard follow.

"Can I keep it?" Leonard asks Brown, flashing those puppy dog eyes. Nope, Brown tells him, and walks away. Leonard hands it over, and the number 3 vanishes, too.

In a few months these numbers will be reassigned. Young men will compete for them, make sacrifices to wear them, value them as new extensions of their changing identities. Eleven of those young men will be named to Pride Panel, and a few will be elevated to the captain's line. They'll hear stories of the craziness that came before them, of the success stories whose footsteps they'll be following, of how much harder coaches used to be on players than they are now.

"You gonna miss me?" Leonte asks Brown as the underclassmen file in. The coach smiles. Miss him? Maybe. Forget him? Impossible.

When the bins and racks are full, players take their places on the weight room floor. Mike and Noel Jr. are sliding trash bags over the speakers, and in the training room the sound of clinking glass is traveling around a wall.

This is the final benediction in the church of Karr, with Norm presiding. This is not the end, he'll say, even for the seniors. You don't stop being a Karr man when the season ends or your eligibility expires. You'll be welcome here forever, unless of course you drop out of college.

"This is not a team for ignorant motherfuckers," Norm says.

Just outside the training room, Nick is pacing. In his hands are two bottles of Korbel, and he shakes them again and again as he waits for Norm to finish. The coaches run this program on dual foundations: incentives and honesty. Among the incentives is a champagne shower, just like the ones Von Miller and Tom Brady have after their teams win the Super Bowl. And because of an airtight commitment to honesty, it can't be sparkling grape juice or soda water. It is, after all, a *champagne* shower, and the kids here know and care about the difference.

Nick keeps listening from behind a cinder-block wall, shaking and shaking, and finally one of the corks surrenders. Champagne douses the bottom of a colleague's pant leg. Nick shrugs when the coach playfully glowers at him, for even against mighty Karr, carbonation is undefeated.

Norm finishes his address, and Brown has a few last words.

"Every team got a different process," he says. "Every team got a different journey. That's why I put you in the purple and gold today: because I knew you was gonna panic. I knew you was gonna say to yourself: 'Oh, he think we're the 2013 team.' Now, I fucked your head up just now."

The kids laugh.

"When I look at y'all, I know what kind of n——s I got 'round me," Brown says. "Aaron putting the ball on the ground; 'Coach take him out!'"

Brown shakes his head.

"*Keep him in*," he says. "Because without him, we can't be here where we at. You don't turn your back on people when our back get against the wall. You know what you do? You *keep* relying on 'em. You *keep* putting 'em in a position where they don't doubt they self."

Brown takes a breath as the young eyes remain on him.

"I know I'm one of your toughest critics, but I'm supposed to be," he says. "At the end of the day, it's about making you better."

Brown's to-do list for the 2019 season is nearly complete.

"Now I'm gonna tell you the stuff that you probably don't wanna hear: Monday, you've gotta come back in this bitch hungry," the coach says. "You've got finals. You've got to finish. You've got to still *finish*! Your best effort is still gonna be asked of you. You come into this motherfucker at 8:45, nine o'clock? I'm gonna be right there waiting on you—times *ten*! You know why? Because everybody else doing this to you."

He pats an assistant coach on the back.

"'Good job. Man, good job. You can go by Coach Brice in the gym.' *Sheeeee*-it!" he says. The youngsters laugh at the absurdity of Brown letting them skate on anything. "You already know that's dead. That's dead like a motherfucker. But, look, you don't understand that's why you a winner. You keep coming to school on time. You keep going to class. You keep doing your job."

"Yes, sir," a few of the kids say.

"You need a *hundred* percent. All the time," Brown says. "That's why you keep winning. It ain't because of the X's and O's. It's because you keep doing what you're supposed to do."

He looks at Fat and a few of the juniors.

"Y'all on the clock: 2021—you're on the fuckin' clock," he says. "You gave us your all. I want you to keep doing that. We gonna end on a prayer."

Brown yields to Leonte, who has a job for the last time.

"Ayy, whose father?" he says, and the other voices join in.

"Our father," they say and begin the Lord's Prayer.

Players and coaches drape an arm onto whoever's next to them, and Nick shakes the sealed bottle once more. When the young voices say amen, Mike touches his phone to blare "In Control" by YoungBoy Never Broke Again through the speakers, and Nick turns the corner and releases the spray.

AND SO, FINALLY, he could rest. Brown plops into a chair in the assistant coaches' office as the champagne flows. Coaches maintain control of the bottles until they're empty, and no players drink from or even hold them. The windows rattle, players' shirts are off, and phones are raised to document this sticky, boozy memory. Dwayne, the young assistant who collected jerseys earlier, climbs onto a counter to dance.

"I love you, baby!" Fat tells Omari, and they stand there and hug it out.

Norm slips into Brown's office to look for something hidden. A moment later he emerges with a bottle of Hennessy. He twists it open and offers Brown the first red cup off a fresh sleeve. The big man waves him off.

"Gave it up," Brown says. He watches his staffers take long pulls before reaching into a tub of ice and twisting open bottles of Miller Lite and Heineken.

He'll say this is how he celebrates: by experiencing victory through the eyes of others. That and replaying the game in the iPad of his mind. He and the staffers are debating the decisive two-point conversion attempt. With a running back as good as Clayton, Brown says he would've handed it off to the power rusher and taken his chances.

"You gotta give the ball to 2," he says.

"You knew it was a fake," Omari says.

"It was over!"

This goes on for a while, and Brown periodically closes his eyes. He opens them, scans the weight room, and notes that Nick seems to have disappeared. He asks if anyone saw him leave, and the other coaches shrug. Rhonda George walks in with a poster she bought at the Superdome, and this momentarily alters the conversation. The unofficial team mother, she congratulates Brown and suggests the coaches avoid Behrman Avenue when they head home. A double shooting near Karr's home stadium has snarled traffic and illuminated the misty air with flashing blue lights. They speak of this in noticeably matter-of-fact terms, though Brown expresses exasperation at the city's relentlessness.

Rhonda offers everyone one last hug before leaving. But her warning has Brown worried. Where the hell did Nick go? He removes his phone to see a missed call from Nick's brother. He calls Nick.

"You have reached the voice mailbox of . . ." the recording says, and Brown ends the call.

He tries to move on, reviving the football discussion to distract himself from his fear. But coaches are leaving the school and heading to the next party. Brown stands to see the last of the players trickling out. He decides to head home, assuring himself his phone will ring and relieve his concerns by the time he turns off the lights and locks up. Neither happens, so he tries Nick again.

"You have reached the . . ."

The gears in his mind are turning, grinding through possibilities. He hates this feeling, one he knows well. He climbs into the driver's seat of his Silverado, and on his way to the Cut-Off, Brown's phone finally rings. It's Nick.

Shortly after Nick sprayed the kids with champagne, his brother called. Their dad died tonight. Nick, who has spent the last few months as Ethridge Foster's caretaker, is beating himself up because he hadn't been there at the end.

Brown listens and tries to ease his friend's conscience. They finish the call, and Brown can feel the deluge of more emotions: guilt, in particular, and regret. He allowed the good ones in, so here come the rest. He should've never celebrated as he did tonight. The headache wasn't the hangover. This was. He should never have allowed himself to get so high. Not in a city and community like this, where time and again, no achievement is without cost. Too often that cost is tragedy.

As self-punishment, Brown discards his plans of heading home and crawling into bed. He thought he'd given 100 percent of himself, but perhaps he has a little more to give. He turns the truck around and drives toward the hospital, where he'll sit with Nick and provide counsel until three in the morning. Brown tries to convince himself that, with his assistants out drinking and his players out in the city feeling invincible, he would've never gone to sleep anyway.

EPILOGUE

FOUR HOURS BEFORE the end of 2019, a man named Michael Hollins Sr. crumpled onto a street in the Lower Ninth Ward. Hollins worked odd jobs and had two sons. Now, two days after his forty-second birthday, he lay dying with two bullets in his head.

Hollins was the year's 120nd, and last, person to be shot dead in New Orleans. City officials would point to 2019, whose murder tally was the lowest since 1971, as evidence Mayor LaToya Cantrell's new fifty-year plan to study and reduce violent crime was showing promise. Seven of the city's eight police districts would report fewer murders. The only one where shooting deaths remained on the rise included the continually decaying New Orleans East, where Omari Robertson heard gunfire increasingly often through the walls of his family's home.

New Orleans still had the United States' fourth-highest murder rate, which was eight times the national average in 2019. But police leaders praised improved data analytics, commonsense policing, and annual training seminars for the NOPD's robbery and homicide investigators.

"We're using intelligence," police superintendent Shaun Ferguson would say in an interview. "Just a boots-on-the-ground approach."

But behind the scenes, some detectives believed the downturn was a mirage. That the supposedly new tactics were toothless. In fact, some blew off the supposedly mandatory retraining courses. They faced neither discipline nor follow-up from their superiors. Some rolled their eyes at the department's trumpeting of analytics, insisting that despite the unreliability of person-to-person witness harvesting, there's no substitute for old-fashioned policing. Some looked forward to the expiration of the city's consent decree, when cops could get back to law enforcement tactics of yesteryear. Point being, residents were just desperate not only for results, but for hope.

"I don't care where you live in New Orleans, right now, you believe you're in a city under siege," District Attorney Leon Cannizzaro said in an interview a few months before announcing he wouldn't seek a third term. "People believe they're under siege, and not a whole lot is being done about it."

If progress had been made under Cantrell's mandate, in mid-December 2019 that ground to a halt. New Orleans declared a state of emergency following a widespread and highly sophisticated ransomware attack on the city's computer network. The immediate recovery effort involved taking thirty-four hundred computers and devices (including those in police cars) offline. Residents couldn't so much as pay bills online or report a pothole, let alone expect swift developments following a loved one's murder.

The city set aside $7.5 million to recover and update its system. But along with an estimated $110 million economic shortfall as a result of the coronavirus pandemic's strain on New Orleans tourism, this led to a new spending freeze on anything unrelated to the cyberattack. When the department's homicide detectives were again allowed to access their computers, they'd often find email in-boxes emptied and hard drives erased. Witness contacts and possible leads were gone. Some investigators had to start from scratch. A few called detectives in neighboring cities just to ask them to look up a suspect's known associates.

New Orleanians, though, took no breaks from shooting each other.

Eight people were shot dead in the first nine days of 2020, and as the months passed and a national surge in gun violence intensified, bullets kept flying and phones kept ringing.

On January 2, 2020, Brown was in San Antonio, Texas, accompanying Tygee Hill and Fat to the US Army All-American Bowl's national combine. That evening, he noticed a missed call from Nick Foster.

Over the crowd noise at the Alamodome, Brown heard Nick say something about one of Karr's players. It was something he'd hoped to never hear again.

"Coach," Nick said, going on to say that one of their sophomores had been shot.

RAYELL JOHNSON CAUGHT his first murder of 2020 on New Year's Day. His phone rang shortly after sunset, and the detective slowly made his way to a notorious intersection in Central City. There was a forty-five-year-old man hunched over in his car, with bullet casings scattered in front of a daiquiri shop.

"Business booming . . . unfortunately," Johnson posted on Twitter.

Like alcohol, social media became one of his many methods of escape. He posted videos of himself climbing out of a Rolls-Royce, selfies with celebrities, photos of himself as he visited the NOPD's gym, and documentation of his picture-perfect health.

"Mr. Cool," Johnson would say. "I'll go rap and have some drinks, because I clear all my cases."

It was, as social media often promulgates, an act. Just another role. The truth was that Johnson's blood pressure was high, his doctor told him to cut back on the cigars and booze, and he increasingly felt boxed in by some of his profession's realities. His caseload remained untenable, and some of Johnson's friends gave him shit about being a Black man and a cop.

In summer 2020, not long after the murder of George Floyd set off global protests and renewed a national conversation about criminal justice reform, Johnson read social media posts by a white NOPD homicide sergeant. In a post sharing a news story of a St. Louis protester who'd been run over by a delivery truck, the sergeant wrote that the individual "got what he deserved."

"I am running them over and shooting if lethal force were my only way out," he wrote. In a separate response to a Black writer's suggestion that protests had been largely peaceful, the sergeant wrote: "Blow up her car and see if she still feels the same way."

Johnson had previously worked cases with the sergeant, but that didn't stop him from reporting the posts to their supervisors. The sergeant was suspended, decommissioned of his police duties, and later fired. Johnson says he's the person who reported the sergeant. Though he'd been granted anonymity upon submitting the complaint, he insisted during a follow-up interview that he be identified. He said he wanted the sergeant to know it was him.

"The blue code and that kind of shit, I don't really so much believe in that," Johnson said. "Because I believe in wrong or right."

He nonetheless chipped away at old cases, and in late 2019 he closed a murder from five years earlier. Producers from *The First 48* visited to film an update to an episode that'd never aired, filling Johnson with fresh enthusiasm. He signed up for acting lessons, researched how to get an agent, hired a photographer to shoot promotional headshots of Johnson wearing a green V-neck and an easy smile. When a director called to offer an in-person audition in Dallas the next day, Johnson checked the homicide up-list and had to say no. He was scheduled to catch the next murder.

"That hit me in the gut so hard," he says. Johnson wonders if that might've been his big break. "I do love homicide cases, but I do want to do something in the entertainment world more than anything. I'll never let it happen again. I will find a way."

Producers from a different series cast him in a true crime show about women who'd broken the law in the name of love. It was something to do. And it seemed to refresh him. He thought more and more about Tonka's case and the things it'd take to crack it. Early in 2020, Johnson read about Cellebrite, an Israeli mobile forensics company and a contractor for the US government. The firm was believed to have helped the FBI unlock the iPhone of one of the perpetrators in the 2015 mass shooting in San Bernardino, California. Johnson wondered if it could do the same with Tonka's phone. He thought it was worth a try.

By then a year had passed since he'd spoken with Rhonda George. She'd stopped calling and texting as she attempted to solve her son's murder.

"I'll never move on," she said. Rhonda still threw birthday parties for Tonka, even if she was the only one celebrating. She still visited him most days at the cemetery, promising justice even when she started accepting that she lived in a place where such a thing feels impossible. She found purpose and therapy in establishing relationships with Karr players, especially those who wore the 5 in the past or might wear it in the future. She called and counseled them. She delivered frequent hugs and told them about Tonka. She listened as they described their goals, hopes, and fears.

Rhonda said they had become her family, and she looked at them like sons.

THE KARR PLAYER WAS ALIVE. In a most New Orleans way, Brown knew that immediately. Nick had said the kid got *shot*. If he was dead, he'd have said the player got *killed*.

Brown, therefore, carried on in San Antonio. He watched Fat run the fastest forty-yard dash at the Combine, rocketing him up college coaches' wish lists. Just a junior, Fat had another year of recruiting ahead. Tygee, a sophomore, has two more years of this. Signing day for Karr's seniors—Leonard, Joe, Leonte, and others—was only a few weeks away. Brown needed time to untangle some futures, including his own.

For reasons he'd struggle to explain, he couldn't say no to Barret Rey and St. Aug. And Nick wasn't letting Brown off easily. He kept talking about this being an important move to catapult their system forward. Despite their four state championships, major college programs weren't calling to offer jobs. St. Aug had produced NFL stars and rappers, mathematicians and mayors. Karr may have the hardware, but St. Aug had something you can't win: prestige. Nick told Brown that if they could turn around a struggling program in the Seventh Ward, that would prove the Karr Method could be transferred.

Brown put him off. At first he promised Nick, and Rey, and himself, that he'd make a decision after the state championship game. Then no later than January 6, which is when students return from Karr's holiday break. Both came and went.

The eight-hour drive from San Antonio would give him time to think. On one hand, Brown and Nick are Karr men. They've built the program to last while providing direction to what is becoming a generation of young Black men. A new campus would be opening the following year, a time of widespread transition. A fifth consecutive state championship would be . . .

"You going to sleep?" Fat says in the back seat on the way back from San Antonio. Brown, leaning against a pillow, says he's not.

But Fat just saw Brown nodding off. He'd swear to it.

"I didn't go to sleep!" Brown says.

"I watched you!"

Anyway, a fifth straight state title . . .

"Give me your pillow," Fat says. After lunch at Hooters, they stopped at Walmart, and Tygee's mother loaded up on discounted stuffed animals. Fat is resting his head on one.

Brown refuses, telling Fat to please shut the hell up. He's trying to focus. Fat keeps talking. Brown asks if he hands over the pillow, will Fat be quiet? Fat says he no longer wants the pillow.

"But you *do* want it," Brown says.

Eventually they move on, the pillow never changes hands, the miles pass. Fat falls asleep. Brown is texting with Rey, negotiating assistant coaches' salaries and possible modifications to St. Aug's restrictive dress code. Brown is a strong believer in people being themselves. You can alter their self-destructive instincts, but you shouldn't tinker with their self-expression. Brown sees this as the first wisps of honesty emerging from a kid who otherwise conceals who he actually is and what he wants to be. In fact he thinks it's essential to assembling a successful team. But St. Aug's student handbook requires hair to be kept less than an inch long, prohibits beards and sideburns, and expressly forbids "Afros, flattops, twists, dread locks, or other exotic or faddish haircuts."

Between texts, Brown is mentally weighing the pros and cons of staying and going. The kid who got shot is somehow both. It's a reminder of the endless stress he deals with, but also of Brown's necessity. If he leaves, who will do what it takes to save them? Who'll commit themselves as Brown has?

"Half of you is tired of it," he says of his dual role at Karr. "Half of you know it's necessary."

He'll learn later that the young man had been walking with a friend near the Fischer when a car pulled up. Someone from inside started shooting, both the kids started running, and one of the rounds caught the Karr player in the back of his left leg. He'd be treated and discharged from a hospital the same day, and would be fully recovered in time for spring football.

The player was a classic Karr kid on the edge, another Ronnie or Joe. His mother was in jail, and he'd bounced between his grandmother's house and foster care. He could be talked into anything, which made him both moldable and a persistent headache. Brown wasn't sure he had it in him for another massive project. He hadn't even finished the one with Joe, who a month before signing day still has college to figure out.

The thought of restarting felt suffocating.

Rey keeps texting. At one point he invites Brown to visit St. Aug on the evening of a basketball game. Just to get a sense of the place, its people, its game-day atmosphere. Brown knows what attending would indicate. It'd be an unmistakable signal he'd be taking the job.

But Brown knows he needs something. A fresh challenge. When he texts back, he tells Rey he'll be at the game.

It's national Signing Day, and six Karr seniors are standing in a hallway outside the school library. Joe isn't here.

In ten minutes, the doors will open and the players will file in. The elaborate ceremony will allow each player to announce his college choice, and with family members watching and television cameras documenting the occasion, they'll sign their national letters of intent. Leonard is enjoying the attention his bright red blazer is generating. Jamie is cracking jokes one moment, acting serious the next—whatever the moment calls for. Leonte, who just two days ago learned that Navarro College in Texas had offered him a scholarship, is pacing as he practices his speech.

"*Now* you're nervous?" Norm asks. Leonte issues an embarrassed smile.

Signing day had weighed on Norm for months, and Joe had been the ultimate case study of the Karr program's ability to transform lives. Coaches tried for months to convince Joe, and themselves, that his limitations could be overcome. He was too short, too thin, too under-hyped, too raw. In the back of their minds, coaches knew getting Joe from Algiers to a college campus was probably a long shot. And Norm knew that if they couldn't, Joe wouldn't be able to sit in the audience and cheer on his teammates as they put pen to paper.

Karr students have been excused from classes today. The library is a makeshift press room, with two tables pushed together near a window. Parents are taking their places in several rows of seats.

Then five minutes before the ceremony begins, a door opens near the school's main office. Joe comes dashing in, apologizing for being late. He gives fist bumps to teammates, administrators, coaches. Brown offers his fist, along with a dubious glare.

"I caught a flat," Joe insists.

"Mm-hmm," Brown says. Joe disappears down a hallway. He came here with Ms. Diane, and Keyoke told Joe she's on the way.

During the Super Bowl four days earlier, Brown had watched from his grandparents' house. It hit him that Joe, even after his postseason heroics, still had no scholarship offers. Two schools expressed interest but backed away because of concerns about Joe's height. So Brown sent texts to recruiters at a few small colleges. The major programs, along with most of the minor ones, had offered the scholarships they were going to offer. The college football supply chain had nearly been satisfied.

But in the final hours of recruiting season, programs such as Texas Wesleyan University were always looking for a few more players to fill their scholarship allotments. When Brown texted Dwayne Taylor, a New Orleans native and Texas Wesleyan's recruiting coordinator, he praised Joe's leadership, drive, and professionalism. He could thrive in the right system. He just needed a chance.

"What can you do?" Brown says he wrote to Taylor.

Taylor asked for some time, and the next morning he forwarded

Joe's hastily produced highlight video to the Rams' linebackers coach. Joe had posted it on his Twitter page ten days earlier.

"Not bad for a no star," he'd written. The two-minute video, set to a mellow song by Future about hard work and survival, shows Joe tackling an elusive Carver ball carrier and taking down a Neville wide receiver. There are three angles showing his adjustment and tackle on Easton's Jewell Holmes, the failed two-point conversion attempt that preserved Karr's championship streak.

As Brown and Nick had indicated, the team's advancement in the playoffs had given Joe opportunities to display his skills. The audiences were larger, the stakes higher. And Joe had stepped up in the most important moments.

The day after the Super Bowl, Taylor called Brown. Texas Wesleyan had one more scholarship. If Joe wanted it, it was his. Though he'd never visited the Texas Wesleyan campus, and in fact had no idea it was in Fort Worth, he said yes. Both recruit and team had formed a union, mostly sight unseen. Beyond major college football's megaproduced, made-for-TV glitz, this is a glimpse into how hundreds of players and programs find each other every year.

Joe, who a few months ago got by almost entirely on McDonald's, would be heading to a private Methodist college whose annual tuition and fees total $27,000 per year. He wouldn't learn until months later that Texas Wesleyan's coaching staff had added someone Joe knew. Chris D, who'd moved from Virginia-Wise to Alvernia University in Pennsylvania, was now coming to coach offensive line at Texas Wesleyan. Another part of his job, of course, was keeping an eye on Joe, and they'd talk almost every day.

For now, Cassidy helped Joe research basic facts about the school, and Ms. Diane would drive him to Fort Worth a week after signing day.

"I'm ready. It ain't nothing new," Joe said as he prepared to sign the papers.

Except it is. And it's an extraordinary thing to witness. Joe was born into a place where residents in a particular socioeconomic and educational class tend to stay there. The cycle of poverty, drug abuse, and crime depends on this complacency. It's such a powerful force in the US that seven in ten Americans born into a lower-class home grow into adults who remain on the bottom rung of that economic ladder. This is a system that doesn't want to be changed, and which resists subversion by making college, earning money, and overall success a confounding and socially divisive notion.

What Brown and Karr provide isn't exceptional. Or at least it shouldn't be. All Brown did was invest his time in Joe, and a few dozen kids like him, who say they want to play ball, win games, be part of something special. Then he asks them to prove it, day after day, year after year. *Not in what you say. But in what you do.* Joe did more than most, and in exchange, all Brown did was call a friend and ask for a favor. This final part of the sequence might change, or save, a life. It could alter his family forever.

This process isn't about football, despite what Joe and others might think. It is, for once, about kids using the college football system to *their* advantage. Brown may not be physically gone from New Orleans after coming home from Grambling. But he knows the way out and what it takes, and more than just how to identify the Cover 3, this is what he's teaching them after having reached them.

On this afternoon, the library doors open. Joe walks in after Kendrick Rogers and Josh Randall. He tries not to smile, but it overpowers him. Leonte, Leonard, Jamie, and Rodney Johnson follow, and they take their places at the long table.

Relatives stand, applauding and capturing cell-phone video. Joe sees Cassidy and Ms. Diane, but not his mother. Kendrick announces he'll be attending Arkansas Baptist College, and Josh says he'll also be signing with Texas Wesleyan. Joe keeps hoping Keyoke makes it in time to hear him say the words, but she does not. He tells the crowd where he'll be attending college, and Ms. Diane claps and smiles. Leonard says he's signing with Nicholls State, where Ronnie will again be his teammate. Jamie announces for Louisville, Rodney for Stephen F. Austin.

Keyoke walks in at last. She's dressed up, wearing a white dress shirt with blue and red polka dots and a red bow tie. Though she has missed Joe's signing, it's clear this is a big day for her. Ms. Diane is nonetheless furious.

"Where *were* you?" she says in a steely whisper. Keyoke shrugs and walks away. Ms. Diane steps into the hallway, trying to avoid saying something she'll regret. Keyoke heads outside to have a cigarette and wait out a passing storm.

And it's alone under this covered area, away from an audience, that Keyoke lets down her guard. In the world she still inhabits, defensiveness and intimidation are keys to survival. She never had a Coach Brown to show her a different way, but regardless of how she acquired her education, she's wise enough to know that an unfamiliar world exists. It's one she pushed Joe toward, even if like him, Keyoke couldn't quite imagine it.

Her methods are unorthodox, but they worked. For Joe. For New Orleans.

Standing here just beyond the raindrops, Keyoke takes another long drag. She doesn't curse or shout. Her voice is soft, her tone reflective.

"It just— It was not easy," she says. "Not knowing how to read and stuff, it was kinda hard. Since I can't do it, let me go ahead and try to get somebody to help him. What I couldn't do, I pushed into him."

Keyoke looks across the pavement and considers what today means to her.

"The trials and tribulations me and him went through, it made me push harder," she says. "And me being incarcerated, it made him push harder. I told him that nothing gonna come to you unless you go get it, and he showed me he went and got it."

Back inside, Joe is helping to carry the two tables back to the library's study area. He hugs Cassidy before sitting down to take a deep breath. Today has been emotional, and Joe, like his coach, tries to put off confronting emotions. Deep down he knows that, as many obstacles as he has cleared, Joe's biggest crossroads lay ahead. If he gets homesick, or receives a bad grade, or gets benched—how will he respond?

What will he do if Keyoke calls and asks him to come home? What if something happens that requires it?

"I always put people before me," he says. "And I need to stop doing that. Because they could burn me in the end. But I'm working on it."

He pauses, like his mom, trying to find the right words.

"It's just the way my heart is," he says.

Joe admits the symbolism of today hasn't fully hit him. Eventually, he says, he'll think about the distance that separates where he came from and where he's headed, the rungs on that educational, social, and socioeconomic ladder he's trying so hard to climb. Perhaps then he'll understand how remarkable his journey truly is.

"The show ain't over yet," he says. "Brice always talking about reflecting. I ain't reflect yet. So I might do it tonight, you know?"

There's that smile and those braces.

"It might come across my mind," he says. "Like: 'Dang. I really made it.'"

WITH ALL OTHER DECISIONS FINALIZED, Brown was finally ready to make his. His public visit to St. Aug had caused a stir and generated headlines. Rey was ready to celebrate.

"Shit, I got him," he'd recall thinking.

Nick, Norm, and Mike would join Brown's new staff across town. Rey couldn't do much about the dress code, considering five members of the school's board of directors are members of the clergy. But Brown told himself he could live with it. It was something new he wanted, after all.

"Let's roll," Brown says one of his assistant coaches texted one day.

Before Brown said good-bye, he decided to spend a Monday afternoon with Fat. At some point he'd share the news: Fat, the presumptive team captain and Pride Panel's first chair, would have a new coach for his senior season. Their first stop is Step 'N Style Fashions, where Brown accompanies Fat while he picks out new school pants. They continue to a small embroidery shop, and the young man asks the clerk to sew "FATASTIC" above the Karr crest on his purple polo shirt.

"I came up with that nickname," Brown says when they're both back in the Silverado.

"Am I supposed to give you the credit?" Fat says.

"You plagiarized."

They both chuckle, and Brown is both amused and frustrated by the kid's stubbornness. Fat challenges him. On everything. Ronnie and Joe craved authority and always yielded to their coach's wisdom and presence. They'd have never talked to Brown this way. One of the things he loves about Karr is that he almost always gets his way. It's also why he stays bored. Eventually the truck reaches the parking lot at New Orleans Seafood & Spirits. This is as good a place as any to be honest with Fat.

They head inside and make their way to a booth. Brown orders his usual: voodoo rolls and an Arnold Palmer, sweet. Fat asks for ice water. Brown reads from the menu and, as he often does, makes suggestions. Fat ignores them and does his own thing. He orders the fried shrimp and catfish.

When the plates arrive, Brown is on the phone with Norm. Fat dives into the voodoo rolls, which come with a plastic cup of the restaurant's secret Tiger Sauce. It's sweet and mustardy, and soon Fat is dunking his shrimp into the cup. Brown still has the phone to his ear when he notices Fat carefully trimming the tails off the shrimp with a fork. He's so befuddled that he tells Norm he'll call him back. The tails have already been removed. He's cutting off actual shrimp meat! This, to Brown, is an atrocity that cannot stand.

Fat pulls away the breading, unsatisfied to just trust his coach's word. Indeed Brown is correct. But if Pride Panel taught Fat one thing, it is that you never change your answer. That'd be a show of submission, and at Karr, you must make a choice and live with it. So he carries on cutting off the ends of the shrimp.

"Well, what the *fuck*?" Brown says. Fat laughs at the psychological hold he seems to have over his coach.

They keep eating, and following three voodoo rolls and maybe a dozen shrimp, Fat leans back and pats his belly. It's a big dinner, but not the biggest Brown has seen.

"You're not no Joe Thomas," he says, and at this moment he realizes something interesting. Not only is Fat nothing like Joe, he's not much like Leonard or Ronnie or Munchie or even Tonka. Or anyone, really. He is confident, lighthearted, weird. Kind of a pain in the ass. He's among the most naturally gifted players to ever pass through Brown's offense. And with the right amount of guidance, love, and honesty, he could reach heights no other Karr man has.

Fat, like so many kids in New Orleans and beyond, needs a Brice Brown. But the truth is, Brown also needs a Fat. He's been looking for a new challenge, and there's a mighty one right here in the booth with him. With this in mind, Brown will call Rey in a few days. But rather than accept the job or continue negotiating, he withdraws his name from consideration. Brown will be staying at Karr for at least one more season. He still has business there, and those closest to Brown know it can never be finished.

St. Aug must nonetheless hire a coach, and Brown offers a recommendation. Rey winds up hiring the man Brown suggests, and in early spring, St. Aug will introduce the twelfth head coach in program history.

His name is Nick Foster.

Brown has spent two decades calling his plays and reshaping lives, and with futures still unwritten on Racey, Ronnie, and Joe, it's Nick—who chose football over quick cash, purpose over shortcuts—who has come further than anyone. He fully committed to the Karr program and allowed it to change him, and it has. Nick's departure nonetheless leaves a hole on Brown's staff; he didn't just coach running backs and signal plays. He was the program's fixer. He did the dirty work. Brown being Brown, at once creative and self-loathing, he taps none other than Omari to replace Nick as his top lieutenant. He'll later hire Munchie Legaux to coach quarterbacks, a decision that lightens Brown's considerable responsibility load.

On this evening, Brown finishes his meal and sees Fat still picking at his mountain of shrimp. He uses one to scrape the last ribbons of Tiger Sauce from the cup. Brown says they can get another serving, if he wants it. Fat waves him off.

"Just say you want it," Brown says.

"I already got one," Fat says.

"Look at all that shit you got left!"

Fat says nothing, smiling as he nibbles. Brown crosses his arms and sighs. No what the fucks.

"Gentlemen, y'all okay?" the server asks.

"Can I have an extra Tiger Sauce?" Fat says, and Brown's eyes widen.

"You *just* said you don't want the sauce!" he says. A moment later the woman returns with a to-go box and two cups of Tiger Sauce. Brown asks for the recipe, but the chef has sworn her to secrecy.

Fat opens the first one, dunks another shrimp, and pops it into his mouth. Brown does the same.

"Honey," Fat says.

"And probably a little cinnamon," Brown says.

"I don't think it's cinnamon."

Brown shakes his head before offering Fat his leftovers. He packs them into the box, and the coach and his next team captain carry on arguing. Brown opens *Toy Blast*, Fat ridicules him for how often his coach plays it, and Brown locks his phone and puts it away. Neither is willing to submit, even as both laugh at the absurdity of whatever they're currently haggling over. Pride Panel begins in a few weeks, and considering who'll be in the first chair, Brown is already looking forward to some merry late-night battles.

"I'm *gonna* interject," he says.

"Might as well," Fat says.

The coach plunges a pinkie into the open cup of Tiger Sauce.

"I just need to recuse myself from that whole situation," Brown says, tasting the sauce on his finger and trying to solve yet another puzzle. "It'll just be unhealthy."

ACKNOWLEDGMENTS

There's just no way this book, or any such look into life on the West Bank and at Karr, would've been possible without the honesty and trust of Brice Brown. During a highly stressful season, I don't remember him ever telling me "no" when I asked for a little more of his time, for a few more details, for one more time going over the differences between Cover 3 and Cover 3 match.

I'll be forever thankful to Brown, and despite being a staunch believer in journalistic objectivity, I also don't believe it's possible to spend as much time as I did with Brown and the Karr program without developing an emotional attachment. These are human beings, and so am I. To this end, I am in no way ashamed to tell you that I came to view Brown and several current and former members of his coaching staff as friends. I developed a deep admiration for Joe, a fascination with his mother, an appreciation for the resolve of Rhonda George, and a respect for the divergent paths and personalities of Leonard, Leonte, and Fat. I don't believe it made me, or makes me, any less objective to tell you that I'll be rooting for these people, and for Karr, for a long time.

Speaking of, I'll also acknowledge that you might be wondering what some of these people have been up to since the story ended in early 2020. Brown is still at Karr, albeit in a gleaming new campus whose head coach's office is so spacious and nice he almost never sets foot in it. He almost always crams into a cramped shared space, usually with others, for he still dislikes being alone. Due to the coronavirus pandemic, Karr played a shortened season in 2020 but still reached the state championship game. This time, though, Carencro High was just too powerful and snapped Karr's state championship streak at four.

Both Joe and Chris D are still at Texas Wesleyan, and despite the challenges of his freshman season, Joe rarely went home. If he did, he always came back. This has perhaps been made easier because Keyoke has stayed out of trouble and remained supportive of her only son's education and future. Leonard remains a backup quarterback at Nicholls State, and though Ronnie can be a continuing source of stress for his coaches, he is expected to be a redshirt sophomore at Nicholls in 2021. Fat signed with Florida State, and Tygee Hill and Aaron Anderson committed to play at Louisiana State. Though Leonte is no longer at Navarro, he insists his football career is not finished.

As for Trent Washington, his legal case is still pending. Mike Thompson has been unable to give up on him, and though he never returned to the Karr football team, Mike offered to help train Trent during his spare time. Trent never took him up on that, though, in part because he has a baby daughter. When I stopped by Karr in April 2021, Mike told me Trent would be graduating from Karr, and Mike planned to attend the ceremony to offer his support.

As of now, no arrest has been made in connection with the killing of Tonka George, and Rhonda said she and Rayell Johnson have not spoken since March 2019. But in late 2020, Johnson learned something interesting. The NOPD's digital forensics team had, at long last, opened Tonka's iPhone.

I am incredibly thankful for the support and guidance of Chad Luibl, my agent with Janklow & Nesbit. Chad has no idea how perceptive, strategic, and just . . . *good* . . . he is. Through this process, I have learned that if Chad believes in something, that something is worthwhile. And that Chad is usually right. I am proud to call him a friend, and the ever-present angel on my shoulder.

There were many editors, official and unofficial, involved in turning this from idea to rough project to manuscript to book. Sydney Rogers, my editor at HarperOne, was my conscience at every turn, reminding me to think about or describe things more specifically or with greater nuance. Miles Doyle provided exceptional advice early on and is responsible for the book's title, which I love and think sounds like a Bruce Springsteen album. Laurie McGee was a careful and highly talented copy editor who pushed back on word choices and sentence structure. Writers like to pretend they're solely responsible for a project like this, but that's part of the industry's mythology. The truth is that it takes confident editors such as Sydney, Miles, and Laurie to save us from lazy writing, bad habits, and sometimes ourselves.

Jeff Asher, the New Orleans-based crime analyst, was an invaluable resource on statistics, charts, and context when it comes to violent crime and shootings in the city. Joan Niesen, a tremendously skilled sports journalist, was this book's fact checker and wrote much of the contextual material that appears in the Notes and Citations section. She was meticulous, demanding, thorough, and I'm so lucky she offered her expertise of New Orleans and an incredible eye for detail. Jerry Brewer, a three-dimensional thinker whose insights and reminders helped elevate this book's scope and empathy, never told me to stop asking for his opinion. Jeff Dooley, an assignment editor at *The Post*, who in summer 2018 emailed me a Nola.com story about a high school football coach named Brice Brown, kept reminding me of this story's importance and how many Joe Thomases are out there, and how few Coach Browns. Jeff and Dayana Sarkisova are remarkable people, terrific friends, and people whose hearts belong to New Orleans. My friends Jeff Duncan and Greg Bishop helped me brainstorm and, perhaps more helpfully, occasionally put this project aside for a few hours.

Emily Kask, a talented photojournalist based in New Orleans, took and processed the images you saw in the insert section of this book. My longtime friend Walter Bethea brought an artist's touch to the play diagrams that begin each chapter.

Chris D became my football whisperer, and because of his patience and teaching skill, I learned more about football in these eighteen months than I did covering college and pro football for more than a decade. Football coaches, especially those who complain about how little some fans and reporters understand about this complex game, should be more like Chris and share their knowledge with those who actually want to learn. If we can all see the game a little better, even if it's not precisely the same way, our conversations will be richer and our coverage more informative. Alex Moran was an enthusiastic friend who helped me understand this world, and its people, a little better all the time.

My sincere thanks to my editors at *The Post*, in particular Matt Rennie and Joe Tone, and many friends in and around journalism. At various levels, for various things, I bent the ears and tested my theories with Robert Klemko, Will Hobson, John Woodrow Cox, Eli Saslow, Roman Stubbs, Jesse Dougherty, Ava Wallace, Candace Buckner, Benjamin Hochman, Sam Mellinger, Baxter Holmes, Amie Just, Larry Holder, Ben Strauss, Todd M. Adams, Gerry Ahern, Nick and Diane Mathews, Charles Robinson, Rick Maese, Ben Schpigel, Mike Rosenberg, Ross Dellenger, Elizabeth Crisp, Rustin Dodd, Randy Covitz, Brett Dawson, Michael Mooney, Mike Jones, Les Carpenter, Mike Sielski, Sam Fortier, Elton Hayes, Jon Gold, Phil Kaplan, Steve Politi, Joe Person, Jeff Passan, Kevin Spain, Jeff Pearlman, McKenna Ewan, Kareem Copeland, Bryce Miller, and Jorge Rojas. A special thanks to Nick Alvarez, Michael McCleary, and Tyler Waldrep, and the inspiring and self-made Louisiana sports reporter Jeremiah "GSportz" Gray. Research is easy when it involves reading the impressive journalism of Ramon Antonio Vargas, Matt Sledge, Michelle Hunter, Christopher Dabe, Andrew Lopez, Rod Walker, and countless others. Much appreciation to Brett Anderson, Brett Dawson, Brett Michael Dykes, Brett Martin, Brett Martell, and all the other Bretts out there. Thanks to Jared Barber and Cam Haggerty for not joining me in New Orleans that once, and to Joel Thorman for never declining my calls. Additional gratitude to Kendra Sampson, Dave Wagner, and Bill Matthews.

When a journalist interviews a political figure or luminary, there often are folks who help coordinate these discussions. For their assistance scheduling these valuable conversations, I offer my gratitude to Ken Daly, Ken Jones, Beau Tidwell, Stacy Astaud, and Ryan Berni. Historians Gaynell Brady, Erin Greenwald, and Donald Costello volunteered their time and knowledge to this project, and helped me to explain, and understand, some of the many obstacles that New Orleanians face.

Whitney is the world's greatest partner, and I'm so lucky that I married a person who understands (or claims to) why I have to go to New Orleans nineteen times in a single year. With help from Susan and Bill, and Grey and Linda, Whitney kept the home train on the tracks, and Lilah (and Charley the dog) cared for, while I was away doing whatever it is I do.

Like Joe and Ronnie and Brice and Tonka, I am the son of a single mother. I didn't grow up on the West Bank, but I nonetheless believe moms have the hardest job in America. I have no idea how my mother, June, raised and supported three of us by herself. Men continually made and broke promises, and so in many ways did our society. Financial and emotional support were always just out of reach, something that had to be fought for, and guidance on how to carve out a better life for her children felt shrouded in mystery. She had to choose between working or being a parent, and sometimes between feeding us or herself. She had to keep refusing to give up. And, like Keyoke, she pushed us forward in the best ways she could. Like so many of the people named in this book, my mother sacrificed on the promise that something better—or at least different—was out there for us. She forfeited meals, her mental and physical health, and much of her identity. She made these choices, yes. But the cost shouldn't be so damn high.

No American should have to give a life to save or change a life, and we as a nation must do a better job not just of supporting the young people who live across the river or through the trees or in the shadows. We have to do a better job of caring for the women who raise us, who tell us this invisible thing is possible, or at least make it a little less hard.

NOTES AND CITATIONS

Author's Note

Page iii: . . . saw the cotton . . . Cotton is still a major crop in Mississippi, which boasts about 825 cotton farms and produces about 1.4 million bales of the fiber each year.

Page iv: . . . Marv himself was one of Karr's first Black students . . . Marv was three years old when New Orleans schools began to desegregate in 1960. Both schools were in the Lower Ninth Ward, which even then was a predominantly low-income area, though it was far more racially integrated than it is today. The students—Leona Tate, Tessie Prevost, and Gail Etienne, who attended McDonogh 19 Elementary and became known as the McDonogh Three, and Ruby Bridges, who attended nearby William Frantz Elementary—faced harassment daily, and the US Marshals were called in. It would take another ten years for the city's schools to fully integrate.

Page iv: . . . expand on a 2018 article . . . Kent Babb, "'Our Call Is to Save Them,'" *Washington Post*, Aug. 23, 2018.

Page iv: . . . a city where, in 2016, an eighteen- or nineteen-year-old Black male was fifty-six times more likely to gunned down than the national average . . . According to data collected by Jeff Asher, the New Orleans–based crime analyst who provided statistics for this book, the murder rate for this demographic group was 297 per 100,000 residents. The national average in 2016 was 5.3 per 100,000 residents.

Epigraph

Page ix: This is for the kids . . . Langston Hughes, "Kids Who Die," in *The Collected Works of Langston Hughes Vol. 1*, ed. Arnold Rampersad (Columbia: Univ. of Missouri Press, 2001), 138–139.

Introduction: The West Bank

Page 2: . . . Algiers, a community just outside downtown New Orleans. Also known as the Fifteenth Ward, Algiers is a 397-acre tract that actually sits to the east of downtown, spanning from Algiers Point and the banks of the Mississippi River to Terry Parkway to the south to Sullen Place to the east.

Page 2: . . . Karr admits students from all over the city. According to the website for the charter school network InspireNOLA, in the aftermath of Hurricane Katrina, Edna Karr High School "reopened as an open access college preparatory high school, accepting students from all over Orleans Parish with an open admissions policy."

Page 2: . . . its third Class 4A title in a row. David Folse II, "Three-Peat: Karr Beats Warren Easton to Claim Class 4A Crown," Nola.com, Dec. 8, 2018.

Page 2: . . . twenty-seven-game winning streak . . . Nathan Brown, "As Two High School Football Titans Clash, John Curtis and Karr See Thursday's Matchup as Tuneup for Title Pushes," Nola.com, Sept. 4, 2019.

Page 2: It, too, is a New Orleans football institution . . . According to 14-0 Productions, a historical database for Louisiana prep sports (www.14-0productions.com), John Curtis has won twenty-six state football championships. This does not include its 2013 championship, which the school forfeited in 2016 as a result of rule violations.

Page 3: . . . cut through the thick summer air. The trend of shootings spiking during the summer months is not unique to New Orleans; in fact, in colder-weather cities, it might be more pronounced due to weather inciting people to spend more time outside. Still, even in the sticky humidity of a New Orleans summer, shootings tick up, in large part because of the lack of summer programming and employment opportunities for at-risk youth. In the summer of 2018, for instance, there was a two-week stretch in New Orleans in which thirty-four people were shot in seventeen shootings. Seven of them died.

Page 3: . . . he led Karr to its first state title game in eleven years. Before 2010, Karr's previous appearance in the state championship game was in 1999, when it reached the final as the number eleven seed in Class 3A. Amite High defeated Karr, 41–7, for its third state title.

Page 3: . . . a dreadful milestone every year: at least a hundred murders. Of the nine US cities that tally triple-digit homicides, New Orleans—population 390,000—is by far the smallest." According to Jeff Asher, the other cities with at least one hundred homicides during this span were Baltimore, Chicago, Houston, Dallas, Detroit, New York, Los Angeles, and Philadelphia. Each of those cities has a population of at least 600,000 people. Population figures are based on data provided by the US Census Bureau. The New Orleans metro area, though, has a population of 1.3 million; that said, the crime stats considered here are for just Orleans Parish. In Louisiana, "parish" is synonymous with "county," and Orleans Parish covers urban New Orleans.

Page 4: . . . neighborhood on the forgotten side. Massoud Hayoun, "Impoverished District Seeks to Secede from New Orleans," Al Jazeera America, May 26, 2015.

Page 4: Parts of Algiers are a mere half mile from the city's bustling French Quarter . . . As the crow flies, the distance separating the French Quarter and Algiers is as little as nineteen hundred feet, according to Google.

Page 4: . . . New Orleans is one of the nation's most rapidly gentrifying cities. According to a March 2019 report issued by the National Community Reinvestment Coalition, New Orleans joined Washington, DC, and Richmond and Charlottesville in Virginia as the cities with "the highest percentages of black displacement at the tract level." The report stated that 17 percent of New Orleans's Black population left the city from 1990 to 2010.

Page 4: A third of the residents of Old Algiers, the oak-lined historic district, live below the poverty line. Chelsea Brasted, "As New Orleans Grows, Are We Forgetting Algiers?," Nola.com, June 6, 2018.

Page 4: Life expectancy is nearly a decade less than the national average . . . A 2015 report issued by the Robert Wood Johnson Foundation titled "Mapping Life Expectancy" suggested that the life expectancy of babies born to mothers in New Orleans "can vary by as much as 25 years across neighborhoods just a few miles apart."

Page 5: The Irish Channel and the Tremé . . . used to be Black neighborhoods. Kate Rose, "Gentrification a Growing Threat for Many New Orleans Residents," Louisiana Fair Housing Action Center, July 24, 2020.

Page 5: . . . $600-a-night Airbnbs. New Orleans saw such a surge of Airbnb rentals in the early years of the site's popularity that it had to enact stricter laws about the short-term rentals, as houses were being bought up all over the city and turned into rentals, worrying leaders that communities like the residential French Quarter would be destroyed.

Page 5: . . . people from one neighborhood don't often trust anyone from a different neighborhood. New Orleans is one of the more segregated cities in the South, especially when it comes to residential housing. Urban renewal projects like the Claiborne Avenue overpass have, in recent decades, destroyed traditionally Black neighborhoods. Still, the city has high population density and a small footprint, so often a predominantly Black neighborhood is a matter of steps from a predominantly white one—and then within a matter of blocks, pedestrians might find themselves back in another largely Black area.

Page 6: Between 2010 and 2018, only a third of the city's 1,434 homicides resulted in an arrest. Investigative team, "Murder with Impunity," *Washington Post*, Jan. 9, 2019.

Page 7: It was as if a second line . . . A "second line" in New Orleans is a parade in which most people are on foot.

Page 7: Brown parked near a neutral ground . . . A "neutral ground" is what New Orleanians call a median.

Page 7: In 2016 alone, there were 486 shootings in New Orleans . . . Matt Sledge, "NOPD: Major Crimes Rose 4.4 Percent in 2016, Up 30 Percent in Last Six Years," Nola.com, Mar. 21, 2017.

Page 7: . . . Will Smith had dinner with his wife and a friend . . . A. J. Perez, "Restaurant Employee Says Will Smith's Dinner Before Shooting Raised No Suspicions," *USA Today*, Apr. 10, 2016.

Page 7: . . . Hayes produced a .45-caliber Ruger from a holster and unloaded eight rounds . . . Michael McCann, "A Closer Look at Jury's Verdict That Found Will Smith's Shooter Guilty of Manslaughter," *Sports Illustrated*, Dec. 12, 2016.

Page 8: "A tragedy," Mayor Mitch Landrieu told reporters . . . "Landrieu: Will Smith Shooting Does Not Reflect Overall Safety of City," WDSU-TV, Apr. 13, 2016.

Page 8: . . . since his father held the office in the 1970s. Mitch had won by promising to curb violent crime . . . Sarah Goodyear, "Inside the High-Stakes Effort to Stop Murder in New Orleans," Bloomberg CityLab, Dec. 23, 2014. Landrieu, the son of former New Orleans mayor Moon Landrieu, ran for mayor first in 2006, losing to the incumbent, Ray Nagin. Nagin was term-limited in 2010, paving the way for Landrieu to win the election that year handily. Five years after Hurricane Katrina, Landrieu took over a city where recovery had stalled. The city's finances were disastrous, and its police department was under investigation by the Department of Justice. In 2014, Nagin was convicted of twenty counts of bribery, corruption, and fraud and sentenced to ten years in federal prison. He was released early in 2020 amid the coronavirus pandemic.

Page 8: . . . the city's $9-billion-a-year tourism industry. "New Orleans Tourism Visitation and Visitor Spending Break Records in 2018," New Orleans Tourism Marketing Corporation, Nov. 22, 2019.

Page 8: . . . ten bar crawlers, among them a twenty-five-year-old tattoo artist . . . Phil McCausland and Alastair Jamieson, "Bourbon Street, New Orleans Shooting Leaves 1 Dead, 9 Hurt: Police," NBC News, Nov. 27, 2016.

Page 8: "New Orleans is safe," Louisiana Governor John Bel Edwards insisted. Michael Isaac Stein, "New Orleans Surveillance Program Gives Powerful Tools to a Police Department with a History of Racism and Abuse," *The Intercept*, Mar. 6, 2018.

Page 8: . . . in Terrytown, and the other driver shot him three times. Michelle Hunter, "Ronald Gasser Sentenced to 30 Years in Joe McKnight Road Rage Killing," Nola.com, Mar. 15, 2018.

Page 8: Police cycled through leadership . . . Between 2005 and 2019, the New Orleans Police Department had five superintendents.

Page 9: When two teenagers were shot outside the Karr gymnasium . . . Kelsey Davis, "Chaos Erupts After Two People Killed in Shooting Outside Edna Karr High School," WDSU-TV, Feb. 1, 2017.

Page 9: . . . each day a hundred emotionally vulnerable young men gather . . . Ages fifteen to eighteen are conventionally regarded as the peak years for a child to engage in violent behavior. According to a 2001 report on youth violence from the Office of the Surgeon General, commitment to school, recognition for involvement in conventional activities, and friends who engage in conventional behavior are three protective factors against youth violence.

Page 10: . . . the three dozen former Karr players who, between 2017 and 2019, used football to get a college education . . . Eleven Karr players signed to play college football in 2017, twelve in 2018, and thirteen in 2019.

Page 11: . . . the spotlight placed on traumatic brain injuries . . . Since 2006, when the forensic pathologist Bennet Omalu discovered a link between playing football and chronic brain injuries, football at all levels has faced intense scrutiny. Participation in youth football has plummeted, and the professional and college games have attempted—with dubious results—to make football safer for players.

Page 12: . . . the team's first loss in two years. Before its 42–39 loss to John Curtis, Karr hadn't lost a game since September 2017, when De La Salle snapped Karr's sixteen-game win streak with a 28–26 victory.

Chapter 1: Karr Men

Page 15: This swamp-side campus about an hour southwest of New Orleans . . . Thibodaux is mostly west and a little south; most of what's south of New Orleans in Louisiana is uninhabitable wetlands, and Thibodaux lies on a narrow strip of land along Louisiana Highway 1, which bisects the state from its northwest corner to its southeastern, eroding tip.

Page 17: Exertional heatstroke kills . . . James Bruggers, "'This Was Preventable': Football Heat Deaths and the Rising Temperature," *Inside Climate News*, July 20, 2018.

Page 17: A football helmet can add ten degrees . . . When former NFL offensive lineman Korey Stringer died of heatstroke in 2001, his core body temperature was 108 degrees when he arrived at a hospital. Marshall Shepherd, "Is Excessive Heat and Youth Football a Dangerous Mix?," *Forbes*, July 15, 2016.

Page 17: . . . Brandon Spincer, a ninth-grade offensive lineman . . . All football players at Karr are required to have their legal guardian sign a waiver that grants permission to media outlets, the school, or InspireNOLA to use a student's name and likeness in promotional materials. This includes students who haven't yet turned eighteen. Though the overwhelming number of interviews for this book took place on school grounds or with a parent or coach present, some fell in what the author considered gray areas. In those cases, noted in this section, some parents were asked for additional permissions to use their child's name, descriptions, or circumstances.

Page 18: . . . overhydration can be similarly deadly. Too much water dilutes salt in the body and can cause severe swelling of the cells, including those in the brain. In fact, the symptoms so closely resemble dehydration that some on-field medical personnel treat overhydration with more fluids, which makes the problem worse. Tamara Hew-Butler, "Stay Hydrated, but Drinking Too Much Water Can Be Deadly, Doctors Warn," CBS News, Aug. 8, 2018.

Page 21: "Coach of the year shit" . . . The New Orleans Saints nominated Brown in 2017 for the Don Shula NFL High School Coach of the Year Award, and the boxed detritus in his floorboard included this clear trophy, still in its plastic wrapper, along with a 2017 award for mentoring by the Alliance of Diversity and Excellence.

Page 22: . . . Keyoke Thomas was arrested and charged . . . Details of Keyoke's arrests are part of the public record, as are those of anyone convicted of a crime in Orleans Parish. Those included in this book are attributable to the Criminal District Court Docket Master Search of the Orleans Parish Sheriff's Office. Any additional details and/or context of Keyoke's crimes and experience in the criminal justice system came directly from the two on-the-record interviews she conducted with the author.

Page 31: . . . what he learned playing college football . . . A spokesman for Southern University athletics confirmed that Omari played football for the school.

Page 35: . . . how to properly line up and salute the flag during "The Star-Spangled Banner." When Colin Kaepernick protested police violence and brutality toward

Black Americans by taking a knee during the playing of the national anthem at NFL games throughout the 2016 season, he inspired athletes in various sports and at various levels of competition to participate in similar acts of protest. Though this was highly polarizing, and in general, opinions fell along political and racial lines, Brice Brown made it clear that Karr players were prohibited from demonstrating during the anthem. Brown would say later that, though he personally believed Kaepernick's protest wasn't aimed at the military or US service members, he couldn't know that everyone believed the same. In part because Karr's staff included Marvin Rose, a Navy veteran, Brown said he told the team that any player or coach who attempted to protest during the national anthem would be asked to leave the sideline, and coaches would be fined a month's salary.

Chapter 2: The Boy Who Played with Trucks

Page 44: McDonoghville Cemetery to talk to Tonka . . . Like most cemeteries in New Orleans, McDonoghville Cemetery consists mostly of aboveground graves because the city sits below sea level. This particular cemetery was established in the first half of the nineteenth century by John McDonogh, a wealthy landowner who was known for making large bequests to public schools. The people he enslaved were originally buried there, and he was also laid to rest for a time there before being moved to his native Baltimore.

Page 44: . . . cross the Crescent City Connection . . . McDonoghville Cemetery is just three blocks from the Mississippi River and another three blocks south from where the bridge soars over it, taking drivers into the heart of New Orleans.

Page 44: . . . the most anticipated high school game in Louisiana . . . John Curtis was ranked No. 26 in the MaxPreps preseason top 100 to begin 2019. Both teams won their respective brackets in 2018; Edna Karr competes in Class 4A and John Curtis in Division I, against other private schools.

Page 45: Norm Randall, who coaches special teams and defense . . . Norm Randall provided verbal permission to include this anecdote involving his older son, Baylon, and additional references to Baylon and Liam.

Page 45: That's my brudda. "Brudda" is a slang term of extreme endearment that means you consider the person like a brother. More casual friends are generally referred to in New Orleans as one's "potnas."

Page 49: The seventy-three-thousand-seat building became an emergency shelter . . . Three days before Hurricane Katrina hit New Orleans, National Hurricane Center models placed the likelihood of a direct hit to the Crescent City at 17 percent, and that probability increased over the next forty-eight hours to 29 percent. Even that low of a chance still signaled potential disaster because more than three-quarters of the New Orleans metro area lies below sea level—especially areas closer to Lake Pontchartrain.

Page 49: Rapes, murders, and suicides were common . . . "How New Orleans Descended into Post-Katrina Chaos," by BBC News, July 14, 2010.

Page 49: . . . shared restrooms overflowed with people and their various fluids. Scott Gold, "Trapped in the Superdome: Refuge Becomes a Hellhole," *Seattle Times*, Sept. 1, 2005.

Page 49: . . . spray-painting an *X* on the walls as a code to other recovery workers of what they'd find inside. The most important note of the *X* was that bottom quadrant, though when residents returned to New Orleans in 2006, they struggled to decode the graffiti that now adorned their homes. Once the mystery was solved, people reacted differently to their *X*'s. Some households removed them immediately, while others ignored or even preserved theirs as a testament to what the city had endured.

Page 49: . . . lacked adequate insurance . . . The school district had about $200 million in property insurance, but damages immediately following the storm were estimated at $800 million. The district also lost three hundred school buses, and replacing them cost $15 million. Steve Ritea, "Schools in Disarray," *New Orleans Times-Picayune*, Nov. 21, 2005.

Page 49: After estimating that 126 facilities . . . Ritea, "Schools in Disarray."

Page 49: . . . many of them at ages seen as particularly important for emotional development and behavior regulation . . . David Abramson, Yoon Soo Park, Tasha Stehling-Ariza, and Irwin Redlener, "Children as Bellwethers of Recovery: Dysfunctional Systems and the Effects of Parents, Households, and Neighborhoods on Serious Emotional Disturbance in Children After Hurricane Katrina," National Center for Disaster Preparedness, Columbia University Mailman School of Public Health, Sept. 4, 2010.

Page 49: But three dozen schools had sustained zero or minor damage. Susan Finch, "Some Orleans Schools to Open on West Bank; New Registration to Begin Sept. 26," *New Orleans Times-Picayune*, Sept. 17, 2005.

Page 49: . . . Edna Karr Magnet School was among those that'd be recommissioned as a charter high school . . . Steve Ritea, "Charter Schools Will Get a Federal Grant; Charter Schools Could Open Nov. 28," *New Orleans Times-Picayune*, Nov. 5, 2005.

Page 50: "I don't care where you were before Katrina . . . Now you're all Cougars." Steve Ritea, "Charter Schools Hit Ground Running; 1,300 Pupils Attend First Day of Classes," *New Orleans Times-Picayune*, Dec. 15, 2005.

Page 50: Rhonda George was among the quarter million residents who'd evacuated. Though Rhonda left with Tonka and Tiffany, New Orleans is a city that likes to ride out storms—or liked to, before Katrina. The 2005 evacuation order from Mayor Ray Nagin was the first mandatory evacuation in the city's history, and some residents were resistant. In the end, it's estimated that 80 to 90 percent of New Orleanians left the city via contraflowed highways, but many residents remained in their homes or in the Superdome.

Page 50: She went to his park ball games . . . This is what New Orleanians call their youth football leagues, and in general kids are signed up at the park nearest their home.

Page 51: Jabbar Juluke was Karr's head coach . . . Juluke, who'd coached at some of the area's best high schools before Karr, took the Cougars to three state championship games, winning one. He left Karr after 2012 to coach running backs at Louisiana Tech; he has since coached at LSU and Texas Tech, and in 2021 he was the assistant head coach and running backs coach at Louisiana. He did not reply to calls and text messages requesting an interview for this book.

Page 51: Though it peaked in the 1970s at the University of Houston . . . Coach Bill Yeoman invented the veer offense in the 1960s, but it didn't go mainstream until he used the ball-control attack to win four conference championships and eleven bowl games. Though the veer has evolved through the decades, it is actually the most influential ancestor of the read-option offense that's primarily run these days from the shotgun formation.

Page 51: . . . Karr made it to the second round of the Louisiana state playoffs. According to playoff brackets published by 14-0 Productions (www.14-0productions .com), Karr lost to Franklinton in 2007 and Northside in 2008.

Page 52: But in 2010, Munchie was playing for the University of Cincinnati. LeGaux enrolled at Cincinnati after graduating from Karr. A dual-threat quarterback, he played in parts of five seasons for the Bearcats, starting at times, but battled injuries toward the end of his career.

Page 52: . . . led victories against Destrehan and Jesuit . . . Though these opponents were in rebuilding mode after their playoff appearances a year earlier, Karr's victories over Class 5A teams were nonetheless impressive because Karr is assigned to Class 4A, indicating a smaller student body and a slightly shallower talent pool. Regardless, Karr went 9–1 during the 2010 regular season.

Page 53: . . . Karr beat Wossman and Northside in the playoffs. Considering Karr was the number one seed in the Class 4A playoffs, these weren't exactly upsets. Its twenty-five-point quarterfinal win against Northside, followed by its shutout of Teurlings Catholic, was considerably more impressive.

Page 54: . . . Franklinton High, a school in the easternmost part of Louisiana. A small town in the toe of Louisiana's "boot," it's actually only about seventy miles from New Orleans, though it feels more like Mississippi, whose state line is about a dozen miles away.

Page 58: On that fateful evening in June 2016 . . . This account of Tonka George's final walk was constructed primarily from interviews with relatives, friends, and sources within various municipal offices and private organizations within New Orleans. Because the investigation into Tonka's killing remains open, several of these sources provided the author, on the condition of anonymity, with vital background information and previously unreleased details, along with access to notes, phone and text records, and surveillance video. Additional information on the night of Tonka's death came from the following news reports: Ben Meyers, "Former Edna Karr Standout Tollette George Victim in Fatal Algiers Shooting Friday, Family Says," Nola. com, June 25, 2016; "Former Edna Karr Football Standout Tollette 'Tonka' George Shot Dead in Algiers," *The Advocate*, June 25, 2016; Beau Evans, "'Somebody Knows Something': Family of Slain Edna Karr Football Standout Seeks Answers," Nola.com, Mar. 19, 2017; and Greg Adaline, "Family Remembers Former Football Star as They Search for Answers Surrounding His Shooting Death," WVUE-TV, Mar. 19, 2017.

Page 60: . . . the fully loaded pistol he ostensibly carried for protection. Louisiana has some of the most relaxed gun laws in the country, and it's hardly uncommon for someone of Tonka's age and socioeconomic status to carry one. Though the state requires permits for concealed carry, it allows open carry without a permit, as long as the gun owners are eighteen years old and have nothing on their records to prevent them from carrying a firearm.

Page 62: Tiffany George, Carlie's mother and Tonka's sister . . . Tiffany George granted verbal permission to use her underage daughter's name in the anecdote before Karr's game against John Curtis at Behrman Stadium.

Page 64: Behrman Memorial Park . . . Behrman stadium was built in 1938 as part of the Works Progress Administration during the Great Depression. It's about a ten-minute drive by bus from the Karr campus, and it's only a few blocks from the cemetery where Tonka is buried. The stadium is run by the city of New Orleans, and it's long been the home of high school teams. Right now, Karr shares it with a rival school, Landry High. Behrman fell into disrepair as its neighborhood declined over the second half of the twentieth century. It's been the site of much gun violence—the first shooting there happened in 1979—but overall conditions have improved since 2011, when the Saints, in partnership with the NFL Youth Football Fund, helped renovate the premises.

Page 65: . . . from the Krewe of NOMTOC, a social club on the West Bank . . . Mardi Gras social clubs are a huge part of the festivities that happen every winter in New Orleans. They hold parades—Rex is the most famous parade held by a predominantly Black club—and balls. NOMTOC is one of the two Mardi Gras krewes to roll its parade on the West Bank. It's a predominantly Black krewe with more than five hundred members.

Page 65: . . . locals press cold drinks and smuggled-in beer cans . . . In certain parts of the country, it's a "soda" or a "pop"; in the author's home state of South Carolina, most every soft drink is referred to as a "Coke"; but in New Orleans, it's a "cold drink." New Orleans has no open container laws (unless people are in vehicles), so it's common to see someone walking down the street with a can of beer in hand. That said, it's frowned upon to take alcoholic beverages into bars, restaurants, or even stadiums from outside when they can be purchased within.

Chapter 3: Intersection

Page 73: . . . she'd sometimes drive him to an unfamiliar neighborhood, Slidell or the East, and demand he get out. She'd instruct him to find his way home. Nearly ten miles separate the Seventh Ward and far-flung New Orleans East. If Joe had the money for bus fare and the ability to find a stop, it would have taken him an hour to get home. Or he could have wound his way across the Industrial Canal and through the city on foot. Slidell, all the way across Lake Pontchartrain to the east, is even farther: thirty miles from the Seventh Ward and inaccessible by bus.

Page 75: . . . Katrina forced Keyoke and Joe to Houston. Katrina is considered to have caused the largest climate-driven migration since the Dust Bowl in the 1930s, and Houston was the most popular destination for displaced New Orleanians. It's estimated that about one hundred thousand evacuees to Houston had yet to return to the Crescent City a decade after the storm.

Page 75: . . . she'd teach Joe to never trust anyone wearing orange . . . The gang is extremely active in Houston and has turf throughout the city. It gained widespread attention in 2017, when a member shot two Houston police officers. Before the author's first visit to Cypress Park to interview Keyoke Thomas, Joe strongly encouraged the author to change out of a pair of orange shorts. But she didn't suspect the author was a possible gang member; instead, she repeatedly asked whether he was an undercover police detective. "You look like the people who locked me up," she said.

Page 75:... on the Gert Town corner of Olive and Fern Streets. This cross section is in Gert Town, which is nestled up against I-10 and is home to Xavier University, is a working-class neighborhood that is well known in New Orleans jazz history. Post-Katrina, it was slow to recover because of extreme flooding and has yet to reach its pre-Katrina population levels.

Page 79:... two additional "municipal attachments"... Roughly one in seven New Orleans residents has what is locally known as a "ghost warrant" out for their arrest—often with no idea why. So when someone is stopped for a traffic violation, for instance, that person can be jailed for years-old charges they weren't even aware they faced. Emily Lane and Greg LaRose, "WDSU Investigates: 'Ghost Warrants' Backlog Haunts Accused in New Orleans Municipal Court," WDSU-TV, Sept. 28, 2020.

Page 80:... in the Magnolia Projects in Central City... The Magnolia Projects were constructed in a low-income portion of Uptown in the 1940s and 1950s and were one of the largest projects in New Orleans, housing more than two thousand people. Magnolia is the home of many bounce and rap artists, including Juvenile, but it had become extremely violent and dilapidated by the 1980s. The city began gradual demolition in 1998, and by the time Katrina hit in 2005, Magnolia was largely empty. Since the storm, it's been redeveloped into Harmony Oaks, another low-income housing community.

Page 81:... he walked down Claiborne Avenue to the Superdome. Claiborne is one of New Orleans's largest arteries, bisecting the city and mimicking the curve of the Mississippi with its path; between the Tulane University area, Uptown, and downtown New Orleans, it cuts through Central City with a wide neutral ground where one can often find residents barbecuing, drinking, or simply gathering at all hours.

Page 92:... a bit more prestigious than Arkansas... There's very little science to college football programs recruiting a player or the players who select a school. Major choices often come down to familiarity and comfort with a coach or just how the program has done in recent years. When Jamie Vance decommitted from Arkansas, the Razorbacks were in the midst of a 2–10 season that would lead to the firing of head coach Chad Morris. Louisville, meanwhile, went 8–5 in 2019 before taking a major step back in coach Scott Satterfield's second season.

Page 93:... borrowing from Greedy Williams... Williams, who grew up in Shreveport, Louisiana, and attended Louisiana State, got his nickname not because he's a stingy defensive back, but because an aunt babysat him once as a memorably hungry infant. Jim Halley, "The Opening: LSU Commit Greedy Williams Has Formula for Success—and Great Nickname," *USA Today*, July 8, 2015.

Page 94:... looking for defensive leverages and mismatches... Brown speaks often about "leverages," usually inside or outside. This is football jargon that refers to a defensive back's positioning before the snap. "Inside leverage," for example, would be a stance that's a step closer to the inner part of the field, rather than lining up directly in front of a receiver. This can tip off any number of things, or nothing at all. In general, though, it signals the cornerback's guess that the play is heading toward the middle, or inside, part of the field and that he's willing to concede some terrain closer to the sideline.

Chapter 4: Sunken City

Page 99: . . . eight penalties, three fumbles, seven dropped passes. In the interest of transparency, the statistics referencing the fumbles and dropped passes differ from those posted by local media covering the John Curtis game. These were internal numbers collected by Karr coaches, and because the scene's context is their confrontations with players about these mistakes, the author opted to use the statistics being referenced.

Page 100: . . . an estimated 135,000 enslaved Africans were bought and sold in and around the French Quarter . . . Faimon A. Roberts III, "Efforts Underway to Mark New Orleans Sites Where Slaves Were Bought and Sold," Nola.com, May 5, 2018. Slave ships sailed into New Orleans, and though some men and women were purchased off the ships' decks at the port, most were taken to slave pens in the city. In 1829, it became illegal for traders to erect slave pens in the French Quarter, so they became prevalent around its edges. One of the most notorious was at the intersection of Esplanade Avenue and Chartres Street. The St. Louis Hotel, just southwest of the touristy Jackson Square, was the site of many slave auctions.

Page 100: . . . in 2015 it took police an average of an hour to dispatch an officer following a 911 call. "New Orleanians on Average Wait over 1 Hour for Police to Arrive," Nola.com, Oct. 27, 2015.

Page 100: . . . harsh emotional burdens that, in particular for children, can lead to higher risk of anxiety and depression. According to the psychologist and scholar Thomas A. Vance, research has begun suggesting that traumatic experiences actually cause biological change in some individuals and that some of those changes can be passed down through the generations. In other words, racism and trauma don't have to be experienced directly. This research suggests they can be inherited. Thomas A. Vance, "Addressing Mental Health in the Black Community," Columbia University Department of Psychiatry, Feb. 8, 2019. For further reading, see Greta Anderson, "The Emotional Toll of Racism," *Inside Higher Ed*, Oct. 23, 2020.

Page 100: . . . the median income in Black households . . . "Racial Wealth Divide in New Orleans," Prosperity Now, October 2016.

Page 101: Not in net worth or home ownership . . . An average Black family's net worth was $17,150 in 2016, while the average white family was worth $171,000. Kriston McIntosh, Emily Moss, Ryan Nunn, and Jay Shambaugh, "Examining the Black-White Wealth Gap," Brookings Institute, Feb. 27, 2020. Nearly three-quarters of white Americans own homes, compared with roughly four in ten Black Americans who own homes. Jung Hyun Choi, "Breaking Down the Black-White Homeownership Gap," Urban Institute, Urban Wire, Feb. 21, 2020.

Page 101: . . . not in admissions at top colleges or approvals on loan applications . . . Jonathan Rothwell, "Black Students at Top Colleges: Exceptions, Not the Rule," Brookings Institute, Feb. 3, 2015. Black borrowers have the highest rate of being denied for a mortgage loan, while white applicants represent the smallest percentage of those turned down. Tendayi Kapfidze, "LendingTree Analysis Reveals Mortgage Denials at Cycle Low," LendingTree, Oct. 7, 2019.

Page 101: . . . not in incarceration rates or even life expectancy. Black Americans are incarcerated in state prisons at five times the rate of whites. Ashley Nellis, "The Color of Justice: Racial and Ethnic Disparity in State Prisons," Sentencing Project, June 14, 2016. White males are expected to live nearly four years longer than Black males in the United States. Elizabeth Aria, "Changes in Life Expectancy by Race and Hispanic Origin in the United States, 2013–2014," Centers for Disease Control and Prevention, National Center for Health Statistics, Apr. 2016.

Page 103: The Wolves went 4–1 against the Cougars during that span. According to team schedules posted on MaxPreps.com, St. Paul's defeated Karr in 2010, 2011, 2013, and 2015 by an average margin of nearly nineteen points. Karr's only victory during this span came in 2013, when it won 34–12.

Page 105: . . . told him to line up in the "three-technique" . . . The "three-technique" is a relatively new responsibility for interior defensive linemen, and Warren Sapp made it famous while playing with the Tampa Bay Buccaneers in the early 2000s. Having an athletic and instinctive player such as Sapp control the line of scrimmage helped Tony Dungy and Monte Kiffin perfect their modified Cover 2, known as the "Tampa 2," and would eventually lead Sapp and Dungy to the Pro Football Hall of Fame.

Page 105: . . . nearly half of all college football players in the United States are Black while only about one in ten head coaches is an American of color. In 2020, 10.6 percent of all Division I football head coaches were a person of color, a slight increase from the 10.3 percent reported in 2019. Athletic directors and school leadership also tends to be overwhelmingly white, while 48.5 percent of all football players at the Football Bowl Subdivision level were Black. Richard E. Lapchick et al., "The 2020 Racial and Gender Report Card," Institute for Diversity and Ethics in Sport, Feb. 24, 2021.

Page 106: . . . brought home an America Online disc . . . During the dawn of the internet age in the mid-1990s, the pioneering company AOL actually mailed physical compact discs to people to get them to sign up for a trial period of internet use. This usually came in the form of a few hundred free hours, and by the turn of the twenty-first century, these free discs were everywhere: at stores, in newspapers and magazines, and as part of promotions at retailers and fast food restaurants.

Page 107: . . . walked in carrying a Sno-Ball . . . New Orleanians chafe at the confusion between their Sno-Balls and the snow cones the rest of the country consumes. Sno-Balls are made with much more finely shaved ice than snow cones, so they're lighter and fluffier and better able to keep the syrup from draining to the bottom of the dish. Sno-Ball season lasts from March to October.

Page 108: . . . DK Metcalf . . . Kent Babb, "DK Metcalf Went Viral for His Muscles. With Seahawks, He Has a Chance to Show More Range," *Washington Post*, July 25, 2019.

Page 110: . . . *Stand and Deliver* and *Dangerous Minds* . . . Both movies tell stories of teachers put in tough schools and forced to learn to cope.

Page 114: . . . notorious for his "Omaha" pre-snap . . . John Breech, "Retired Peyton Manning Finally Explains the True Meaning of His 'Omaha' Call," CBS Sports, Apr. 12, 2017.

Page 114: . . . has earned him a $17 million annual salary . . . Andrew Marchand, "NFL Analyst Tony Romo Agrees to $17M per Year to Stay at CBS," *New York Post*, Feb. 28, 2020.

Page 118: . . . a 53–6 record and outscored opponents by an average of twenty-four points . . . This is according to scores posted on MaxPreps.com.

Page 123: . . . Catholic High, an all-boys private school with $12,000-a-year tuition, fields a football team that's about 70 percent white. The $12,000 tuition figure comes from the admissions section of Catholic's official school website. The 70 percent white football team was an estimate by former head coach Gabe Fertitta. Not quite 3 percent of Catholic's student body is Black; its football alumni include Major Applewhite, Jeremy Steward, Derrius Guice, and Clyde Edwards-Helaire.

Page 123: . . . fans would see that Catholic has big, strong, fast athletes . . . After receiving questions about why he would schedule a team such as Karr, Fertitta tweeted the following on his personal account on September 26, 2019: "Honest ansr: I wanted ppl to get out of the old tired stereotypes. 'Cath is discplnd and well coached/Karr is fast and has great athletes.' People will [eyeballs emoji]. We have grt aths. Karr is extremely discplnd and well coached."

Page 123: . . . a horseshoe-shaped structure . . . Memorial Stadium is part of a nearly forty-five-acre complex right off Interstate 110 in downtown Baton Rouge, not far from the governor's mansion. It opened in 1952, and its seating capacity is 21,500 people.

Chapter 5: One Foot In

Page 133: . . . Guy Henderson Sr. had been gunned down . . . The spot where Guy Sr. was shot is just about a mile east of Karr's campus, on the 6400 block of Isadore Street. The NOPD spokesperson said at the time that the motive was a dispute over money, though media reports at the time suggest Guy Sr. had been gunned down in retaliation for his role in a robbery. Tara Young, "Robbery Led to Pal's Murder, Friend Says," *New Orleans Times-Picayune*, Apr. 3, 1999.

Page 134: . . . when his dad, Burnell, was stabbed near an intersection close to the Fischer Projects . . . The Fischer Projects were the last conventional housing projects built in New Orleans, in the mid-1960s. They consisted of one high-rise and fourteen mid-rise buildings. From almost the moment they opened, they were known for crime and violence. Drug use and sales were rampant, and the project became the scene of many high-profile murders. In the early 1980s, there were reports of a sniper stationed atop the Fischer high-rise, ready to fire at police. Things got so bad that public transit through the area had to cease at night.

Page 135: . . . as the state's number ten seed . . . The Gators ranked twenty-third . . . The seedings for both Karr and South Terrebonne High are from 2003 Louisiana state football playoff brackets found at www.14-0productions.com.

Page 135: . . . **South Terrebonne 24, Edna Karr 14.** The Karr loss was the biggest first-round upset of the 2003 playoffs.

Page 136: . . . **didn't return to Grambling after his freshman year.** Melvin Spears, Grambling's football coach when Guy Henderson played for the team, blamed poor grades as the reason Guy left school following his freshman year. Guy's obituary on Nola.com points out that he "briefly" attended the school before transferring to Southern University. Dan Lawton, "Aunt Suspects 'Set-Up' in Algiers Killing," Nola. com, Apr. 11, 2015.

Page 136: . . . **a 1997 project called Iridium** . . . Ambitious as it was, Motorola's $5 billion venture was a colossal failure. The project filed for bankruptcy in 1999 after it attracted only ten thousand subscribers for an early cell phone service that required $3,000 per handset and charged $5 per minute. Douglas A. McIntyre, "The 10 Biggest Tech Failures of the Last Decade," *TIME*, May 14, 2009.

Page 137: Bill Walsh used the "West Coast" offense to win three Super Bowls. Though it helped to have Joe Montana running his offense, Walsh used his pioneering pass-first attack to build the NFL's dynasty of the 1980s. His 49ers won Super Bowl XVI against the Cincinnati Bengals, Super Bowl XIX against the Miami Dolphins, and Super Bowl XXIII in a rematch against the Bengals.

Page 137: . . . **assistant coach for Doug Williams** . . . Starting for Washington, Williams was the first Black starting quarterback to lead a team to the Super Bowl. He was named most valuable player of Super Bowl XXII after Washington defeated the Denver Broncos, 42–10, following the 1987 season.

Page 137: . . . **helped Grambling win three consecutive Black college national championships.** It's technically true that in 2000, 2001, and 2002 Grambling can claim championships as the best football team among the nation's historically Black colleges and universities. But as many as six media organizations named a champion during this period, leading to debate over which program was actually the year's best. None was ever unanimous, and in 2000, more of the voting bodies selected Tuskegee (which finished the season 12–0) as national champion over Grambling (which went 10–2), whose designation came from only the American Sports Wire.

Page 139: . . . **Louisiana state championship game four years in a row.** Between 2010 and 2013, Karr appeared in the Class 4A title game every year. Its only championship during that span was its defeat of Neville in 2012, capping a perfect season for the Cougars and leading to Jabbar Juluke's leap to the college game.

Page 142: . . . **he could see Guy's blue Kia** . . . Dan Lawton, "Aunt Suspects 'Set-Up' in Algiers Killing," Nola.com, Apr. 11, 2015.

Page 145: . . . **occupies a demographic group that is more likely to suffer from depression and anxiety while being less likely to actually seek out professional help.** According to psychologist and scholar Thomas A. Vance, stigma is persistent in the Black community when it comes to mental health and seeking treatment. Adult Black Americans are 20 percent more likely to experience major depressive disorder or generalized anxiety disorder than white adults, but Vance writes that some Black adults refuse to discuss their thoughts with peers or seek out professional resources because many "believe that a mental health condition is a personal weakness." Thomas A. Vance, "Addressing Mental Health in the Black Community," Columbia University Department of Psychiatry, Feb. 8, 2019.

Chapter 6: Tulane and Broad

Page 151: "We've got a thirty" . . . The list of signals used by the New Orleans Police Department actually includes four possible designations for a "thirty." A "thirty-S," for instance, is a shooting, and a "thirty-D" would be for a killing in a domestic situation. New Orleans Police Department Operations Manual, "Police Complaint Signals and Dispositions," distributed by the NOPD and dated Jan. 14, 2018.

Page 151: . . . one of the victims refused to identify the gunmen . . . "Second Victim Identified in Edna Karr Shooting," Fox8Live.com, WVUE-TV, Feb. 2, 2017.

Page 152: . . . Gregory Neupert drove his cruiser into the Fischer Projects. The "Algiers 7" case has been extensively written about and analyzed for four decades, but details used in this book primarily came from news accounts during the ordeal's immediate aftermath along with look-back pieces that examined the long-term fallout. "7 Officers Indicted in New Orleans," *New York Times*, July 10, 1981; "Timeline: NOPD's Long History of Scandal," PBS *Frontline*, Law & Disorder; "City to Pay $2.8 million for 'Algiers 7' Violence," United Press International, Apr. 2, 1986.

Page 152: But a New Orleans judge threw out criminal charges . . . Brendan McCarthy, "Infamous Algiers 7 Police Brutality Case of 1980 Has Parallels to Today," *New Orleans Times-Picayune*, Nov. 7, 2010.

Page 154: . . . sipping his Martell straight. Martell is a brand of cognac.

Page 154: . . . cleared 38 percent of his cases. Of the NOPD detectives with ten or more cases as the lead detective between 2015 and 2017, Rayell Johnson's 38 percent clearance rate ranked fifth among the department's nineteen homicide investigators. Those were particularly challenging years for homicide, and though clearing just over a third of Johnson's twenty-four cases may seem low, it was actually above average for the unit. Debra Normand led the division with 45 percent of her cases solved. "The Trace Obtained Data on 4.3 Million Violent Crimes from 50+ Police and Sheriff's Departments," The Trace.

Page 154: . . . that makes an arrest in only one in three murders . . . Those numbers aren't improving, either. In 2020, the city's murder rate spiked after four years of improvement, and that November, murder arrests were down 16 percent compared with the previous year. Kimbriell Kelly, "In a Home Surrounded by Homicide," *Washington Post*, Nov. 16, 2018.

Page 154: . . . had the second-highest murder rate in the US . . . Kate Abbey-Lambertz, "These Are the Major U.S. Cities with the Highest Murder Rates, According to the FBI," *Huffpost*, Nov. 12, 2014.

Page 154: . . . the murder rate among Black male New Orleanians . . . Jeff Asher, "The Demographics of Murder in New Orleans," NOLA Crime News, June 14, 2016.

Page 156: . . . Apple and law enforcement agencies were battling over privacy rights. The dispute began after a December 2015 mass shooting in San Bernardino, California. The FBI petitioned Apple to help the bureau gain access to the shooter's phone so it could learn more about the shooter's and his wife's actions before and after the crime. Apple argued that it would have to write new software in order to do so and that being forced to would violate its due process.

Page 156: A murder in broad daylight . . . Johnson's case wasn't even that unique. According to the Orleans Parish Coroner's Office, NOPD, and Nola.com, there were at least four murders in broad daylight in New Orleans East alone that summer.

Page 157: . . . **a thirty-six-year-old father of ten shot dead in Algiers** . . . That case was solved; a man was charged in 2018 for committing the murder, a woman in 2017 as an accessory.

Page 157: . . . **a triple shooting near Behrman Stadium.** The NOPD had an easier time with this case, which was a shootout that left two dead and one shooter injured. That shooter, a nineteen-year-old former Grambling State student, was charged with second-degree murder after a bloody series of events that left his cousin dead. According to the surviving shooter, he'd been shot at while driving, and he and his cousin had then driven to the home of the men he suspected. That's where the triple shooting occurred.

Page 157: . . . **more than twice the workload** . . . The Bureau of Justice Assistance, a watchdog agency, recommends homicide detectives take on no more than six new cases each year. The BJA commissioned a report on the NOPD homicide division in 2010, which also recommended the department staff thirty-two homicide detectives. In recent years, the actual number has been about half that.

Page 157: . . . **detectives gave up tracking their scant closures on the whiteboard** . . . Ken Daley, "'We Are Completely Broken,' NOPD Detective Says of Struggling Homicide Unit," Nola.com, Apr. 14, 2017.

Page 157: Since 2013, when a consent decree . . . A consent decree is a court-enforceable agreement between two parties that solves a dispute without an admission of guilt. In the case of the NOPD, it resolved the Department of Justice's findings in an investigation into the department, which found that the NOPD had engaged in unconstitutional conduct. Under the decree, the NOPD agreed to reform. The Department of Justice press release announcing the decree on January 11, 2013, stated: "This order is a critical milestone in reforming the long-troubled NOPD and is an important step in dealing with the public safety crisis in New Orleans and in restoring community confidence in the New Orleans criminal justice system."

Page 157: . . . **the death of Henry Glover** . . . In total, five officers were charged in the Glover murder, and none was arrested until 2010. David Warren faced the most serious charges. The two officers who assaulted Glover's relatives and burned Glover's body were also arrested, as were two others who were charged with obstructing justice and lying to the FBI. Three officers—Warren; Gregory McRae, the officer who drove Glover's car to the levee; and Travis McCabe, who helped cover up the crimes—were convicted. Two were acquitted. Warren's conviction was overturned by an appeal. McRae was sentenced to seventeen years in prison, which was eventually reduced to eleven years and nine months. In spring 2021 he remained incarcerated. McCabe was also granted a retrial, but before it could happen, a judge dismissed all the charges against him.

Page 157: . . . **$55 million bill to taxpayers.** Emily Lane, "'Substantial Work' Remains on NOPD Consent Decree, Feds Tell City in Tense Letter Exchange," Nola.com, Jan. 11, 2019.

Page 158: Leon Cannizzaro, the city's district attorney . . . Cannizzaro announced in July 2020 that he would not be seeking a third term. He had served as the Orleans Parish district attorney since 2008.

Page 158: . . . **overspent its overtime budget and paused new hiring.** Mike Perlstein, "Still Not Enough? NOPD Faces Uphill Battle to Meet Hiring Goals," WWL-TV, 2016 [no date].

Page 158: The NOPD had no crime lab . . . Hurricane Katrina destroyed the city's crime lab. A new one was slated to open in the fall of 2021.

Page 158: . . . **attended autopsies in a fire-damaged former funeral parlor** . . . Pathologists at the facility worked out of a trailer, and the ventilation system caused the smell of decomposition to spread through the building and surrounding neighborhood. A new facility opened in 2016. Jim Mustian, "Left with a Decomposing, Neglected Agency, Orleans Parish Coroner Said He Wants to 'Right the Ship from Years Past,'" Nola.com, May 18, 2015.

Page 158: An average of ten cops a month left the force . . . "New Orleans Police Pay Increase Is Attempt to Stop 'Terrible' Attrition Rate," WVUE-TV, July 6, 2017.

Page 158: . . . **in a city of 390,000 residents and 175 homicides.** The NOPD's official number for that year is 174. It does not count the unborn child of a woman who was murdered in November 2016 when she was nine months pregnant. The local paper counts the child in its stats because it was of a viable age. Regardless, the murder total for 2016 was the city's highest since 2012.

Page 164: . . . **Shaun Ferguson, the NOPD superintendent and Algerine** . . . Though Ferguson attended high school in Algiers, he was raised in the Lower Ninth Ward before moving there.

Page 165: . . . **Mayor LaToya Cantrell, who succeeded Landrieu** . . . Members of Cantrell's communications team initially agreed to make her available for an interview for this book before failing to respond to follow-up requests.

Page 165: . . . **unveiled her own fifty-year crime plan.** "Mayor Cantrell Releases 'A Generational Gun Violence Reduction Plan,'" City of New Orleans and the Office of Mayor LaToya Cantrell, Aug. 20, 2019.

Page 167: . . . **ended its contract with** *The First 48* . . . Mike Scott, "New Orleans Ending Contracts with A&E's 'First 48' and 'Nightwatch'; Here's What to Know," Nola.com, June 2, 2016.

Chapter 7: Hitch

Page 171: . . . **had been married since 2003** . . . According to a wedding announcement in the *New Orleans Times-Picayune*, Trent Washington Sr. and the former Gwendolyn Alexander were married in November 2003.

Page 171: . . . **Trent Sr., is a bus driver** . . . This is according to a LinkedIn profile associated with Trent Washington Sr. He did not reply to repeated attempts to reach him for an interview.

Page 174: . . . eventually led him to Louisiana College. Louisiana College is a D-III Baptist School in Pineville, Louisiana. Thompson graduated in 2014.

Page 174: . . . family's home in nearby Gretna . . . Gretna is just upriver (that's southwest) from Algiers.

Page 175: . . . near a Family Dollar, a struggle ensued . . . Michelle Hunter, "Man Shot During Attempted Carjacking in Terrytown Friday Night: JPSO," Nola.com, Aug. 26, 2019.

Page 176: . . . charged Trent with attempted second-degree murder . . . Michelle Hunter, "In Terrytown Robbery and Shooting, DA's Office Charges 16-Year-Old Suspect as Adult," Nola.com, Oct. 8, 2019.

Page 176: Karr's players and coaches would claim they were unaware when this second domino fell . . . Though the coaching staff, Trent's teammates, and the school pled ignorance, Trent's name had been attached to the crime in news reports for more than a week. He'd been arrested and charged on October 3, 2019, and the *Times-Picayune* reported as much on October 8.

Page 177: . . . the rapper Lil Wayne went there . . . "Lil Wayne Goes Back to Former High School," *XXL*, Feb. 21, 2008.

Page 177: . . . and subsequent release on bail . . . This is according to Gwen Washington.

Page 178: . . . Mustangs his stress ball . . . McMain High would go 2–8 in 2019.

Page 178: . . . passes to a sophomore and junior who rarely participated. Junior wide receiver Vernon Fulton and sophomore Edwin Joseph each caught touchdown passes in Karr's 44–0 win against McMain.

Page 179: . . . Gwen would recall Trent insisting . . . Gwen Washington conducted two on-the-record telephone interviews for this book, totaling about an hour. Asked directly for permission to use her underage son's name and descriptions of his legal entanglements, Gwen said, "Absolutely." She did not make Trent available for an interview.

Page 180: . . . there was a silver car waiting. This and other details of the shooting that involved the young woman are attributable to the Major Offense Log of the NOPD's superintendent from October 18 and 19, 2019. Though her name was not included in this report, additional information was present that could potentially identify her. Because she was underage at the time of the incidents, along with the highly sensitive nature of these events, the author made the editorial decision to omit some details from the narrative.

Page 182: . . . against cross-town rival Landry-Walker. Amid the national protests in the weeks following the murder of George Floyd, the Algiers Charter Schools Association announced it would drop the name of former superintendent Oliver Perry Walker, who supported school segregation before his death in 1968. The school was renamed L. B. Landry High School, after Dr. Lord Beaconsfield Landry, and was the first school in Louisiana to be named for a Black person. "Landry-Walker Drops Walker from School Name After Vote," WWL-TV, July 31, 2020.

Chapter 8: Homecoming

Page 188: . . . Joe looked so much like Ms. Diane's son . . . In New Orleans, it's common for people to call their elders by a prefix—Ms. for women and Mr. for men—and then their first name.

Page 188: . . . (a Louisiana prison system trying to decompress its notoriously overcrowded facilities). In 2017, more than thirty-five thousand people were incarcerated in Louisiana prisons, many of them for drug offenses passed down from the antiquated "War on Drugs," and the overwhelming majority of them were Black. In fact, though Louisiana's population is only one-third Black, its *prison* population is two-thirds Black. In 2019, the American Civil Liberties Union challenged Louisiana to cut its prison population in half by 2025. Grace Toohey, "Could Louisiana Slash Prison Population in Half by 2025? It Could Happen, ACLU Says; Here's How," *The Advocate*, Apr. 5, 2019.

Page 190: . . . the six hundred thousand Americans released from prisons each year . . . In addition, about 9 million people cycle through jails every year, and on any given day, about 6.9 million Americans are in prison, in jail, on parole, or on probation. "Incarceration & Reentry," US Department of Health and Human Services website, Office of the Assistant Secretary for Planning and Evaluation.

Page 190: . . . among the 27 percent of formerly incarcerated people who are unemployed . . . These numbers come from the Prison Policy Initiative and cite statistics from 2008, the most recent year in which unemployment numbers for the formerly incarcerated are available. Unemployment peaked during the Great Depression at 25 percent, and during the first full month of the COVID-19 pandemic in 2020, it surged to 14.7 percent—still far lower than that of formerly incarcerated people. Looking at the segment of the population aged thirty-five through forty-four, formerly incarcerated white men have the best employment numbers—only 18.4 percent of them were out of work in the 2008 report—compared with Black women, who have a 43.6 percent unemployment rate. Lucius Couloute and Daniel Kopf, "Out of Prison & Out of Work: Unemployment Among Formerly Incarcerated People," Prison Policy Initiative, July 2018.

Page 190: . . . women face greater risk of mental health disorders than men . . . Aleks Kajstura, "Women's Mass Incarceration: The Whole Pie 2019," Prison Policy Initiative, Oct. 29, 2019.

Page 190: . . . during the first months after release, are at an elevated risk of major depressive episodes and suicidal thoughts. Doris J. James and Lauren E. Glaze, "Mental Health Problems of Prison and Jail Inmates," Bureau of Justice Special Report, September 2006.

Chapter 9: One Foot Out

Page 205: . . . it hammered Karr, 27–6, for Neville's tenth state title. According to 14-0 Productions (www.14-0productions.com), Neville was the top seed in the 2011 playoff bracket in Class 4A. Karr was No. 7 and pulled upsets of St. Thomas More and Lutcher en route to the championship game. That marked the second straight year Karr had lost in the state title game. The previous season, with Tonka at quarterback, it fell to Franklinton, 34–28, in overtime.

Page 205: . . . it was Karr that hoisted the championship trophy. The final score of that game was 29–22.

Page 207: . . . during the long trip to Wossman High . . . That game was a 41–28 Karr victory.

Page 208: . . . **fund-raising efforts such as a fish fry** . . . Fund-raisers haven't all gone off without controversy. In 2019, the school held a fish fry to benefit athletics programs during school hours. According to *Big Easy Magazine*, for $10, students could purchase a plate with fried fish, potato salad, macaroni and cheese, peas, and cake. Students who couldn't afford to purchase a plate or didn't want to were told they'd be able to have a regular school lunch—but the school's cafeteria workers were tied up with the fund-raiser, so those students got one slice of turkey between two pieces of bread and a few carrots. InspireNOLA spoke out against the fish fry, calling it unauthorized, and condemned the fund-raiser. Jenn Bentley, "Inspire NOLA Issues Apology After Edna Karr Fish Fry Fiasco," *Big Easy Magazine*, Mar. 21, 2019.

Page 210: Saints coach Sean Payton . . . knew Brown's name. In February 2017, Brown was honored as the Saints' coach of the year nominee and sat next to Payton during a ceremony at an Italian restaurant in Metairie. "Sean Payton, New Orleans Saints Honor Local High School Coaches," NewOrleansSaints.com.

Page 210: . . . **Racey McMath, a star wide receiver.** McMath played in all of LSU's games in 2019 and 2020, his junior and senior seasons, winning a national title following the 2019 season.

Page 211: . . . **return to Ronnie's side.** Ronnie would never play at the University of Texas–San Antonio. By fall camp in 2019, his freshman year, he was enrolled at Nicholls State. He redshirted that season, and Nicholls's 2020 season was canceled because of the coronavirus pandemic.

Page 214: . . . **Black parochial school in New Orleans's Seventh Ward.** This means St. Augustine High is operated by the Archdiocese of New Orleans.

Page 215: . . . **and national media outlets reported on it** . . . In addition to being heavily covered by local media, the video of a St. Aug football assistant coach leading a pregame chant that included the N-word—and the subsequent firing of three coaches—led to stories in the *New York Post, USA Today*, and ABC News.

Page 215: . . . **a wrongful termination and defamation lawsuit** . . . After the dismissal of Nathaniel Jones's lawsuit, the author requested an interview with Jones for this book. His attorney, Willie Sanders Sr., acknowledged the request via email but did not make Jones available. Chris Slaughter, "Federal Judge Dismisses Suit Filed Against St. Augustine High School by Fired Football Coach," WDSU-TV, Aug. 7, 2020.

Page 218: . . . **Noel Ellis Jr., a twenty-five-year-old former high school All-American** . . . Ellis played at Karr under Brown's predecessor, Jabbar Juluke, and went on to play cornerback at Texas A&M. He'd been coaching at Warren Easton since graduating college.

Page 222: . . . **his biological father, from whom Fat is estranged.** Fat's full name, which he used throughout the 2019 season and the reporting of this book, was Destyn Pazon, which he shared with his father. But during the 2020 season, he asked local media to identify him as Destyn Hill, the surname of his grandfather, Gregory Hill. It's unclear whether he legally changed his name. Christopher Dabe, "Dabe: Karr Wideout Destyn Hill Wants to Make His Grandfather Proud; Then He'll Choose Between LSU and 4 Other Schools," Nola.com, Dec. 26, 2020.

Page 224: . . . **the Mississippi Mass Choir's mighty soloist, Mosie Burks** . . . The

Mississippi Mass Choir is a gospel choir based in Jackson, Mississippi, and has been releasing music since 1988. Inez Andrews is credited with writing "I'm Not Tired Yet" and, with her gospel group The Caravans, recording it in 1958.

Chapter 10: Penumbra

Page 227: . . . its lowest ranking since 2015. Karr was the number one seed in 2018 and 2017. In 2016 it was the number two seed, and in 2015 it was the number fourteen seed—though it made it all the way to the state title game before losing to Neville.

Page 227: . . . on the north side of Lake Pontchartrain . . . Mandeville, where Lakeshore is located, is 92 percent white and only 5 percent Black. Median household income there is $52,500, compared with $37,468 in New Orleans.

Page 227: . . . stomped opponents by nearly thirty-two points per game. This average comes from scores posted on Lakeshore football's official website.

Page 228: . . . when Karr upset Franklinton? That was the third upset of Karr's 2015 run. As a fourteenth-seeded team, it beat number three seed Cecilia in the second round, number eleven seed Bastrop in the quarterfinals, and then finally number ten seed Franklinton to get to the state title game.

Page 228: Remember "Big Cat"? The Big Cat drill was born during the Les Miles years at LSU, and it continues as a tradition at the school today.

Page 229: . . . a history professor with a doctorate from Tulane. Clyde Robertson is now the director of the Center for African and African American Studies at Southern University.

Page 230: . . . such as *The Mis-Education of the Negro* and *Countering the Conspiracy to Destroy Black Boys* . . . Both books cover educational issues facing Black students. *The Mis-Education of the Negro*, published in 1933, puts forth the theory that Black students are indoctrinated in schools and taught to seek out inferior social status. Written fifty years later, *Countering the Conspiracy to Destroy Black Boys* is a kind of guide to raising Black boys.

Page 230: . . . 145-mph winds and dumping 2.3 trillion gallons of rainwater . . . Peggy Mihelich, "Storm Surge the Fatal Blow for New Orleans," CNN, Sept. 7, 2005. Jason Samenow, "No-Name Storm Dumped Three Times as Much Rain in Louisiana as Hurricane Katrina," *Washington Post*, Aug. 19, 2016.

Page 230: . . . an upper-middle-class Black enclave . . . Jennifer Larino, "8 Reasons Why New Orleans Neighborhoods Remain Segregated," Nola.com, Apr. 6, 2018.

Page 230: . . . as a result of *lowering* the terrain . . . Richard Campanella, "How Humans Sank New Orleans," *The Atlantic*, Feb. 6, 2018.

Page 231: . . . believed to sit between eight and twelve feet below sea level. New Orleans East contains some of the lowest points in the city, dipping to more than ten feet below sea level. The ground along Lake Pontchartrain there is extremely low, with just a tiny sliver of land above sea level next to a giant body of water. Just to the west, across the Industrial Canal, blocks and blocks of high ground separate more affluent pockets of the city from the lake.

Page 231: . . . federal government had largely left New Orleans for dead. Chris Edwards, "Hurricane Katrina: Remembering the Federal Failures," CATO Institute, Aug. 27, 2015.

Page 231: The Robertsons rebuilt on the same tract they'd called home for years. According to a 2014 paper by Narayan Sastry, a population studies scientist, about 53 percent of New Orleanians had returned to the city a year after Katrina. Less than one-third of those people were living in their pre-Katrina homes. Breaking down that total number of returnees by race, only 44 percent of African Americans returned within a year, compared with 67 percent of the rest of the population.

Page 231: . . . recommissioned as a citywide charter school . . . After Katrina, New Orleans completely reconfigured its public school system, transitioning to a charter school model. Karr was one of the first schools to reopen after the storm, and its rigorous admissions standards were no more.

Page 232: Shak introduced Omari to fellow defensive back Jordan Sullen . . . Shak Smith and Sullen played together for Tulane, a fifteen-minute drive across the river and uptown from Karr. Shak jokes now that his accent was so thick that Sullen acted as his "translator" while at Tulane, especially when communicating with white teammates. Sullen went on to play briefly in the NFL, for the Bears and Steelers.

Page 233: . . . would later be named team captains at Karr. Omari, Shak, and Jordan all played at Karr under head coach Jabbar Juluke. Pride Panel hadn't yet been established, nor were the high-pressure captains' "campaigns" that now take place during summer training camp.

Page 238: Karr makes easy work of Cecelia . . . Karr won the game, 49–21.

Page 238: . . . Kenilworth Mall had been shuttered. Melinda Daffin, "More Dead Shopping Centers in New Orleans: Vintage Photos," Nola.com, Dec. 29, 2016.

Page 239: The Fischer Housing Development, the grisly site . . . The city had begun demolishing housing projects before Katrina. Part of Fischer was imploded in 2004.

Page 239: . . . the author and academic James K. Glassman wrote in January 2006. Glassman wrote those words in a *Wall Street Journal* op-ed, and he wasn't the only person who framed Katrina as a rebuilding opportunity for the city.

Page 239: . . . handed out free food and tobacco. Carl Nolte, "The Great Quake: 1906–2006 / Rising from the Ashes," SFGATE, Apr. 18, 2006.

Page 239: . . . the city council voted unanimously to tear down . . . Adam Nossiter and Leslie Eaton, "New Orleans Council Votes for Demolition of Housing," *New York Times*, Dec. 21, 2007.

Page 239: . . . pepper sprayed and Tasered. Jenny Jarvie, "A Fury in New Orleans as Housing Demolition OKd," *Los Angeles Times*, Dec. 21, 2007.

Page 239: . . . locked out of their homes, prohibited from retrieving their belongings . . . Roberta Brandes Gratz, "Who Killed Public Housing in New Orleans?" *The Nation*, June 2, 2015.

Page 239: If vouchers were honored at all by landlords . . . Pam Fessler, "After Katrina, New Orleans' Public Housing Is a Mix of Pastel and Promises," NPR, *Morning Edition*, Aug. 17, 2015.

Page 239: . . . rents were on average 35 percent higher . . . David Schrayer, *New Orleans Affordable Housing Assessment: Lessons Learned*, July 2007.

Page 240: . . . Keyon was a senior who entered the game with eleven touchdown

catches. Ken Trahan, "Karr Faces Rematch with Carver," *Crescent City Sports*, Nov. 16, 2017.

Page 241: . . . Skyler Perry, Karr's quarterback and Brown's protégé, hit Anthony Spurlock . . . Hank Brady, "Karr 40, Carver 35: Anthony Spurlock Grabs Winning TD as Cougars Withstand 21-Point Rams Rally," Nola.com, Nov. 18, 2017.

Page 241: . . . the Pelicans' surprising win in the NBA draft lottery. The Pelicans had just a 6 percent chance of winning the top pick in the NBA draft lottery that year.

Page 241: . . . headed to a playground in Metairie . . . Metairie is a mostly white suburb that lies just to the west of the city of New Orleans.

Page 241: Keyon and Darrell "DJ" Clark . . . DJ had also been a prep football star in New Orleans and was supposed to play his senior season that fall. He missed 2019, and Grambling did not play a season in 2020 because of the coronavirus pandemic. DJ was on Grambling's roster for its shortened spring 2021 schedule.

Page 242: Keyon Clark died . . . Ramon Antonio Vargas, "Grambling Player Wounded, His Brother Killed in Triple Shooting in Jefferson Parish," Nola.com, June 20, 2019.

Page 242: . . . Jefferson Parish Sheriff's Office deputies approached a suspect . . . Danny Monteverde, "Questions Linger for Family After JPSO Deputies Kill Man in Metairie," WWL-TV, July 18, 2019.

Page 245: . . . noticed Carver in Cover 1 man-free . . . In Cover 1 man-free, defenders are in man-to-man coverage, and a free safety covers the center of the field.

Chapter 11: Crabs in a Bucket

Page 255: . . . the $4.1 billion college sports industry . . . *USA Today* released that number in April 2020, and it covers only the fifty-three public schools in the Power Five conferences. Steve Berkowitz, "Major Public College Football Programs Could Lose Billions in Revenue If No Season Is Played," *USA Today*, Apr. 14, 2020.

Page 255: . . . Leonard—smart and talented but undersized at five foot ten . . . Though Nicholls State would list him at six feet one, this is an extremely generous description of Leonard's height.

Page 255: . . . more than ten thousand new players join nearly seven hundred college football teams . . . According to Next College Student Athlete, an organization that helps athletes navigate the occasionally complex recruiting process, there are in fact 893 colleges and universities that offer football. That's an increase of more than 120 programs just in the past few years. While roster size varies, a different report in 2016 estimated that seventy thousand players participate throughout the expansive college football landscape. "Number of Colleges and Universities Offering Football Reaches All-Time High of 774," National Football Foundation and College Hall of Fame, June 14, 2016.

Page 257: The coach told him to remain calm . . . Ronnie Jackson is describing a conversation he said he had with Frank Wilson, his former head coach at the University of Texas–San Antonio. Wilson graduated from St. Augustine High School, went on to play at Nicholls, and has coached since then. He worked his way up from coaching high schools in New Orleans to the Power Five, and he made his name as LSU's running backs coach and recruiting coordinator. His reputation for swaying top players earned him his first collegiate head coaching job, at UTSA, but he was fired the winter after Ronnie went home after a 4–8 season. A month later, he took the head coaching job at McNeese State. The author attempted to interview Wilson and collect his side of the story involving Ronnie Jackson, but neither Wilson nor McNeese athletics spokesman Matthew Bonnette responded to multiple messages.

Page 262: . . . Nick Saban has won seven national championships . . . In January 2021, Alabama defeated Ohio State for Saban's seventh title, pushing him past legendary Crimson Tide coach Paul "Bear" Bryant for most all-time.

Page 262: "Houston is, probably—I would say probably—four conferences underneath them." Playing in the American Athletic Conference, Houston is one of the top programs among the Group of Five conferences, one (unofficial) level below the Power Five.

Chapter 12: Little Shit

Page 267: . . . first ten passes in a 51–14 victory. Against Breaux Bridge, Karr scored more points than it had in any game all season but one. In fact, it hadn't scored so many points in a playoff game since it put fifty-four on Buckeye in the first round in 2017.

Page 268: . . . 26–24, then got the final defensive stop. There wasn't much media coverage of Neville's quarterfinal victory against Westgate, so these details come from a telephone interview with Westgate coach Ryan Antoine.

Page 270: . . . Ouachita Parish's population is nearly two-thirds white . . . In 2019, the US Census Bureau reported that the parish was 59.6 percent white and 37.7 percent Black.

Page 270: . . . Florida State University found that Monroe was the thirteenth-most-segregated city in the United States. In fact, the Florida State University study found that only three cities in the South are more segregated than Monroe: Birmingham-Hoover, Alabama; Gadsden, Alabama; and Beaumont–Port Arthur, Texas. John R. Logan and Brian J. Stults, "The Persistence of Segregation in the Metropolis: New Findings from the 2010 Census," US2010 Project, Mar. 24, 2011.

Page 271: They mill rice and make aluminum . . . Louisiana is one of six states that produces the majority of the 8.9 million metric tons of rice produced each year in the United States. Kennedy Rice, a manufacturer in northeast Ouachita Parish, converts more than 136,000 metric tons per year of rough rice into polished white rice. Sapa Extrusions, which manufactures products that include aluminum sliding doors and football stadium seats, is in nearby Delhi, Louisiana.

Page 271: . . . send conservative politicians to the state house and US Capitol. In the most recent election for state representative, Monroe voters didn't even have a Democrat on the ballot.

Page 271: . . . five times less likely to be enrolled in gifted and talented courses . . . According to a consent decree issued in 2015, only 5.5 percent of the school district's 7,306 Black students were enrolled in gifted and talented courses, compared with 30.2 percent of the district's 1,011 white students. The court's filing also found that predominantly white schools in Monroe offered far more college-preparatory classes than predominantly Black ones; Black students had nowhere near an equal opportunity to enroll. *Andrews and US v. Monroe City School Board—Second Amended Consent Decree*, US Department of Justice, Civil Rights Division, July 12, 2016.

Page 271: . . . NFL quarterback Bubby Brister. A Neville grad, Brister played college ball at Northeast Louisiana (now the University of Louisiana–Monroe). He went on to play fifteen seasons in the NFL for the Steelers, Eagles, Jets, Broncos, Vikings, and Chiefs.

Page 272: . . . scheduled the game against Wossman . . . Wossman is in the predominantly Black southeast section of Monroe, and in that 2016 Department of Justice report, it was often used as a foil for Neville in terms of student opportunity.

Page 273: . . . NOW/RPO IS 2ND PRIORITY . . . RPO stands for "run-pass option," and it's a play in which the quarterback has both a run and a passing option he can choose between, depending on how the play unfolds. The term has become extremely popular in the NFL and in college football in recent seasons. But the RPO was born in high school ball and worked its way up the ranks.

Page 274: . . . must release it in 2.3 seconds . . . That's as fast as the best NFL quarterbacks get rid of the ball. In 2020, Ben Roethlisberger led the league with an average release time of 2.29 seconds.

Page 274: TAKE CHANCES IN JET FORMATION. Jet formation is when players line up for a jet sweep play, where a wide receiver runs parallel to the line of scrimmage, receiving the ball via a pitch or handoff from the quarterback.

Page 275: . . . festooned with eighteen championship and runner-up banners. Neville has won a dozen state championships, the most recent of which came in 2015, which it won against Karr. The next year, Karr got revenge and added that sixth runner-up banner to the stadium fence.

Page 275: . . . just approved the construction of a massive video scoreboard . . . Zach Parker, "MCSB to Buy $558,000 Scoreboard for Neville," *Ouchita Citizen*, Sept. 18, 2019.

Page 281: Tikey Reese, a senior defensive tackle . . . Reese signed to play college football at Southern University a few months after this game.

Page 281: "Fuck them boys on three." This comes from video footage posted on GSportz, the Louisiana prep sports outlet, collected by Jeremiah Gray.

Chapter 13: Good Luck

Page 290: . . . an agonizing choice: pay out of pocket for expensive medication, or deal with other financial responsibilities . . . Howard LeWine, "Millions of Adults Skip Medications Due to Their High Cost," Harvard Health Publishing, Harvard Medical School, Jan. 30, 2015.

Page 292: . . . quarterback Stephen Banford Jr. abruptly, and surprisingly, told coaches he'd be transferring . . . After transferring from Easton to Belle Chasse High, where Banford played his sophomore season, he again transferred to nearby Shaw High. Garland Gillen, "Warren Easton QB Dayshawn Holmes Easing into Elevated Role Ahead of Rematch with Edna Karr," WVUE-TV, Aug. 15, 2020.

Page 292: . . . Lance LeGendre's star turn . . . LeGendre was one of three quarterbacks whose senior years were featured in season three of Netflix's *QB1: Beyond the Lights*.

By the time the show aired, LeGendre had enrolled at Maryland, where he's been a backup quarterback since 2019.

Page 292: . . . head coach Jerry Phillips . . . Easton coach Phillips graduated from Karr in 1996 and won two basketball state championships there.

Page 294: . . . team lunch at Boomtown Casino . . . The Boomtown Casino is just that: a casino and hotel in an industrial neighborhood on the West Bank, far from the lights of Bourbon Street and New Orleans's downtown Harrah's.

Page 299: . . . All-American Devante "Speedy" Noil highlighted . . . Noil is perhaps the biggest star to come out of Karr since Juluke and Brown modernized its offense and turned the team into a Louisiana power. ESPN's recruiting rankings pegged Noil, at six feet tall and 161 pounds, as the nation's seventh-best player in the 2014 class, which also included such phenoms as Deshaun Watson, Dalvin Cook, and fellow New Orleanian Leonard Fournette. Noil played for Texas A&M but was undrafted and briefly played in the Canadian Football League and the short-lived Alliance of American Football.

Page 299: . . . lost to East Jefferson . . . East Jefferson had never made the title game before that season. It was the number four seed in the Class 4A tournament bracket, and Karr was the number two seed.

Page 304: . . . the sixth-ranked senior in Louisiana. ESPN listed Easton running back Ashaad Clayton as the state's sixth-best player in the class of 2020.

Page 307: . . . practicing one play under center would just confuse players. Fans at all levels of football express dismay when their favorite team, needing one yard, lines up in the shotgun formation—with the quarterback and running back about four yards behind the line of scrimmage. Plays under center are much closer to the line, and the center puts the ball directly into the quarterback's hands rather than tossing it to him from between his legs. When the objective is to chew clock and be conservative, that appears to make more sense. But the truth is, experience and comfort are major factors in success on the football field. In this case, Karr's offense was accustomed to its quarterback lining up in the shotgun, and Brown believed asking players to line up in an unfamiliar formation might have caused them to tense up and make a game-changing mistake. It was a risk, to be sure, but lining up under center would have been one as well.

Page 318: A double shooting near Karr's home stadium . . . The shooting took place just about five blocks from the entrance to the park where Karr plays its football games. Both victims were hospitalized.

Page 318: Their dad died tonight. "Ethridge Foster Obituary, 1954–2019," *New Orleans Times-Picayune*, Dec. 25, 2019.

Epilogue

Page 321: . . . with two bullets in his head. Matt Sledge, "Man Sought for Questioning in New Year's Eve Slaying," Nola.com, Mar. 5, 2020.

Page 321: . . . the year's 120nd, and last, person to be shot dead . . . Ramon Antonio Vargas, "New Orleans 2019 Murder Total Increases to 120 After 1 Victim Left Off Initial NOPD Tally," Nola.com, Feb. 5, 2020.

Page 321: . . . whose murder tally was the lowest since 1971 . . . Chris McCrory,

"New Orleans Sees Lowest Murder Total in Nearly 50 Years for 2019," WWL-TV, Dec. 31, 2019.

Page 321: **Seven of the city's eight police districts would report fewer murders.** Emily Lane, "New Orleans Murders in 2019: Explore a Map of the Killings," WDSU-TV, Mar. 28, 2020.

Page 321: **The only one where shooting deaths remained on the rise . . .** Emily Lane, "New Orleans Murders in 2019: What the Data Tells Us," WDSU-TV, Feb. 13, 2020.

Page 321: **. . . the United States' fourth-highest murder rate . . .** Ramon Antonio Vargas, "New Orleans Was Fourth-Deadliest U.S. City in 2019. Here's What 2020 Ranking Could Look Like," Nola.com, Sept. 29, 2020.

Page 322: **. . . the expiration of the city's consent decree . . .** Rob Masson, "NOPD Discusses End of Consent Decree in 2020," WVUE-TV, Dec. 20, 2019.

Page 322: **. . . declared a state of emergency . . .** Davey Winder, "New Orleans Declares State of Emergency Following Cyber Attack," *Forbes*, Dec. 14, 2019.

Page 322: **. . . taking thirty-four hundred computers and devices (including those in police cars) offline.** "City of New Orleans Says It Will Take Months to Recover from Recent Cyber Attack," WVUE-TV, Jan. 15, 2020.

Page 322: **. . . couldn't so much as pay bills online or report a pothole.** Jessica Williams, "Cyberattack Update: Most Systems Are Back at City Hall, but Access to Public Records Still Delayed," Nola.com, Jan. 13, 2020.

Page 322: **. . . set aside $7.5 million to recover . . .** Jessica Williams, "New Orleans Tech Chief Says City Continues to Recover After Cyberattack, Though Coronavirus Has Brought New Challenges," Nola.com, Jan. 16, 2020.

Page 322: **. . . an estimated $110 million economic shortfall . . .** Michael Isaac Stein, "Mayor Cantrell Plans to Partially Furlough All City Employees Through End of the Year," *The Lens*, Oct. 5, 2020.

Page 322: **. . . led to a new spending freeze . . .** Jennifer Crockett, "New Orleans 80 Percent Recovered from Ransomware Attack Last Year," WDSU-TV, June 16, 2020.

Page 323: **. . . in the first nine days of 2020 . . .** Through the end of January, New Orleans was on a pace for 192 murders for 2020, which at the time felt like a staggering number. This was before the coronavirus pandemic added extreme stress to residents. The numbers actually wound up being worse, and the city logged 195 murders, the most in nearly a decade. Chris McCrory, "Counting the Dead: 16 People Were Murdered in New Orleans Last Month," WWL-TV, Feb. 1, 2020.

Page 323: **. . . a forty-five-year-old man hunched over in his car . . .** "NOPD Investigating Two Homicides on New Year's Day," WWL-TV, Jan. 1, 2020.

Page 324: **. . . wrote that the individual "got what he deserved."** Chris McCrory, "NOPD Strips Sergeant of Power, Investigating Social Media Posts About Protesters," WWL-TV, June 12, 2020

Page 325: **. . . Cellebrite, an Israeli mobile forensics company . . .** Michael Hayes, "Exclusive: Inside New York City's Partnership with Israeli iPhone Hacking Company Cellebrite," Medium OneZero, Oct. 7, 2019.

Page 325: **The Karr player was alive.** Brown and others shared this player's identity with the author, along with specific details about the events surrounding this

NOTES AND CITATIONS

shooting. However, because this individual was a minor at the time, and there was no police report associated with the incident, the author made the editorial decision to omit the player's name and other information that could identify him.

Page 325: . . . the fastest forty-yard dash at the Combine . . . Glen West, "2021 Receiver Destyn Pazon's Elite Speed, LSU Football Ties Makes Him Intriguing Prospect for the Tigers," *Sports Illustrated*, June 18, 2020.

Page 327: But St. Aug's student handbook requires . . . An electronic version of the school's student policies, which outlines rules about discipline and campus culture, is posted on its official website.

Page 330: . . . a private Methodist college . . . Tuition and fees are based on those posted on its official school website before the 2020–2021 term, which was Joe Thomas's freshman year.

Page 331: . . . seven in ten Americans born into a lower-class home . . . "Pursuing the American Dream: Economic Mobility Across Generations," Pew Charitable Trusts, July 2, 2012.

Page 336: His name is Nick Foster. Rod Walker, "Nick Foster Named St. Augustine's New Head Football Coach After Six Years as Assistant at Karr," Nola.com, Apr. 1, 2020.

ABOUT THE AUTHOR

Kent Babb has been a staff writer at *The Washington Post* since 2012 and is currently assigned to its Sports and Society investigative and enterprise team. He previously wrote columns and covered professional football for *The Kansas City Star*, and before that, he was a reporter with *The State* in Columbia, SC. A proud graduate of the University of South Carolina, Babb often examines sports' intersections with culture and politics in his work.

His first book was the widely acclaimed *Not a Game: The Incredible Rise and Unthinkable Fall of Allen Iverson*, which was shortlisted for the PEN/ESPN Award for Literary Sports Writing. His journalism appeared three times in the prestigious anthology *The Best American Sports Writing*, and the annual Associated Press Sports Editors contest has honored three of his features as the best in the country. He lives in the Washington, DC, area with his wife, Whitney, and their daughter.